THE
LATINO
ENCYCLOPEDIA

THE
LATINO
ENCYCLOPEDIA

Volume 1

Abejeños – Chicano movement

Editors

RICHARD CHABRÁN AND RAFAEL CHABRÁN

Marshall Cavendish
New York • London • Toronto

Published By
Marshall Cavendish Corporation
99 White Plains Road
Tarrytown, New York 10591-9001
United States of America

∞ The paper in these volumes conforms to the American National Standard for Permanence of Paper for Printed Library Materials, Z39.48-1984.

Library of Congress Cataloging-in-Publication Data

The Latino encyclopedia / editors, Richard Chabrán, and Rafael Chabrán,
    p.   cm.
    Includes bibliographical references and index.
    1. Hispanic Americans—Encyclopedias.   I. Chabrán, Richard   II. Chabrán, Rafael
E184.S75L357 1995
973′ .0468′003—dc20   95-13144
ISBN 0-7614-0125-3 (set).   CIP
ISBN 0-7614-0126-1 (vol. 1).

First Printing

PRINTED IN THE UNITED STATES OF AMERICA

Contents

Publisher's Note

From its roots in Spain, Portugal, and the indigenous cultures of the Americas through its modern expression, Latino culture has become the focus of educational debate and public attention in recent years. Modern scholars have argued for a more inclusive approach to American history, one that would rescue from undeserved obscurity the contributions and achievements of groups that have been neglected in the historical record. Latinos, who as a group are growing as a proportion to the U.S. population as a whole, are widely recognized as deserving greater attention in the classroom and in public and academic discourse. This multicultural perspective offers fresh insights into the history of the Americas, presenting the perspective of the indigenous people as well as that of European explorers and settlers. This perspective highlights the diversity of backgrounds, interests, and opinions within American society as a whole as well as within Latino society.

Although numerous works in the fields of Chicano studies, Latin American studies, and other area studies have been published in recent years, the information in these works is often specialized and widely scattered, making it less accessible to the general public. By collecting essential information on Latino life, culture, and history and incorporating the rapidly expanding scholarship in the broad area of Latino studies, the articles in this encyclopedia challenge preconceptions about Latinos. The encyclopedia presents the facts about the Latino experience in the United States. Readers are allowed to form their own opinions on the many issues and points of view involved in controversial topics. *The Latino Encyclopedia* has been designed to provide the most up-to-date, contemporary multivolume source on the subject of Latino life while maintaining the highest standards of accuracy and objectivity.

Among the controversial issues involved in the study of Latinos is the question of appropriate language. The editors of the set have made strong efforts to avoid racist, sexist, or otherwise biased language. The decision to use the term "Latino" in most cases was based on an emerging consensus; however, it is recognized that the term "Hispanic" also is widely used, particularly in government statistical reports. Both terms are used throughout the encyclopedia to refer to a person of Mexican, Puerto Rican, Cuban, Central or South American, or other Spanish culture or origin, regardless of race. It is further recognized that many Latinos prefer not to be categorized as part of such an inclusive group, instead labeling themselves in reference to their countries of origin—as Cuban Americans, for example, rather than as Latinos—or simply calling themselves Americans. The editors have attempted to use specific designations whenever possible and to avoid generalizations about Latinos as a group that may not be true of particular Latino subgroups or individuals. The word "American" has been added to the names of immigrant groups, such as Salvadoran Americans, to differentiate people living in the United States from those in the country of origin; although the countries of Central and South America are also "American," this usage was chosen for consistency and workability. Acceptable and preferred group names are constantly in flux, reflecting both changing group identity and social roles. Similarly, the terms "ethnic," "racial," "cultural," and "minority" to describe groups tend to be used interchangeably and inconsistently, suggesting the evolving nature of these concepts.

Further issues arise in use of non-English words, phrases, personal names, and organization names. Words and phrases that have not yet been incorporated into mainstream English appear in italics, often with definitions following in parentheses. Many of these terms are defined in separate entries. Some terms may have culturally specific meanings or may differ in meaning among Latino subgroups. Entries were designed to be as inclusive as possible given the constraints of space. Contributors often use the term "Anglo" to refer to non-Hispanic U.S. residents of European descent. Although this term carries strong cultural meanings in some contexts, contributors most often use it neutrally, simply as a shorthand expression to avoid awkward language. Personal names are spelled as they are most commonly found in printed sources or as individuals have expressed preferences; diacriticals therefore do not appear consistently on identical surnames or given names, and many personal names have been Anglicized ("Roberto," for example, becoming "Robert," "Bert," "Bob," or "Bobby"). In addition, many individuals are referred to only by their first familial name: For example, baseball player Rodney Cline Carew y Scott is referred to as Rod Carew. Organization names also are provided as they most often appear in published sources. Most organization names in Spanish therefore have diacriticals where appropriate. The decision was made to use the English alphabet for indexing and alphabetization purposes. The Spanish-alphabet characters *ch, ll, ñ,* and *rr* thus are treated, respectively, as separate letters *c* and *h,* two *l*'s, the letter *n,* and two *r*'s. In indexing and alphabetization, no distinction is made between letters with and without diacriticals. Another convention of indexing and alphabetization concerns articles as a part of speech. Articles ("the," "an," and "a" in English; *el, la, las, los, una,* and *uno* in Spanish) appear following the substantive part of the title of an entry: For example, El Grito de Lares is listed alphabetically as "Grito de Lares, El."

Organized in traditional encyclopedic format, the six volumes feature entries on people, organizations, geographic locations, history, entertainment, military activity, religion, family life, court cases, cultural movements, and other facets of life that have a unique expression among Latinos. The space limitations of this project made it necessary to be selective, particularly among the people profiled. The profiles of some well-known celebrities and historical figures deliberately were kept short in order to allow more balanced coverage of lesser-known individuals in various fields. Important individuals and their accomplishments will also be mentioned in various overview articles. In-depth treatment was accorded to those individuals, events, organizations, and concepts of central importance within the following broad categories: Civil Rights; Customs and Traditions; Economic and Labor Issues; Education and Scholarship; Exploration; Family Life; Food and Foodways; Geographic Areas of Settlement; Immigration and Immigration Issues; Languages and Language Issues; Laws, Acts, Treaties, Legal Cases, and Legal Issues; Latino Subgroups; Literature and the Media; Military Relations and the Military; Organizations; Performing and Visual Arts; Politics and Government; Prejudice, Discrimination, Assimilation, and Intergroup Relations; Regions of Origin; Religion and Religious Groups; Science, Technology, Medicine, and Health; Social Movements and Issues; and Sports.

Entries vary in length from one paragraph to several pages. The twenty-eight longest articles, approximately 4,000 words in length, provide broad overviews of major aspects of Latino life, showing the relationships among many of the topics addressed in shorter entries and interpreting the implications of central concepts and events. These articles include bibliographic references to sources for further study, annotated to evaluate the usefulness of these works for the nonspecialist. Approximately 80 articles, each about 2,000 words, cover topics of slightly smaller scope in a similar format. Approximately 120 articles of about 1,000 words each cover, in detail, specific concepts, groups, and events of major importance, offering unannotated bibliographies to guide readers to other sources of information. Shorter articles provide capsule summaries of significant people, organizations, events, and concepts, along with providing definitions of terms. Topics covered in separate entries are cross-referenced in the text through the use of small capital letters.

In the final volume, readers will find lists of Latino broadcast media; businesses; educational institutions and programs; films; social, political, and cultural organizations; and serial publications. These lists are followed by a time line of important events in Latino history. Two bibliographies follow the time line. The first covers literature, including novels, autobiographies, short stories, poetry, essays, drama, anthologies, and criticism. The second lists reference works and is organized around topical areas. Next, each entry in the encyclopedia is listed by subject matter, organized in two ways: by the Latino group or groups involved and by field of study. Finally, a comprehensive index allows the user to locate the various individuals, organizations, events, terms, and concepts mentioned in the text.

Many hands went into the creation of this work, from the academicians who prepared the list and those who contributed articles (a list of whom appears in volume 1) to the editors who researched information and selected photographs, maps, and tables to illustrate the entries. Their efforts are most gratefully acknowledged.

Acknowledgments

We thank the scores of people who helped to bring *The Latino Encyclopedia* to completion. We would like to thank especially the editorial consultants for the project: Shifra M. Goldman, Michael Heisley, Vilma Ortiz, Nélida Pérez, Raymond A. Rocco, Vicki L. Ruíz, and Michael Soldatenko-Gutierrez. Their critical advice throughout the project was greatly appreciated. We also thank the many individuals who took time to write entries contained within these volumes. Many others contributed other forms of support. In particular, we thank Lillian Castillo-Speed from the Chicano Studies Library at the University of California, Berkeley, and Pat Dawson from the Coleccion Tloque Nahuaque, who provided information that helped us identify possible entries. Our home institutions of Whittier College and the University of California, Los Angeles, provided needed institutional support. Finally, we thank our families, who shared us with this project: Gail, Gabriel, Paco, Ann, Melissa, Rhonda, and Rafael.   —*Richard Chabrán and Rafael Chabrán*

Editors

Richard Chabrán
University of California, Los Angeles

and

Rafael Chabrán
Whittier College

Editorial Consultants

Shifra M. Goldman
University of California, Los Angeles

Michael Heisley
University of California, Los Angeles

Vilma Ortiz
University of California, Los Angeles

Nélida Pérez
Hunter College of the City University of New York

Raymond A. Rocco
University of California, Los Angeles

Vicki L. Ruíz
Claremont Graduate School

Michael Soldatenko-Gutierrez
Santa Monica College

Contributors

Walter Randolph Adams
Brown University

Richard Adler
University of Michigan-Dearborn

Maria Angela Aguilar
University of Texas at Austin

Yara I. Alma Bonilla
Massachusetts Institute of Technology

María L. Alonzo
Independent Scholar

Melissa Amado
University of Arizona

Angel A. Amy Moreno de Toro
Roxbury Community College

Peggy J. Anderson
Wichita State University

Debra D. Andrist
Baylor University

Francisco A. Apodaca
Independent Scholar

Sylvia P. Apodaca
Independent Scholar

Pablo R. Arreola
Saint Michael's College

Keith Atwater
California State University, Sacramento

Susan Auerbach
Independent Scholar

Hector Ignacio Avalos
Iowa State University

James A. Baer
Northern Virginia Community College

Silvia P. Baeza
Independent Scholar

Susan Benforado Bakewell
Kennesaw College

Russell Barber
California State University, San Bernardino

Cynthia Bily
Adrian College

Jorge A. Brea
Central Michigan University

Elise M. Bright
University of Texas at Arlington

John A. Britton
Francis Marion University

Ray F. Broussard
University of Georgia

Kendall W. Brown
Brigham Young University

Walton Lyonnaise Brown
Central Connecticut State University

Laura R. Broyles
Independent Scholar

David E. Camacho
Northern Arizona University

Michael Candelaria
St. John's College

Byron D. Cannon
University of Utah

Robert Carballo
Millersville University of Pennsylvania

José Carmona
Hudson County Community College

Peter E. Carr
TCI Genealogical Resources

Rafaela Castro
University of California, Davis

Rafael Chabrán
Whittier College

Richard Chabrán
University of California, Los Angeles

Lorenzo Chavez
VISIONES Magazine

Manuel Chavez
Independent Scholar

Jonathan Clark
San Jose State University

M. Cecilia Colombi
University of California, Davis

Patricia Constantakis-Valdés
University of California, Santa Cruz

Marguerite Cotto
Northwestern Michigan College

Antonio de la Cova
West Virginia University

David A. Crain
South Dakota State University

Stephen Cresswell
West Virginia Wesleyan College

Jennifer Davis
University of Dayton

Linda Prewett Davis
Charleston Southern University

Richard A. Dello Buono
Rosary College

Michael Delucchi
University of Hawaii-West Oahu

Victoria Díaz Méndez
Independent Scholar

Steven L. Driever
University of Missouri-Kansas City

Jorge Duany
University of the Sacred Heart

Víctor Manuel Durán
Millikin University

Susan Ellis-Lopez
Heritage College

Loring D. Emery
Independent Scholar

Dionne Espinoza
Cornell University

John W. Fiero
University of Southwestern Louisiana

Horacio R. Fonseca
Los Angeles City College

Gregory Freeland
California Lutheran University

Guadalupe M. Friaz
University of Washington

Angelica C. Fuentes
Lewis University

Elizabeth Fuller
Independent Scholar

Kelly Fuller
Independent Scholar

Cecilia M. Garcia
Congressional Hispanic Caucus Institute

Matt Garcia
Claremont Graduate School

Juan Garcia-Castañón
California State University, Fresno

Angela I. Garcia-Holtzman
Chicago Public Library

Lisa Garza
Texas Woman's University

Beaird Glover
Independent Scholar

Juana Iris Goergen
DePaul University

Shifra M. Goldman
University of California, Los Angeles

Marc Goldstein
Independent Scholar

Luz E. Gonzalez
California State University, Fresno

Fernando González de León
Springfield College

Gloria Gonzalez-Kruger
Independent Scholar

F. Gonzalez-Lima
University of Texas at Austin

César A. González-T.
San Diego Mesa College

D. Douglas Graham
Independent Scholar

Teresa Lupe Grenot
Independent Scholar

Richard L. Haiman
California State University, Chico

James K. IV Hayes-Bohanan
Independent Scholar

Pamela Hayes-Bohanan
McAllen Memorial Library

Alberto H. Hernandez
Boston College

Stephen R. C. Hicks
Rockford College

Carl W. Hoagstrom
Ohio Northern University

Robert L. Jenkins
Mississippi State University

Jeffry Jensen
Independent Scholar

Angélica Jiménez Narain
Arizona State University

Bruce E. Johansen
University of Nebraska at Omaha

Ludmila Kapschutschenko-Schmitt
Rider College

Glenn J. Kist
Rochester Institute of Technology

Nathan R. Kollar
St. John Fisher College

Wendy Lamb
Independent Scholar

David Laubach
Kutztown University

Thomas T. Lewis
Mount Senario College

José Manuel Lezcano
Keene State College

Darrell B. Lockhart
Arizona State University

Melissa A. Lockhart
Arizona State University

Janet Alice Long
Independent Scholar

Dolores Lopez
Independent Scholar

Grace McEntee
Appalachian State University

Robert R. McKay
Clarion University of Pennsylvania

Michelle McKowen
Independent Scholar

Paul D. Mageli
Independent Scholar

Russell M. Magnaghi
Northern Michigan University

Krishna Mallick
Bentley College and Salem State College

Bill T. Manikas
Gaston College

Barry Mann
Independent Scholar

Philip Martin
University of California, Davis

John Martinez
University of California, Irvine

Manuel Luis Martinez
Stanford University

Oscar J. Martínez
University of Arizona

Lynn M. Mason
Lubbock Christian University

Delia Méndez Montesinos
University of Texas at Brownsville

Barbara Mendoza
Santa Barbara City College

Ruben G. Mendoza
California State University, Monterey Bay

Linda J. Meyers
Pasadena City College

Laurence Miller
Western Washington University

Bruce M. Mitchell
Eastern Washington University

Dario Moreno
Florida International University

Silvia M. Nagy
Catholic University of America

Irene Narvaez
Independent Scholar

Armando Navarro
University of California, Riverside

Jose Alfredo Nunez
University of Akron

Max Orezzoli
Florida International University

Kurt C. Organista
University of California, Berkeley

William Osborne
Florida International University

Maria A. Pacino
Azusa Pacific University

Yolanda C. Padilla
University of Texas at Austin

Juan Vicente Palerm
University of California, Santa Barbara

JoAnn Pavletich
University of Texas at Austin

Jaime Pelayo
Yale University

Manuel Peña
University of Texas at Austin

Maria E. Perez y Gonzalez
Brooklyn College of the City University of New York

Andrés I. Pérez y Mena
Long Island University, Brooklyn Campus

Julia L. Perilla
Georgia State University

Hugh Phillips
Independent Scholar

Jorge del Pinal
U.S. Census Bureau

Francis C. Poole
University of Delaware

Victoria Price
Independent Scholar

Johnny Ramirez
Atlantic Union College

Susan E. Ramírez
DePaul University

Carlos I. Ramos
University of Illinois at Urbana-Champaign

Douglas W. Richmond
University of Texas at Arlington

Edward A. Riedinger
Ohio State University

Blanca Rivera
State University of New York College at Fredonia

Francisco L. Rivera-Batiz
Columbia University

John Robinson
Abilene Christian University

St. John Robinson
Eastern Montana College

Carlos Rodriguez
Independent Scholar

Victor M. Rodriguez
Concordia University

Moisés Roizen
West Valley College

Mary Romero
University of Oregon

Daniel Rothenberg
University of Chicago

Vicki L. Ruíz
Claremont Graduate School

Wendy Sacket
Independent Scholar

José F. Salgado
San Diego City College

David A. Sandoval
University of Southern Colorado

Pedro Santoni
California State University, San Bernardino

Louis Sarabia
New Mexico State University

T. M. Scruggs
University of Iowa

Burl E. Self
Southwest Missouri State University

Clayton M. Shotwell
Augusta College

R. Baird Shuman
University of Illinois at Urbana-Champaign

Alissa Simon
University of California, Los Angeles

Sanford S. Singer
University of Dayton

Amy Sisson
Independent Scholar

Genevieve Slomski
Independent Scholar

Suzanne Smith
Independent Scholar

William L. Smith
Georgia Southern University

Daniel Smith-Christopher
Loyola Marymount University

James N. Snaden
Central Connecticut State University

A. J. Sobczak
Independent Scholar

Robert M. Spector
Worcester State College

Susan A. Stussy
Independent Scholar

L. J. Sullivan
Independent Scholar

Andrew Sund
Saint Augustine's College

Robert Talbott
University of Northern Iowa

Nancy Conn Terjesen
Kent State University

Leslie V. Tischauser
Prairie State College

Luis A. Torres
University of Southern Colorado

Ignacio Orlando Trujillo
Stanford University

Abel Valenzuela, Jr.
University of California, Los Angeles

Jesse M. Vázquez
*Queens College of the City University of
New York*

Santos C. Vega
Arizona State University

Francisco A. Villarruel
Michigan State University

Maria Isabel Villaseñor
New Mexico State University

Hari Vishwanadha
Santa Monica College

Marilynn I. Ward
University of Findlay

M. C. Ware
*State University of New York College at
Cortland*

Michael A. Warren
Tulane University

Joyce E. Williams
Texas Woman's University

Maria Wilson-Figueroa
Portland State University

Michael Witkoski
Independent Scholar

Anna Witte
Eastern Washington University

Regina Howard Yaroch
Independent Scholar

Marisol Zapater-Ferrá
University of California, Berkeley

THE
LATINO
ENCYCLOPEDIA

A

Abejeños: Term describing CALIFORNIOS and MEXI-CANOS living in the southern two-thirds of Spanish and Mexican California. People living in the southern two-thirds of California under Spanish and Mexican rule resented the disproportionate political power wielded by *arribeños* in the north, living near the capital at Monterey. This resentment intensified, particularly during the Mexican era (1821-1848), while the central government in Mexico City debated whether to centralize or federalize the new Mexican government. During this period, relations between these rival groups degenerated into personal jealousies, intrigues, and revolts. The division between these two factions facilitated the conquest of California by the United States in 1846 and the fall of Mexican rule in Mexico's most northern province.

acculturate by maintaining their original heritage as a part of their new culture. In the context of the Latino experience, this question involves choices of language and customs, among other lifestyle characteristics.

The Need to Adapt. People, as a matter of survival, respond to changes in their environment. This adaptation process is usually gradual and often goes unnoticed, as in the adaptation to wearing warmer clothes when the weather turns cold. Environmental changes for immigrants represent fundamental shifts in their world. Adaptation becomes a conscious and deliberate act.

The most appropriate form of adaptation has been the subject of controversy. Although it is generally agreed that cultural adaptation is a two-way process that involves reorientation on the part of the immigrant

Food booths at this fiesta in San Antonio, Texas, illustrate the intermixing of cultures, with traditional Mexican foods sold alongside American favorites. (James Shaffer)

Acculturation versus assimilation: No one disputes that immigrants need to adjust and adapt to their new homelands. The question is whether immigrants should assimilate by shedding their original cultural heritage and adopting that of their new home or instead

as well as acceptance on the part of the host culture, disagreement arises concerning how much adaptation is desirable. Proponents of complete assimilation believe in maximum adaptation; that is, they believe that immigrants should attempt to sever cultural and ethnic ties to their native lands and adopt the symbols, rituals, and values of the dominant group. Pluralists or multiculturalists, on the other hand, advocate minimum adaptation, or acculturation. They believe that society is best served when groups maintain, celebrate, and harmoniously blend their respective cultural identities.

History of American Assimilation. The concept of assimilation is a familiar thread in the fabric of American society. It is the basis for the United States' image as "the melting pot," a place where differences are dissolved and a new national identity is forged. Many factors affect an individual's potential to assimilate, such as age and racial or other physical characteristics, but of critical importance is the receptivity of the host culture to the new immigrant.

The desirability of assimilation went nearly unchallenged for most of the twentieth century. During the 1980's, the growing voices of women, African Americans, and other groups, together with shifting demographic patterns that foreshadowed a change in the ethnic makeup of the United States, called assimilation into question. Pluralists began advocating a different means of ethnic adaptation. They conceived of the United States not as a melting pot where all combine to form the same, but as a mosaic where differences remain but join to form a rich and colorful whole.

The trouble with assimilation, according to multiculturalists, is that it subverts the interests of minorities to the expediency of the dominant group. The MELTING POT THEORY suggests a warm and generous welcome to immigrants and the promise of belonging to a force greater than one's self. The United States, however, has not been able to translate that idea into reality. The "melting pot" historically was most open to white men, leaving women and Latinos, as well as other people of color, excluded from the dominant culture.

Assimilation poses other problems. Immigrants are forced to choose between their heritage and their future. Those who attempt to break away from their

Nearly ten thousand people were sworn in as U.S. citizens in a 1984 ceremony in Miami, Florida. (AP/Wide World Photos)

cultural traditions in order to more fully assimilate may be unfavorably viewed by other immigrants. Perhaps the most objectionable issue of assimilation is the way it has been institutionally enforced, resulting in the civic, economic, and educational oppression of minorities. For example, assimilation has resulted in the suppression of languages other than English. Education and voting ballots in Spanish were scarce until the 1970's, leaving generations of Latinos living and learning far below their potential.

Problems of Multiculturalism. As early as 1915, social commentator and Harvard University instructor Horace Kallen decried the U.S. emphasis on assimilation and called for what he termed "CULTURAL PLURALISM," citing his utopic vision of a collection of individual ethnic communities. Decades passed before Kallen's philosophy gained popular acceptance, and criticism remained. The main arguments against pluralism and acculturation center on their potential to weaken American society. Education is often cited as an example. In grade schools and high schools, according to critics, MULTICULTURALISM is too often implemented as an exercise in minority self-esteem, with lessons in literature and history left unlearned. In colleges and universities, multiculturalism requires that information be scanned from many perspectives; it is thoroughly probed from none. Learning and discovery, therefore, become superficial. Additionally, multiculturalism is criticized because by emphasizing differences it serves to divide society rather than unite it.

The Question for Latinos. It appears that, for Latinos, assimilation is not the most workable form of cultural adaptation, for two reasons. First, Latinos, as compared to European, African, and Asian immigrants, live relatively close to their native lands, making visits home and regular contact with friends and relatives more likely. This closeness heightens and strengthens the Latino sense of cultural tradition, which then decreases the likelihood of advanced assimilation. Second, Latinos are unlikely to assimilate completely because of the support network offered by the Latino community. The situation is ironic, as ethnic communities developed because white society had rejected minorities' attempts to integrate. What earlier had served to keep immigrants segregated and insulated now acts as an active agent of cultural pride and a primary tool of adaptation through acculturation.

Assimilation and acculturation are terms that describe how an immigrant adapts to the cultural environment of his or her new home. Proponents of assimilation adhere to the image of the United States as the melting pot, in which individual differences are replaced by pride in unity and conformity. Those who favor acculturation support a pluralistic society in which differences are acknowledged and embraced, and in which ethnic identities combine to form a mosaic American culture. For a number of reasons, Latinos are more likely to successfully acculturate than to assimilate into U.S. society. —*Regina Howard Yaroch*

SUGGESTED READINGS: • Feuer, Lewis S. "From Pluralism to Multiculturalism." *Society* 29 (November, 1991): 19-22. • Robeson, Paul, Jr. *Paul Robeson, Jr., Speaks to America.* New Brunswick, N.J.: Rutgers University Press, 1993. • Rose, Peter I., ed. *Interminority Affairs in the U.S.: Pluralism at the Crossroads.* Thousand Oaks, Calif.: Sage Periodicals Press, 1993. • Schaefer, Richard T. *Racial and Ethnic Groups.* 3d ed. Glenview, Ill.: Scott, Foresman, 1988. • Schlesinger, Arthur M., Jr., and Nathan Glazer. "Does Multicultural Education Contribute to Racial Tensions?" *CQ Researcher* 4 (January 7, 1994): 17.

Acequias: Irrigation canals or ditches, also referred to as *zanjas.* The *acequias* represented the main water source for people living in Spanish/Mexican territories in the nineteenth century and earlier. A canal known as the *acequia madre* or *zanja madre* transported water from springs, creeks, and rivers to people living in pueblos. Iberian custom and law regarded the *acequia* as a public resource and responsibility. Spanish and Mexican settlers therefore were obliged to construct, maintain, and use the canal as a community, respecting everyone's right to the resource. This egalitarian relationship to water continued throughout the Spanish and Mexican eras but was radically changed after the American conquest of the Mexican Southwest.

The Espada Aqueduct is an eighteenth century acequia *located near the mission of San Juan Capistrano in San Antonio, Texas.* (Ruben G. Mendoza)

Aceves, José (1909, Chihuahua, Mexico—1968): Painter. Aceves was born in Mexico and moved with his family to El Paso, Texas, in 1915. Aceves was a self-taught artist whose desert landscapes and regional murals helped record the historical heritage and regional character of the American Southwest.

Aceves was one of many Mexican American painters commissioned to paint murals for the Federal Art Project of the Works Progress Administration from the mid-1930's through the early 1940's. Although the subject matter of Aceves' murals was decidedly Southwestern American, his work drew on the stylistic traditions of great muralists of his native Mexico. The public nature of the MURAL ART drew attention to Latino artistic talent and helped make a place for Latinos in the art of mainstream America.

Achiote: Red seed of a shrub, used to color food, particularly in the Caribbean. The hard, red seeds of *achiote* were used by some American Indians before Columbus to paint their bodies and color their foods. The latter practice continues, especially with rice dishes. Seeds usually are ground dry (Mexico), soaked and ground into a paste (Yucatán), or cooked in oil to color it (Caribbean). A paste form is available commercially in blocks. The term is derived from a Taino Indian word; its most common synonyms are "annatto" and *roucou*, both derived from Carib Indian words.

Acosta, Manuel Gregorio (May 9, 1921, Villa Aldama, Veracruz, Mexico—Oct. 25, 1989, Houston, Tex.): Painter, muralist, and sculptor. Acosta gained national recognition when his portrait of labor activist César CHÁVEZ was published on the cover of *Time* magazine in 1969. His reputation rests primarily on evocative paintings of Mexican Americans, as well as on frescoes and murals depicting the history of the American Southwest.

Acosta emigrated to El Paso, Texas, with his family when he was a child. He studied at the University of Texas at El Paso and at the Chouinard Art Institute in Los Angeles, California. In the 1950's, Acosta was commissioned to paint historical murals and frescoes for a museum, a motel, and several banks in New Mexico and Texas. His easel paintings, noted for their humble subjects and human warmth, include El Paso scenes and portraits of Mexican American friends, neighbors, and relatives. These include oil and watercolor paintings of a domestic worker, a dancer in regional costume, a wrinkle-faced Mexican elder, and young men urging people to toss them pennies from a bridge.

Acosta's work can be found in the National Portrait Gallery in Washington, D.C., as well as in permanent art collections in Texas, New York, New Mexico, and Colorado.

Acosta, Oscar "Zeta" (b. Apr. 8, 1936, El Paso, Tex.): Writer and lawyer. Acosta is perhaps the most mysterious and infamous Mexican American novelist. His two works *The Autobiography of a Brown Buffalo* (1972) and its sequel *The Revolt of the Cockroach People* (1973) are uncompromising explorations of the author's struggle to define his ethnic identity within the larger dominant culture of the United States. His "autobiographies" are in reality novels, but the protagonist in both works closely parallels Acosta. A year after the publication of his second book, Acosta disappeared without a trace.

Born in Texas, Acosta spent his childhood in California's San Joaquin Valley near Modesto. At his father's insistence, Acosta spoke no Spanish in California. This alienated him from the other Mexican Americans in his neighborhood. Acosta's estrangement from his cultural heritage set the stage for his career choices and his novels.

After serving in the Air Force and attending college, Acosta became a lawyer in 1966. In defending several Mexican American clients in famous trials, he established himself as a successful attorney in East Los Angeles. Both Acosta's legal works and his writings are recognized as pivotal in the CHICANO MOVEMENT of the 1960's and 1970's.

Acosta-Belén, Edna (b. Jan. 14, 1948, Hormigueros, Puerto Rico): Educator. Acosta-Belén immigrated to the United States in 1967 to complete her undergraduate education. She received a B.A. (1969) and M.A. (1971) from the State University of New York at Albany (SUNY, Albany). In 1977, she received her Ph.D. from Columbia University. She has held postdoctoral fellowships at Princeton and Yale universities.

Acosta-Belén began teaching as a part-time instructor at SUNY, Albany, in 1970, then became a lecturer and an assistant professor. In 1981, she became an associate professor, with her primary appointment in the department of Latin American and Caribbean studies. She has held joint appointments in the department of women's studies and the department of Hispanic and Italian studies. She eventually earned promotion to the rank of Distinguished Service Professor, the highest rank at SUNY, Albany, conferred to those with outstanding records of service to the institution, the community, the profession, and the nation.

Early in her career, Acosta-Belén became involved in the educational and civil rights plights of the Puerto Rican community on the U.S. mainland. She is among the pioneers in the ethnic and women's studies movements at SUNY, Albany, where the PUERTO RICAN STUDIES PROGRAM began in 1971 and became a department three years later. The department of Latin American and Caribbean studies is one of the major centers in the United States for the scholarly study of the Puerto Rican experience.

Acosta-Belén has made significant scholarly contributions to the study of Puerto Rican women and the mainland Puerto Rican community. Her book publications include *The Puerto Rican Woman: Perspectives on Culture, History, and Society* (1979), *The Hispanic Experience in the United States* (1988), and *Researching Women in Latin America and the Caribbean* (1993).

Acquired immune deficiency syndrome (AIDS): AIDS was identified as a public health problem in 1981. It is an opportunistic disease of the immune system that has disproportionately affected the black and Latino communities.

According to the Centers for Disease Control, more than 100,000 people had died from AIDS by the end of 1993. Of these, 59 percent were homosexual or bisexual men, and 21 percent were women or heterosexual men who were intravenous drug users. During 1990, the rate of death for Hispanics was 22.2 per 100,000 population, compared to 29.3 for African Americans, 2.8 for Asians/Pacific Islanders, 2.8 for American Indians/Alaskan Natives, and 8.7 for whites.

Initially, AIDS was considered to be a "white gay disease." Not until drug users were recognized as a population at risk were women and children considered to be at risk. Many Latino cases were heterosexual male drug users who were in contact with female partners who were having babies. The disease manifested itself differently in women, resulting in women not qualifying for treatment because they were misdiagnosed. The same thing happened with children. In the 1990's, those most at risk for the disease were people of color, with an increasing number of these being Latino women and children.

As of the end of 1990, 15.9 percent of persons who died of AIDS were Hispanic. More than five thousand children and adolescents had died of AIDS. In 1988,

AIDS was the leading cause of death among Hispanic children between the ages of one and four in the state of New York.

The National Center for Health Statistics identified human immunodeficiency virus (HIV) infection as the eighth leading cause of death among Hispanics in 1990. HIV infection is a precursor to AIDS. Of all Americans with AIDS, 46 percent were people of color. A 1992 report on teenagers and AIDS noted that the number of people with AIDS between the ages of thirteen and twenty-four was rising. Nearly half the cases were found in New York, New Jersey, Texas, California, Florida, and Puerto Rico, all of which had large Hispanic populations.

According to a study published in 1988, 77 percent of women infected with AIDS in 1987 were black or Latina. In a 1993 report, the Centers for Disease Control revealed that 43 percent of Hispanic females who contracted the disease did so through intravenous drug use and 41 percent from heterosexual contact, principally with an injecting drug user. The majority of Latino men and women diagnosed with AIDS were between the ages of twenty-five and thirty-nine. There were, however, nine hundred children under five years of age and four hundred persons over the age of sixty-five (mostly men) diagnosed with AIDS. Nearly

AIDS-RELATED DEATHS, 1982-1991

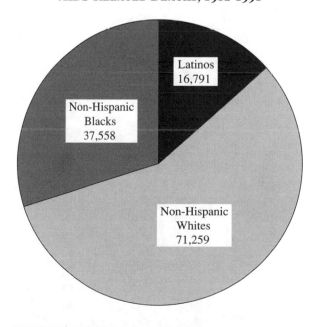

Latinos
16,791

Non-Hispanic
Blacks
37,558

Non-Hispanic
Whites
71,259

Source: Data are from Marlita A. Reddy, ed., *Statistical Record of Hispanic Americans* (Detroit: Gale Research, 1993), Table 387.

Rudy Acuña addresses a rally opposing California's controversial Proposition 187, which proposed restricting the rights of unauthorized residents. (Tony Cuevas)

90 percent of HIV-positive infants were born to black or Hispanic women.

Acuña, Rodolfo Francis "Rudy" (b. May 18, 1932, Los Angeles, Calif.): Educator and activist. Acuña is perhaps best known for his book *Occupied America: The Chicano's Struggle Toward Liberation* (1972), in which he discusses the Mexican American experience as framed by colonialism within the United States. In a revised version, *Occupied America: A History of Chicanos* (1981), he abandoned the model of internal colonialism. A third edition appeared in 1988.

Acuña was a pioneering scholar in the study of the Mexican American people. He was perhaps the first person to teach a course in the history of the Mexican American people, at Mount St. Mary's College (Los Angeles) in 1966. Later, he founded the department of Chicano studies at California State University, Northridge.

After graduating from Loyola High School in 1951 and serving in the U.S. Army, Acuña earned his B.A. in social science at Los Angeles State College in 1957. He earned his M.A. from the same institution in 1962, then a Ph.D. in Latin American history at the University of Southern California. He held several teaching positions before joining the faculty at California State University, Northridge, in 1968. Acuña is also known for his community involvement and for participation in the CHICANO MOVEMENT.

Adams-Onís Treaty (1819): Also known as the Transcontinental Treaty, this agreement was negotiated by Secretary of State John Quincy Adams and Spanish diplomat Luis de Onís. Spain ceded its remaining territory in eastern Florida—more than seventy-two thousand square miles—to the United States. Spain also agreed to set the western boundary of the Louisiana Territory at the banks of the Sabine, Red, and Arkansas rivers up to the Continental Divide. In addition, Spain ceded all claims to the Oregon Territory. In return, the United States paid some $5 million to American citizens who had filed claims against Spain. The treaty brought numerous Spanish settlers under American rule while firming up the border between the United States and Mexico's Texas territory.

Adelitas: Mexican women who served in the Mexican Revolution (1910-1921) as assistants, wash women, supporters of male troops, and occasionally soldiers. *Adelitas* were also known as *SOLDADERAS*. The term has been associated mostly with camp followers, or women who did not engage in combat. These women made tremendous sacrifices for male combatants, cleaning their equipment, nursing their wounds, and preparing their meals. The devotion of the *adelitas* inspired *CORRIDOS* that soldiers sang on the front. Although some women demonstrated their courage in battle, most soldiers who sang about "La Adelita" focused not on her valor but rather on her beauty, desirability, and loyalty.

Adobe: Sun-dried brick made of compressed mud and straw. Adobe construction is among the oldest in the world and has been widely used in the southwestern region of the United States and in Mexico, Peru, and other Latin American countries. Although adobe is generally used for building simple earthen walls and rural structures, multistory constructions that combine adobe and stone can be found in various areas of New Mexico and Latin America. The oldest examples of adobe-type monumental construction date from around A.D. 1000 and are found in the city of Chan Chan, Peru, the imperial city of the Chimú Kingdom. It is the world's largest adobe city.

This wall and doorway at the mission of Nuestra Señora de los Angeles de Porciúncula is constructed of adobe. (Ruben G. Mendoza)

Adoption: Adoption is the voluntary acceptance of the responsibility of parenthood by an adult for a child who is not the adult's biological offspring. Adoption is an established and diverse practice in Western culture. Stories of adopted and orphaned children abound in libraries, in both fictional and historical accounts. One of the first early American institutions to aid in adoption was the Children's Aid Society, founded in New York City by Loring Brace in the 1800's. He facilitated adoption of children by farm families in the West and arranged for their transportation.

Adoption has taken diverse forms as the traditional family has changed. With single parenthood on the rise, more children are being adopted by stepparents who marry a child's biological parent. The U.S. Bureau of the Census reported that 2.9 percent of all children were living with unrelated adoptive parents in 1980. The figures were 1.9 percent in 1985 and 2.1 percent in 1990. Separate figures for Hispanic adoptions were not reported before 1990. Reports indicate that during the 1970's, 96 percent of adoptive families were white, whereas between 1980 and 1987, 87 percent were white and 13 percent were minority.

Statistics from the 1987 National Health Interview Survey and the 1982 National Survey of Family Growth show some surprising data for minority families. In white families, most adoptions were of unrelated children. Black families adopted related and unrelated children equally. Hispanic families tended to adopt related children more often than unrelated children in 1982. In 1987, the number of adoptions of related children was similar to that in 1982 for Hispanic families, but adoptions of unrelated children had increased.

A growing number of adults want to adopt children of races other than their own. From 1970 to 1987, 7.6 percent of adoptions of unrelated children involved a mother and child from different races. Of all unrelated adoptions, 4.8 percent involved white mothers and a child other than black (Hispanics being the largest group). Minority mothers and white children were 1.6 percent of the group. Children from other countries are being adopted with less frequency than in the past. Between 1980 and 1987, 9.7 percent of adoptions of unrelated children involved children from other countries.

A 1990 report from the National Center for Health Statistics confirmed the belief that Hispanic families have usually adopted related children. Hispanic families tend to have strong extended family ties and lower rates of childlessness than other groups. When a child loses a home, the extended family tends to take the child in as a form of familial fostering that has the potential to lead to legal adoption. The growth of the middle class in the Hispanic population, however, is beginning to cause an increase in rates of unrelated child adoption. Also affecting adoption practices are the prevalence of single-parent homes, abortion, medical advances regarding infertility, and the tendency for single mothers to keep their out-of-wedlock children.

Advertising. *See* **Marketing and advertising**

AFDC. *See* **Aid to Families with Dependent Children**

Affirmative action: Affirmative action is the practice of using an individual's sex, race, or religion or some other criterion of group membership as a significant factor in hiring or admissions decisions.

Context. Bigots are people who are intolerant of members of other racial, sexual, religious, and ethnic groups. For most of human history, various types of bigotry have been widely practiced (*see* DISCRIMINATION, BIGOTRY, AND PREJUDICE AGAINST LATINOS). For example, people have historically believed that making slaves of members of other races is entirely natural; members of virtually all races have believed their race to be inherently superior to other races. For most of human history, moreover, most men have believed that males are inherently superior to females; this belief has led to the common practice of denying women equal social and legal status.

Throughout history, many wars have been fought over ethnic and religious differences. An extreme example of religious warfare occurred in the twentieth century in Germany, before and during World War II: The ruling Nazi Party, led by Adolf Hitler, attempted to exterminate all members of the Jewish religion and succeeded in killing several million Jews.

Although there is widespread agreement that bigotry is immoral, there are disputes about how best to combat it. One of these disputes focuses on the practice of affirmative action.

A major part of the dispute in the United States has concerned interpretation of Title VII of the CIVIL RIGHTS ACT OF 1964, which forbids the government to discriminate on the basis of race or sex. Legal tests of affirmative action have yielded no clear judicial position on its overall validity. In *Johnson v. Santa Clara* (480 U.S. 616, 1987), the Supreme Court upheld the hiring of a female applicant over a male who had more experience and a better test score. In *United States v.*

Paradise (480 U.S. 149, 1987), the Court upheld a one-to-one promotion scheme for black and white Alabama State Police troopers. The scheme was to remain in effect until the number of black troopers equaled 25 percent (the percentage of black people in Alabama's labor market) of the total number of troopers.

In an earlier case, the famous *Regents of the University of California v. Bakke* (438 U.S. 265, 1978), at issue was the fact that a white male was denied admission to medical school even though he had significantly higher grades and test scores than several minority-group members who were admitted. The Court ruled that the affirmative action program at Davis was illegal.

Governor Pete Wilson has advocated elimination of affirmative action programs in California. In 1995, the regents of the University of California voted to abolish affirmative action guidelines for that university system.

Arguments in Favor. Advocates of affirmative action offer two major arguments. The first is based on the goal of equal economic outcomes. Currently, some groups in North America (for example, Latinos, African Americans, and women) do not have economic equality with other groups (such as Asians, whites, and males). Perhaps the current inequalities are the legacy of past acts of bigotry, or perhaps they are caused by current acts of bigotry. It is argued, however, that society as a whole has certain overarching goals, one of which is the attainment of economic equality for all groups. Accordingly, achieving economic equality requires positive action to overcome the legacy of bigotry or to counterbalance current bigotry. Therefore, special preferences should be given to less-than-economically-equal groups.

The second argument in favor of affirmative action is a collective version of the first. In North America, some groups (most notably, white males) have in the past benefited as a class from acts of bigotry against other groups. This was unjust. Descendants of those who benefited directly have as a class benefited from those past acts of injustice, while the descendants of those who were discriminated against have as a class been harmed by those acts.

According to the arguments, justice requires that those who benefit from an injustice pay compensation

Affirmative action programs attempt to find jobs for members of minority groups in occupations in which they traditionally have been underrepresented. (Jim West)

to those harmed by the injustice. Therefore, modern whites and males owe compensation to contemporary women and minorities. Preferential hiring and admissions on the basis of race or sex are ways to make such compensation. Therefore, advocates claim, preferential hiring and admissions are justifiable.

Arguments Against. Opponents of affirmative action reject these arguments and argue that affirmative action programs institutionalize the same bigoted practices they were supposed to oppose. Opponents of affirmative action argue that society should teach and practice the principle of judging others as individuals rather than as members of groups and that, concomitantly, society should judge everyone by the same standards, never on the basis of morally irrelevant criteria such as race or sex. Affirmative action, however, gives some groups special advantages because of their sex or SKIN COLOR.

Opponents also charge that affirmative action policies unfairly harm innocent individuals. For example, a well-qualified man may be denied a job so that a less-qualified woman may have it. Because the man was better qualified, opponents argue, justice requires that he get the job. Because he is not the person who committed the past acts of bigotry, they argue further, it is unfair to make him pay compensation for the immoral actions of others.

Finally, opponents of affirmative action argue that preferential hiring and admissions reinforce negative racial, sexual, and ethnic STEREOTYPES. If it is known that members of some groups receive their positions

because of affirmative action, members of those groups will be viewed as less competent and as less able to earn their positions through open competition. If the members of those groups are thus viewed as less competent, critics claim, then affirmative action is contributing to the very problem it is supposed to solve.   —*Stephen R. C. Hicks*

SUGGESTED READINGS: • Capaldi, Nicholas. "Affirmative Action." In *Commerce and Morality*, edited by Tibor Machan. Totowa, N.J.: Rowman & Littlefield, 1988. • Ezorsky, Gertrude. *Racism and Justice: The Case for Affirmative Action*. Ithaca, N.Y.: Cornell University Press, 1991. • Newton, Lisa. "Bakke and Davis: Justice, American Style." *National Forum (The Phi Beta Kappa Journal)* 58 (Winter, 1978): 22-23. • Sowell, Thomas. *Preferential Policies: An International Perspective*. New York: William Morrow, 1990. • Thomson, Judith Jarvis. "Preferential Hiring." *Philosophy and Public Affairs* 2 (Summer, 1973): 364-384.

Afro-Cubans: Cubans of African descent. Spain took possession of Cuba in 1511. Initially, the conquistadores used the islands as a base for their expansion into other Latin American territories. Prior to the emergence of the sugar plantation system, Cuba's economy was composed of mostly independent peasant farmers and squatters. By the nineteenth century, Cuba had been transformed into the "bourbon and sugar capital" of the region as a result of its large output of sugarcane, and the demand for African slave labor increased dramatically.

History of Slavery. As in the majority of Latin American colonies, African slaves produced wealth for Europe, both in terms of the slave trade itself and through the profits earned from the products sold in European markets as a result of their labor. The wealth of Cuba's plantation system depended on African slaves.

In 1789, in order to meet the Cuban needs, King Charles IV of Spain permitted unlimited importation of slaves into Havana. In 1792, Cuban slave merchants began to import Africans directly from the African continent. Havana became not only a major source of slaves for Spanish America but also a source of illegal slave traffic to the United States, where the slave trade was banned in 1829.

Before the nineteenth century, free persons of African descent were more numerous in Cuba than anywhere else in the Western Hemisphere. Free Africans were able to participate in all sorts of trades and activi-

LATINO ATTITUDES TOWARD JOB AND ADMISSION QUOTAS					
	Response (percentages)				
	1	2	3	4	5
Mexican Americans	19.4	11.9	30.2	9.3	29.3
Puerto Ricans	24.0	9.9	34.8	6.1	25.2
Cuban Americans	11.9	6.3	17.8	7.0	56.9
Non-Hispanic Whites	1.7	4.7	21.1	20.4	52.0

Source: Data are from the Latino National Political Survey, which polled a representative sample of 1,546 Mexican Americans, 589 Puerto Ricans, and 682 Cuban Americans in forty metropolitan areas in 1989-1990. See Rodolfo O. de la Garza et al., *Latino Voices: Mexican, Puerto Rican, and Cuban Perspectives on American Politics* (Boulder, Colo.: Westview Press, 1992), Table 7.36.

*Respondents were asked to rank their opinions on a scale of 1 to 5, with 1 indicating approval of government quotas for college admissions and hiring to ensure Hispanic representation and 5 indicating the belief that college admissions and hiring should be based entirely on merit.

Thousands of balscros *left Cuba in 1994 and attempted to reach the United States in makeshift boats.* (Impact Visuals, Steven Fish)

ties. Racial exclusion and color barriers, however, remained a constant reminder of separate societies in Cuba.

The expansion of the slave trade and slave populations increased the frequency of slave rebellions. As occurred elsewhere in Latin America and in the United States, slaves often ran away and established separate communities. Escaped Cuban slaves established communities called *pallenques*. Nine major slave revolts occurred between 1795 and 1843 in the provinces.

Movements Toward Equality. Abolition of SLAVERY was one product of the Ten Years' War (1868-1878) against Spain. One major anticolonial movement, led by Carlos Manuel de Cespedes, was begun by that leader's statements in El GRITO DE YARA. Cespedes freed his slaves and enlisted them into his army. People of African descent fought on the side of independence and composed a significant portion of the anticolonial army. Towns occupied by revolutionary forces often appointed freed slaves to municipal positions. Manuel Muñoz, a black Cuban, was appointed to a municipal council in eastern Cuba and orchestrated the Cuban national anthem.

Along with emancipation and the end of the Ten Years' War came the first attempts at the creation of racial equality in Cuba. Cuba's national hero José MARTÍ became a major advocate of racial equality. General Antonio Maceo, a black Cuban, was also a major force during the revolution. During the second war of independence (1895-1898), black military leaders included Flor Crombet, Perico Perez, and Isidro Acea. Cuba came under control of the United States as a result of the SPANISH-AMERICAN WAR (1898).

The Cuban Republic, established in 1902, began with vestiges of anti-Africanism and RACISM. Efforts were made to erase African influences in the culture and repress the practice of African-based religions such as SANTERÍA. People of African descent were also barred from holding public office. Protests were organized, and the Association of Black Independents was created to protect the rights of black persons. The organization served as the base for the development of Cuba's first black independent political party.

U.S. Presence in Cuba. The Independents rebelled in 1912, and the United States intervened in Cuba in order to protect the sugar estates in the eastern prov-

Participants in an Afro-Cuban dance class in Havana. (Hazel Hankin)

inces. The majority of Cuba's black population remained in the rural agricultural regions. Black persons in urban areas tended to be in the lower economic classes.

The presence of U.S. forces added confusion to the Cuban racial hierarchy. The system of racial classification commonly followed in the United States, whereby persons with small amounts of African heritage were considered black, was different from the classification systems used in Cuba and much of Latin America. The system from the United States slowly became the norm in Cuba, with many more people being classified as black as a result.

The Cuban Revolution. Racial and class inequalities in Cuba set the stage for the success of Fidel CASTRO's revolution in 1959. Afro-Cubans were split in their support of the revolution. Unlike other Cuban (and other Latin American) leaders, Castro admitted racial inequality and injustice in Cuban society, making these matters a subject of political debate.

Steps to deal with the political, economic, and social problems of racial inequalities were evident from the beginning of the new regime. The achievements of the postrevolutionary regime in the area of race relations are, however, subject to debate. Black Cuban author Carlos Moore, for example, emerged as one of the leading critics of failure to deal with RACISM.

Moore saw the Castro regime as trying to suppress African components of Cuban culture, with religion as evidence of the regime's continued preference for white, European culture and values. Moore has also criticized the regime's failure to fully integrate Afro-Cubans into the higher ranks of government and the professions.

Proponents of the CASTRO regime argue that racial equality has been achieved and that only traditional cultural manifestations that have opposed the revolution have been repressed. SANTERÍA, for example, has been repressed. Between 1969 and 1971, some *santeros* (practitioners of the religion) were alleged to have been involved in black market activities. Questions about revolutionary Cuba's achievement of racial equality will continue to be posed for some time.

Impact. The CUBAN REVOLUTION provoked the migration of large numbers of middle- and upper-class Cubans to the United States. Compared to other Latino migrants in the United States, the first wave of Cuban migrants to the United States, those who left Cuba during and immediately following the revolution, fared well both economically and politically. Black Cuban immigrants who followed often suffered from discrimination, both from their fellow Cubans and on the part of U.S. society.

Afro-Cubans have been a vital part of the creation of Cuban culture and Cuba's political and economic history. Because a large proportion of Cubans are of African descent, it is clear that the African influence will remain an important part of the Cuban future.

—*Walton Lyonnaise Brown*

SUGGESTED READINGS: • Clytus, John. *Black Man in Red Cuba*. Coral Gables, Fla.: University of Miami Press, 1970. • Cole, Johnnetta. *Race Toward Equality*. Havana, Cuba: J. Martí, 1986. • Moore, Carlos. *Castro, the Blacks, and Africa*. Los Angeles: Center for Afro-American Studies, University of California, 1992. • Nodal, Roberto. "The Black Man in Cuban Society: From Colonial Times to the Revolution." *Journal of Black Studies* 16 (March, 1986): 251-267. • Rout, Leslie. *The African Experience in Spanish America*. New York: Cambridge University Press, 1976.

Afro-Hispanics: People of African descent have played important roles in the histories of Spain and various Latin American countries. In ways paralleling their struggles in the United States, they rose out of SLAVERY to become integral members of their communities.

Moorish Influence. The overthrow of the Visigoths in 711 by Africans who had recently converted to Islam began eight hundred years of Moorish rule on the Iberian Peninsula. This was the first phase of African influence in the development of Hispanic culture, society, and history.

The period of Moorish domination has been considered to be one of Arabic rather than black or African influence because of the belief that the term "Arab" refers to a race of people. The term more accurately describes a vast multiracial conglomerate of Arabic-speaking people. "Moor," a term that originated during the Renaissance, refers to people with very dark skin. Many scholars assert that Moors were the North African ancestors of the present-day peoples of the Sahara and the Sahel, primarily the Fulani, the Tuareg, the Zenagha of southern Morocco, the Kunta and Tebbu of the Sahelian African countries, the Traza of Mauritania and Senegal, the Mogharba, and other Sudanese peoples, such as the Chaamba of Chad and Algeria.

The Moorish invasion of Iberia in the eighth century succeeded because of the military skills and leadership of Africans. Tarik, who led the invasion, is immortalized in the geographic name Gibraltar, meaning Ger-

This fort building in San Diego, California, shows Moorish influence in its design. (Diane C. Lyell)

ber Tarik (hill of Tarik). Tarik's army comprised approximately seven thousand men, of whom more than six thousand were Moorish Africans and three hundred were Arabs.

Yusuf Ibn Tashifin, the leader of the second black Moorish dynasty, routed Alphonso VI's army in 1086 and assumed leadership in Spain in 1091. The Almoravids ruled from Senegal to the Ebro River in Spain. Tashifin is also credited with conquering Algeria and Morocco. The third black Moorish dynasty, the Almahords, came to power after Yakub al-Mansur conquered Spain and Portugal, overthrowing the Almoravids, in 1184.

The Moors transformed the agricultural technology of the Iberian Peninsula by introducing advanced drainage and irrigation systems, reservoirs, aqueducts, storage facilities, marketing, and transportation and trading networks. Moorish city planners introduced gardens, parks, public baths, mosques, lush inner courtyards, and steady supplies of pure water. Moorish homes included bathrooms with supplies of hot and cold water. Architectural designs created cooling currents of fresh air in the summer and included pipes that conveyed warm air to provide heat in the winter. The Moors brought such crops to the peninsula as cereals, beans, peas, rice, olives, almonds, and various fruits including oranges, pomegranates, bananas, and coconuts.

The Moors influenced Iberian music, poetry, and dress. Ziryab, known as the blackbird because of his black complexion and his voice, arrived in Spain in 822. He introduced crystal tableware, new perfumes and deodorants, new fashions in dress and dress materials, and new forms of cooking. Moorish advances in mathematics and medicine included new concepts in trigonometry, vivisection, the dissection of dead bodies for research, and delicate surgical operations.

African Slave Trade. The era of African SLAVERY in the New World began with Portuguese and Spanish expansion in the Western Hemisphere and with the approval of popes Martin V (1454) and Calixtus (1456). The slave trade existed from the late fifteenth century until the late nineteenth century. Ironically, Christopher Columbus' navigator on the *Niña*, the pilot ship of his first voyage, was an African named Alonzo Pietro.

Goree Island, off the coast of Senegal, was occupied by Portugal in 1444. Over the course of three centuries, nearly twenty million slaves were brought to the island for transport to the Americas. Slightly more than twenty million others were transported directly to the Americas from Benin, Dahomey, Ghana, Guinea, Mozambique, and Angola. Yorubas from Nigeria, Mandinkas, Seres, Fulani, and Wolofs were sold in large numbers.

African slaves were dispersed throughout Latin America and the Caribbean. The profitability of the slave trade, along with the slaves' labor on plantations (particularly the large-scale sugarcane plantations) was a source of wealth throughout Latin America and the Caribbean. Slaves also introduced new agricultural techniques, crafts, and artisan skills.

Statistics on the number of slaves imported into Brazil range from ten million to twenty-five million. For the rest of South America, the figure is approximately 400,000. The Brazilian economy, like a few other plantation-dependent colonies of Latin America and the Caribbean, depended on a constant supply of slaves.

In Mexico, the largest concentrations of slavery were in Oaxaca and the cities of Veracruz and Pueblo.

At one time, Mexico rivaled Cuba in terms of the number of African slaves imported. Like Cuba, Mexico became a major source of slaves for North American slave dealers and plantations.

Throughout South America, African slaves and free Africans provided labor for agricultural plantations and mines. In the Andean nations of Uruguay, Chile, and Argentina, plantation slavery was not considered profitable. In the early 1800's, Peru found the slave system profitable. In most of these nations, national racial doctrines that emerged in the mid-1800's virtually eliminated African influence from cultural and political futures. Ecuador, the only nation in the region that allowed the immigration of free Africans, had a large population of Afro-Ecuadorans in the southern region of Loja and in three northern provinces in the 1990's.

Afro-Colombians and Afro-Venezuelans maintained their numerical significance and cultural integrity from the eras of slavery to the end of the twentieth century. A few Afro-Colombians emerged as leading politicians in the Liberal Party during the 1930's and 1940's. Jose Rafael Revenga was one of the first black people in Venezuela to become a member of congress

Afro-Hispanic culture combines elements with roots in Africa, Latin America, and Spain. (Hazel Hankin)

(1844-1848). He later became the secretary of internal affairs.

Cultural Impact. Efforts were made throughout Latin America to de-Africanize the slaves, through banning use of the drum and prohibitions against speaking African languages and practicing African rituals. Non-Islamic African-based religions, rituals, and forms of social organization nevertheless were retained by large numbers of people.

The Afro-Brazilian religions Umbanda and Candomblé, as well as the Afro-Cuban SANTERÍA, continue to be practiced throughout Latin America. These religious practices have been traced to traditions of the Yoruba and Bantu-speaking people of Africa. The slaves' African religions merged with European Catholicism; traditional African deities became associated with Catholic saints.

Latino musical forms such as SALSA, MERENGUE, MAMBO, RUMBA, and *JAROCHO* all have roots in African musical traditions. Percussion instruments associated with Hispanic music—CONGAS, BONGOS, *TIMBALES*, and MARACAS—have deep roots in the percussion requirements of African music. The Brazilian SAMBA and the Dominican merengue are dances that came directly from African slaves. The samba de roda, a dance from the Kimbundu tradition in Angola, has many forms: the circle samba, chanson samba, sambao, and bossa nova samba. The Brazilian national celebration of CARNAVAL is derived from African tradition. Carnival celebrations spread throughout Latin America and into the Latino communities of North America.

Afro-Hispanics also made major contributions to the food and language traditions of Latin America. The use of okra, certain beans, yams, bananas, and plantains derives from African foodways. In Honduras, the GARIFUNA (black Hondurans) preserved a distinct culture and dialect.

Social Impact. Not only were Afro-Hispanics subjected to the cruelties of SLAVERY, but in addition many countries developed rigid classification systems that divided populations into racial strata, perpetuating racial exclusion, degradation, and political and economic inequality. Throughout Latin America, Afro-Hispanics have been disproportionately subject to poverty, poor services, illiteracy, high levels of unemployment, and malnutrition. Their position has been

Dominican American women participate in a parade in New York City. (Richard B. Levine)

worsened by the poor economic conditions and political repression in many Latin American countries.

Although Afro-Hispanics share many problems and concepts, there are some differences in their status in various countries. Few people outside Uruguay, Mexico, Argentina, and Ecuador know of the existence of populations of African descent in those countries. In El Salvador, Nicaragua, and Guatemala, many people of African descent faded into the general Native American population and were relegated to the bottom of the socioeconomic ladder. In Nicaragua, a large black community, the Bluefields, thrives on the western coast. Belize (formerly the British Honduras) has maintained its distinctly African culture. In Costa Rica and Panama, people of African descent have remained significant in number and have historically challenged RACISM in their societies. Most wars of Latin American independence during the nineteenth century and some of the major political democratization movements in the twentieth century owe much to the bravery and support of people of African ancestry.

Brazil, in the late twentieth century, had the largest population of people of African descent outside Africa and the United States. It has been estimated that at least 60 percent of Brazil's population was of African descent in the early 1990's. Afro-Brazilians have actively opposed economic and social repression through groups such as the United Black Movement and have pursued democratization in Brazil.

As part of the immigrant Hispanic populations in North America, Afro-Hispanics are marginally accepted by their non-black compatriots, mirroring conditions in countries of origin, where dark-skinned people are often considered to be socially inferior. Economic reforms in the Americas, movements toward human and civil rights, and increasing appreciation of Afro-Hispanic cultural contributions offered hope for improvement of the status of Afro-Hispanics. —*Walton Lyonnaise Brown*

SUGGESTED READINGS:
- Chandler, Wayne. "The Moor: Light of Europe's Dark Age." In *African Presence in Early Europe*, edited by Ivan van Sertima. New Brunswick, N.J.: Transaction Books, 1985. An informative chapter on the role of the African Moors in Iberian history.
- *The Crisis* 93 (June/July, 1986). A special issue devoted to articles on the African diaspora in the Western Hemisphere, from South America to Canada.
- Davis, Darien J. *The African Dimensions in Latin American Culture*. Wilmington, Del.: Scholarly Resources, 1992. A study of the African dimension of Latin America, including selections on the colonial era, religion, music, and intermarriage.
- Forbes, Jack. *Black Africans and Native Americans*. New York: Basil Blackwell, 1988. A study of the relations between Africans and Native Americans in the New World.
- Fraginals, Manuel Moreno, ed. *Africa in Latin America*. Translated by Leonor Blum. New York: Holmes & Meier, 1984. Fourteen essays on the African experience in Latin America, from the period of slavery on. Originally published in Spanish by UNESCO.
- Jackson, Richard L. *Black Literature and Humanism in Latin America*. Athens: University of Georgia Press, 1988. An examination of Afro-Hispanic literature.
- Rout, Leslie. *The African Experience in Spanish America*. Cambridge, England: Cambridge University Press, 1976. A nation by nation study of the history of Afro-Latinos throughout Spanish-speaking Latin America, from slavery to the mid-1970's.
- Van Sertima, Ivan, ed. *Golden Age of the Moor*. New Brunswick, N.J.: Transaction Books, 1992. An anthology of detailed studies on the role of the African Moors in Iberian history. Special attention should be given to the historical references and extensive bibliography.

Agricultural Labor Relations Act (1975): California law signed by Governor Jerry Brown. For the first time in American history, farmworkers were guaranteed the right to bargain collectively. Unauthorized workers, many of whom were too fearful of deportation to report abuses they witnessed, were encouraged to file complaints with the Agricultural Labor Relations Board (ALRB). They could also vote on whether they would be represented by a union. César CHÁVEZ of the UNITED FARM WORKERS (UFW) and other labor organizers tried to encourage all migrant workers to sign union cards. They were unable to prevent many legal workers from being fired for their union activities. Wealthy growers could afford to appeal the decisions of the ALRB in the courts while most workers gave up their chance for back pay and moved on to find non-union employment elsewhere.

Agricultural unions: Agricultural laborers, who are among the poorest and most disadvantaged workers in the United States, have consistently sought to improve their working conditions by organizing unions. Farmworker unions have struggled against considerable odds to achieve wage increases, improved legislative

Agricultural unions have fought for a variety of causes, including health care and safe working conditions. (David Bacon)

protections, and public recognition of the gross inequities that define the lives of MIGRANT LABORERS.

The history of farmworker unions in the United States is the tale of a continual uphill battle in which workers with few resources have struggled against extremely powerful political forces in an effort to improve conditions in what is perhaps the nation's least desirable job. The achievements of agricultural unions stand as extraordinary testaments to the courage and commitment of both farm laborers and farmworker organizers.

The unskilled and seasonal nature of farm labor makes organization of migrant and other farmworkers particularly difficult. Because most farm work requires no formal education and few special skills, employers can easily replace dissatisfied workers. In addition, because farm labor is highly seasonal, workers often travel long distances in order to piece together enough short-term jobs to earn a living, thereby establishing few close ties or political alliances with the communities in which they work. In addition, farmworkers have almost always been recruited from among the poorest and most disadvantaged members of American soci-

ety, in particular minorities, recent immigrants, and the dispossessed.

In the late twentieth century, farmworkers still were exempted from many basic labor protections. As of 1990, the average annual wage for seasonal farmworkers was $6,500, and more than half of all farmworkers were living in poverty. As a result of the difficult, often exploitative conditions that farmworkers face, work stoppages and spontaneous strikes have been common throughout U.S. farm labor history.

Worker Protections. One of the most significant obstacles facing farmworker unions involves the specific exemption of agricultural workers from the NATIONAL LABOR RELATIONS ACT (NLRA). The NLRA, passed by Congress in 1935 and often referred to as the Wagner Act, provides workers with basic federal protections regarding the rights to organize, strike, and engage in collective bargaining.

Although proposals to include farmworkers under the NLRA have been presented repeatedly in Congress, farmworkers continue to be denied its fundamental worker protections. They are also denied other protections. For example, agricultural laborers are exempted from equal protection under federal minimum wage and child labor laws and remain exempted from equal coverage under numerous state laws, including workers' compensation and unemployment insurance. To a large degree, the special exemption of agricultural workers from protective labor legislation is a function of the relative powerlessness of farmworkers, the limited influence of farmworker unions, and the failure of traditional industrial unions to demand that agricultural laborers be provided with the same rights as other U.S. workers.

Early Twentieth Century Organizing. Throughout the early 1900's, farmworkers engaged in numerous, scattered labor disputes. The INDUSTRIAL WORKERS OF THE WORLD (IWW, known as the "Wobblies") was the first major labor union to organize farmworkers. In 1913, its attempts to improve wages and working conditions among hop workers in California led to the infamous Wheatland riot, in which four people were killed and numerous workers were injured. The event drew national attention to the low wages and poor working conditions of agricultural laborers. In 1915, the IWW helped establish the first farmworker union, the Agricultural Workers Organization. When the United States entered World War I, the initial gains of the IWW were rapidly lost, partially as a result of the movement's antiwar position. In the late 1920's, there was a second wave of farmworker organizing involving growing numbers of Mexican and Filipino immigrant workers.

The 1930's. Between 1930 and 1939, there were more than 140 strikes in California involving more than 125,000 workers. Some of these strikes were spontaneous, and others were planned by the initially successful Cannery and Agricultural Workers Industrial Union (CAWIU). As workers grew increasingly militant, their efforts were met with violent opposition on the part of growers, who hired armed thugs to protect their fields and break up strikes.

By 1935, the CAWIU was dissolved. Organizing efforts faced more difficulties as more than 300,000 Dust Bowl refugees made their way to California, providing growers with an overabundance of cheap labor. In 1937, the Congress of Industrial Organizations (CIO) organized a union of farmworkers, drawing its support from the exploitation of Dust Bowl refugees and the increasingly important connections between organized labor and the Democratic Party.

In 1975, the United Farm Workers went on strike against the Gallo corporation. (Lou DeMatteis)

In 1934, in the rural South, the Southern Tenant Farmers' Union (STFU) was formed to organize tenant farmers and sharecroppers who labored under conditions of extreme poverty and continual debt to landowners. The STFU had notable success in uniting white and black workers in a common labor struggle, and by 1937 the union claimed more than thirty thousand members in seven states. The STFU successfully negotiated improved wages and fought forced evictions but faced opposition, intimidation, and violent resistance from established political interests. After affiliating with the CIO, the STFU experienced a number of organizational problems, and by the early 1940's, the union had lost all but a few hundred members.

Perhaps the most successful farmworker union in U.S. history arose from the CIO's organization of sugarcane and pineapple workers in Hawaii. In the late 1930's, after successfully organizing dockworkers into the International Longshoremen's and Warehousemen's Union (ILWU), the CIO began organizing farm laborers working in fields owned by the same employers. Although the ILWU staged a number of successful strikes, its most significant victories resulted from the election of a number of prolabor political candidates and the passage of the Employment Relations Act of 1945, which gave farmworkers the right to form unions in Hawaii.

As other farmworker protections were signed into law, Hawaii gradually created a system in which farm work was redefined as a relatively stable form of employment that offered reasonable worker protections and decent, competitive wages. The conditions of farmworkers' lives in Hawaii stood in stark contrast to those of agricultural workers virtually everywhere else in the United States.

In addition to seeking worker empowerment, the farmworker organizing efforts of the 1930's focused public attention on the oppressive living and working conditions of the nation's farm laborers. Public outrage at the treatment of farm laborers was also fueled by the publication of John Steinbeck's *The Grapes of Wrath* (1939), a novel about Dust Bowl refugees laboring in California, and Carey McWilliams' *Factories in the Field* (1939), a journalistic exposé of the plight of farm laborers. In response to public concern, a commission headed by Congressman Robert La Follette conducted a series of hearings in 1939 and 1940. The hearings revealed the severe mistreatment of farm laborers and

César Chávez leads the United Farm Workers in a 1987 demonstration. (Impact Visuals, Rick Gerharter)

Immigrant Mexican landscape gardeners demonstrated in San Jose, California, for their right to organize a union. (David Bacon)

the growers' illegal use of violent intimidation against union members and organizers. Although the La Follette Committee proposed legislative changes to include farmworkers within the NLRA, these were never enacted because the committee's report was not issued until 1942, by which time the United States had entered World War II.

Wartime and Postwar Developments. During World War II, virtually all the previous gains of farmworker unions were reversed. Many farm laborers were drafted into the military or found higher-paying jobs in war production plants. Around the same time, large western growers began to bring thousands of Mexican farmworkers to the United States through the BRACERO PROGRAM (1942-1964), sponsored by the U.S. government. The Bracero Program severely hindered farmworker organization by enabling the entry of a total of four to five million Mexican workers, who were contracted to work for specific employers and then sent back to Mexico at the end of each season. It was extremely difficult to organize braceros because they were foreigners who could be repatriated to Mexico for almost any reason. In 1946, the American Federation of Labor (AFL)

chartered the NATIONAL FARM LABOR UNION (NFLU). Under the direction of Ernesto GALARZA, the NFLU sought to organize California's largely Latino farm labor force and struggled against the Bracero Program.

In 1959, the combined AFL-CIO decided to become involved in farm labor organizing and set up the Agricultural Workers Organizing Committee (AWOC). This group staged a number of strikes during the 1960's but was never particularly successful, largely because of its reliance on traditional, hierarchical organizing strategies. A more grassroots approach to organizing grew out of the efforts of Mexican American activists who formed the COMMUNITY SERVICE ORGANIZATION (CSO) in 1952, as well as the work of Thomas McCullough, a Roman Catholic priest who organized the Agricultural Workers Association (AWA) in 1958.

The United Farm Workers. César CHÁVEZ gained his early training in the CSO. In 1962, he formed the Farm Workers Association (FWA), which was later renamed the NATIONAL FARM WORKERS ASSOCIATION (NFWA) in recognition of the group's objective of creating a national union of agricultural laborers. Unlike traditional industrial labor organizers, Chávez sought to build a grassroots movement to empower farmworkers to achieve goals arrived at through consensus and a critical understanding of their situation. In 1965, the NFWA became increasingly involved in labor strikes. Through its affiliation with the AFL-CIO, it was renamed the United Farm Workers Organizing Committee (UFWOC).

The UFWOC signed its first contract in 1966. The union's highly successful national boycott of table grapes led to negotiation of 150 contracts in California by 1970. In 1972, the UFWOC was granted a union charter and was renamed the UNITED FARM WORKERS (UFW). The UFW went on to organize farmworkers in Texas, sign a major contract with Minute Maid to harvest oranges in Florida, and play a crucial role in educating the American public about the plight of the nation's farm laborers. Despite extraordinary achievements, however, UFW membership declined from more than 100,000 in the 1970's to approximately 20,000 by 1992.

Other Modern Unions. Although the UFW is by far the largest and most visible farmworker union, a number of others were operating in the United States in the early 1990's. These include the Comite de Apoyo al Trabajado Agricola (CATA), which began organizing Puerto Rican farmworkers in 1979 in New Jersey; La Union del Pueblo Entero (LUPE) in Arizona; and the FARM LABOR ORGANIZING COMMITTEE (FLOC), based in Ohio.

The FLOC is a particularly interesting farmworker union because its most significant gains occurred in the 1980's, a difficult decade for organized labor. The union was founded by Baldemar VELASQUEZ in 1967. After many years of grassroots organizing and a successful six-year boycott, the FLOC signed its first contract with the Campbell Soup Company in 1986. Since then, the FLOC has had considerable success, negotiating a number of cooperative agreements between farmworkers, vegetable growers, and food processing corporations.

Conclusion. The organizing gains of the 1960's and 1970's led to improvements in wages and working conditions and, in some states, the passage of relatively progressive labor legislation. In addition, the UFW GRAPE BOYCOTT and other highly public actions increased the public's awareness of the exploitation of migrant farmworkers.

Many of these gains, however, have been undercut by massive changes in the nation's economic and political climate. In particular, the steady drop in the real value of the minimum wage and the increased immigration of undocumented Latino workers willing to accept low wages and poor working conditions have significantly affected farmworker unions. According to the National Agricultural Workers Survey, in 1990, less than 1 percent of the nation's farmworkers were referred to their jobs through a union hiring agreement.

By the early 1990's, the future of farmworker organizing was uncertain. Unless social and political conditions changed dramatically, it seemed unlikely that farmworker unions would gain enough political authority to significantly improve the living and working conditions that characterize migrant farm work. Nevertheless, continued struggles on the part of agricultural unions will no doubt play an important role in protecting existing farmworkers' rights and in pressuring American society to provide migrants with the same fundamental protections afforded other workers.

—*Daniel Rothenberg*

SUGGESTED READINGS:

- Goldfarb, Ronald. *Migrant Farm Workers: A Caste of Despair*. Ames: Iowa State University Press, 1981. An excellent review of how farmworkers have been exempted from basic labor protections, coupled with an argument that grassroots union organizing is necessary for improvements in the lives of workers.
- Jenkins, J. Craig. *The Politics of Insurgency: The Farm Worker Movement in the 1960s*. New York: Columbia University Press, 1985. A detailed discussion of the rise of the UFW, with an overview of agricultural labor organizing in California from the 1940's through the 1980's.
- Majka, Linda, and Theo Majka. *Farm Workers, Agribusiness, and the State*. Philadelphia: Temple University Press, 1982. A detailed review of farmworker organizing in California. Focuses on the relationship between the state and large-scale agriculture.
- Matthiessen, Peter. *Sal Si Puedes: César Chávez and the New American Revolution*. New York: Random House, 1969. An exceptionally well-written account of the life of Chávez and the organizing activities of the UFW.
- Meister, Dick, and Anne Loftis. *A Long Time Coming: The Struggle to Unionize America's Farm Workers*. New York: Macmillan, 1977. Comprehensive and highly readable account of the history of farm labor movements in the United States.

Agriculture, Latino contributions to: The indigenous peoples of the Americas provided staple foods for the Western Hemisphere and colonists. They contributed

Latinos contributed many of the practices now common in the cattle industry. (University Libraries, Arizona State University, Tempe)

methods for growing crops in difficult conditions, introduced plants and grains now considered to be basic and necessary foods, and helped to develop the art of cattle husbandry on the North and South American continents.

Maize. Maize is perhaps the most important agricultural contribution of the peoples of the Americas. When Christopher Columbus arrived in the New World, maize (Indian corn) was unknown in Europe. The Spanish found this grain growing throughout South America and Mexico. They quickly adapted Incan, AZTEC, and American Indian methods to grow it in Europe and export it to other countries. Corn quickly became a staple food worldwide.

Indian tribes greatly improved the variety, growth potential, and cultivation of MAIZE. The Hopi of Arizona developed "pure" varieties of the plant. The Aztecs and Incas developed strains of the corn plant that reduced the complex system of branches to a simple stem, yielding maximal amounts of the grain. Indian methods isolated the strains of corn that gave the highest yields with the least amount of effort. Indian tribes provided these corn strains to the Spanish colonists as well as teaching cultivation methods, undoubtedly saving many of the colonists from starvation.

Tribes from Mexico and Central America cultivated corn with stalks as high as twenty feet, with stems so large and firm that they were used to build houses and fences. The most beneficial use of corn, however, was as a food with high nutritional value. Modern society owes much to Latin American, Mexican, and Southwestern Indians for the development and generous introduction of the maize plant.

The Chile Pepper. The chile pepper and its myriad strains and varieties were also cultivated by native Indian tribes in what is now the southwestern United States, Mexico, and Latin America. Its cultivation quickly spread throughout Europe and East India. It has remained an important crop in the Southwest. It is used as a condiment as well as for various medicinal purposes.

Fabian Garcia led scientific studies of chiles and their uses, heading the New Mexico Agricultural Experiment Station during the 1920's. Scientists have confirmed that the chile plant is an important and healthy source of riboflavin, thiamin, and critical minerals. In a region where food was often scarce, the chile was, and remains, an important source of nutrition.

Other Food Products. The Incas grew many crops that were overlooked by the Spanish and subsequent

Latinos, particularly Basques, are known for a tradition of sheep raising. (AP/ Wide World Photos)

colonizers. Recently, scientists have begun to study the cultivation of crops that may have nutritional and medicinal value. Although the crops have not been forgotten by the Indian tribes of the Andes, they have been overlooked by the mainstream of international science and people outside the region. Most of these crops were developed by indigenous groups, some before the time of the Inca Empire. By the time of the Spanish Conquest, the Incas had developed advanced methods of cultivation for these plants and had dispersed methods for planting and harvesting them throughout the Andean region.

Agronomists and ethnobotanists working in the Andes are now studying these traditional Latin American Indian foods. The cultivation of many of these plants has begun around the world. Quinoa (a grain) is being grown successfully in the United States, oca (a tuber) has been planted in Eastern Europe, and cherimoyea (a fruit) has been an important crop in Spain's agriculture.

At the time of the Spanish Conquest, the Incas not only cultivated as many species of plants as the farmers of Asia and Europe, but they also did so in harsh and challenging topographical regions. They had to contend with steep mountainsides up to four kilometers high along the ridges of a large continent that varied in climate from tropical to polar. These peoples successfully grew a wealth of roots, grains, legumes, vegetables, fruits, and nuts without iron, wheels, or work animals for plowing. Pre-Columbian tribes terraced, irrigated, and produced abundant food for more than fifteen million people.

Historians credit the astounding productivity of Incan agriculture to the remarkable public organization and agricultural methods of the Incas. Francisco Pizarro's conquest of the Incas led to their crops being thrown into obscurity even though they included some widely adaptable, uncommonly nutritious, and delicious foods. According to the National Research Council, which led research into reviving these crops in the late twentieth century, Inca staple foods have the potential to become important new sources of sustenance for today's population.

Agricultural Methods. Tribes such as the Mimbres of southwestern New Mexico had developed water conservation structures, check dams, terrace systems, irrigation canals, and bordered fields hundreds of years before the Spanish came to the Americas. Such methods for farming in dry regions taught European colonists how to survive in harsh climates.

Latinos have also contributed to the cattle industry. Hispano-Mexican practices established enduring patterns of livestock husbandry in the Southwest. Mexican and Southwestern Latino cattle breeders were instrumental in helping to develop hardy breeds of cattle. The growth of the cattle industry in the Southwest depended on Mexican-Latino methods in development since the sixteenth century.

Conclusion. The Latino-Hispanic and indigenous tribal contributions to agriculture lie in both agricultural methods and crops. Although many people of the twentieth century have perceived Latinos primarily as field workers, there is a strong tradition of agricultural innovation and successful experimentation within the Latino culture. —*Manuel Luis Martinez*

SUGGESTED READINGS: • Advisory Committee on Technology Innovation, Board on Science and Technology for International Development, National Research Council. *Lost Crops of the Incas: Little-Known Plants of the Andes with Promise for Worldwide Cultivation.* Washington, D.C.: National Academy Press, 1989. • Dethloff, Henry C., and Irvin M. May, Jr., eds. *Southwestern Agriculture: Pre-Columbian to Modern.* College Station: Texas A&M Press, 1982. • Soustelle, Jacques. *The Daily Life of the Aztecs, on the Eve of the Spanish Conquest.* Translated by Patrick O'Brian. London: Weidenfeld and Nicolson, 1961. • Wallace, Henry A., and William L. Brown. *Corn and Its Early Fathers.* Rev. ed. Ames: Iowa State University Press, 1988. • Weatherwax, Paul. *Indian Corn in Old America.* New York: Macmillan, 1954.

Agringado: Negative term for a person of Latino ancestry who rejects his or her ethnic background. This derogatory term is used by Latinos to refer to a Latino who has become Anglicized in culture and language. The term literally means "like a gringo." Its implication is that a Latino has rejected Latino culture and ethnicity in favor of mainstream Anglo culture.

Aguilar, Robert Peter (b. Apr. 15, 1931, Maderas, Calif.): Attorney and U.S. district court judge. Aguilar completed his undergraduate studies at the University of California, Berkeley, in 1954. He earned a law degree at Hastings College of Law in San Francisco. Aguilar practiced law from 1960 to 1979, with the firms Mezzetti and Aguilar, Aguilar and Aguilar, and Aguilar and Edwards.

Aguilar's first appointment to the bench occurred in 1979, when he was named to serve as California Superior Court Judge for Santa Clara County. In 1980, President Jimmy Carter appointed Aguilar to the U.S. District Court for the Northern District of California.

Robert Aguilar was acquitted of a charge of obstruction of justice in 1990; his later conviction on another charge was overturned. (AP/Wide World Photos)

Aguilar served as a federal judge for the U.S. District Court in San Francisco until 1990. He was found guilty that year of illegally disclosing wiretap information. On April 19, 1994, the U.S. Court of Appeals for the Ninth Circuit reversed Aguilar's conviction for racketeering.

Aguilera-Hellweg, Max (b. 1955, Fresno, Calif.): Photographer. Aguilera-Hellweg is known for unusual and often eccentric portraits of a wide range of subjects including Disney studio executives, exotic priestesses, and surgeons at work in operating rooms.

Aguilera-Hellweg's unique perspective is evident in a 1989 project for *Savvy* magazine. Assigned to photograph a top American neurosurgeon, he brought his camera to the operating room and captured on film the exposed spine of a patient undergoing the removal of vertebrae. Fascinated by the patient's vulnerable interior, Aguilera-Hellweg began work on a book of photographs of surgery.

In the 1990's, Aguilera-Hellweg focused on the motion picture and entertainment industry. He was one of seventy-five people commissioned to photograph celebrities for the book *A Day in the Life of Hollywood* (1992).

Aguinaldo: Religious and secular Christmas song indigenous to the Iberian Peninsula, Puerto Rico, and Venezuela. *Aguinaldos* or *villancicos* (the names are used interchangeably) descended from the sixteenth century Spanish *villancico*. Resembling the Puerto Rican SEIS, their melodies are in two-four or six-eight meter with some syncopation, ascribed to African influences. *Aguinaldos* are performed by *aguinalderos*, groups of young singers accompanied by wooden, gourd, or metal *charrascas* (scrapers), MARACAS, *tamboras* (double-headed drum that hangs from the player's shoulder), *cuernos* (horns), guitars, and CUATROS.

Aid to Families with Dependent Children (AFDC): Main U.S. welfare program providing for families with needy children, including many poor Latinos. AFDC was created in 1935 by President Franklin D. Roosevelt as part of a bill that became the Social Security Act. It eventually covered families put in need

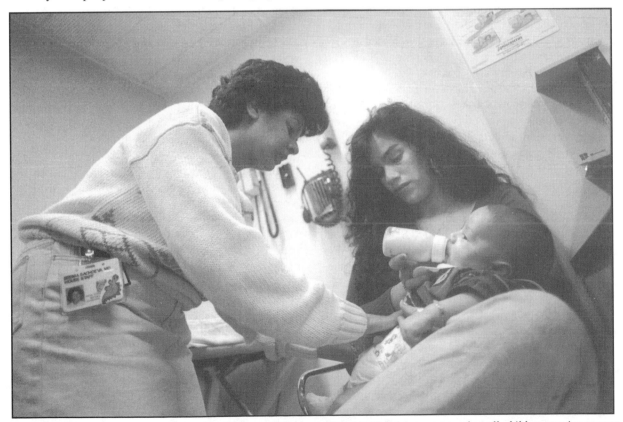

This mother may be able to afford medical treatment for her child; AFDC helps to ensure that all children receive proper care. (Hazel Hankin)

by the death, continued absence, unemployment, or incapacity of a parent.

AFDC is administered as a grant-in-aid program, in which the federal government matches state expenditures in varying amounts, depending on the state. States with lower per capita incomes receive a higher percentage of their expenditures as federal matching funds. Each state decides its own definition of need standards and what is covered in the standards (such as housing, food, clothing, and utilities).

AFDC operates on the principle that the government is responsible for ensuring that needy children are cared for in their own households. The government views AFDC support as a temporary option for families after all other possible sources of income have been exhausted.

Over the years, AFDC expanded to include social services. During the 1960's, as women became an increasing proportion of the work force, the federal government decided that women no longer needed to stay at home to care for their children until they were grown. The result was the Work Incentive Program (WIN), which required every AFDC participant over the age of sixteen to register for job training or employment unless attending school, caring for a child under the age of six, or otherwise unable to enroll in such programs. In 1990, WIN was replaced by Job Opportunities and Basic Skills Training (JOBS). This program offered help in passing the high school equivalency test, basic education including English training for nonfluent speakers, job skills training, job search assistance, community work experience, work supplementation, and childcare.

About 17 percent of AFDC families were Latino in the early 1990's. The utilization of AFDC programs among various Latino groups varied greatly, however. The largest two groups of Latinos in the United States, Mexican Americans and Puerto Ricans, made up about 75 percent of all Latinos in the United States and about 80 percent of the Latino poor. Puerto Ricans tended to settle in urban northeastern areas where the economy was worsening. A growing number of their families were headed by single women, which led them to use AFDC more than Mexican Americans. The latter group more often settled in the Southwest, where new jobs were on the rise, and had more two-parent families. Undocumented status, however, prohibited some Mexicans and Central Americans from applying for AFDC. Refugees and asylees may be eligible for AFDC, although if they are sponsored by agencies, they are ineligible for three years unless the agency loses the ability to provide for them.

AIDS. *See* **Acquired immune deficiency syndrome**

Alabado: Religious hymn sung in parts of the American Southwest. An *alabado* is a religious hymn sung in Catholic worship, celebrations, and funerals; sometimes it is a part of daily worship in the home. The *alabado* tradition exists in New Mexico and southern Colorado, where it has been preserved by the Penitent Brothers of the Third Order of St. Francis, a once-flagellant society in New Mexico that has held onto Spanish roots with tenacity. In the religious context *alabados* are sung as ritual music, but they are also sung at nonliturgical events. The contents and origins of *alabados* vary. Some were written in honor of God, the Virgin, or saints; some deal with human sin. Some *alabados* have Spanish origins, some are from Mexico, and some were written by local New Mexico and Colorado poets. *Alabados* traditionally are sung without accompaniment, with solo parts followed by congregational response. They traditionally begin with the words *Alabado sea* (blessed be), referring to the Sacraments.

Alacranes Mojados, Los: Music group. Los Alacranes Mojados were a group of four Chicanos from San Diego, nicknamed El Chunky, El Prieto, El Diablo, and El Chulo. They were based at the Centro Cultural de la Raza in San Diego and played in such settings as farmworker camps, public schools, universities, prisons, factories, and hotels. Their music mixed MÚSICA NORTEÑA, *veracruzana*, and other Latin American styles. The group was active in the 1970's.

Alambrista: Term for an illegal entrant into the United States from Mexico. The term comes from the word *alambre* (wire) and refers to someone who crosses the high wire fence along northwestern portions of the Mexico/United States border, especially between California and Baja California Norte. The *alambrista* presumably has climbed over the fence or gone through a gap or hole. The term is pejorative, equivalent to the term MOJADO (wet one), used to describe undocumented immigrants who have supposedly crossed the Rio Grande into Texas.

Alamo, Battle of the (Feb. 23-Mar. 6, 1836): In this battle, Texas rebels fighting the Mexican government used an old Spanish mission as a military fortress. After two weeks of siege, the Mexican army defeated the Texans, and all the Alamo's military defenders met their death.

A wire fence in some places forms the only barrier separating the United States and Mexico. (Impact Visuals, Imagen Latina)

The Battle of the Alamo. (Library of Congress)

During the early part of the TEXAS REVOLT, the rebels succeeded in forcing Mexican soldiers to retreat from the region. General Sam Houston, commander of the Texas forces, wanted to concentrate his troops, and he ordered his subordinates to destroy the fortifications at San Antonio and to abandon the place. A number of Texans disagreed with this plan, however, and about 145 of them decided to defend San Antonio. Among these were Davy Crockett, frontiersman and former Tennessee congressman; Jim Bowie, another noted frontiersman; and Lieutenant Colonel William Travis. When Mexican general Antonio López de Santa Anna arrived with nearly four thousand men, the Texans retreated to within the walls of an old Spanish mission called the Alamo.

Founded in 1718 as the mission of San Antonio Valero, the Alamo was one of the earliest Mexican outposts in the region. Although the towers and roofs had since collapsed, the Alamo provided some defense for the rebels; for example, its walls were four feet thick and twenty-two feet high. On the other hand, the walls did not have military towers for sharpshooters. Within the walls were a chapel and a barracks. The area enclosed by the walls was about three acres.

On February 24, the Texans refused Santa Anna's demand for surrender, instead opening fire with their cannon. Travis sent out a call for reinforcements, and on March 1, Captain Albert Martin arrived with thirty-two men, bringing the total to about 185 soldiers. Eight of these men were Mexican Texans who chose to cast their lot with the rebels. Also present in the Alamo compound were between fifteen and twenty women, children, and slaves.

On March 6, the Mexican army repeatedly assaulted the Alamo. The Texans were able to turn back the first two assaults, but on the third try, Mexican soldiers made it over the wall. Fierce hand-to-hand combat followed, but the cause was hopeless for the outnumbered defenders.

All the soldiers defending the Alamo died on March 6. Most were killed in the fighting, and a handful were killed after capture, on the orders of General Santa Anna. The general spared the noncombatants who were present. Mexican casualties were also heavy, numbering about one-third of their force.

The fall of the Alamo sent Texas into a panic. General Sam Houston was angered by the defenders' decision to disobey his orders, but before the Battle of San Jacinto, General Houston urged his troops to "Remember the Alamo!" The Texans won that battle, on April 21, 1836, and captured Santa Anna. The Treaty of Velasco, signed by Santa Anna after his defeat, provided for the independence of Texas.

Alarcón, Norma (b. 1943?, Monclova, Mexico): Writer. Alarcón is a respected Chicana feminist scholar who has written seminal essays on some of literature's most highly acclaimed Chicana writers. She is an editor, writer, and founder of Third Woman Press, based at the University of California, Berkeley, where she has taught in the departments of Chicano studies and ethnic studies. Alarcón has published creative work but is known primarily for her scholarship.

A bilingual scholar, Alarcón translates literary criticism and feminist essays into Spanish. Her translations include her published dissertation *Rosario Castellanos' Feminist Poetics: Against the Sacrificial Contract* (1983; *Ninfomania: El discurso feminista en las obra poetica de Rosario Castellanos*, 1992) and, with Ana CASTILLO, the influential collection *Esta puente, mi espalda: Voces de mujeres tercermundistas en los Estados Unidos* (1988; *This Bridge Called My Back: Writings of Radical Women of Color*, 1988), which also contains an essay by her.

Alarcón's essays appear in several journals and collections. She has also collaborated on several scholarly texts, including the *Bibliography of Hispanic Women Writers* (1980) with Sylvia Kossnar. With Cherríe MORAGA and Ana Castillo, she edited *The Sexuality of Latinas* (1989) and *Chicana Critical Issues* (1993).

Alatorre, Richard (b. May 15, 1943, Los Angeles, Calif.): Legislator. Alatorre completed his undergraduate studies at California State University in 1965 and

Councilman Richard Alatorre following a 1994 press conference announcing a pay increase for Los Angeles police officers. (AP/Wide World Photos)

went on to the University of Southern California for a master's degree in public administration. Alatorre served as western regional director for the National Association for the Advancement of Colored People (NAACP) Legal Defense Fund in 1967. He also taught at both the University of California, Irvine, and California State University.

Alatorre's career in public service began with his election to the California State Assembly in 1972. He served as an assemblyman until 1985, when he was elected to the Los Angeles City Council. He began service as a member of the Democratic National Credentials Committee in 1972 and continued to hold that position into the 1990's, serving as chairman of this committee at the 1984 Democratic National Convention.

Albizu, Olga (b. 1924, Ponce, Puerto Rico): Painter. Albizu is recognized for her abstract paintings reproduced on album covers of Latin-inspired music. She became widely known for covers done for the albums of Stan Getz in the late 1950's and continued to do covers in the 1960's.

Under the guidance of Spanish painter Estéban Vicente, Albizu studied at the University of Puerto Rico and was graduated in 1948. That year, she went to New York, New York, on a University of Puerto Rico fellowship for postgraduate study. Albizu held her first art exhibit in 1956, the year she moved to the United States. Soon after, she began receiving coverage in leading art magazines. By the 1960's, she was well known in New York art circles. A student of abstract expressionist pioneer Hans Hofmann, she represented the abstract tradition in New York.

Albizu gained national recognition with *Growth* (1960), an abstract oil work in warm colors that was reproduced for the cover of a bossa nova album by musicians Getz and Gilberto. Albizu was subsequently commissioned to paint album covers for other companies. Because the albums themselves were popular, her art was recognized in record shops and homes across the United States. In 1966, Albizu's paintings were included in an international exhibition at the Organization of American States building in Washington, D.C.

Albizu Campos, Pedro (Sept. 12, 1891, Ponce, Puerto Rico—Apr. 21, 1965, San Juan, Puerto Rico): Nationalist leader. Albizu earned a law degree from Harvard University in 1923. At Harvard, he became interested in world liberation trends and also saw (and perhaps experienced) American racial prejudice.

Shortly after returning to Puerto Rico, Albizu joined the Nationalist Party, which had been established in 1922 to pursue independence for Puerto Rico. Albizu repeatedly pointed out that Puerto Ricans needed complete control of their affairs to successfully attack problems such as overpopulation and illiteracy. He became head of the Nationalist Party in 1930. Defeat in the 1932 elections, however, convinced Albizu that Puerto Rico would not achieve independence through the democratic process. Albizu then pursued this goal through direct revolutionary action.

Albizu was arrested in 1936 for conspiring against the United States. He and other Nationalists were taken to the United States and convicted of seditious conspiracy. He returned to Puerto Rico in 1948, where he and other Nationalists continued to emphasize violence as one way of eliminating the American presence in Puerto Rico. The government returned Albizu to jail after four Nationalists went on a shooting spree at the visitors' gallery of the U.S. House of Representatives in 1954, but his deteriorating health forced his transfer to San Juan's Presbyterian Hospital two years later.

Albóndigas: Meatballs made from ground meat or fish. *Albóndigas* vary greatly from region to region throughout Latin America. South American *albóndigas* usually are made from one kind of meat (or two kinds blended together) and are mildly spiced; Mexican *albóndigas* usually are made from one kind of meat, fish, or shellfish and often are more heavily spiced. *Albóndigas* usually are served in soup, but they also can be served with sauce or in other dishes. Both the name and the dish derive from Arabic predecessors transmitted through Spain to the Americas.

Albuquerque, New Mexico: Largest city in New Mexico, Albuquerque is a leading center for industry, trade, transportation, and research in the Southwest.

Albuquerque has long been a crossroads in the Southwest, beginning with the original inhabitants. The first Spanish settler was Luis Carbajal, a soldier. He built a hacienda and laid out an *estancia*. During POPÉ'S REVOLT (1680), an uprising of local Indians, the hacienda was destroyed, and the inhabitants fled.

The Spanish population returned in 1706, the beginning of the town's official records. Francisco Cuervo y Valdés persuaded twelve families of the town of Bernalillo, nineteen miles north, to settle in the new area. To charter the city, Cuervo claimed to have thirty families settled. This number made the area a villa, or city, instead of a town. It was eventually named La Villa de

Pedro Albizu Campos at a 1936 gathering. (AP/Wide World Photos)

LATINO POPULATION OF ALBUQUERQUE, NEW MEXICO, 1990

Total number of Latinos = 178,310; 37% of population

Puerto Ricans 0.6%   Cuban Americans 0.3%

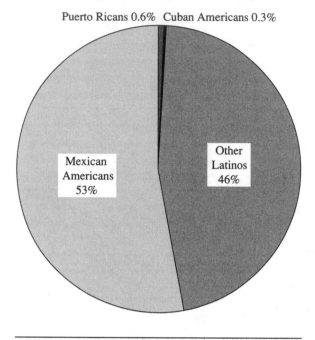

Mexican Americans 53%

Other Latinos 46%

Source: Data are from Marlita A. Reddy, ed., *Statistical Record of Hispanic Americans* (Detroit: Gale Research, 1993), Table 110.

Note: Figures represent the population of the Metropolitan Statistical Area as delineated by the U.S. Bureau of the Census. Percentages are rounded to the nearest whole number except for Cuban Americans and Puerto Ricans, for whom rounding is to the nearest 0.1%.

San Felipe de Neri de Alburquerque (the first "r" was later dropped from the spelling). The patron saint was changed from the original St. Francis to St. Philip Neri at the demand of the Spanish government. Boundaries were set at one league in all directions from the central plaza. These boundaries overlapped other grants, and confusion existed for almost three hundred years.

The town grew steadily in the decades after its resettlement. Church records from 1769 give a population of 1,814. Irrigation provided water for grain and tobacco fields, orchards, and vineyards. In 1826, gold was discovered in the mountains east of Albuquerque, and coal was discovered to the north. The town became a center of supplies for both types of mining, and with this prosperity came more people. In spite of these mining booms, by 1870 the largest industry in the area was sheep ranching.

The face of the town changed with the coming of the railroad. The Atlantic and Pacific Railway laid rails west from Albuquerque. From the east came the Atchison, Topeka and Santa Fe railroad. The AT&SF preferred to build close to the old plaza in the town, but owners of land needed for the railway wanted to make a large profit and priced their land accordingly. The railroad decided on a cheaper route and built two miles east. As a result, businesses and people concerned with the railroad moved east, and Old Town declined in its fortunes.

Present-day Albuquerque has changed since its early, provincial years. World War II marked a turning point for the city, as the beginnings of nuclear research were centered there. Since the late 1940's, scientific and military research installations have brought people into the area. In 1950, a large uranium deposit was found near Grants, New Mexico, fifty miles west of Albuquerque. This ensured the continuance of a research presence in the city.

Albuquerque has a long history of ethnic mixing. The community adapted as the Anglo presence increased. In order to alleviate some discrimination problems arising in the early 1950's, the city commission passed an antidiscrimination ordinance with heavy penalties. The University of New Mexico attracts students from throughout the country and the world, and the smaller University of Albuquerque attracts much of the area's Latino population.

Albuquerque Walkout (May, 1966): Protest. Early in 1966, the Equal Employment Opportunity Commission met in Albuquerque, New Mexico, to hear testimony on DISCRIMINATION against minorities, especially Native Americans, in the Southwest. Fifty Chicano leaders staged a protest by walking out of the meeting, charging that the commission had failed to consider the problems of Mexican Americans. They demanded a meeting with President Lyndon B. Johnson and a White House conference on the needs of La Raza (the race).

Johnson heeded their call and scheduled a meeting for May in El Paso, Texas. Hundreds of prominent Latino leaders were invited, but three key spokesmen, César CHÁVEZ, Rodolfo "Corky" GONZÁLES, and Bert N. CORONA, announced they would boycott this meeting to protest the government's lack of concern for farmworkers. They held a counterconference, called the La Raza Unida Conference, in El Paso's largest barrio. This meeting brought together many community and youth groups for the first time and was important in creating a national Latino CIVIL RIGHTS MOVEMENT.

Alcapurrias: Puerto Rican banana or plantain cro-
quettes with meat fillings. *Alcapurrias* are based on a
dough consisting of grated green bananas or plantains,
sometimes admixed with grated taro or other starchy
vegetables and usually colored with *ACHIOTE*. A bit of
any of various savory-seasoned meat fillings is thrust
inside a ball of this dough, which then is closed and
deep-fat fried until golden brown. *Alcapurrias* are a
typical snack from Puerto Rican take-out restaurants in
both Puerto Rico and New York City.

Alcoholism: Alcoholism is a disease that increasingly
affects the Latino community. Assessing the extent of
the problem of alcoholism in the Latino community is
difficult because there are few existing studies of alcohol use by Hispanics. There are some indications that

the problem is serious. According to a 1993 report by
the Centers for Disease Control and Prevention,
among the ten leading causes of death for Latinos were
chronic liver disease and cirrhosis, accidents and ad-
verse effects, and homicide and legal intervention, all
frequently associated with alcohol consumption.

Raul Caetano began studying patterns of drinking
among Latinos in 1984. He found that 22 percent of
Latino men and 47 percent of Latino women abstained
from use of alcohol. Latino males drank the heaviest in
their thirties, with alcohol consumption declining after
the age of forty-nine. Latinas drank most heavily during their forties and fifties. For both sexes, abstention
increased after the age of sixty. There was also evidence that drinking patterns for Latino males were
positively associated with drinking by spouses.

Consumption of alcohol is accepted as part of many social activities. (Impact Visuals, Arvind Garg)

A review of the data by national origin revealed that Mexican American men had both higher rates of abstention and higher rates of heavy drinking than Latinos of Cuban, Puerto Rican, and other Latin American origin. Mexican American women drank more heavily than women of Cuban, Puerto Rican, or other Latin American origin, although they also had the highest rate of abstention. Puerto Rican women were the most moderate drinkers.

Drinking among Latino males has been considered socially acceptable. There is also evidence that the number of Latinas who drink is rising. In a 1988 national household survey, 17 percent of Latino youths aged twelve to seventeen reported using alcohol during the most recent month, and more than 60 percent of young adults between the ages of eighteen and twenty-five reported using alcohol.

At risk from alcohol use are pregnant women and their fetuses. Drinking contributes both to low birth weight and fetal alcohol syndrome, which is the leading preventable cause of birth defects and mental retardation. Even when consumed in small quantities, alcohol has been associated with learning disabilities, neurological deficits, birth defects, and low birth weight.

Alcohol has been linked to accidents, family violence, social problems, and health problems. A 1987 congressional report from the secretary of health and human services related that foreign-born Mexican American men had a higher reported prevalence of social problems than did mainland Puerto Ricans and Cuban Americans.

By the early 1990's, some studies reported that chemical addiction had reached epidemic proportions among Latinos. Alcoholism ranked third in the causes for admission to state and county mental health hospitals among Latinos. Nevertheless, only 11 percent of those admitted for treatment for alcohol abuse were Latino, according to a 1990 report by the U.S. National Institute on Drug Abuse and the U.S. National Institute on Alcohol Abuse and Alcoholism. That rate was slightly higher than the proportion of Latinos in the population as a whole.

Alfonso, Carlos (1950, Havana, Cuba—Feb. 19, 1991, Miami, Fla.): Artist. A well-known artist in Cuba before he arrived in the United States in 1980, Alfonso is famous for abstract paintings dealing with oppression, exile, magic, and religion.

After serving in the Cuban army, Alfonso studied at Havana University and the Academia de Bellas Artes San Alejandro in Havana. He taught art history in the early 1970's before becoming a studio art instructor for Cuba's ministry of culture.

Alfonso's paintings, which critics often compare to the surrealistic work of Spanish painter Pablo Picasso, are known for their lush compositions and primitive and mysterious imagery. In Cuba, Alfonso developed an abstract style that enabled him to express feelings without raising suspicion from the authorities. Many images in his later works are drawn from Christianity and Afro-Cuban religions. The image of a knife through a tongue, an Afro-Cuban idiom for keeping quiet, appears often in his paintings, as do a cross representing spiritual sacrifice and tears that symbolize exile.

In the United States, Alfonso's work has been included in group shows in New York, Florida, and North Carolina. His awards include a 1983 Cintas Fellowship in the Visual Arts, a 1984 grant from the National Endowment for the Arts, and a 1985 commission for a ceramic mural in a Florida metrorail station.

Algarín, Miguel (b. Sept. 11, 1941, Santurce, Puerto Rico): Writer. Algarín is an award-winning writer and a leading figure among New York City's Puerto Rican literary community. He identifies himself as "Nuyorican" rather than Puerto Rican. According to Algarín, "Nuyorican," a term that combines the words "New" (from New York) and "rican" (from Puerto Rican), better describes the generations of immigrants from Puerto Rico who made the United States, and New York City in particular, their home.

Besides teaching English literature, Algarín extols Nuyorican culture inside and outside academia. He helped create a PUERTO RICAN STUDIES PROGRAM at Rutgers University in New Brunswick, New Jersey, opened a literary center known as the NUYORICAN POETS' CAFÉ, and collected writings by NUYORICANS for an anthology. Algarín also writes poetry that is noteworthy for capturing the poetic sound of Nuyorican speech, an urban, working-class language in which English is filtered through Spanish and black English. Algarín sees this new language as a key component of his cultural identity.

Algarín's work includes editing (with Miguel PIÑERO) *Nuyorican Poetry: An Anthology of Puerto Rican Words and Feelings* (1975) and his own books *Mongo Affair* (1978), *On Call* (1980), *Body Bee Calling from the Twenty-first Century* (1982), and *Time's Now/Ya es tiempo* (1985), winner of the Before Columbus Foundation American Book Award for 1985.

Algaze, Mario (b. Oct. 4, 1947, Havana, Cuba): Photographer. Algaze is famous for photographs of Latin American subjects, which range from images of LITTLE HAVANA—the bustling community of Cuban expatriates in Miami, Florida—to intimate glimpses of daily life in Costa Rica, Colombia, Ecuador, Mexico, and other Latin American countries.

The son of Cuban lawyers who risked imprisonment under the regime of political leader Fidel Castro, Algaze fled Havana with his father in 1960. His mother followed in 1961. The family settled in Miami, where Algaze continued to live and work into the 1990's.

Algaze took his first photographs at the age of twenty, when he served as an apprentice to a professional photographer. In 1974, he made his first trip to Latin America, capturing on film the charm of Latin American street vendors, schoolchildren, housewives, and others engaged in their daily business.

Algaze specializes in photographs taken in the natural light of early morning. In addition to people, his photos record the courtyards, stairways, balconies, and other elements of Latin American architecture.

Photographic records of Algaze's frequent journeys to Latin America were presented in a 1991 solo exhibit of his work, Portfolio Latinoamericano. His work has been included in group and individual shows at many Florida museums.

Alianza Hispano-Americana: Mutual aid society in the southwestern United States and overseas. The Alianza was founded in 1894 in Arizona as a fraternal brotherhood and mutual aid society to provide life insurance for its members and increase unity within the Latino community. Belief in the brotherhood of all Latinos aided in the organization's expansion to other states and Latin American countries.

The focus of the group changed to include political issues. In the 1920's, the Alianza developed a legal defense fund for poor Mexicans; in the 1950's it helped to end legal segregation in Arizona, fought cases of unjust deportation, and established a civil rights division. In 1960, the group changed focus again, aligning itself with John F. Kennedy's presidential campaign. Idealistic and economic splits among the group's factions arose during this period, with some members seeing leaders as acting out of desire for power in the Anglo world. These internal struggles and financial mismanagement led the group to disband in the mid-1960's.

Alicia, Juana (Juana Alicia Montoya, b. 1953): Painter Juana Alicia, as she signs her works, expresses through her art her personal experiences and dreams, as well as the social and economic concerns of Latinos.

Juana Alicia came of age working in the celery and lettuce fields of Salinas, California, and she participated in the farmworker movement for labor rights. Years later, she recaptured her memories of those experiences in *Las Lechugeras* (1983; the lettuce workers). Painted on a building in the MISSION DISTRICT, the Latino hub of San Francisco, California, the mural is both a tribute to farmworkers and a criticism of the irresponsible use of pesticides. Montoya's other Mission District murals include *Para las Rosas* (1986; for the roses) and *Illuminations* (1986), a work she completed with three other artists. She has been involved in the women's and Chicano movements and sees her art as a contribution to social change.

Alien Contract Labor Law (1885): IMMIGRATION LEGISLATION. This federal law was designed to restrict migration of foreign-born laborers to the United States. It banned American employers from tendering labor contracts directly to alien workers. Although it was passed as a result of anti-immigrant fervor, the law was laxly enforced. Most employers simply instructed their labor agents to wait until foreign-born workers had crossed the border before signing them up to work. Until 1891, enforcement of the law was left to individual states. In that year, the newly created Bureau of Immigration took over responsibility for the law's enforcement. Regulation was not intended to impede immigration of Mexican workers; it was primarily aimed at restricting Chinese workers and members of other proscribed groups from entering the United States via Mexico or Canada.

Alien smuggling: A method of illegal immigration. The smuggling of people into the United States in the 1990's often was accomplished by an individual known as a COYOTE or a team of coyotes. The relationship between coyote and *pollo* (literally "chicken," but used to refer to the coyote's client) at that time existed mainly along the border that divided Mexico from California, Arizona, New Mexico, and Texas.

When one decides to enter the United States illegally through Mexico, the choices are twofold: to attempt to enter alone or with a group of unorganized individuals, or to contract the expertise of a coyote. The price of the coyote varies according to his or her reputation and the services to be rendered. A typical fee per person in the early 1990's was between $150 and $200 to get an undocumented individual across the

Border Patrol agents work on roads into the United States as well as at the borders, looking for people being smuggled into the United States by car or truck. (Impact Visuals, Jeffrey D. Scott)

border. After that, additional fees sometimes were paid so that one could be smuggled farther into the United States, generally to a populated urban area. Often a portion of the original fee was used to bribe a U.S. border official, and a portion was turned over to the Mexican border inspector to prevent him or her from revealing the coyote's name to the U.S. official.

The majority of coyotes were hired by individuals or groups attempting to cross the border illegally for the first or second time. The use of coyotes also varied depending on where one wished to cross the border. For example, crossing the Mexican border into areas such as South Texas less often involves a coyote and usually involves a relatively low fee. The cost and frequency of coyote usage to cross the border into California typically have been much larger. The higher price stemmed both from the future benefits to the undocumented immigrant—wages were higher in California than in Texas—and from the greater diffi-

culty of crossing the border there. The California-Mexico border has been more tightly secured and patrolled than the Texas-Mexico border, and the highway between the California border and Los Angeles was notorious for its many IMMIGRATION AND NATURALIZATION SERVICE (INS) checkpoints.

The methods of alien smuggling and the treatment of the *pollos* by the COYOTES differed markedly. Crossing from Mexico to Texas often required only a raft trip or a swim timed in accordance with the INS officials' movements. To be successfully smuggled from Mexico into an urban California city usually required a mode of transportation by which immigrants were concealed to evade checkpoint officials. Immigrants were packed in the backs of cargo trucks, hidden in the trunks of cars, concealed under back seats, or even strapped to the bottoms of automobiles. Coyotes often took advantage of immigrants' desperation and lack of familiarity with the process of illegal immigration.

Immigrants, especially first-timers, were frequently robbed, beaten, or killed. Women could be robbed or raped. Those who suffered the most at the hands of coyotes were often people from Central and South America who lacked both experience in the alien-smuggling process and familiarity with Mexican bordertown customs, habits, and geography.

Alienz, The: East Los Angeles Chicano music group. The Alienz, formerly called Los Amigos Cosmicos, formed in East Los Angeles in the late 1980's. The three-member group, including saxophonist Mario Flores and bassist Jesse Rangel, played rock and rhythm-and-blues music, with the addition of Mexican and other Latin elements. The band has played as an opening act for such stars as Rubén BLADES.

Aliso-Pico (East Los Angeles, Calif.): Public housing project. Aliso-Pico, built in the early 1930's, is located within the Boyle Heights neighborhood of EAST LOS ANGELES. Its ethnic composition was largely Hispanic and primarily Chicano.

In the 1970's, Aliso-Pico became the center of a growing Hispanic cultural awareness movement. This activity continued through the 1980's and into the 1990's. In the 1990's, the Lord's Mission Church, located in the Aliso-Pico area, became an important sanctuary for Central and South Americans seeking refuge from political persecution in their home countries. In 1994, the barrio, which was governed by the Los Angeles Housing Authority, went under reconstruction.

Allen v. State Board of Elections (Mar. 3, 1969): Voting rights case. This U.S. Supreme Court decision (393 U.S. 544) contains four consolidated cases under the VOTING RIGHTS ACT OF 1965. Chief Justice Earl Warren used this decision, considering three Mississippi cases and one Virginia case, to strengthen the rights of private citizens to seek redress under the act and give the act the broadest possible interpretation to cover minor changes in state election laws.

These four cases applied the Voting Rights Act to Mississippi and Virginia. Both states were covered by the Voting Rights Act because of their history of discrimination against black voters.

All the cases considered in this decision focused on section 5 of the Voting Rights Act. Under section 5, states covered by the act could not deprive persons of their VOTING RIGHTS based on changes in their election laws enacted after November 1, 1964, without ap-

proval of the United States District Court for the District of Columbia or submitting the new enactments to the attorney general.

Allen v. State Board of Elections involved a bulletin issued by the Virginia Board of Elections in an attempt to comply with the act. Functionally illiterate voters objected to the bulletin, which they thought could lead to discriminatory procedures at the polls.

Bunton v. Patterson, another of the consolidated cases, involved a minority challenge to changes in section 6271-08 of the Mississippi Code. These changes allowed eleven counties to change the office of county superintendent of education from elective to appointive. The minority voters who challenged the change were potential candidates who wanted the change disallowed unless section 5 procedures were applied.

Fairley v. Patterson involved a 1966 amendment to section 2870 of the Mississippi Code of 1942. It allowed county boards of supervisors to issue an order providing that supervisors would be elected on an at-large basis. Minority voters feared a dilution of their voting power. They sought a declaratory judgment that the amendment was subject to section 5.

Whitley v. Williams involved a 1966 amendment to section 3260 of the Mississippi Code that changed election procedures for independent candidates. The plaintiffs challenging this amendment were potential independent candidates whose nominating petitions were rejected based on the amendment.

Despite the broad interpretation he gave to the Voting Rights Act, Chief Justice Warren did not order the stringent remedies requested by the plaintiffs. He gave only prospective (future) application to his decision, and he was unwilling to overturn certain elections that already had taken place.

The major victory won by plaintiffs in these cases was the right to sue as individuals under the Voting Rights Act. Although the plaintiffs in these cases were all African Americans, their struggle for greater voting rights also benefited Hispanic Americans in some states. Chief Justice Warren remanded all four cases for further lower court action. The consolidated decision expanded the scope of changes in voting procedures that could come under judicial review in the light of the VOTING RIGHTS ACT OF 1965 and other laws.

Allende, Isabel (b. Aug. 2, 1942, Lima, Peru): Novelist. A noted journalist in Chile, Allende fled that country after the assassination of Chilean president (and her father's first cousin) Salvador Allende in 1973. Unable to find work as a journalist in exile, Allende turned her

Author Isabel Allende. (AP/Wide World Photos)

efforts to creative writing. Her internationally best-selling novel *La casa de los espíritus* (1982; *The House of the Spirits*, 1985) received worldwide critical acclaim. It has been printed in more than twenty languages and was made into a feature film in the United States in 1994. The novel, considered too politically provocative by the military government in Chile, was banned in that country until 1989.

Allende's first novel mixes fantastic elements and characters with strong political realism as it follows several generations of the Trueba family. Because of this narrative mixing, within the school of Magical Realism characteristic of much Latin American postwar literature, Allende's novel is often compared to Gabriel GARCÍA MÁRQUEZ's *Cien años de soledad* (1967; *One Hundred Years of Solitude*, 1970). Unlike most of her contemporaries, Allende couples her Magical Realism with a feminist perspective, making her novels unique.

Allende's other novels include *De amor y de sombra* (1984; *Of Love and Shadows*, 1987), *Eva Luna* (1987), and *The Stories of Eva Luna* (1991). She has also published a collection of essays titled *The Infinite Plan* (1993).

Alliance for Progress: International alliance. The Alliance for Progress was organized on August 17, 1961, by delegates from twenty-one American republics (only Cuba abstained) as a response to the initiative presented by President John F. Kennedy as part of the Inter-American Economic and Social Council, one of the organs of the Organization of American States. The declaration signed by representatives of these countries stated a commitment to "immediate and concrete actions to secure a better life, under freedom and democracy, for the present and future generations." The Inter-American Committee on the Alliance for Progress (CIAP) was established in November, 1963, in São Paulo, Brazil.

The CIAP was composed of eight members, one from the United States and seven from Latin America. Its mission was to help coordinate the activities of the Alliance for Progress, which included external financial and technical assistance and internal reform of each of the charter members. The financial assistance offered by the Alliance for Progress was to be carried out through two independent financial institutions, the Inter-American Development Bank and the United Nations Commission for Latin America.

The bolder plans of the Alliance for Progress called for political, social, and economic reforms in each charter member country. Specifically, the charter called for fighting illiteracy, alleviating poor housing and health conditions, and shifting the economic base of the charter members from a few agricultural and mineral products to a broader base following the implementation of land and tax reforms. The charter also called for improvement of industry, agricultural techniques, and infrastructure.

The initiatives of the Alliance for Progress have been carried out by the Permanent Executive Committee of the Inter-American Economic and Social Council (Americas) of the General Secretariat of the Organization of American States. Founded in 1974, it had thirty-one charter members. This council is project oriented and accepts proposals dealing with economic and social development.

Almeida, Laurindo (b. Sept. 2, 1917, São Paulo, Brazil): Composer and Spanish acoustic guitarist. Almeida immigrated to the United States in 1947. He played with Stan Kenton, making a name for himself before forming his own trio. He furthered his reputation by playing an unamplified guitar with his own trio in Los Angeles. He became known for his BOSSA NOVA style.

In 1962, Almeida's album *Viva Bossa Nova* reached number thirteen on the charts. He also wrote music for a number of films, including *Viva Zapata!* (1952), *The Old Man and the Sea* (1958), and *Maracaibo* (1958). Almeida toured with the Modern Jazz Quartet in 1964. He is also a respected classical guitarist.

Since the late 1960's, Almeida has had a concert career as a classical guitarist. On a number of occasions, his wife, soprano Deltra Eamon, has performed with him. Almeida has worked frequently with Bud Shank. Over his long career, he has recorded many successful Latin jazz and classical albums; he won a Grammy Award for the 1964 album *Guitar from Ipanema*.

Alomar family: Baseball players. Sandy Alomar, Sr. (Santos Alomar y Conde; b. Oct. 19, 1943, Salinas, Puerto Rico) grew up in Puerto Rico at a time when many Latin Americans were successfully moving into major league BASEBALL in the United States. In much of Latin America, baseball was exceptionally popular. Residents of Puerto Rico and other Latin American countries saw baseball as a young man's route to success. Even if a youngster failed to make the North American big leagues, he could make more money as a baseball player in his native country than in most

Roberto Alomar began playing for the Toronto Blue Jays in 1991 and helped the team win consecutive World Series. (Toronto Bluejays)

other jobs. Baseball players, especially those who became major leaguers, were idolized.

As a result of this situation and the year-round baseball weather in Latin American countries, the playground baseball fields of Latin America have been to baseball what the neighborhood basketball courts of U.S. cities are to basketball. Many successful baseball players have come to the big leagues from Latin American countries, and the Alomars are representative of the considerable Puerto Rican contribution.

Sandy, Sr., played in the big leagues from 1964 to 1978. He was the California Angels' second baseman for all or part of six seasons and made the American League All-Star Team in 1970. He was a utility player for several other teams and played every position but pitcher and catcher at some time during his career, though his specialties were second base and shortstop. He was a switch hitter with a lifetime batting average of .245. He was also an excellent defensive player and base runner. He managed and coached in Puerto Rican winter baseball during his playing career and was a coach with the San Diego Padres when his sons first reached the major leagues with that team.

Sandy, Jr. (Santos Alomar y Velazquez; b. June 18, 1966, Salinas, Puerto Rico) played catcher for the San Diego Padres and Cleveland Indians. In 1990, he appeared in 132 games and batted .290, winning a Gold Glove and earning the American League Rookie of the Year Award. He had a .263 lifetime batting average at the end of the 1993 season and had appeared in three All-Star games.

Roberto (Roberto Alomar y Velazquez; b. Feb. 5, 1968, Ponce, Puerto Rico) played second base for the Padres from 1988 to 1990. Before the 1991 season, he was traded to the Toronto Blue Jays. He hit .310 for the Blue Jays in 1992 and .326 in 1993, compiling a lifetime batting average of .297 by the end of the 1993 season. He became a perennial All-Star and Gold Glove Award winner, and he was chosen as the most valuable player of the 1992 American League Championship Series. His hitting and exceptional defensive play were instrumental in the consecutive world championships the Blue Jays won in 1992 and 1993.

The Alomars have been role models for Latin American youth in Puerto Rico and in North America. Their return to Puerto Rico to play in the winter leagues has been a reminder of the success achieved by many Latin American ballplayers. Their careers have been an inspiration and a source of pride for many Latino youngsters.

Alonso, Maria Conchita (b. 1957, Cuba): Actress. Alonso came from a financially secure family that relocated to Venezuela when she was five years old. She was Miss Teenager of the World in 1971 and Miss Venezuela in 1975. She began her acting career in Venezuela, where she appeared in four films and ten soap operas. As a recording artist, she earned one platinum and four gold albums.

Alonso studied acting with Lee Strasberg in Los Angeles and made her U.S. film debut in 1984 as an Italian immigrant in *Moscow on the Hudson*. Other film credits include *A Fine Mess* (1986), *Touch and Go* (1986), *Extreme Prejudice* (1987), *The Running Man* (1987), *The Vampire's Kiss* (1988), *Predator 2* (1990), *The House of the Spirits* (1994), and the 1988 feature *Colors*, about gang violence in Los Angeles. On television, she has been seen in the miniseries *An American Cousin*, the specials *Viva Miami* and *Night of the Super Sounds*, and the television film *Blood Ties*. She also starred in the short-lived pilot *One of the Boys*, based loosely on her own experiences as a Latina actress in Los Angeles. She is best known for her work in the 1991 series *McBain*.

In addition to her film and television work, Alonso in the late 1980's recorded several rock albums, for which she garnered two Grammy nominations. A confirmed vegetarian, Alonso has spoken out on issues such as AIDS and put her support behind candidates in Venezuelan political elections.

Alou family: Baseball players. Cubans were the first Latin American BASEBALL players to have a large effect on the North American game, but the Dominican Republic has produced more major leaguers per capita than any other country. The Alou brothers were pioneers in the influx of Dominicans into the major leagues.

Felipe Rojas y Alou (b. May 12, 1935, Santo Domingo, Dominican Republic) played outfield and first base for the San Francisco Giants, Milwaukee and Atlanta Braves, and several other teams from 1958 through 1974. His lifetime batting average was .286, and he hit 206 home runs. He was on the National League All-Star Team in 1962, 1966, and 1968. His best year probably was 1966, when he played with the Atlanta Braves. He had the second highest batting average in the major leagues (.327, behind his brother Matty's .342), leading the league in hits (218) and runs scored (122). He also hit 31 home runs. He coached and managed in the Dominican Republic winter league throughout his career, then in the Mon-

Matty Alou. (AP/Wide World Photos)

treal system after he retired as a player. In June of 1992, he became the manager of the Montreal Expos, and in 1994 he was named National League Manager of the Year.

Matty (Mateo Rojas y Alou; b. Dec. 22, 1938, Haina, Dominican Republic) followed Felipe to the majors in 1960 and played until 1974, primarily as an outfielder for the San Francisco Giants and Pittsburgh Pirates. He had an exceptional lifetime batting average of .307. In 1966, his first year as a Pirate, he had the highest batting average in the major leagues (.342). He was on the All-Star team in 1968 and 1969.

Jesús María Rojas y Alou (b. Mar. 24, 1942, Haina, Dominican Republic) played in the major leagues from 1963 to 1979, with the San Francisco Giants, Houston Astros, Oakland Athletics, and New York Mets. He had a good lifetime batting average of .280. Jesús joined the Giants at the end of the 1963 season, and Felipe was traded to the Braves before the 1964 season, so for about a month the three brothers were on the same team. They started one game together as the three Giant outfielders. Jesús played for the Athletics when they won back-to-back world championships in 1973 and 1974.

Felipe's son Moises (b. July 3, 1966, Atlanta, Ga.) became a regular Montreal Expos outfielder in 1992. In 1993, he batted .286 with 18 home runs and 85 runs batted in before breaking his leg late in the season.

Some Latin American baseball players have been at a disadvantage because of language problems, and some have experienced discrimination based on their skin color. Many had difficulty adjusting to the realities of segregation, still a fact of U.S. life in the 1960's, in part because they had played on mixed teams all of their lives in their homelands. Felipe wrote a book (*Felipe Alou: My Life and Baseball*, 1967) in which he recounted and explained some of his own and other players' experiences. His explanations enhanced understanding of the problems that Latin American players faced in the United States.

The Alous have made important contributions to the community throughout their baseball careers. They returned to the Dominican Republic regularly to play, coach, and manage in winter leagues. While there, they also worked with Dominican youths in baseball camps.

Alta California: Beginning in the 1700's, Spanish settlements were established at sites along the California coast. After the establishment of a mission and fort at San Diego de Alcala in 1769, the territory was split into the two administrative provinces of Alta California in the north and BAJA CALIFORNIA to the south.

The first Europeans who appeared along the coast of present-day California during the mid-1500's were greeted by a large number of indigenous peoples. Estimates of the number of natives at that time range as high as 300,000 persons, organized into numerous tribes. Following the conquest of the Mexican Aztecs by Hernán CORTÉS between 1519 and 1521, Spanish explorers moved across Mexico toward the Pacific, discovering Baja, or lower, California in the process.

Cortés' successor, Antonio de Mendoza, hired a Portuguese navigator, Juan Rodríguez CABRILLO, to explore the coast of what was thought to be an island. Cabrillo and his successor, Bartolomeo Ferrelo, explored the coast as far north as the present border between Oregon and CALIFORNIA. The land was called "California" in reference to the island paradise of a medieval romance popular at the time. The name may have been one of derision, since neither gold nor jewels were discovered in the region.

Colonization of California by Spain was as much a reaction to English exploration as it was to the potential of newly discovered riches. A party led by Sebastián Vizcaíno in 1602 set out to explore the coast. Although beset by poor weather and devastated by scurvy, the party discovered Monterey Bay (named for the Viceroy de Monterrey) and urged that Spain establish settlements through the region. Spain was more interested in the colony of Mexico, however, and interest in the north died.

By the mid-eighteenth century, Russian and English colonization of western North America began to alarm Spain. In 1757, Andres Burriel published *Noticia de la California*, in which he argued that if Spain failed to establish settlements on the coast of California, foreign governments would surely do so. In addition, Christian proselytizers had long had an interest in the region. Jesuit friar Eusebio KINO, who had preached the gospel to the Indians of BAJA CALIFORNIA as early as the 1680's, had supported the idea of missions in the area. It is likely that Kino was the first to refer to the northern region as Alta California. In 1769, Franciscan friar Junípero SERRA established the first California mission at present-day SAN DIEGO. By the time Spanish rule ended in 1822, twenty-one missions had been established along the California coast, each about a day's travel from its neighbors.

With Mexican independence in 1821, Alta California consisted of the present state of California as well as portions of Colorado, New Mexico, and Wyoming.

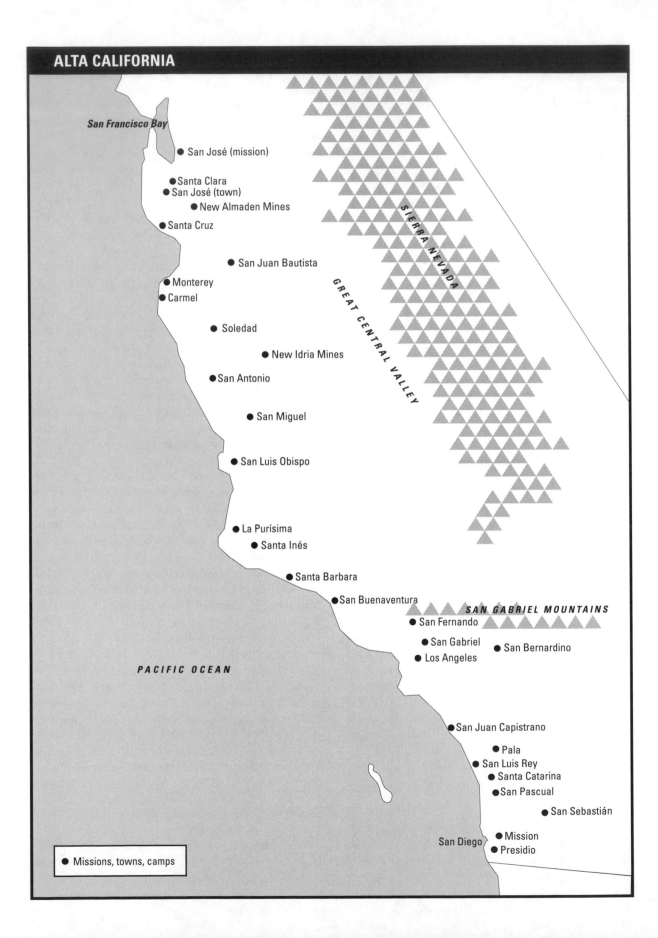

ALTA CALIFORNIA

San Francisco Bay

● San José (mission)

● Santa Clara
● San José (town)
● New Almaden Mines
● Santa Cruz

● San Juan Bautista

● Monterey
● Carmel

● Soledad

● New Idria Mines

● San Antonio

● San Miguel

● San Luis Obispo

SIERRA NEVADA

GREAT CENTRAL VALLEY

● La Purísima
● Santa Inés

● Santa Barbara

● San Buenaventura
● San Fernando   *SAN GABRIEL MOUNTAINS*

● San Gabriel
● Los Angeles   ● San Bernardino

PACIFIC OCEAN

● San Juan Capistrano

● Pala
● San Luis Rey
● Santa Catarina
● San Pascual

● San Sebastián

San Diego   ● Mission
● Presidio

● Missions, towns, camps

The province was effectively self-governing, although the governor was appointed in Mexico City. Increasing settlement by U.S. citizens eventually led to attempts by the United States to annex California. As part of the TREATY OF GUADALUPE HIDALGO, which ended the MEXICAN AMERICAN WAR in 1848, California was ceded to the United States.

California was admitted as the thirty-first state in 1850. Its population boomed after World War II, as defense workers and servicemen settled in the region. In the 1970's, the state began another expansion, as large numbers of emigrants from Asia, Mexico, and Central America swelled the "minority" population.

Altamirano, Ignacio Manuel (Nov. 13, 1834, Tixtla, Mexico—Feb. 13, 1893, San Remo, Italy): Writer. Altamirano is Mexico's greatest nineteenth century novelist and was a prolific man of letters. Born of Aztec parents who spoke only Nahuatl, Altamirano overcame cultural oppression to receive a degree in law. He was later elected to the Mexican Congress and the Supreme Court, on which he served as chief justice. His interests went far beyond law. At various times he worked as a historian, professor, literary critic, orator, and diplomat to Spain and France. He also founded several literary journals.

Considered to be a major literary influence and the originator of the modern Mexican novel, Altamirano wrote three major novels. *Clemencia* (1869; *Clemency*, 1907) was made into a feature film in Mexico in 1935. He also published *La Navidad en las montañas* (1871; *Christmas in the Mountains*, 1961) and *El Zarco, espisodio de la vida mexicana en 1861-63* (1901; *El Zarco, the Bandit*, 1957). Praised for their concise structures and astute observations, Altamirano's works are studied throughout the world.

Altamirano also wrote novelettes and literary criticism. His works include *Obras completas* (1949; *Complete Works*, 1986) and two volumes of *Paisajes y leyendas: Tradiciones y costumbres de México* (1884; landscapes and legends: traditions and customs of Mexico).

Altars, home: The home altar has been a part of Latino life for centuries. Altars are dedicated to a particular saint, the Blessed Virgin, or Our Savior. Some religious cults and sects also use altars in their ceremonies.

The worship of a household god or the image of a supernatural protector is as old as humankind. The native civilizations of the ancient Americas used gold to decorate their places of worship and adorn themselves. It was the high visibility of this precious metal that attracted the conquistadores to the New World. With the SPANISH CONQUEST came the conversion of the native Americans to the Catholic faith.

The replacement of images of native gods with Christian religious figures was a necessary step in the conversion of the native peoples. As colonization proceeded, gold was still used, but now it adorned great cathedrals. To attest their faith, the indigenous people sought a personal yet religiously significant holy place. This led to the popularity of the home altar. Individuals fashioned places of worship and veneration specific to their households. The altar was dedicated to a patron saint possessing certain powers of intercession. Prayers were offered for health of family, abundance of crops, cures for illness and disease, and relief from famine or drought.

Because of heavy reliance on agriculture as a means of earning a living, villages were widely scattered. Town centers or marketplaces were far away from many people. This meant that the church also was far away. In order to keep their faith alive, the early converts to Catholicism fashioned home altars. These altars gave the presence of their new-found faith even when they could not get to a church.

The altars were also seen as a testimony to the household's conversion. In the early days of the Conquest, the native population struggled to accept their new faith. The altars in their homes were symbols of their conversion to the CATHOLIC CHURCH.

Vestiges of pre-Columbian times can be seen in the structure of the home altar. The altars are tiered, like the ancient pyramids. Most are decorated with flowers and candles. The central figures, statues or pictures of saints, attest the Catholic faith. The offerings of flowers, food, and clothing all demonstrate the cultural heritage of the community. A picture of a departed relative can be present on the altar so that family members can pray for repose of the soul.

Celebration of El DÍA DE LOS MUERTOS (the day of the dead) in Mexico shows a specific use of the home altar. A celebration of this kind makes clear the role of community participation and also reflects the social order prevalent in the community. Festival observances differ from town to town, but the principle is the same: to remember the departed, to celebrate their memory with offerings and gifts, and then to share the offerings with others in the community.

The use of the home altars also represents a mechanism of integration for the community, enhancing the

A home altar might hold a collection of photos of people for whom prayers will be said. (James Shaffer)

sense of social cohesion. It also serves to demonstrate a reaffirmation of the values and traditions that have shaped the existence of the community.

Alternative education: Classes for academic supplementation, cultural enrichment, or motivational empowerment outside a student's formal schooling or instead of mainstream schooling. Alternative education has been practiced in the Hispanic community in diverse forms but with one primary motivation, the lack of comprehensive education being offered to Hispanics.

Precursor forms of alternative education were used in the missions of the frontier, which educated the Indians to preserve Spanish political, cultural, moral, and religious values but virtually ignored academic subjects. The primary sources of academic education were the family and community on the pueblos and presidios.

When Mexico gained its independence from Spain in 1821, the missions began to fade in importance. The Mexican government called for elimination of distinc-

tions of race or class. The missions were seen as institutions that oppressed Indians, and the church was perceived to be in the service of colonizers. An influx of colonizers brought popular support for public education.

Public schools, however, did not serve the entire community of Hispanics well. Even though compulsory school attendance was mandated in 1802 by Governor Juan Elguezábal of Texas, it was not enforced. During the early 1800's, the family continued to be the primary source of education, with the church as a supplemental or alternative (but valued) educational forum.

In the late 1800's, the CATHOLIC CHURCH, Protestant groups, and governments founded schools. Government-run schools often had a primary goal of "Americanization" of indigenous people and Hispanics. They taught academic subjects but concentrated on practical skills such as homemaking, farming, carpentry, and ranching.

Public schools came to dominate education, with American academic subjects and values being empha-

Alternative schools like this one in Crystal City, Texas, foster cultural awareness and pride as well as teaching academic subjects. (AP/Wide World Photos)

sized. Hispanic students, as a result of segregation and lack of finances, often were denied an equal education. The MISSION SCHOOLS were no longer available to participate in cultural preservation.

Beginning in the 1960's, Hispanic reform groups urged BILINGUALISM, cultural education, and community awareness. Because public schools failed to provide all that was desired in the way of role models, forms of supplemental education known as alternative education were created by various civic and religious groups. The Catholic church set up schools to educate undocumented aliens before the federal government mandated access to public schools in 1982.

Alternative schools focus on academic subjects and achievement through programs that enhance the students' self-esteem. The Valued Youth Partnership Program in San Antonio, Texas, for example, has helped at-risk teens to feel valued by training them as tutors for younger elementary students. Youth Community Service in Los Angeles, California, works with high school students to develop leadership skills through community goodwill projects. Programs such as the National Hispanic Institute in Austin, Texas, have helped Hispanic high school students gain admission to and graduate from college.

Most contemporary alternative education community programs have shared goals. They want to serve small numbers of students and give personal attention. They strive to enrich education, not fix deficiencies. They reinforce self-esteem, validating the language and culture of students, and they provide role models.

Alurista (Alberto Baltazar Urista-Heredia; b. Aug. 8, 1947, Mexico City, Mexico): Poet and activist. Alurista is a leading literary figure of the CHICANO MOVEMENT. Alurista migrated to San Diego, California, at the age of thirteen. His early adult years in the United States coincided with the growing Chicano movement, and the young writer's art and activism were strongly influenced by that movement. As a college student at San Diego State University, in 1967 Alurista helped establish the student group MECHA (MOVIMIENTO ESTUDIANTIL CHICANO DE AZTLÁN), which later opened chapters on campuses across the United States. He also helped organize the CHICANO STUDIES PROGRAM in 1968 and the Centro de Estudios Chicanos in 1969 at that same university.

Alurista's poetry reflects his social and political activism. Issues of identity, liberation, and self-determination recur throughout his work. Alurista's poems are revolutionary in their multilingualism.

Writing in both Spanish and English, with names and words frequently taken from Nahuatl (the language of the Aztecs still spoken in Mexico), Alurista uses and mixes several languages within single works. Alurista's works include *Floricanto en Aztlán* (1971), *Timespace Huracán: Poems 1972-1975* (1976), *A'nque* (1979), *Return: Poems Collected and New* (1982), and *Spik in Glyph?* (1981).

Alvarado, Juan Bautista (1800-1882): Politician. During the early nineteenth century, CALIFORNIA remained largely unconcerned with Mexican politics. In 1834, however, its administration was affected by political turmoil in Mexico City. At that time, General Antonio López de Santa Anna led a revolt to abolish federalism and establish a centralist form of government.

Alvarado thwarted Santa Anna's efforts to impose centralism in California. In November, 1836, Alvarado led a rebellion declaring the sovereign state of California, which would remain independent until Mexico agreed to restore the federal constitution of 1824. Alvarado declared himself provisional governor, retaining the position until 1842. During this time, California enjoyed de facto autonomy within the Mexican Republic.

During his tenure as governor, Alvarado encouraged Americans to settle by making it easy for them to obtain land. This development, as in Texas and New Mexico, contributed to the loss of the province to the United States in 1846. Following the MEXICAN AMERICAN WAR, Alvarado declined an offer to become either interim governor or secretary of state, instead living as a ranchero. In doing so, Alvarado lost an opportunity to speak for the rights of CALIFORNIOS as the century progressed.

Alvarez, Cecilia Concepción (b. 1959): Artist. The paintings of Seattle-based Alvarez bring together decorative elements of Latino art, goals of the Chicana movement, and an individual outlook on beauty.

Alvarez's 1979 painting *Las Cuatas Diego* presents a closeup of two young women against a decorative floral background. Although not directly political in its impact, the painting suggests a positive, feminine view of family, domesticity, and inner strength, views shared with Chicana artists of the 1970's whose works are less subtle in their message.

Alvarez sees her art as intimately connected to the Latino experience and a broader social context. People, art, and society, she believes, have an obligation to advance humanity and find solutions to the problems threatening human coexistence and survival. Such concerns motivate her artistic production.

Alvarez, Julia (b. Mar. 27, 1950, New York, N.Y.): Writer. Alvarez is a writer and educator whose first prose work garnered critical and popular success. Although she previously had published several volumes of poetry, the novel *How the García Girls Lost Their Accents* (1991) brought her national attention. The novel won the 1991 PEN Oakland/Josephine Miles Book Award and was selected as one of the best books of 1991 by *Library Journal*. The book is a collection of fifteen interwoven stories about the four García sisters, who are forced to leave the Dominican Republic after their father is branded as a political enemy of the state. The book is divided into three chronological periods, with the stories presented in reverse chronological order. Alvarez puts a spin on traditional immigrant narrative by having the novel begin in the United States and end in the Dominican Republic.

In 1960, Alvarez and her family left the Dominican Republic, where she was reared, for the United States. She has degrees in literature and creative writing and has taught at Middlebury College in Vermont. She has received writing grants from the National Endowment for the Arts and other foundations. Her other works include *The Housekeeping Book* (1984) and *Homecoming* (1984).

Alvarez, Luis Walter (June 13, 1911, San Francisco, Calif.—Sept. 1, 1988, Berkeley, Calif.): Physicist. Alvarez received his B.S. in physics in 1932 from the University of Chicago and his Ph.D. in physics, also from the University of Chicago, in 1936. He completed most of his life's work at the University of California, Berkeley, where he worked from 1936 until his death in 1988. Most of his work was carried out at the Lawrence Livermore Laboratory, where he served as associate director from 1954 to 1959 and 1976 to 1978. Under the direction of Alvarez, the Berkeley proton linear accelerator was able to produce free protons in 1947.

Julia Alvarez is pictured in front of fellow authors Ana Castillo (back) and Denise Chávez (middle). (Impact Visuals, Donna DeCesare)

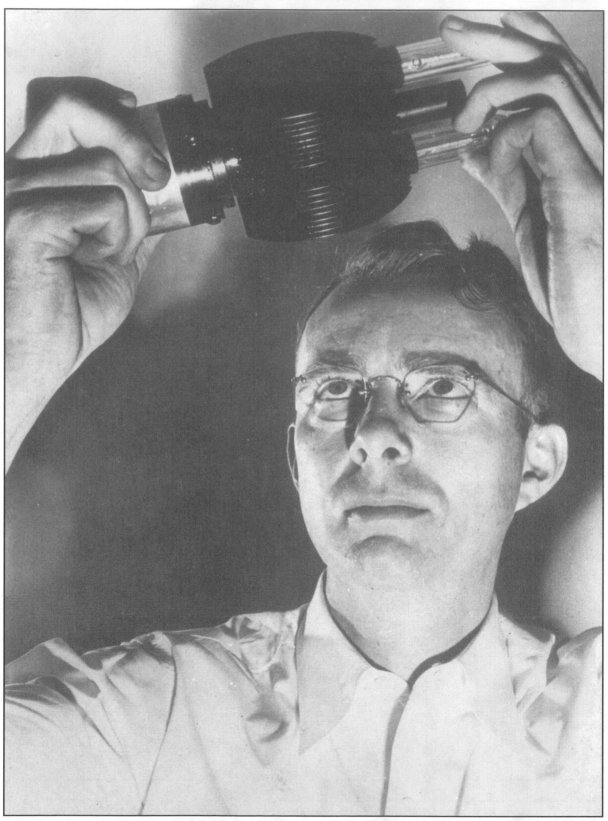

Luis Alvarez's accomplishments included discoveries in radar technology and particle physics. (AP/Wide World Photos)

In 1960, Alvarez announced his discovery of short-lived subatomic particles that were called "resonances." In 1968, he was awarded the Nobel Prize in Physics for this discovery. Among Alvarez's other important awards are the Collin Trophy (1946), the Scott Medal (1953), the Einstein Medal (1961), and the National Medal of Science (1964). His chief areas of research were particle physics, astrophysics, optics, geophysics, and air navigation.

In 1980, he was part of a team of scientists, including his son Walter, that postulated that the extinction of the dinosaurs was caused by a large body, such as an asteroid or comet, that crashed into the earth. Alvarez was one of the most distinguished and respected physicists of his time.

Álvarez de Pineda, Alonzo: Explorer. Álvarez de Pineda was the Spanish explorer who first saw the Mississippi River. In addition, he discovered that Florida was not an island but instead part of a much larger land mass.

In 1519, Antón de Alaminos, the pilot who traveled with Juan Ponce de León to Florida, spoke with the governor of Jamaica, Francisco de Garay. Alaminos mentioned the riches available in Florida. Garay arranged for a new expedition under the leadership of Álvarez de Pineda.

Álvarez de Pineda sailed straight to the northern boundary of the Gulf of Mexico. He then headed south, along the western shore of Florida. Weather conditions did not permit him to round the cape of Florida, so he returned north and sailed along the northern coast of the Gulf of Mexico. He made notes of all the rivers and bays, including the Mississippi River. He reached Tampico, where he met Hernán Cortés.

Álvarez de Pineda returned to Garay in 1520, bringing news of the lands he had seen. His voyage was significant as one of exploration, not of conquest or settlement.

American Baptist Churches in the United States v. Thornburgh (Jan. 31, 1991): Case involving political asylum. This decision bears the case number Civ. No. C-85-3255-RFP. District Judge Peckham approved a settlement between the American Baptist Churches and Richard Thornburgh, the United States attorney general. As a result of this settlement, a defined class of Salvadorans and Guatemalans living in the United States as illegal residents gained access to unappealable asylum adjudication including a dispute resolution mechanism. The plaintiff represented churches

and individuals active in the SANCTUARY MOVEMENT. This decision represented a significant victory for Central Americans seeking refugee status and those aiding them. (*See* REFUGEES AND REFUGEE STATUS and ASYLUM POLICIES.)

This case should be read in conjunction with *American Baptist Churches in the United States v. Meese* (712 F. Supp. 756). The American Baptist churches had a history of supporting those opposed to the 1980's U.S. government policies in Central America and of supporting Salvadorans and Guatemalans who were in the United States illegally and were seeking asylum.

The 1991 settlement negotiated by the plaintiff provided generous treatment for asylum seekers belonging to a recognized class. This class consisted of all Salvadorans in the United States as of September 19, 1990, and all Guatemalans in the United States as of October 1, 1990.

Members of the recognized class who had not been convicted of an aggravated felony according to the terms of the Immigration and Nationality Act received the right to an unappealable asylum adjudication before an asylum officer. The adjudication would include a new interview. The regulations used were to be those in effect on October 1, 1990. The rights of asylum seekers who obtained an interview with an asylum officer between October 1, 1990, and November 23, 1990, did not include a new asylum interview or a new first asylum officer adjudication, but all other rights were the same as for other asylum seekers under this settlement. Class members who were apprehended by the Immigration and Naturalization Service (INS) after the date of the preliminary approval of this settlement would not obtain the one-time-only rights provided in the agreement.

As part of the agreement, the defendant agreed to publish terms of the settlement in English and Spanish. All class members who could benefit from the settlement were entitled to receive notice by publication. Certain subgroups of the protected class of asylum seekers, including especially individuals who were involved in ongoing legal or administrative proceedings, were entitled to written notice by first class mail under the terms of the agreement. Those members of the protected class detained under INS authority had the right to notification by personal service from the INS.

In addition to delineating the protected class and increasing its asylum rights, the settlement also described in detail how members of the protected class should apply for asylum and the procedural norms of the process. The case established that in asylum hearings it is not relevant, in determining whether an applicant has a fear of persecution, whether the United States supports or opposes the applicant's home-country government.

American G.I. Forum: The largest organized Latino group of American military veterans, founded in 1948. Like patriots worldwide during World War II, Félix Longoria served his country proudly. He died in battle in the Pacific, on the island of Luzon. The refusal of the Three Rivers Funeral Home to allow the burial of this warrior and citizen, simply because his heritage was Mexican, enraged the South Texas Mexican American community. The racism evidenced by Longoria's funeral motivated South Texans of Mexican descent to address the discrimination that greeted them in their community each day, even after they had served gallantly in the war. The community's outrage

found expression in the *corrido*, "Discrimination Against a Martyr," written in 1949.

Héctor Pérez GARCÍA, a physician in Corpus Christi, Texas, championed the cause of Longoria's family, finally forcing the funeral home to hold a wake for the slain soldier. Garcia and the Longoria family put the funeral home's burial offer to a vote in a Mexican American town meeting in Corpus Christi. Those at the meeting decided to reject the offer and instead to bury Longoria with full military honors at Arlington National Cemetery in Washington, D.C.

After World War II, Mexican Americans sought political power by drawing on their outstanding war records. García's ongoing efforts on behalf of Longoria brought national attention to the Mexican American civil rights movement and the American G.I. Forum, an organization founded by García with the intent of helping Mexican American veterans sort through the

The American G.I. Forum supports recognition of the military roles played by Latinos such as Everett Alvarez, Jr., the first American pilot lost over Vietnam; after being held as a prisoner of war, he was released to the United States. (AP/Wide World Photos)

bureaucratic red tape associated with health, educational, and employment benefits. The American G.I. Forum gave Mexican Americans in South Texas a vehicle through which they could funnel information, and it quickly became a valuable political tool.

The American G.I. Forum began to embrace the goal of raising Mexican Americans to political prominence in an area of the country they inhabited in large numbers, yet whose major political and economic decision-makers were all white non-Hispanics. The American G.I. Forum became the second major Latino civil rights organization to advance the political concerns of Mexican Americans through patient organizing and voter registration drives, following the League of United Latin American Citizens.

García's methods were subtle and not threatening to the established political community, to some degree because the white community was unaware of the breadth of the movement. García's efforts through the forum helped to produce the first and second generation of Mexican American policymakers, and it remained a potent political force in South Texas.

By the 1990's, the forum's membership of twenty thousand was addressing such social issues as education, youth activities, housing, and women's programs. The large number of Mexican Americans serving as elected officials in Texas is evidence of the foundation

laid by García and of the political genius and success of the American G.I. Forum.

Americanization programs: Educational practices encouraging assimilation or elimination of a nondominant culture. Areas of influence are language, culture, dress, recreational activities, family traditions, education, and politics. (*See* ACCULTURATION VERSUS ASSIMILATION.)

The practical goal of Americanization is to allow and facilitate full participation in American society. The rationale for Americanization programs developed from the belief that immigrants traditionally have had a desire to escape oppression, participate in democracy, and adopt American values and customs.

Historically, Mexican Americans have experienced Americanization as a process of conquest and annexation. Other Hispanic groups have had the experience of migration for asylum and the experience of conquest in varying degrees. Mexican Americans are the dominant Latino group in America, and their experience with Americanization tends to define the practices that have been instituted.

The earliest institutions for Americanization of Latinos were the churches in the late 1800's. Prior to that, schools of the Southwest had promoted Hispanic ideals because the Southwest was still part of Spain or, later,

This class photo of Arizona schoolchildren in 1920 shows both Hispanic and Anglo youngsters; Hispanic students were placed in segregated Americanization programs in many schools. (University Libraries, Arizona State University, Tempe)

Mexico. Most education was carried out by the family, presidio, and ranch community units on an informal basis. Catholic parochial schools became a significant force as Americanizing influences for Hispanic students in California in the 1850's. They usually allowed Hispanic students to keep their own culture.

Between 1848 and 1900, native Mexicans not only were excluded from the governing bodies of the public educational system, but their religious heritage, culture, and language were excluded as well. Most schools wanted instruction in English only, with Anglo culture to be taught. Tolerance of the Spanish language in local government, in schools, and in newspapers was accepted only for the purpose of assimilating the first generation of Spanish speakers. At the end of the 1800's, only New Mexico still used Spanish officially in schools.

Hispanic students were sent to vocational and agriculture classes because it was thought that this was the best way to Americanize people who were culturally and socially not ready for academic tracks. Schools emphasized personal health, civics, English, sewing, home economics, carpentry, farming, and shop classes. They tried to keep intact the ethnic character of family relationships and home life. Adults were taught similar subjects in evening and weekend classes. Teaching of English was aimed at practical, conversational usage for specific manual labor occupations.

Mexican Americans' strong cultural ties have been enhanced by virtue of proximity to Mexico, familial ties, and constant contact with migrants. Mexican Americans appeared to be the least likely Latino group to be assimilated. Most Americanization programs viewed education as valid only if it promoted Anglo-American middle-class culture. The most advantageous situations enabled Hispanics to affirm their own culture while learning American ways, but there were few such programs.

Amnesty: An overlooking or pardon of past offenses by a ruling authority. In contemporary international politics, amnesty takes several forms. Of particular relevance to the U.S. Latino community were amnesty provisions of the IMMIGRATION REFORM AND CONTROL ACT OF 1986, which stated that persons who had entered the United States without documentation but had maintained continuous residence for a stated period would be granted amnesty for their illegal immigration and would be eligible for citizenship.

On a broader scale, a nation might, as happened in Haiti during the first week of October, 1994, enact legislation to grant amnesty to usurpers who overthrew the duly elected government. The United States sent troops to Haiti to force the restoration of the regime of Jean-Bertrand Aristide, the country's first democratically elected president. In order to reinstate Aristide's regime peaceably, both houses of Haiti's parliament voted to grant amnesty to those who overthrew it, in this case Lieutenant General Raoul Cedras and his followers, who grasped power shortly after Aristide's election and forced his exile.

In an arrangement brokered by former U.S. president Jimmy Carter, Cedras' government agreed to relinquish power on October 15, 1994, provided that its members could remain in Haiti, where new elections would occur in 1995. The amnesty voted by Haiti's parliament appeared to be a reasonable solution to a difficult problem.

On the other hand, some human rights violations are endemic, with citizens arrested and held incommunicado for long periods of time. Outside pressures for the release of such political prisoners, over time, encourages repressive governments to grant amnesty to prisoners of conscience in exchange for acceptance by the international community.

In 1965, after allegations of gross human rights violations came to the attention of Amnesty International, a neutral but powerful multinational organization with a mission of publicizing human rights abuses throughout the world, the organization launched a campaign to protect human rights in Brazil. Brazil was undergoing economic turmoil, and the government in power was unflinchingly authoritarian and oppressive.

Citizens critical of the government were snatched from the streets by government agents and held for extended periods without access to legal assistance, often with no communication to the outside world, including family. Incontrovertible evidence confirmed that these prisoners were brutally tortured, frequently to the point of death.

Amnesty International, which works worldwide for the unconditional release of prisoners whose opposition to government has been nonviolent, dealt with the Brazilian problem for sixteen years. In 1979, it achieved its greatest victory by forcing Brazil to reform its oppressive Law of National Security and to release all but fifty-six of its political prisoners. Brazil also agreed to permit the return of political exiles. Amnesty was granted to both groups. Brazil refused to release and grant amnesty to political prisoners who had been violent in their antigovernment protests.

Romelia Salazar displays the work authorization granted to her in 1987 under the immigration amnesty program. (AP/Wide World Photos)

AMNESTY APPLICATIONS BY COUNTRY OR AREA OF CITIZENSHIP

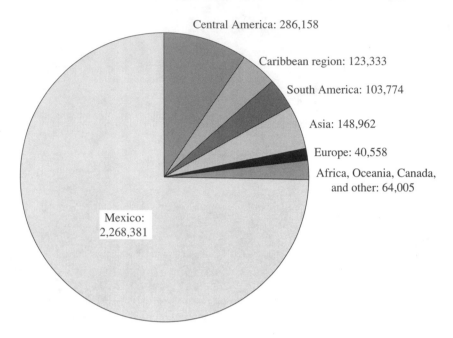

Central America: 286,158

Caribbean region: 123,333

South America: 103,774

Asia: 148,962

Europe: 40,558

Africa, Oceania, Canada, and other: 64,005

Mexico: 2,268,381

Source: Data are from Immigration and Naturalization Service, *Statistical Yearbook of the INS, 1990* (Washington, D.C.: Government Printing Office, 1991), Table 22.

Note: Numbers reflect applications for legalization processed as of May 12, 1991. The three primary categories of applicants were persons who entered illegally prior to 1982, persons who overstayed nonimmigrant visas prior to 1982, and seasonal agricultural workers.

Amnesty International has worked tirelessly in Guatemala, El Salvador, and Nicaragua on behalf of political prisoners, many of whom, particularly in Guatemala, have been snatched from the streets and summarily executed without trial. The organization has made a greater impact in Nicaragua than in any other Central American country, where the half-century regime of the Somoza family was derailed by the Sandinistas in 1979.

Anarco-syndicalism: Social and political philosophy. Under this philosophy, trade unions, through the use of the general strike, attempt to achieve the goal of individual liberty within a shared, nongovernmental society. This philosophy competed with many others in Mexican and Mexican American communities during the tumultuous period of the Mexican Revolution (1910-1921). The anarco-syndicalist movement led by Ricardo FLORES MAGÓN established areas of influence in the United States, particularly in South Texas and Los Angeles, where significant populations of Mexican refugees resided. Considered one of the most radical philosophies developing out of the revolution,

anarco-syndicalism was publicized by Flores Magón and his followers in their Los Angeles-based newspaper, *Regeneracion.*

Anaya, Rudolfo Alfonso (b. Oct. 30, 1937, Pastura, N.Mex.): Novelist and dramatist. Anaya won critical acclaim and international recognition for his first book, *Bless Me, Ultima* (1972), which won the Second Annual Premio Quinto Del Sol in 1971. Critical acclaim was matched by popular success; with sales exceeding two hundred thousand copies, Anaya's book was one of the all-time best-sellers by a Mexican American.

Using his native New Mexico as the backdrop, *Bless Me, Ultima* is the coming-of-age story of a rural New Mexican boy in the years during and following World War II. The novel mixes elements of storytelling, folklore, folkloric mysticism, and local color, elements that greatly interested Anaya. His interest in native oral history forms such as the Spanish *cuentos* (tales) led him to co-edit and publish an anthology titled *Cuentos Chicanos* (1980) and write plays based on cultural legends, including the one-act *The Season*

Rudolfo Anaya uses his native New Mexico as the setting for many of his written works. (AP/Wide World Photos)

of La Llorona, about the legendary "wailing woman" who murdered her children and now mourns for them. Anaya's other works include the novels *Heart of Aztlán* (1976), *Tortuga* (1979), and *Alburquerque* (1991); a collection of short stories titled *The Silence of the Llano* (1982); and the autobiographical *A Chicano in China* (1986).

Anaya, Toney (b. Apr. 29, 1941, Moriarty, N.Mex.): Governor of New Mexico. Anaya was born into a family of ten children. In his early childhood, Anaya and his family shared an adobe home with no electricity or plumbing. The Anaya children were strongly encouraged by their parents to earn an education. Anaya obtained a scholarship to attend New Mexico Highlands University. From there he went to Washington, D.C., where he earned a degree at Georgetown University as well as a law degree from American University. Prior to his graduation from law school in 1967, Anaya worked for Senator Dennis Chávez (D-N.Mex.). Later, he worked for Senator Henry Montoya, also of New Mexico.

Anaya's political career began when he moved back to his home state and successfully ran for attorney general in 1974. He ran unsuccessfully in 1978 against Senator Pete Domenici. Four years later, Anaya was elected governor of New Mexico. He served until 1986.

Andujar, Joaquín (b. Dec. 21, 1952, San Pedro de Macoris, Dominican Republic): Baseball player. Andujar, a hard-throwing right-handed pitcher, made his major league debut in 1976 with the Houston Astros. In 1977 and 1979, he was named to the National

Toney Anaya celebrates victory in the Democratic primary on his way to winning the governorship of New Mexico in 1982. (AP/Wide World Photos)

Joaquín Andujar in a 1982 game. (AP/Wide World Photos)

League All-Star Team, but he also struggled at times and quarreled with Houston manager Bill Virdon.

Traded to the St. Louis Cardinals in the middle of the 1981 season, Andujar blossomed. In 1982, he posted a fine 15-10 record and excelled in postseason play, winning the final game of the National League Championship Series and games three and seven of the World Series.

After a poor 1983 season, Andujar in 1984 led the National League with twenty wins, four shutouts, and 261 innings pitched. In 1985, he won twenty-one games and again led St. Louis into the World Series, but he also cemented his reputation as a hothead when he had to be restrained from attacking an umpire during the decisive game. The fallout from the incident led to Andujar being traded to the Oakland Athletics before the 1986 season. He was never able to recapture his earlier form, and his major league career ended after two frustrating seasons with Oakland and one more with Houston.

Anglo: Ethnic designation used primarily by Latinos. "Anglo" is a general term used by Latinos to describe non-Latino persons of European ancestry. The term as most often used is descriptive and not derogatory. It probably originated in the mid- to late 1800's in the southwestern United States, where the term differentiated people of European ancestry from those of Mexican or other Latino ancestry. Most Anglos of this period adhered to Anglo-Saxon religious and cultural values.

Annual Awards in the Hispanic Arts (Washington, D.C.): Beginning in 1986, the Hispanic Institute for the Performing Arts, Inc. (HIFPA) began recognizing individuals or groups of Hispanic artists and performers by giving its annual HIFPA Star Awards. It also has recognized Hispanics and non-Hispanics who have interpreted or in some way contributed to the development of Hispanic arts. The awards are presented at a gala celebration in November.

Antivagrancy Act (1855): Legislation passed by the California State Legislature that limited the freedom of California residents of Mexican descent. The racist language of the act's restrictive second section, in which people of Mexican descent were identified as persons "commonly known as Greasers," led this act to be commonly known as the Greaser Law. The act ostensibly was designed to restrict the undesirable activities of all individuals known to be vagrants and to limit local municipal responsibility for the care of im-

poverished drifters. Although the act was amended in 1856 in order to remove the reference to "Greasers," its harsh language reflected the widespread prejudices of white settlers against Californios.

Antojitos: Mexican snacklike foods made from corn. *Antojitos* include many of the Mexican dishes best known to Anglo Americans: TACOS, TAMALES, ENCHILADAS, TOSTADAS, *CHALUPAS*, and *QUESADILLAS*. All these dishes are made from *MASA* or its derivative, TORTILLAS. In Mexico, *antojitos* are associated with fiesta time. *MENUDO* and other dishes not based on corn sometimes are included in the category. *Antojitos* are eaten as snacks or as parts of light meals.

Anza, Juan Bautista de (1735, Fronteras, Mexico— Dec. 19, 1788, Arizpe, Mexico): Soldier and explorer. Anza was a frontiersman of Spanish descent whose father and grandfather, both soldiers, had served the Spanish colonial government of Mexico. In 1753, Anza too became a soldier, and within two years he was a lieutenant. Beginning in the 1760's, as captain of the garrison of Tubac, Anza participated in sporadic warfare against the rebellious Apache, Seri, and Pima Indians. By his mid-thirties, Anza was famous for his role in suppressing Indian uprisings throughout Sonora. In one battle, he vanquished an important Indian chief in hand-to-hand combat.

In January, 1774, Anza led an expedition that included fathers Juan Díaz and Francisco GARCÉS and identified an excellent land route from Sonora to California. As a result of this discovery, Anza was promoted to lieutenant colonel. Anza led many other expeditions, including those associated with the founding of Monterey and San Francisco, although he was prevented from establishing a permanent Spanish colony at the latter site. After 1777, Anza was the commandant of Sonora and governor of New Mexico. He retained the latter position for about ten years and explored New Mexico thoroughly until his sudden death at Arizpe.

Anzaldúa, Gloria (b. Sept. 26, 1942, Jesus María, Tex.): Writer. Anzaldúa's career, like most of her writing, defies simple categorization. As a scholar, educator, and writer, her interests span several disciplines. Born on a South Texas ranch settlement, Anzaldúa experienced the hardships of migrant labor, cultural sexism, homophobia, and European American oppression. These experiences deeply affected her later writings and scholarship.

Teaching at several universities across the United States, Anzaldúa established herself as a leading lesbian feminist and scholar. Anzaldúa's major work *Borderlands: The New Mestiza = La Frontera* (1987) is a mixture of genres (prose and poetry), languages (Spanish and English), and issues (autobiographical passages to discussions of history, sociology, and literature). Anzaldúa's work contains all of these interests under the symbols of borders and boundaries. Although she previously had published short stories in smaller presses, this collection won her more critical recognition as well as the Before Columbus American Book Award for 1987.

Anzaldúa has also edited two feminist collections. *This Bridge Called My Back: Writings by Radical Women of Color* (1981, with Cherríe MORAGA) won the Before Columbus American Book Award for 1986. *Making Face, Making Soul=Haciendo Caras: Creative and Critical Perspectives by Feminists of Color* was published in 1990.

Aparicio, Luis Ernesto (b. Apr. 29, 1934, Maracaibo, Venezuela): Baseball player. Aparicio, a diminutive shortstop renowned for his defensive prowess, was born into a baseball family in Maracaibo, Venezuela's second-largest city. Aparicio began playing professionally in Caracas at the age of sixteen and in 1953 succeeded his father as shortstop for the Maracaibo Gavilanes. After only a brief stint with the Maracaibo team, Luis, Jr., accepted an offer from the Chicago White Sox of the American League.

After two seasons in the White Sox minor-league system, Aparicio replaced Chico Carrasquel, a perennial all-star, as Chicago's starting shortstop. He dazzled American League fans with his range afield, led the league with twenty-one stolen bases, and batted a solid .266, a performance that won him the league's Rookie of the Year Award.

For the next six years, Aparicio was the defensive mainstay of the Chicago infield, and he also served as the team's leadoff hitter, leading the league in stolen

Often successful in stealing bases, Luis Aparicio was tagged out at home in this 1959 game. (AP/Wide World Photos)

bases for nine consecutive years. In 1959, he and teammate Nellie Fox led the White Sox to an American League pennant, and Aparicio finished second to Fox in the voting for the league's Most Valuable Player Award.

After the 1962 season, Aparicio was traded to the Baltimore Orioles, and he was the starting shortstop for Baltimore's 1966 world championship team. In 1968, he returned to the White Sox, and he finished his career in 1973 after three seasons with the Boston Red Sox. When he retired, he had won nine Gold Glove Awards and ranked as the all-time major-league leader among shortstops in games played, assists, and double plays. In 1984, he was inducted into the National Baseball Hall of Fame, becoming the first Venezuelan to be so honored. The same year, the White Sox retired his uniform number, 11.

Apodaca, Jerry (b. Oct. 3, 1934, Las Cruces, N.Mex.): Governor of New Mexico. Apodaca was born in an area of New Mexico where his family could trace its roots back more than one hundred years. After his graduation from the University of New Mexico in 1957, Apodaca worked as an educator and in business. His political career began in 1966, when he ran a successful campaign for the New Mexico State Senate as a Democrat.

Apodaca served in the state senate until 1974, when he was elected governor. He was the first Latino since 1920 to serve as the state's governor. Known as a moderate, Apodaca was able to draw votes in the growing urban areas of the state. Apodaca was later appointed as chairman of the President's Council on Physical Fitness and Sports by President Jimmy Carter. Apodaca returned to business after the Carter Administration. He maintained an active interest in civic and political affairs.

Aragón, José Rafael (c. 1796-1862): Sculptor and painter. Aragón was a *santero*, or maker of religious images, who had a productive career in Spanish colonial New Mexico during the nineteenth century. He

As governor of New Mexico, Jerry Apodaca addressed the 1976 Democratic National Convention. (AP/Wide World Photos)

was one of the most important artists in the area between 1820 and 1860.

In 1815, Aragón was married in Santa Fe, New Mexico. He and his family lived in a woodworkers' district in Santa Fe. After the death of his first wife, Aragón remarried and traveled through various mountain villages in northern New Mexico's Santa Cruz Valley, where much of his signed and dated work remains in churches.

Aragón's work includes sculptures of saints, paintings of biblical stories, altar screens, and other accessories for homes and chapel interiors. These items, made of cottonwood root or pine common in New Mexico, were coated with artist's plaster before being painted. Aragón used water-based pigments from New Mexico and Mexico. Although Aragón and his contemporaries drew inspiration from religious prints imported from Mexico, they developed an innovative painting style distinguished by fluid, bolder lines, elongated body proportions, sharp color contrasts, and imaginative decorative motifs.

Aragón's religious images played an important part in the spiritual life of the Spaniards who settled in New Mexico. Used for contemplation or veneration, the images made God seem more accessible and were important sources of inspiration among settlers in a lonely new land.

Arce, Julio (Jan. 9, 1870, Guadalajara, Jalisco, Mexico—November, 1926): Writer. Arce wrote under the pen name Jorge Ulica. He was a journalist and editor for more than thirty years. Born into a family of distinguished physicians, Arce at an early age exhibited a different career inclination, showing an avid interest in journalism. When he was ten years old, he started a neighborhood newspaper. By the age of fourteen, he was editing a student newspaper, *El hijo del progreso* (the child of progress), critical of the Mexican government. After earning a degree in pharmacy, Arce, in his early thirties, edited two newspapers in the city of Culiacán. As editor of *El diario del pacifico* (Pacific diary), he expressed his opposition to the Mexican Revolution. His opposition to the government forced him to flee Mexico for his safety.

In 1915, Arce arrived in San Francisco, California, where he worked as a journalist. He later became editor of *Hispano-America*. Under the pseudonym Jorge Ulica, Arce published a series of biting satirical sketches called *Crónicas diabólicas* (diabolical chronicles). These sketches commented on the social life and issues of San Francisco's Hispanic community.

Some of these pieces are critical of the emerging Chicano culture. Arce had a sharp tongue, and his satirical works are notable for their biting wit.

Archaeology: The earliest civilizations in Mexico left artifacts and pyramids. Archaeologists' studies of these ancient buildings and relics have helped people of the modern era to better understand the heritage of Latinos in the United States. As applied to the cultures of the Americas, archaeology has found most use in the study of the Preclassic (2000 B.C.E. to 300 C.E.) and Classic (300 to 900 C.E.) periods.

Archaeology is the study of the human past, discovered through excavation of human material remains. These may include pottery, stone objects, tools, and remains of housing. Occasionally written documents are found with the remains, and the extinct society may speak for itself. Theories about how people lived in the past are generated by careful examination of the material remains.

Preclassic Period. Central Mexican cultures have more in common with cultures of Guatemala than they do with cultures of the southwestern United States or the Caribbean islands. Patterns of religion, calendrical dating, human sacrifice, ball games, and architecture are remarkably similar in several groups from the Mexican-Guatemalan complex.

The first people to enter the New World came from Asia across the Bering Straits of Alaska. They were following large game such as the woolly mammoth across the land bridge, and they continued chasing game down through the Americas. They reached the basin of present-day Mexico in about 20,000 B.C.E.

Just as the discovery of rice in Asia and wheat in Europe had given nomadic and foraging people a reason to settle, the discovery of corn inspired permanent settlements in Mexico. With corn cultivation, the hunter and gatherer lifestyle was no longer necessary. People could settle in an area and cultivate crops.

The first traceable civilizations of Mesoamerica are from the Preclassic period. During this time, basic patterns of Mesoamerican civilization were formulated. (*See* MESOAMERICAN NATIVE COMMUNITIES.)

All succeeding Mexican and MAYAN CIVILIZATIONS have their roots in the Olmec civilization. OLMECS introduced a rich artistic tradition to Mexico. Enormous heads, altars, and figures appear in the Olmec heartland of southern Veracruz and western Tabasco. The tallest stone heads found by archaeologists are nine feet high and weigh up to twenty tons. Moving some of the huge stone carvings would have required at least a thousand men; the stones themselves were quarried more than thirty miles from the site where they eventually rested. Olmec art differs from the later Mayan art in that space, particularly blank space, is very important. By contrast, the Maya tended to neatly fill in the entire artistic field.

Guerrero, the land of gold, tin, silver, and the semi-precious stone jade, became a prominent part of the Olmec economy. Jade was often the focal point of the art created in Guerrero. Portable Olmec art treasures such as green stone plaques, masks, figures, and celts were produced there. Two caves near Chilpancingo decorated with paintings in the pure Olmec style are thought to be some of the oldest artistic works of the New World.

TEOTIHUACÁN emerged around 200 B.C.E. and grew to be the center of culture in the Mexican highlands by the Classic period. A joint archaeological project in 1964, composed of Mexicans headed by Jorge Acosta and students from the University of Rochester headed by René Millon, greatly expanded the archaeological knowledge of Teotihuacán.

Teotihuacán is famous for the Avenue of the Dead and the Pyramids of the Sun and Moon. The Pyramid of the Sun has weathered but is still enormous, seven hundred feet wide at the base and two hundred feet high. The city of Teotihuacán grew and blossomed in the Classic period as new cultures emerged in the Mexican lowlands and the Yucatán.

Classic Period. The beginning of the Classic period is marked by the Long Count inscriptions left in the lowland Maya area. The recording of dates and other hieroglyphic inscriptions may be the most important contributions of the Maya Indians to Mesoamerican civilization. The Mayan calendrical system was more accurate than any other in the world until 1582.

The Mayan system of writing consisted of about four hundred simple characters and two hundred compound characters. A Spanish bishop, Diego de Landa, studied these and attempted to learn the language but found that many of the symbols could easily have several meanings, thus invalidating his prior work. In his anger and frustration, he gathered and burned many Mayan documents. The writings that remained after

This lionlike head decorates the wall of Quetzalcóatl Temple in Teotihuacán, Mexico. (Claire Rydell)

The Temple of Warriors at Chichén Itzá. (Claire Rydell)

his rampage have not been interpreted adequately.

During the Classic period, many pyramids were built across the lowlands, and the Maya moved into the Yucatán. By the end of the period, villages and trade routes were firmly established across the Yucatán peninsula.

Chichén Itzá, the largest Maya ceremonial center in Mexico during the period, is now one of the greatest archaeological sites in the world. Its beginnings may have been as early as 450 C.E. Over the centuries, Chichén Itzá went through many phases, including times when it was uninhabited, destroyed, and rebuilt.

Chichén Itzá holds the God of the Plumed or Feathered Serpent, originally more than one hundred feet tall, and the Temple of the Warriors, with its brilliant feathered serpent columns and a large ball court.

The serpent motif was the focus of Mayan art, and it became the defining characteristic of much subsequent art in Central America and Mexico. Variants of this Maya serpent motif are most clearly seen in later art and architecture of the Toltecs and Aztecs.

Mayan civilization declined toward the end of the Classic period. The Toltecs overran Chichén Itzá, and a new culture emerged. In Chichén Itzá, the temple structures with interior columns and long colonnaded courts are of Toltec design. After establishing themselves in Chichén Itzá, the Toltecs soon dominated the Yucatán, and the Classic period ended.

—*Beaird Glover*

SUGGESTED READINGS: • Crow, John A. *The Epic of Latin America.* 4th ed. Berkeley: University of California Press, 1992. • Hammond, Norman, and Gordon R. Willey, eds. *Maya Archaeology and Ethnohistory.* Austin: University of Texas Press, 1979. • Kelly, Joyce. *An Archaeological Guide to Mexico's Yucatán Peninsula.* Norman: University of Oklahoma Press, 1993. • Reed, Alma M. *The Ancient Past of Mexico.* New York: Crown, 1966. • Rippy, J. Fred. *Historical Evolution of Hispanic America.* 2d ed. New York: F. S. Crofts, 1940. • Schezen, Roberto. *Visions of Ancient America.* New York: Rizzoli, 1990. • Weaver, Muriel Porter. *The Aztecs, Maya, and Their Predecessors: Archaeology of Mesoamerica.* New York: Seminar Press, 1972.

Architecture and architects: The influence of Hispanic architecture since Spanish Colonial times has been large; some of the most innovative and sought-after architects working in the last quarter of the twentieth century have been of Hispanic ancestry.

Spanish Influence in American Building. In 1519, Spanish conquistador Hernán Cortés looked down into the valley of Anahuac and saw the last great Indian city, Tenochtitlán, which seemed to float in the midst of a still lake, tethered to the shore by causeways. Most of the buildings were no more than two stories, with flat roofs that often held roof gardens. The skyline was level and harmonious, punctuated with temples held aloft by pyramids. Cortés believed the Aztec capital to be the most beautiful city in the world.

The Aztecs, the Maya, and the Toltecs each had ruled large areas of Mexico, erecting temples, palaces, and public buildings built of stone block and sometimes covered with a layer of plaster stucco. The Toltecs preferred small, brightly painted, cut stones laid like mosaics in geometrical motifs. The Maya carved scenes, usually of a religious nature, on their walls and attached masks of deities, much as gargoyles and saints were later used in Europe.

The architecture of Spain in Cortés' day was quirky, often vulgar, and original only in how it managed to jumble gothic, Romanesque, and Renaissance features alongside Moorish motifs, even in the cathedrals. Church building was in full swing in the sixteenth century. Soon after Cortés brought Spanish rule to Mexico, the friars began to sail for the New World. The Indian temples were knocked down, and the bricks and stone blocks from them were used to build churches that looked much like the churches in Spain. In Mexico, however, craft workers and Indians added details of their own. Around the front doors, where decoration was heaviest, they carved fruits and grains, especially MAIZE, that grew only in Mexico. An angel might have the face of a local chief. Upon a frieze, the sacred symbols of sun and moon might appear innocently, but significantly, in the Christian heavens.

The conquistadores who explored the north toward the end of the sixteenth century served the Spanish king, but for many of them Mexico was home. Missions, forts, and governors' palaces were built from California to Florida. The Pueblo Indians had built mud dwellings that were four and five stories tall, but it was the Spanish who taught the Indians to mix the mud and sand with straw and pour it into molds. They

This train station in San Antonio, Texas, shows a Spanish style of architecture. (Bob Daemmrich Photography)

called these bricks by the Arabic name of ADOBE. Because the threat of Indian attack was large until after the Civil War, most houses in the Southwest were within walled settlements. Large haciendas (*see* HACIENDA SYSTEM) provided their own defenses, including rooftop ramparts. Windows were few, very small, and covered with a wooden (later iron) grille. Doors and windows opened onto the *placita*, or patio, around which the buildings were arranged. No room could be wider than the logs procured for the roof, and the Spanish followed the Indian practice of allowing the logs to protrude through the walls, casting long shadows against the plastered adobe.

Missions and Mission Style. In Spain and Mexico, some of the friars were trained architects. The determined padres who sought souls on the hostile frontier were able builders but of far less skill. The degree of sophistication found in Mexican architecture of the period was never reached in the North American colonies. Only in Arizona, at SAN XAVIER DEL BAC, and in Texas did the Churrigueresque—the Spanish brand of Baroque that seemed to cover every inch of given wall space with a riot of fanciful detail—make its appearance. The façade around the portal of Mission San Jose y San Miguel de Aguayo was carved in limestone and is considered the equal of anything in Mexico. In California, adobe was used to build missions, but so were bricks made of burned clay. Red roofing tiles, called terra cotta, topped the white stucco-covered walls. Garden patios were planted in the middle of the mission complexes and were surrounded by arcades.

The California building designed for the 1893 World's Columbian Exposition was a massive mission-style structure complete with arcades, bell towers, and terra cotta tile. It was the first serious consideration by architectural firms in California of a Hispanic-based regional architecture, although a popular fascination with Spanish colonial buildings had begun in the 1880's. The Mission Revival style influenced public and residential design throughout the United States until the 1920's. Art Deco proved particularly suitable for adaptations of pre-Columbian bas-reliefs, as seen on the Mayan Theater in Los Angeles, and for borrowings from the pueblo adobe style, popular in New Mexico. Santa Fe style, a late twentieth century trend that peaked in the 1980's, was notable for its use of white or near-white pastel textured wall surfaces and rounded interior corners.

Latino Architects. Throughout the twentieth century, Latin America has produced internationally acclaimed architects such as Oscar Niemeyer of Brazil, Carlos Raul Villanueva of Venezuela, and Mario Pani and Ricardo Legorreta of Mexico. Some have erected significant buildings in the United States and maintained offices there. Several have made a permanent home in the United States.

The most prominent of those who have chosen to become U.S. citizens is Cesar PELLI. Born in Tucuman, Argentina, in 1926, Pelli accepted a scholarship to study architecture at the University of Illinois. After working as a project designer for Eero Saarinen, he moved to the firm of Daniel, Mann, Johnson & Mendenhall in Los Angeles. He became a partner in Gruen Associates in 1968. Throughout the 1970's, 1980's, and 1990's, Pelli was one of the most sought-after architects in the world. Among his many noteworthy commissions are the Pacific Design Center in West Hollywood, California, and New York's Museum of Modern Art and Museum Tower. The Miglin-Beitler Tower in Chicago, begun in 1988, was expected to be the world's tallest building when completed, boasting 125 floors and rising to 2,000 feet. Pelli's son Raphael also chose to become an architect.

Martin del Campo, founder and principal architect of Del Campo & Maru, was born in Guadalajara and was graduated from the National University of Mexico. He worked with the university's architect, Enrique del Moral. While still a student, del Campo formed his first partnership, but the venture did not prosper. Del Campo moved his family to Detroit, where he hoped to learn more efficient business practices. Three years later, del Campo moved to San Francisco, where, in 1957, he founded his own firm. Del Campo & Maru uses state-of-the-art computer technology to aid in its design work, and the personal involvement of del Campo and the firm's other principals has earned the company a reputation for design excellence and administrative reliability. Among the firm's commissions are the New International Terminal of the San Francisco International Airport, the Mexican Heritage Cultural Center and Gardens in San Jose, California, and a number of state and federal buildings.

Florida Architects. Florida is home to a number of notable architects of Hispanic descent, including Andres Dwany, designer of the planned community of Seaside, Florida. Spillis Candela & Partners is one of the oldest (founded in 1926 as Ferendino-Grafton) and largest architectural firms in Florida. Cuban American Hilario Candela joined the firm in 1960 and later became its president; a number of the firm's partners are also Latino. Among the firm's many award-winning commissions are the four campuses of the Miami Dade

Cesar Pelli designed the World Financial Center in New York City. (Richard B. Levine)

This Cuban American architect was one of the early middle- and upper-class refugees from Cuba. (Library of Congress)

Community College system, the Museum Tower Office Building in downtown Miami, the University of Miami's Mailman Center for Child Development, and the American Automobile Association Corporate Headquarters in Orlando. Candela has been credited with leading the movement to preserve and restore many of the historic Mediterranean style buildings in Coral Gables, Florida.

One of the most dynamic architectural designers in the United States is Bernardo Fort-Brescia, cofounder of Arquitectonica. Drawing from his Peruvian heritage, Fort-Brescia's innovative designs have won for him international recognition. His extensive work in the United States includes the Center for Innovative Technology in Herndon, Virginia, and the Disney All-Star Resorts in Orlando. Fort-Brescia has had major commissions in Luxembourg, France, and Hong Kong. Many of his most notable buildings are in Latin America: the U.S. Embassy in Lima, Peru; Palos Grandes Condominium Towers and the Altamira and Bello Campo centers in Caracas, Venezuela; and the Parque Fundidora Convention Hotel and the Rio Nazas Office Building in Monterrey, Mexico. The Atlantis, a ninety-six-unit condominium high-rise in Miami, is one of the most recognized buildings in Florida. Made familiar by the television series *Miami Vice*, the Atlantis is a slender rectangle of glass accented with red columns and capped asymmetrically by a red triangle.

Another Florida architect, David Castro-Blanco, was born in Barranquilla, Colombia, and moved to the United States to study architecture at Columbia University. In 1965, the year he became a U.S. citizen, he cofounded the firm of Castro-Blanco, Piscioneri, and Associates. A fellow of the American Institute of Architects (AIA) and senior partner of one of the largest Latino-owned architectural firms in New York, Castro-Blanco is a vocal and dedicated advocate of the Hispanic community, actively recruiting talented minority architects. He has served in various offices of the New York chapter of the AIA, including acting as president in 1992. His commissions include the McGuire Unaccompanied Enlisted Personnel Housing at McGuire Air Force Base and the Schomberg Plaza Development in Manhattan.

Urban Work. Renovation and redevelopment make up the bulk of many architects' work load. Upgrading, redesigning, or rescuing from decay a standing structure is a costly and challenging proposition, but it is often preferable to razing and rebuilding. La Marqueta, a community-based indoor marketplace and retail and entertainment complex in New York, is one such project. Still in the planning stages in the mid-1990's, the $15 million commission was given to New York City architect Raymond Plumey. Plumey, in a joint project with Lee Borrero, also designed the Julia de Burgos Latino Cultural Center in Manhattan. A member of the faculty at the architectural school of City College of the City University of New York, Plumey is active in the AIA and in the Society of Spanish Engineers, Planners and Architects.

Second-generation Mexican American Ernesto Vasquez was born in East Los Angeles and was graduated with honors from California Polytechnic State University in San Luis Obispo. After establishing his reputation for innovation and high standards in the firm of McLarrand, Vasquez & Partners, he was made vice president in 1984. As president of MV&P International in Costa Mesa, California, the company's minority arm, which he founded in 1989, Vasquez has made his firm a top competitor in the fields of urban planning and commercial and residential design. His redevelopment projects have included the twenty-eight-story Metropolitan Transportation Authority head-quarters in Los Angeles. The River Oaks and Renaissance developments in San Jose, California, are representative of his groundbreaking designs in high-density housing developments that have garnered for him more than 250 design awards and the distinction of being named the 1990 Architect of the Year by *Professional Builder* magazine.

By 1994, the American Institute of Architects listed among its members more than nine hundred Latino architects and about two hundred Latino interns and associates. The numbers were growing, as were the reputations of many talented architects of Hispanic ancestry. Organizations, such as the Society of Spanish Engineers, Planners and Architects and the National Organization of Minority Architects, as well as the AIA itself, support and encourage the careers of Latinos, and financial aid is available for qualified minority students through the American Architectural Foundation.   —*Janet Alice Long*

SUGGESTED READINGS:

• Breeze, Carla. *L.A. Deco*. New York: Rizzoli, 1991. A beautiful collection of Breeze's photographs of Art Deco buildings in the Los Angeles area. Several close views of the Mayan Theater show the influence of pre-Columbian bas-reliefs. The introduction is by David Gebhard.

• Dunlop, Beth. *Arquitectonica*. Washington, D.C.: American Institute of Architects Press, 1991. A beautiful full-color photographic presentation of the work of Arquitectonica. Contains an informative foreword by Philip Johnson and a bibliography.

• Pelli, Cesar. *Cesar Pelli: Buildings and Projects, 1965-1990*. New York: Rizzoli, 1990. A thorough presentation of Pelli's work up to 1990 that includes works then in progress such as the Miglin-Beitler Tower. Includes essays by Mario Gandelsonas and John Pastier, a brief biographical sketch of Pelli, a selected chronology of buildings and projects, a bibliography, and a list of exhibitions and awards.

• Sanford, Trent Elwood. *The Architecture of the Southwest: Indian, Spanish, American*. New York: W. W. Norton, 1950. A dated but nevertheless informative study of architecture, beginning with the Anasazi and covering the early Spanish period. Illustrated. Includes maps and a very useful appendix. Index but no bibliography.

• Weitze, Karen J. *California's Mission Revival*. Los Angeles: Hennessey & Ingalls, 1984. The third volume in the series California Architecture and Architects, edited by David Gebhard, this is a thorough discussion of Mission Revival buildings throughout the United States. Heavily illustrated with photographs and drawings. Notes, a short but annotated bibliography, and index.

Archives. *See* **Libraries and archives**

Areito: Ceremonial dance of pre-Columbian origin. According to the chronicler Gonzalo Fernández de Oviedo (1478-1557), the *areito* was a circle dance performed by men and women joining hands, imitating the movements of a soloist while accompanied by rattles, MARACAS, and the *mayohuacan* (wooden drum without skin). Song and dance were not separated; they functioned as accompaniments to each other. Themes included love, harvest prayers, and war chants, which were reserved exclusively for men. The *areito* was found in Cuba, Santo Domingo, Mexico, the Greater Antilles, and Central America. Chroniclers agree that neither the melody nor the rhythm of a pre-Columbian *areito* can be fully authenticated.

Arenas, Reinaldo (July 16, 1943, Holguin, Oriente, Cuba—Dec. 7, 1990, New York, N.Y.): Writer. Arenas, a Cuban exile, is an internationally renowned writer who immigrated to the United States in 1980. Suffering from AIDS, he committed suicide ten years later.

He left behind a literary legacy of highly acclaimed short stories, prose poetry, and novels including *Celestino antes del alba* (1967; *Singing from the Well*, 1987), which *Le Monde* named as the best novel of 1969 published in France.

Arenas joined Fidel Castro's CUBAN REVOLUTION (1959) as a teenager. He moved to Havana in 1961 and worked as a librarian, journalist, and editor. His early writings garnered honorable mentions in national literary competitions, but his second novel, *El mundo alucinante* (1969; *The Ill-Fated Peregrinations of Fray Servando*, 1987) was labeled antirevolutionary by the Castro regime and consequently was banned. Accused of being a counterrevolutionary, Arenas was imprisoned from 1974 to 1976. Forced to live life underground because of his homosexuality and his writings, Arenas fled to the United States. Arenas' works include *El palacio de las blanquísimas mofetas* (1980; *The Palace of the White Skunks*, 1990), *Otra vez el mar* (1982; *Farewell to the Sea*, 1986), *The Graveyard of the Angels* (1987), and his autobiography *Before Night Falls* (1993).

Argentinean Americans: Argentinean Americans are primarily a middle-class population with relatively high levels of educational achievement, occupational status, and income. Data from the 1990 U.S. census allow some interesting comparisons. Argentinean Americans displayed high levels of income and education compared to other Spanish-speaking groups in the United States. Argentinean American families had an average of between two and three children, and the median age of Argentinean Americans was 31.0 years. In these and other characteristics, Argentinean Americans were more similar to CUBAN AMERICANS than to any other Latino group.

South Americans represent nearly 5 percent of the Latino population, estimated at 22.3 million by the 1990 U.S. census. Of the people of South American origin in the United States in 1990, only 9.7 percent were of Argentine background.

The Mother Country. Argentina is considerably industrialized, with a per capita gross national product (GNP) of US $2,370 in 1990, estimated by the World Bank. Argentina's population is overwhelmingly Euro-

Argentinean Americans have entered all aspects of U.S. economic life and have added aspects of their culture and traditions. (Robert Fried)

pean—principally Spanish and Italian—in origin. An estimated 97 percent of Argentina's population is of European extraction, with most of the remainder of Amerindian or mixed lineage.

Argentine immigrants to the United States include a large number of European Jews who fled to Argentina in the 1930's and 1940's, as well as many descendants of Italians who emigrated to South America in the early twentieth century.

Occupations. Immigrants from South America have an occupational profile that differs from those of immigrants from Central America. From 1959 to 1975, a high percentage of employed immigrants from South America were professionals. A much smaller proportion, about 4 or 5 percent, of employed South American immigrants were domestic workers. Argentina, together with Colombia, Ecuador, and Uruguay, has sent a high percentage of craftspeople and semiskilled workers to the United States. The most significant

immigrant group from Argentina, however, consists of highly trained and skilled individuals.

Few Argentineans migrated to the United States until the late 1950's, when a "brain drain" of professionals and technicians began. This may perhaps reflect the fact that Argentina ranked among the world's top ten economies (in terms of gross domestic product per capita) until the mid-1950's, when the process of industrialization ran into major difficulties. After that time, higher rates of inflation and slower rates of growth plagued the economy.

According to the U.S. IMMIGRATION AND NATURALIZATION SERVICE, only 3,348 Argentineans immigrated to the United States during the period from 1941 to 1950. In contrast, from 1951 to 1960 there was an immigration of 19,486 Argentineans. In the next decade (1961-1970), 49,721 immigrants from Argentina were admitted to the United States. The 1970's saw 29,897 Argentineans admitted to the United

---

STATISTICAL PROFILE OF ARGENTINEAN AMERICANS, 1990

Total population based on sample: 100,921

Percentage foreign-born: 77%

Median age: 34.4 years

Percentage 25+ years old with at least a high school diploma or equivalent: 75%

Occupation (employed persons 16+ years old)

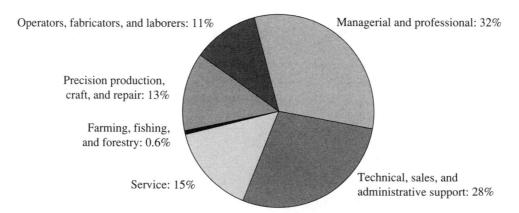

Operators, fabricators, and laborers: 11%

Managerial and professional: 32%

Precision production, craft, and repair: 13%

Farming, fishing, and forestry: 0.6%

Service: 15%

Technical, sales, and administrative support: 28%

Percentage unemployed: 5.1%

Median household income, 1989: $35,202

Percentage of families in poverty, 1989: 7.8%

Source: Data are from Bureau of the Census, *Census of 1990: Persons of Hispanic Origin in the United States* (Washington, D.C.: Bureau of the Census, 1993), Tables 1, 3, 4, and 5.

States, and the 1980's another 27,327. In contrast, the 1991 Canadian census showed a total of only 3,090 residents of Argentine background.

Many Argentineans were attracted to the United States by opportunities for employment in highly skilled professions. Argentinean Americans have made significant contributions in the areas of medicine, science, humanities, and the arts.

Reasons for Immigration. In the 1970's and 1980's, thousands of Argentineans went into exile because of the political turmoil in Argentina. They sought to escape the "dirty war" that the military waged against "subversion" between 1976 and 1983. That campaign left a legacy of more than fifteen thousand *desaparecidos* (disappeared ones) in a country of less than thirty million people.

Political refugees from the "dirty war" included persons from all walks of life, from professionals to those working as unskilled laborers. During the 1970's, the first generation of Argentinean Americans outnumbered the second generation by two to one, reflecting the recent arrival of large numbers of immigrants.

Geographic Location. Throughout the nineteenth and twentieth centuries, Argentinean Americans have congregated in urban areas, especially in the largest metropolitan centers. They concentrated in urban centers in northeastern, Pacific Coast, and Gulf Coast states because their education, occupational skills, and lifestyles were suited to urban society. The four urban areas with the largest numbers of Argentinean Americans in 1990 were New York, New York, and Los Angeles, California (approximately 30,000 each), followed by Miami, Florida (between 15,000 and 20,000), and Washington, D.C. (about 3,000).

Language. Argentinean Americans have opportunities to return home, and a steady stream of newcomers renews the contact of less recent immigrants with the language, culture, and society of Argentina. Argentinean Americans thus retain characteristics of their home culture.

The Spanish language of Argentina is diverse (*see* SPANISH LANGUAGE—VARIATIONS ACROSS LATINO GROUPS). All the varieties share one characteristic that is often puzzling for other Spanish speakers in the United States, although it is well known in Central America. In Argentina, *vos* is used instead of *tú* as the familiar "you." The pronoun *vos* comes from a respectful form of address used in the fifteenth and sixteenth centuries. It is accompanied by different verb forms from those used with *tú*.

Argentinean Americans prefer *vos* when speaking to one another, but many comfortably switch to *tú* when speaking to non-Argentineans. Although there are many *tonadas* (accents or differences in speech patterns) in Argentina, the *rioplatense* or *porteño* (from the River Plate area) is by far the most common. More than one-third of all Argentineans live in or around greater Buenos Aires. The outstanding phonetic feature of this variety is the *yeísmo*, in which the "ll" and "y" characters are pronounced like the "j" in Jill.

—*M. Cecilia Colombi*

SUGGESTED READINGS: • Armstrong, John A. *Nations Before Nationalism.* Chapel Hill: University of North Carolina Press, 1982. • Biggins, Alan, comp. *Argentina.* Santa Barbara, Calif.: Clio Press, 1991. • Business Monitor International. *Argentina 1993.* London: BMI, 1993. • Garzón Valdés, Ernesto. "La emigración argentina—acerca de sus causas ético-políticas." In *El poder militar en la Argentina (1976-1981),* edited by Peter Waldmann and Ernesto Garzón Valdés. Frankfurt: Verlag Klaus Dieter Vervuert, 1982. • Graziano, Frank. *Divine Violence: Spectacle, Psychosexuality, and Radical Christianity in the Argentine "Dirty War."* Boulder, Colo.: Westview Press, 1992. • Rock, David. *Authoritarian Argentina.* Berkeley: University of California Press, 1993. • Thernstrom, Stephan, ed. *Harvard Encyclopedia of American Ethnic Groups.* Cambridge, Mass.: The Belknap Press of Harvard University Press, 1980. • U.S. Department of Justice. Immigration and Naturalization Service. *Statistical Yearbook of the Immigration and Naturalization Service.* Washington, D.C.: Government Printing Office, 1992.

Arguello, Alexis (b. Apr. 19, 1952, Managua, Nicaragua): Boxer. The multitalented Arguello began boxing at the age of fifteen. Under the direction of an influential businessman, the young Nicaraguan would go on to set a high goal for himself—to be the first four-time champion in four different weight classes.

Taking his first title in the 126-pound welterweight class in 1974, Arguello would go on to win the junior lightweight (130 pounds) and the lightweight (135 pounds) classes over the next six years. When he sought his fourth title, in the junior welterweight class, Arguello had amassed an impressive 76-4 record.

The fourth title, however, eluded Arguello. He twice took terrible poundings from Aaron Pryor in title bouts. Their November, 1982, meeting, in which Pryor landed twenty-three consecutive unanswered punches, left Arguello with serious injuries. After a second un-

Competing as a junior welterweight in 1983, Alexis Arguello landed a punch on Vilomar Fernandez. (AP/Wide World Photos)

successful attempt at the title, against Pryor, he retired in 1983.

A national hero, Arguello turned to a different kind of fight when he joined the Contra movement in his homeland, Nicaragua. Financial problems led Arguello, unsuccessfully, to attempt a comeback in 1986.

Argüello, Concepción (1790, San Francisco, Calif.—1857, Convent of Saint Catherine Benicia, Calif.): Nun and part of a famous romantic pair. Concepción Argüello was the daughter of the commandant of San Francisco in the early 1800's. At that time, Russia sought to obtain food for its Alaskan colony at Sitka from the Spanish colonies, the closest source of supply. In one such effort, Nicolai Rezanov, a Russian official, attempted to end a famine at Sitka by obtaining food at San Francisco. Arriving there in April, 1806, he sought unsuccessfully to barter with colonial officials.

Rezanov and Concepción met, fell in love in a whirlwind six-week courtship, and became engaged. Although Rezanov was older by decades and was not Catholic, permission was granted by the Argüello family for the future marriage, contingent on papal approval, which Rezanov was to obtain. He set off for Alaska with the food he had sought in May of 1806. He died in 1807 en route to Russia to report the successful mission. Unaware of this, Concepción waited patiently. Eventually, she became a nun. Later, when her father was appointed governor of Baja California, she accompanied him, staying in that region from 1815 to 1819. She later returned to Alta California. In 1842, Concepción finally learned Rezanov's fate. She is famous for this romance, her kindliness, and her good works.

Arias, Ronald Francis (b. Nov. 30, 1941, Los Angeles, Calif.): Journalist and novelist. Arias is best known for his debut novel *The Road to Tamazunchale* (1975), which was nominated for the National Book Award in 1976. The book tells the story of Don Fausto, who makes an imaginary journey while on the verge of death. An actual Mexican village, Tamazunchale, represents for Fausto the final resting place after death.

Short stories published years earlier had not brought much recognition to Arias. Upon publication of this novel, Arias became recognized as a leading Mexican American writer of Magical Realism, a literary form popularized in South American literature by Gabriel García Márquez. Arias' novel, however, is more a hybrid of American realism and Magical Realism than a pure example of the South American literary form.

Arias' Mexican heritage and travels throughout Latin America have undoubtedly influenced his writing. As a journalist who has worked for newspapers, national and international wire services, and *People* magazine, Arias has a writing style that blends journalism with the magical, fantastic passages associated with Magical Realism.

Arias' other writings include the short stories "El mago" (1970), "The Interview" (1974; adapted into a play, *The Wetback*, 1975), and "The Boy Ate Himself" (1980), along with the nonfiction work *Five Against the Sea* (1989).

Arizona: Arizona has a diverse history of peoples coexisting, including such American Indian tribes as the Apache, Hopi, Navajo, Pima, Tohono O'dham, and Yaqui. Arizona was a Spanish or Mexican possession until the mid-nineteenth century, when it became a territory of the United States. Arizona was formally admitted as a state on February 14, 1912.

Demographics. In 1870, Arizona's population was 9,658. Arizona's Latino population in the nineteenth century remained primarily in southern and eastern Arizona. Thomas Sheridan, in *Los Tusconenses: The Mexican Community in Tucson, 1854-1941* (1986), determined that Tucson's Latino population in 1860 was 653 out of 925 residents. By 1940, Tucson's population had grown to 36,818, and the Latino component was 11,000. The state of Arizona experienced continued population growth from the 1940's through the early 1990's.

Arizona is composed of fifteen counties. The 1990 U.S. census estimated the state's population to be 3.7 million. The state capital, PHOENIX, is located in the largest county, Maricopa, which had a population of 2,285,199. Pima was the second largest county, with a population of 717,209 residents, living primarily in the city of TUCSON. About 688,000 Latinos lived in the state. Latinos lived throughout the state but were found primarily in Maricopa, Pima, Santa Cruz, Pinal, Cochise, and Yuma counties.

History. The origin of the word "Arizona" is unclear. James Officer has noted that early Spanish Basque explorers used the phrases *arritza onac*, which refers to good or valuable rocky places, and *aritza onac*, which refers to good or valuable oaks. These early explorers identified the region as Arizonac, and it was considered to be part of Sonora, Mexico. The region that included Arizona and SONORA acquired the name of Gran Pimería; the far northern region, which became Arizona, was known as PIMERÍA ALTA. The Pimería Alta region was the land of the upper Pima Indians and was considered uncharted and dangerous territory by the Spanish.

Spanish exploration into Arizona started with the Francito Vázquez de Coronado expedition of 1540-1542, which was searching for fabled riches of gold and other mineral wealth. Other early Spanish explorations included Antonio Espejo's expedition of 1582 and Juan de Oñate's expedition of 1604. Settlement was limited to isolated areas of Sonora where agriculture, ranching, and the excavation of mines could develop.

The northward expansion of Spanish and Mexican settlers during the seventeenth century created a need for protection from various indigenous peoples. As Spanish military exploration moved throughout the region, Catholic missionaries were given the tasks of colonizing the indigenous peoples. Father Eusebio Francisco KINO, a Jesuit missionary, was sent to Pimería Alta in 1686. Under Father Kino's plan, missions and smaller churches were located near haciendas, ranchos, mining sites, or Spanish presidios, which offered protection in case of attack. Tucson was a Spanish presidio and still identifies itself as the Old Pueblo, but the presidio buildings no longer exist. The Franciscan order assumed the duties of the MISSION SYSTEM during the eighteenth century. Arizona's best example of a well-preserved Spanish mission is SAN XAVIER DEL BAC, located near Tucson on the San Xavier Indian Reservation. San Xavier del Bac was completed in 1797 and was still in use in 1994.

In 1821, Arizona became a northern frontier outpost for the Mexican government. In 1848, Mexico ceded northern and central Arizona to the United States as part of the TREATY OF GUADALUPE HIDALGO (1848) at the conclusion of the MEXICAN AMERICAN WAR. The GADSDEN PURCHASE (1854) allowed the establishment of a railroad system that would link the continental U.S. territories.

Mining. Arizona had rich mineral resources, including silver, gold, copper, coal, zinc, and iron, that attracted the development of a MINING industry. In 1732, a large reservoir of silver was discovered in the community of Arizonac, approximately seventy miles south of Tucson. This discovery attracted Spanish colonization into the region, contributing to the Pima Indian Revolt of 1751 and the strengthening of the presidio system. The mining industry remained on a small scale because of limited technology and insufficient investment by the Spanish and Mexican governments.

The United States' acquisition of Arizona during the nineteenth century generated mining interests in southern and eastern Arizona. Ratification of the Gadsden Purchase in 1854 and the completion of the railroad in the 1880's provided a means for transporting mineral ore from Arizona to other areas for mass production. Arizona became known for large-scale copper reserves and attracted substantial investments from U.S. mining companies.

During the early part of the twentieth century, Arizona's mining industry evolved into a strong force in the state's economy. Out-of-state mining companies sought to control their labor forces by establishing company towns near mines. Residents of these company towns were at times obligated to purchase basic housing and household products from the company. Wages for Mexican or Mexican American miners typically were set below those of their Anglo counterparts. Mexican miners were used as leverage to keep wages low if resistance to policies of the mining company developed. The companies could threaten to bring in compliant Mexican workers at lower wages.

Labor unions sought to end discriminatory practices within the mines and to provide for improved working and living conditions for miners and their families. Labor unions instigated strikes (*HUELGAS*) and disrupted the production of mineral ore at the mines. Labor unions were seen as a threat to the stability of the MINING industry and to Arizona's revenues. Companies used forced lockouts and law enforcement officers to break the strikes. In 1917, the perception that Mexican nationals were taking jobs and social resources away from Anglos generated support for deporting Mexicans and restricting their hiring.

Arizona's labor unions continued to generate support from miners until the 1970's. In the early 1980's, Arizona's mining industry experienced severe economic hardships. Major mining companies were forced

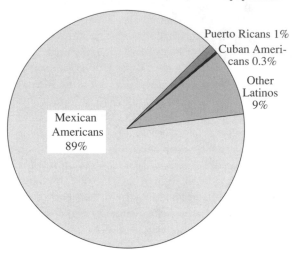

LATINO POPULATION OF ARIZONA, 1990

Total number of Latinos = 688,338; 19% of population

Mexican Americans 89%

Puerto Ricans 1%
Cuban Americans 0.3%
Other Latinos 9%

Source: Data are from Marlita A. Reddy, ed., *Statistical Record of Hispanic Americans* (Detroit: Gale Research, 1993), Table 106.
Note: Percentages are rounded to the nearest whole number except for Cuban Americans, for whom rounding is to the nearest 0.1%.

to shut down their mines or sought concessions from labor unions in order to continue operations. In 1983, the labor union declared a strike at the Morenci mine, located near the towns of Clifton and Morenci. The strike became violent, and Arizona's governor, Bruce Babbitt, ordered state police and military to intervene. The ensuing battle left several people injured and forced governmental inquiries into the use of Arizona state troops in a mining strike.

During the remainder of the 1980's, Arizona's mining industry went into an economic downturn. After the mid-1980's, labor unions were no longer found in every mine, and their membership was low. Profitable mines continued to operate in northwestern, eastern, and southern Arizona.

Education, Politics, and Business. Even though Latinos encountered various forms of discrimination and prejudice, many continued contributing to business development, intellectual life, theater, and art after the GADSDEN PURCHASE. Tucson's Mexican American community supported Spanish-language theater and actively sought Mexican and Latin American plays. The community of Tucson demonstrated active Latino participation in all areas of social and political life.

Latino elected officials served in the territorial senate (council) and local governmental offices. Two major Spanish-language NEWSPAPERS, *El Fronterizo* (1880's-1914) and *El Tucsonenses* (1914-1950's), were available throughout Arizona and Sonora. On January 14, 1894, La ALIANZA HISPANO-AMERICANA, a mutual aid society, was founded in Tucson. La Alianza established lodges throughout the Southwest, in northern Mexico, and as far north as the state of Wyoming.

The public education system in Arizona during the nineteenth century was limited and tended to benefit non-Hispanic school children. Until the 1950's, Arizona's public schools often were segregated by race and ethnicity. Spanish-surnamed children were automatically placed in remedial classes before they could enter the first grade. It was assumed that Spanish-surnamed children could not speak English and needed special help. The remedial classes segregated Mexican American children and were used to detain them for several years. Latino schoolchildren were punished if they were caught speaking any language except English.

The issue of language usage did not disappear from Arizona. In the late 1980's, Arizona state residents passed a law making English the official language for state governmental use. The ENGLISH-ONLY law was found unconstitutional, but continued to be challenged in the legal system. BILINGUAL EDUCATION continued in various public school systems, as well as on many American Indian reservations.

In the 1880's, Arizona's first institution of higher education, the University of Arizona, was established in Tucson. Its first Board of Regents included noted Mexican American businessman and politician Mariano Samaniego. In 1994, the university's president was Manuel Pacheco, the first Latino to head a major U.S. research institution and the first member of a minority group to be the school's president.

Arizona in the Early 1990's. Since Arizona became part of the United States, the only Latino to hold the position of governor was Raúl CASTRO, in the 1970's. Latinos were active in politics, however, and served in local governmental offices. Ed Pastor was elected to the U.S. House of Representatives from Arizona in 1992. Continuous immigration from Mexico and other Latin American countries contributed to the continued use of Spanish throughout the state. Latinos continued sponsoring Hispanic community events, protecting the interests of their community.   —*Melissa Amado*

SUGGESTED READINGS:

• Acuna, Rodolfo. "Sonora Invaded: The Occupation of Arizona." In *Occupied America: A History of Chicanos.* 2d ed. New York: Harper & Row, 1981. Describes the turmoil created between Latinos and Anglos starting in the 1850's.

• Dobyns, Henry. *Spanish Colonial Tucson: A Demographic History.* Tucson: University of Arizona Press, 1976. Traces Tucson's development from 1694 to 1797.

• Kino, Eusebio Francisco. *Kino's Plan for the Development of Pimería Alta, Arizona, and Upper California.* Translated by Ernest J. Burrus. Tucson, Ariz.: Arizona Pioneers' Historical Society, 1961. Details Kino's mission system for Arizona, Sonora, and Upper California in the seventeenth century.

• Officer, James. *Hispanic Arizona, 1536-1856.* Tucson: University of Arizona Press, 1987. Traces the arrival of the Spanish presidios and missions in Arizona in the sixteenth century. Also discusses possession by Mexico and takeover by the United States.

• Sheridan, Thomas. *Los Tucsonenses: The Mexican Community in Tucson, 1854-1941.* Tucson: University of Arizona Press, 1986. Documents Tucson's prominent Hispanic community in social, political, and economic realms.

• Torres, David, and Melissa Amado. "The Quest for Power: Hispanic Collective Action in Frontier Arizona." In *Perspectives in Mexican American Studies* 3

Mariano Samaniego. (Arizona Historical Society)

Pedro Armendáriz escorts Mary Pickford to the 1950 premiere of the film Breakthrough. (AP/Wide World Photos)

(1992): 73-94. Discusses prominent Hispanic business entrepreneurship and elected political officials during the late nineteenth and early twentieth centuries.

• U.S. Department of Commerce. Bureau of the Census. *1990 Census of Population: General Population Characteristics: Arizona.* Washington, D.C.: Government Printing Office, 1990. Census figures for the state of Arizona.

• Wagoner, Jay. *Arizona Territory 1863-1912: A Political History.* Tucson: University of Arizona Press, 1970. Describes territorial Arizona's political life.

• Wagoner, Jay. *Early Arizona: Prehistory to Civil War.* Tucson: University of Arizona Press, 1975. Identifies early indigenous tribes living in Arizona. Discusses the first Spanish explorations, starting in 1540, and settlement of the region.

Armendáriz, Pedro (May 9, 1912, Churubusco, Mexico—June 18, 1963, Los Angeles, Calif.): Actor. Armendáriz was one of Mexico's most successful film stars. He was internationally recognized for work in director Emilio Fernández's *María Candelaria* (1943) and *The Pearl* (1945). He also worked with other major directors including Luis Buñuel and John Ford. He appeared in more than seventy-five films.

Armendáriz's most notable Mexican films include *Rosario* (1936), *Jalisco nunca pierde* (1937, Jalisco never loses), *Mi candidato* (1938, my candidate), *Los olivadados de Dios* (1940, those forgotten by God), *La reina del rio* (1940, the queen of the river), *Guadalajara* (1943), *The Life of Simón Bolívar* (1943), and *La Cucaracha* (1958). His U.S. films include *The Fugitive* (1947), *Fort Apache* (1948), *Three Godfathers* (1949), *We Were Strangers* (1949), *Tulsa* (1949), *Border River* (1954), *The Littlest Outlaw* (1955), *The Wonderful Country* (1959), *Francis of Assisi* (1961), and *Captain Sinbad* (1963). *From Russia with Love* was released in 1963 after his death.

After learning that he had cancer, Armendáriz shot himself to death. His son, Pedro Armendáriz, Jr., also is well known as an actor.

Armijo, Manuel (1792, Albuquerque, N.Mex.—Dec. 9, 1853): Politician. Born into a rich family, Armijo accumulated a substantial fortune in land and mercantile interests during his lifetime. He also served as governor of NEW MEXICO from 1827 to 1829, then again for most of the period between 1837 and 1846.

Armijo's career illustrates the lack of control that Mexico had over its frontier officials. Between 1839 and 1844, Armijo unilaterally streamlined complicated national ad valorem tariff laws because he believed they were detrimental to regional interests. In addition, in the early 1840's Armijo approved an extraordinary number of land grants to encourage private development. Some critics have characterized this land policy as reckless, but it was designed to create a barrier against Indians, Texans, and Americans. Armijo thus hoped to avoid a repetition of the mistakes made by the Mexican government in Texas during the 1820's.

Armijo is remembered for his role in the Mexican American War. When hostilities broke out, Armijo judged the situation to be hopeless and abandoned all defenses, allowing American forces to occupy SANTA FE without immediate resistance. Historians debate whether he accepted a bribe by the Americans or was simply afraid to make a stand. He was imprisoned briefly by the Mexican government on grounds of treason, but charges were dropped for lack of evidence.

Armiño, Franca de (b. Puerto Rico): Dramatist and labor organizer. A poet, essayist, and playwright, Armiño (a pseudonym) used her strong feminist voice for the cause of workers' rights in the 1930's and 1940's. She worked as an organizer, but her major contribution came through her art. The only one of her works still available is a play, *Los hipócritas: Comedia dramática social* (1937; the hypocrites: a social drama), concerning political and social issues arising from the Great Depression and the Spanish Civil War. After several twists in plot, the play ends in triumph with the heroine choosing her own husband—from the working class—rather than marrying her father's choice, a duke. It was performed in New York City in 1933. She is also known to have published another play, *Tragedia puertorriqueña* (Puerto Rican tragedy), a book of essays, and a book of poems. These works have been lost.

Arnaz, Desi, Sr. (Desiderio Alberto Arnaz y de Acha III; Mar. 2, 1917, Santiago, Cuba—Dec. 2, 1986, Del Mar, Calif.): Bandleader and actor. Arnaz and his mother emigrated from Cuba in 1933 to Miami, Florida, where he began playing with such figures as Xavier CUGAT. By 1938, he led his own band. In 1939, he moved to California, where he married actress Lucille Ball. His film debut came in 1940 with *Too Many Girls*. His other features include *Father Takes a Wife* (1941), *Four Jacks and a Jill* (1941), *The Navy Comes Through* (1942), *Bataan* (1942), *Cuban Pete* (1946), *Holiday in Havana* (1949), *The Long Long Trailer* (1954), and *Forever Darling* (1956).

Desi Arnaz, Sr., and wife Lucille Ball formed Desilu, a production company. (AP/Wide World Photos)

In 1950, Arnaz and Ball formed Desilu Productions, which pioneered the three-camera film technique that soon became standard in television. Their show *I Love Lucy* featured Arnaz as bandleader Ricky Ricardo and Ball as his zany wife. It ran until 1961 and became a classic of television situation comedy, continuing for decades in syndication. Desilu also produced such television hits as *Our Miss Brooks*, *The Untouchables*, and *The Danny Thomas Show*. Arnaz and Ball were divorced in 1960. Their children Desi, Jr., and Lucie both followed in their parents' footsteps and became professional performers. For the last film of his career, *The Escape Artist* (1982), Arnaz deferred to his son by returning to the name Desiderio Arnaz.

Arreola, Juan José (b. Sept. 12, 1918, Ciudad Guzmán, Jalisco, Mexico): Writer. Arreola, who was once a professional actor, is widely regarded as one of the outstanding short-story writers of the Spanish-speaking world. Arreola's literary career began in Guadalajara,

where he edited two literary magazines. His short story "Hizo el bien mientras vivió" (1943) earned him recognition as a writer.

Arreola traveled to Paris in 1945 to further his established acting career and returned to Mexico City a year later. He shifted his efforts from acting to professional and creative writing. Arreola received a Rockefeller Foundation scholarship for creative writing in 1950.

Arreola's writing is notable for frequent use of irony and satire. The frequently anthologized "El Guardagujas" (1952; the switchman) is a satire of the Mexican railroad system. The text is compounded with elements of Magical Realism. Arreola's knowledge of literary movements led him to the position as host of a televised show about literary subjects. In 1963, he won the prestigious Xavier Villaurrutia prize. Arreola's works include the short-story collections *Varia invención* (1949; varied invention), *Cuentos* (1950; stories), and *Confabulario* (1952; confabulary), in addition to the novel *La feria* (1963; *The Fair*, 1977).

Arriola, Gustavo Montaño (b. July 23, 1917, Florence, Ariz.): Cartoonist. Arriola is best known as the creator of "Gordo," a long-running comic strip that drew story ideas and characters from Mexican life and people.

Arriola grew up in Los Angeles, California. After graduating from high school in the mid-1930's, he worked in the cartoon story department of Metro-Goldwyn-Mayer's animation studio. Later, he was an animator for Screen Gems and Columbia Pictures.

In 1941, Arriola sold the concept for "Gordo." After only one year of publication, the daily strip had amassed one million readers. At the age of twenty-six, Arriola had to discontinue the strip to serve four years in the military. When he resumed publication in 1946, "Gordo" became one of the most widely published comic strips of its time.

With unique, if somewhat stereotypical, characters—including Gordo himself, the Widow Gonzales, Gordo's nephew Pepito, and chihuahuas and Mexican roosters—"Gordo" gave Mexican life and people exposure on the comics page. The amusing drawings and inventive situations of the comic strip added to its universal appeal.

Arroz: Rice, a common component of meals throughout Latin America. Although it is not the ubiquitous

Rice and beans is a common dish. (Don Franklin)

accompaniment suggested by the combination plate of Mexican take-out restaurants in the United States, rice is a common part of meals throughout Latin America. Originally domesticated around southwestern China, rice was transported to Arab lands, then to Spain, then, by the 1560's, to the Americas. Rice in Latin America usually is eaten boiled, sometimes cooked with vegetable purées or spices. It often forms a course of its own, sometimes admixed with beans. It also can be served along with other dishes. In addition, it is used in soups, casseroles, stews, HORCHATA, and some desserts.

Art, Cuban American: Although the graphics and POSTER ART of revolutionary Cuba were popular in the United States in the 1960's, the work of modern Cuban American artists was only beginning to be recognized outside Miami in the 1980's and 1990's. Cuban exile artists are diverse in style but generally less political than Chicano and mainland Puerto Rican artists.

Historical Background. An examination of U.S. relations with Cuba during the nineteenth and twentieth centuries sheds some light on the social and cultural milieu of Cuban exiles and, in turn, their artistic expressions. The Monroe Doctrine of 1823 declared that the American continents were no longer to be considered ripe for colonization by European powers. After the United States failed to buy or diplomatically win Cuba from the Spanish Empire, it helped Cubans liberate themselves from Spanish rule in the SPANISH-AMERICAN WAR (1898). Cuba passed into U.S. hands, and the island's Hispanic and African cultures continued to mingle in a unique way. Even after Cuba became an independent republic, a series of U.S.-backed presidents terrorized the people with ruthless police forces. In 1959, a rebellion led by Fidel CASTRO toppled the dictatorship and formed a Marxist-Leninist government that would soon break off relations with the United States.

Cubans came to North America in two large waves, with many smaller trickles in between. The first wave, from 1959 to 1962, was made up of those who stood to lose the most under the Castro regime. These immigrants were largely middle-class landowners, business people, lawyers, doctors, technicians, professors, and engineers.

Cuban exiles differed in important ways from other Latino groups. They did not view the United States as a land of opportunity but rather as a temporary haven from the regime in control of their beloved Cuba. Also, they did not face the shock of adjusting to a modern, urban culture; they were already well-educated and prosperous.

These exiles, paradoxically, were among the few Latino refugee immigrant groups to receive substantial financial aid from the U.S. government. Moreover, this aid, teamed with vitality, enterprise, intelligence, and hard work, aided in the relatively quick assimilation and success of Cuban Americans. (*See* ACCULTURATION VERSUS ASSIMILATION.)

The Cuban American community diversified with the arrival of thousands of less advantaged Cubans in the MARIEL BOAT LIFT of 1980. Unlike earlier exiles, the *marielitos* were not necessarily focused on an anti-Castro crusade. This wave also included some persecuted homosexuals and a group of criminals. In general, these immigrants were not well received by the established Cuban community in the United States.

The Cuban American Art Scene. The earliest Cuban artistic manifestation in North America was that of middle-class academy-trained artists from the island. For personal and political reasons, these artists chose not to associate themselves with the "postrevolutionary" art that evolved after Castro's takeover. They chose instead to turn back for inspiration to the Cuban avant-garde of the 1920's. Their art was international in style, universal in theme, and devoid of political content.

Most Cuban exile artists settled in Miami or New York. They eventually grouped themselves by generation and along the lines of race, class, and sexual preference. The sharpest division, as with other Cuban Americans, was between those who wished to overthrow the Castro regime and those who wanted to establish ongoing communication with the island after years of isolation.

The first major exhibition of exile art in the United States was "Outside Cuba/Fuera de Cuba," organized by the Art Museum of Rutgers University and the

Murals such as this one of Cuba decorate outside walls in Miami, Florida. (Otto G. Richter Library, University of Miami, Coral Gables, Florida)

University of Miami Art Museum in 1987. This was followed by "Cuba-USA: The First Generation," a production of Fondo Del Sol, in 1991. Although Cuban American artists were often exhibited and reviewed in Miami, it was harder for them to find mainstream recognition elsewhere.

The quick economic recovery of the early Miami exiles and the government assistance they received in the United States was accompanied by the country's most well-funded support structure for Latino artists. Lowe Art Museum of the University of Miami has a large Cuban collection. Cuban Jose Gómez Sicre, the powerful visual arts director of the Pan American Union of the Organization of American States for forty years and founder of the Museum of Modern Art of Latin America in Washington, D.C., helped Cuban American artists find exhibit venues, patrons, and recognition. The Cintas Foundation was set up in Florida by a wealthy former ambassador with $2 million set aside for Cuban artists outside Cuba. There is also a sizable population of Cuban American art collectors and donors.

Notable Artists. The works of Ana MENDIETA are the best known of those artists who favored establishing a dialogue with Cuba. Mendieta had been separated from her family and sent to the United States in the 1960's. She was trained at the Center for the New Performing Arts at the University of Iowa. In search of a new identity and healing, she expressed herself through the use of her own body in tableaux, performances, and mixed media earth works. Returning to her homeland in 1981, she created a series of carvings inspired by Indian rock paintings in the limestone caves of Jaruco.

Luis Cruz AZACETA grew up in Cuba and studied at the School of Visual Arts in New York. He made "the victim" his principal theme, particularly the plight of the political exile exposed to the brutality of life in New York City. His intense, neo-expressionist works have been exhibited in American and international galleries.

Another artist in exile, Pedro PEREZ, acknowledged feeling "caught between two cultures" and perceived himself as working more in an American tradition than a Cuban one. His early exposure to his parents' jewelry business in Cuba aided him in making remarkable gold leaf constructions. His brilliant *La Esmeralda (Queen That Shoots Birds)* mixes baroque opulence with intelligent humor.

The anguish of exile can be felt in Maria Brito-Avellana's surrealistic installations. These evoke child-hood memories refracted from mirrors or the pain of severance from homeland, demonstrated by a bucket full of monstrous tears.

For some artists, the search for identity is spiritual. Most notable in this category are the works of deceased artists Juan BOZA and Carlos ALFONSO. Both *marielitos* had achieved artistic recognition in Cuba before leaving in 1980. Boza, a Santero, was known for his altars inspired by SANTERÍA practices incorporating objects such as fruits, shells, feathers, and fetishes.

Later generations of Cuban artists have explored technology available internationally and in North America to find new avenues of expression. Susana SORI creates installations of spiraling energy and light reflections. Doris Vila immersed herself in holography, film, and sound to sculpt space with light, shadow, and color.

Perhaps the most notorious Cuban American artist in the 1990's was Andrés SERRANO. His provocative postmodern photography combined Catholic and sexual images in what some considered an offensive or sacrilegious manner. Senator Jesse Helms singled out Serrano's work in 1991 hearings criticizing grants awarded by the National Endowment for the Arts.

—*L. J. Sullivan*

SUGGESTED READINGS: • Beardsley, John, and Jane Livingston. *Hispanic Art in the United States: Thirty Contemporary Painters and Sculptors*. New York: Abbeville Press, 1987. • Fusco, Coco. "Art and Cuba Now." *The Nation*, June 24, 1991, 858. • Hughes, Robert. "Taking Back His Own Gods." *Time*, February 22, 1993, 68. • Plagens, Peter. "The Next Wave from Havana." *Newsweek*, November 30, 1992, 76. • *Six Cuban Painters Working in New York*. New York: Center for Inter-American Relations, 1975. • Turner, Elisa. "Mythic Presence." *ARTnews* 90 (December, 1991): 20.

Art, Latin American: Much regional exchange has occurred among the nations of Latin America in terms of art shows, local and regional biennials, study, research, travel, and the dissemination of artistic motifs, techniques, and styles. In addition, particularly since the 1960's, a growing number of Latin American-sponsored Pan-American and international exhibitions and biennials have underlined the cohesions within the continents, apart from Latin American interchanges with Europe and the United States. Chief among international biennials are the São Paulo Biennial (since 1951, the oldest and the largest), which brought together Latin (and non-Latin) Americans with European artists, and the Havana Biennial (since 1984, changed in 1991 to a triennial), for which works were curated from the Third World. For the 1989, 1991, and 1994 gatherings, Third World artists living within the First World as immigrants or descendants of immigrants were also included. A smaller, but very important, biennial (since 1971) is that of San Juan, Puerto Rico, a graphics exhibition open to artists from Latin America and the Caribbean. French-speaking as well as Spanish-speaking artists are included. Since 1986, Puerto Rico—the Commonwealth designation of which has disguised its colonial status in relation to the United States—increasingly has invited Latino artists born and reared in North America to participate in its convocations and to compete for its prizes and honorable mentions with other artists from Latin America.

Terminology of U.S. Artistic Geography. It is useful to employ the term "Latino" for those artists born in, and those who have spent the major portions of their lives in, the United States and who do not maintain citizenship or an active and ongoing presence in the art worlds of their countries of origin. For those who do, the appellation "Latin American" is preferred, as is reference to their country by name. Such artists would be called Cuban, Argentinean, Mexican, Puerto Rican, Colombian, or Guatemalan, for example, rather than Latino. Generally speaking, neither group (obviously with exceptions) accepts the term "Hispanic" as its preferential designation, although the term is used widely by governmental, educational, and artistic institutions as a catch-all phrase for all persons of Latin American birth or heritage. Even some organizations presenting and representing Latin Americans and Latinos use the term. It has been argued that for grants and other types of public and private funding, the term "Hispanic" is more widely accepted, but on a personal level, the continental term "Latin American" or the national terminology of a given country is preferred.

Older terminologies such as Ibero-Americans (for the Iberian Peninsula), Luso-Americans (from Lusíad in Portuguese, for Brazilians), or Spanish/Hispanic-Americans fell into disuse in the second half of the twentieth century but are still appropriate. The word "American" as a suffix is considered important to distinguish between nationalities of Europe and those of the New World who count among their cultural, social, and biological inheritances the presence of both Native Americans and Africans as the earliest residents before the European conquests, or the earliest after the Spanish invasions.

In a further refinement of terminology, it is useful to refer to the Caribbean separately because three Spanish-speaking nations—Cuba, the Dominican Republic, and Puerto Rico—form a minority language group among the various islands, where a greater number of nations (actually or officially) speak English, French, Dutch, and Portuguese. Anthropologists and sociologists examining the Caribbean as a whole, often with reference to its African American social and cultural attributes, sometimes neglect to mention or consider the Spanish-speaking nations.

The appellation "America" to refer to the United States of America has been called into question. With so many immigrants from the American continents within its borders who also consider themselves "Americans" (from Chile, Mexico, Argentina, Brazil, and other countries), the appropriation of the term by the United States of America has been challenged by artists and writers who argue that "North America" or "U.S. America" are more appropriate designations. In terms of cultural affinities and transnational interchanges, Canada, the United States, and Mexico are all part of North America. In actuality, however, Mexico and Central America (Guatemala, El Salvador, Honduras, Nicaragua, and Costa Rica) share many cultural traits as well as indigenous ethnic groups (such as the Maya) who form large populations in several countries, including the English-speaking nation of Belize. Other sets of countries have their own regional affiliations. For example, the eastern coasts of Mexico and Central America and the countries of Panama, Colombia, and Venezuela—as well as Brazil—share an African American cultural base with the Caribbean nations of Cuba, the Dominican Republic, and Puerto Rico.

U.S. Artistic Geography: Latin Americans and Latinos. One of the most comprehensive exhibitions recording the presence of Latin American artists who visited the United States during the twentieth century or maintained permanent residence in the United States was "The Latin American Spirit: Art and Artists in the United States, 1920-1970." That exhibition set as its goal the documentation of the breadth of Latin American artistic participation in the cultural life of the United States during a fifty-year period, with a special emphasis on Puerto Rican creativity both on the island and in the continental United States. According to checklists issued by the Bronx Museum of the Arts, 167 artists from 15 countries exhibited 233 works. The largest number of artists (28) came from Argentina, Puerto Rico (27), Mexico (22), and Brazil (18); other countries, including Bolivia, Chile, Colombia, Cuba,

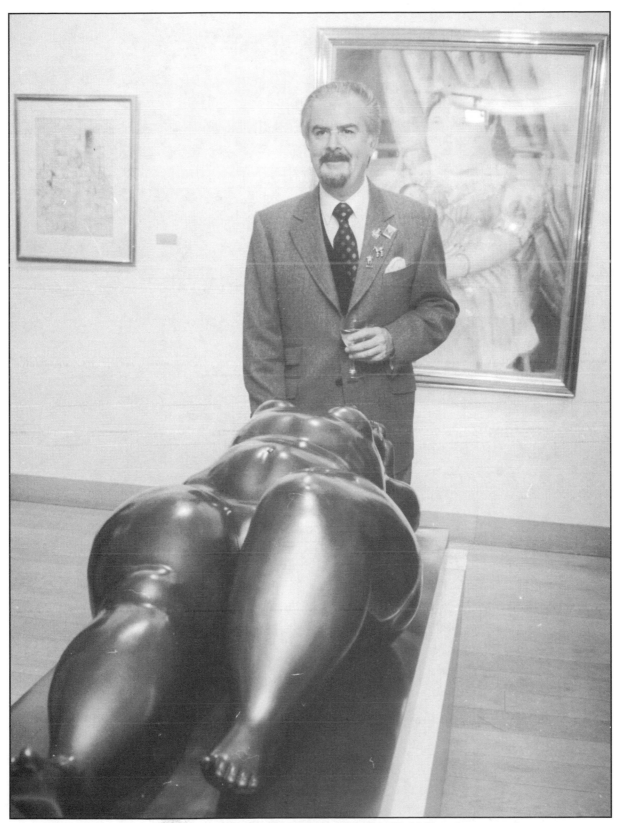

Colombian artist Fernando Botero. (AP/Wide World Photos)

Puerto Rican artist Rafael Tufiño. (AP/Wide World Photos)

Ecuador, Guatemala, Nicaragua, Peru, Uruguay, and Venezuela, had between one and eleven representatives. The catalog included biographies of the artists, an extensive bibliography, and 225 illustrations.

A majority of the artists were Latin Americans who had spent some time in the United States (roughly from one to ten years) and divided their time between their country of origin and several countries abroad. Others resided in Europe, traveling frequently to other sites but identifying themselves with the country in which they were born and educated. About thirty were artists whose first affiliation was with Latin America; they continued to identify with and exhibit in their countries of origin but considered their homes to be in the United States. Some of them became U.S. citizens, but even they functioned as "dual citizens," never relinquishing their original identity and often representing that identity in national and international exhibitions. Furthermore, regardless of the citizenship status of artists, Latin American countries exhibited their work as Latin American nationals, not as North Americans.

Among this group (as represented in the "Latin American Spirit" exhibition) were Marcelo Bonevardi, Jaime Davidovich, Leandro KATZ, Mauricio Lasansky, César PATERNOSTO, and Liliana PORTER (Argentina); María Luisa Pacheco (Bolivia); Enrique Castro-Cid, Juan Downey, Juan Gómez-Quiroz, and Mario Toral (Chile); Leonel Góngora (Colombia); Agustín FERNÁNDEZ, Carmen Herrera, and Emilio Sánchez (Cuba); Rudolfo Abularach (Guatemala); Olga ALBIZU, Rafael Colón-Morales, Rafael Ferrer, Lorenzo HOMAR, Carlos Irizarry, Rafael Tufino, and Pedro Villarini (Puerto Rico); Julio Alpuy, Luis Camnitzer, Gonzalo Fonseca, and Antonio Frasconi (Uruguay); and Angel Hurtado and Marisol (Marisol Escobar) (Venezuela).

Jacqueline Barnitz established prototypes for the monumental "Latin American Spirit" show with three smaller exhibitions that she organized over a period of six years: "Latin American Artists in the United States Before 1950," "Latin American Artists in the U.S., 1950-1970," and "Latin American Artists in New York Since 1970." These exhibitions provide names of other artists resident in the United States for long periods. Among them are Luis Frangella, Leopoldo Maler, Raquel Rabinovich, and Miguel Angel Ríos (Argentina); Maria Martins and Regina Vater (Brazil); Ismael FRIGERIO, Benjamín Lira, Catalina PARRA, Juan Estéban Pérez, Francisca Sutil, Jorge TACLA, and Cecelia Vicuña (Chile); José Urbach (Colombia); Daniel Serra-Badue (Cuba); Camilo Egas and Araceli Guilbert (Ecuador); José Gutiérrez and Ricardo Regazzoni (Mexico); Carlos Baca-Flor, Hugette Franco, and Ramiro Llona (Peru); Edgar Franceschi, Juan Maldonado, and Carlos OSORIO (Puerto Rico); and Horacio Torres (Uruguay). Others, whose names derive from multiple sources, include Norma Bessouet, Juan Carrera Buján, Dina Bursztyn, Pérez Celis, Susana Lago, Silvia Malagrino, Elena Presser, and Andrés Waissman (Argentina); Walter Terrazas (Bolivia); Josely Carvalho, Judite dos Santos, and Jonas dos Santos (Brazil); Guillermo Bert and Alfredo JAAR (Chile); Félix Angel, Yolanda Mesa, Luis Monje, Fanny Sanin, Luis Stand, and Francisco Vidal (Colombia); Rolando Castellón and Magda Santonastasio (Costa Rica); Manuel Maccarrula, Bismarck Victoria, and Freddy Rodríguez (Dominican Republic); Luis Serrano and Santiago Vaca (Ecuador); Alfredo Ceibal and Carlos Laorca (Guatemala); Francisco Alvarado Juárez (Honduras); José Antonio Aguirre, Alfredo Arreguín, Frieda Broida, Guadalupe García, Guillermo GÓMEZ-PEÑA, Gustavo Rivera, and Alejandro Romero (Mexico); Arturo Lindsay and Tabo Toral (Panama); Lydia Buzio, Naúl Ojeda, and Luis Solari (Uruguay); and Elba Damast (Venezuela).

These lists are simply indicators because no survey has been conducted to encompass statistically the number of Latin-born artists in the United States. The artists listed are some of those most available to museum and gallery curators in terms of exhibiting their work. Of the artists of Latin American descent living permanently, or reasonably so, in the United States, the three largest groups, in order of size, are Chicanos (Mexican Americans), Puerto Ricans, and Cubans.

Chicanos, Puerto Ricans, and Cubans. Mexicans, Puerto Ricans, and Cubans not only form the largest contingent of Spanish-language peoples in the United States but also trace their presence within its borders to the interventions practiced by the United States under the rubric of MANIFEST DESTINY. Half of Mexico's national terrain was annexed by the United States in the mid-nineteenth century; the other two countries were taken over in 1898, when the Spanish-American War was used to validate the expropriation of Cuba and Puerto Rico. These three groups have separate histories, though all have roots in conquest. Differences in the details of those histories and in questions of changing cultural practices, class, race, and gender realities have been manifested across three generations of artists functioning in the second half of the twentieth century.

This 1970's mural in Tucson, Arizona, shows many of the themes employed by Mexican American muralists. (Ruben G. Mendoza)

The sustained and influential CIVIL RIGHTS MOVE-MENTS of the late 1950's and the 1960's inspired a generation of primarily working-class young people of Mexican and Puerto Rican descent in the Southwest, the Midwest (where the groups met), and New York. In addition to economic and political issues, the two groups advanced demands for relevant education; respect for racial, cultural, and linguistic particularities; and the need for alternative spaces to disseminate cultural information. All these goals were achieved with great difficulty.

Cuban exiles fleeing Fidel Castro's revolution, on the other hand, did not begin to arrive in large numbers until the 1960's. They were the only Latin American immigrant group at the time receiving substantial financial aid from the U.S. government, a fact that aroused considerable bitterness among impoverished African Americans, Chicanos, and Puerto Ricans.

The earliest Cuban artistic manifestation in the United States was that of middle-class, academy-trained artists from the island who disassociated themselves from the postrevolutionary art beginning to evolve in Cuba in order to look back toward the Cuban avant-garde of the 1920's-1940's. Cuban artistic development in the United States had a different character, for reasons of class, political posture, and chronology. In fact, the militant and political character of Chicano and Puerto Rican artists was such that anti-Castro Cubans were excoriated and ostracized by both groups, while images of Che GUEVARA appeared in East Los Angeles and on the headquarters of the Puerto Rican YOUNG LORDS' headquarters in Chicago.

Chicanos. The term "Chicano" began to be used in the 1960's as a self-designation for young Mexican Americans who wished to separate themselves from what they viewed as the assimilationist tendencies of their forebears. Sociopolitical and economic issues (national and international) formed one thematic nexus; the reclamation of a societally suppressed identity, including Indo-American roots, formed the other. Both prongs of this program served as levers for the establishment of new power relations with the dominant society.

With both murals and graphics, Chicanos underlined their support for the embattled farmworkers of

Diego Rivera and Frida Kahlo are among the best-known artists from Mexico. (AP/Wide World Photos)

California and Texas. Portraits of Mexican and Chicano heroes appeared, such as those of revolutionary Ricardo FLORES MAGÓN and martyred newspaper reporter Rubén SALAZAR. Urban problems of landlord arson and drug use in one California mural borrow from a famous mural composition by Mexican David Alfaro SIQUEIROS. The Chicano engagement with Mexican art and its politics was selective. It was limited to pre-Columbian and contemporary Indians, to the popular (the skeletons of printmaker Posada and folk Catholicism), and to the revolutionary muralists. Some artists painted police brutality and the self-destructiveness of gang warfare, while others illustrated the destruction of mind and culture by U.S. mass media, a process that could be remedied through education in Mexican and Chicano history. Revival by Chicano artists of the zoot-suit PACHUCO culture from the 1940's was accompanied by sympathetic portraits of the "children" of the pachucos, *cholos* and *cholas* in the khakis, oversized T-shirts, and thrift shop chic of the post-1950's generation.

Women's images entered the arena with labor organizers Luisa MORENO and Emma TENAYUCA appearing in murals and posters. By the 1980's, women in particular looked to Frida KAHLO as a role model and prototype for their own lives. Some women reconsidered the Virgin of Guadalupe as a motif and placed the Virgin in scandalous tandem with the Aztec goddess Coatlicue. The ambivalence of identity for a Chicana caught between two cultures, and as a lesbian threatened by homophobia, has been explored most poignantly in the work of one Chicana photographer, while a number of gay men have pictorialized or designed performances about their status in U.S. society.

Border issues were also addressed, including the question of dehumanized Mexican workers in border towns and indictments of the immigration authorities at the U.S./Mexico border who daily crucify undocumented workers. By extension, Chicano artists have questioned all such political/social boundaries. Finally, some artists have confronted contemporary problems of urban alienation, loneliness, competitiveness, and other issues that affect Chicanos and the whole society.

Puerto Ricans. This group has chosen various names, including Puerto Ricans, Ricans, Neo-Ricans, Nuevo Yorrícan (Spanish) and Nuyorican (English) for those in New York City, and Taino Indian designations such as Borinquen (and Boricua as an adjective). Puerto Ricans began coming to the United States in large numbers as economic refugees in the 1940's and in increasing numbers during the 1960's. They came to form a large group in New York, with smaller enclaves in Philadelphia and Chicago. The colonial status of Puerto Rico allows Puerto Ricans to enter the U.S. mainland freely and subjects them to taxation and the military draft but does not provide for representation in Congress. This status has produced, on one hand, a terrible ambivalence about identity and, on the other, a well-defined and militant platform for national independence that serves to strengthen that identity.

Like Chicanos, Puerto Ricans also created murals during the 1970's, largely in New York and Chicago, celebrating national heroes such as Pedro ALBIZU CAMPOS. In Chicago, a Puerto Rican and a Japanese artist collaborated on a history of Latin American and Japanese laborers in the United States. Another collaborative mural protested urban displacement as it affected two poor communities. In 1969, both the Museo del Barrio and the Taller Boricua (Puerto Rican Workshop) were established in New York as cultural outposts for the Puerto Rican community. Rafael Tufiño, a major U.S.-born printmaker and painter from the island, designed the first workshop silkscreen poster. Tufiño worked with Nuyorican and island artists to translate to New York the collectivist and community service principles of San Juan's Centro de Arte Puertorriqueño (CAP), a 1950's organization that advanced the earliest nationalist artists' program on the island. Artists' groups hosted outdoor exhibitions, classes for the community, and cultural activities of all sorts.

The collaboration between island and migrant artists, many born in New York, is unlike any among Chicano and U.S. Cuban artists and those of their home countries. Although Chicanos also established cultural centers, galleries, and art classes across the Southwest in the 1970's, for example, they were set up completely with local participation. Main themes of Puerto Rican art include still lifes of tropical plants, the banana as the staff of life in Puerto Rico, and evocations of the aboriginal Taino Indian. These themes set up important prototypes for NUYORICANS. West African deities (hybridized with Catholic saints in Puerto Rican and Cuban SANTERÍA) and rituals, such as that attending a child's burial among peoples of African descent, reactivate another cultural source.

Political themes remain cogent. They are embodied in works advocating a free Puerto Rico, re-creating Puerto Rico's history as a continuum from the Taino Indians to the New York landscape, detailing abuses of the island, and showing the destructiveness of U.S. military exercises in Puerto Rico. Alienation, loneliness, fractured identity, and the search to recover a whole vision of self and existence are themes of some works, while self-portraits portray interior states of mind.

Cubans. Although sharing many problems with immigrants from elsewhere in the hemisphere, Cuban Americans have a particularly complex relationship with their adopted country owing to the intensity of U.S. involvement in Cuban affairs. Cubans arrived in the United States in two large waves. Approximately 215,000 Cubans left the island between 1959 and 1962. These included light-skinned, politically conservative landowners, businesspeople, and members of the middle class, those who stood to lose the most within the more egalitarian society sought by the revolution. A second wave arrived in the Mariel boat lift of 1980, with many trickling in between these dates. As of 1990, approximately one million Cuban Americans were dispersed across the United States, primarily in Florida, New York, New Jersey, Illinois, and California.

The first group's opposition to the Cuban Revolution was militarized by the United States in what must be considered as another Manifest Destiny intervention in the internal affairs of Cuba. U.S. intervention consolidated the power of the most reactionary forces concentrated in Miami and polarized the entire community, including artists. It has led to terrorism exercised against Cuban Americans who do not support hard-line policies. Such was the case with a bomb that exploded, with considerable damage, outside the doors of Miami's Cuban Museum of Art and Culture on June 14, 1990. That was the second bombing in the museum's brief history. Artists Ana Mendieta and Nereyda García reportedly appeared on "hit lists" for repeatedly visiting Cuba.

The *marielitos* who arrived en masse via a boat lift from Mariel, Cuba, were neither wealthy nor all white; nor were they necessarily focused on a military anti-Castro crusade like the earlier exiles. Their ranks also included persecuted homosexuals. They were shunned by the established community and encountered racism and homophobia in Miami and the United States at large. Cuban American art, therefore, divided itself not only generationally but also by race, class, and sexual preference. It was polarized between those determined to exterminate the Castro regime and those who wished to establish a dialogue with the island.

Best known in this latter respect are the works of Ana Mendieta, who died young. She was wrenched from her family in pre-adolescence and sent to the United States. Her search for self-healing and a new identity employed a feminist language. Another artist who made "the victim" his principal theme, particularly the political exile exposed to the brutalities of New York, used his own persona in connection with alienating and terrifying experiences. Metamorphoses of various kinds appear in Cuban art, as do images emblematic of exile.

The anguish of nostalgia for a lost Cuba was particularly poignant. Many artists were true exiles in that they could not return even if they wished, and many claimed they did not. Some referred to childhood memories and mementos in Cuba; others portrayed the voyage of exile. The search for identity also invoked spiritual beliefs, drawing on rituals of Santería and other Afro-Cuban religions as a major source of imagery and practice. Their parallel generation in Cuba focused on similar subjects, as well as on critical statements, and received international attention for their originality and creativity, ironic developments in the face of Cuban exiles' claims that no art could exist in Castro's Cuba. Another subject explored by Cuban exiles is that of dictators of the twentieth century. Other artists deal with the temptations of consumerism and the unexpected sufferings of the *marielitos* in the United States.

Nostalgia and the search for a personal identity served as a keynote of contemporary Cuban art, which rarely engaged political issues of the United States as they affected so-called minorities. Ethnicity and personal identity also became major motifs for Chicanos and Puerto Ricans in the 1980's, replacing many, if not all, of the social protest themes of the 1970's. In the process, there was an increasing tendency for all three groups to form limited artistic alliances against the second-class status tendered to most Latin American and Latino artists in the United States, even in the face of the "boom" of the 1980's.   —*Shifra M. Goldman*

Suggested Readings: • Barnitz, Jacqueline. *Latin American Artists in the U.S. Before 1950.* New York: Queens College, 1981. • Barnitz, Jacqueline. *Latin American Artists in the U.S. 1950-1970.* New York: Queens College, 1983. • Barnitz, Jacqueline. *Latin American Artists in New York Since 1970.* Austin: A. M. Huntington Art Gallery, College of Fine Arts, University of Texas at Austin, 1987. • Beardsley, John, and Jane Livingston. *Hispanic Art in the United States.* New York: Abbeville Press, 1987. • Cancel, Luis R., ed. *The Latin American Spirit: Art and Artists in the United States, 1920-1970.* New York: Bronx Museum of the Arts, in association with Harry N. Abrams, 1988. • *The Decade Show: Frameworks of Identity in the*

1980s. New York: Museum of Contemporary Hispanic Art, New Museum of Contemporary Art, and Studio Museum in Harlem, 1990. • Fuentes-Pérez, Ileana, Graciella Cruz-Taura, and Ricardo Pau-Llosa, eds. *Outside Cuba/Fuera de Cuba*. New Brunswick, N.J.: Rutgers University, 1988. • Goldman, Shifra M., and Tomas Ybarra-Frausto. *Arte Chicano: A Comprehensive Annotated Bibliography of Chicano Art, 1965-1981*. Berkeley: Chicano Studies Library Publications Unit, University of California, 1985. • Griswold del Castillo, Richard, Teresa McKenna, and Yvonne Yarbro-Bejarano, eds. *Chicano Art: Resistance and Affirmation, 1965-1985*. Los Angeles: Wight Art Gallery, University of California, 1991. • Lippard, Lucy R. *Mixed Blessings: New Art in a Multicultural America*. New York: Pantheon, 1990.

Art, Mexican American: Mexican Americans have a long tradition of art extending back to Indian representations and including religious imagery. This art was shaped by Spanish colonizers.

Santo Art. Mexican American art had its beginnings in the early part of the nineteenth century in the upper Rio Grande Valley of New Mexico. The art produced at the beginning of the nineteenth century was religious art. Its iconography included images of Jesus Christ, saints, the Virgin Mary, and angels. This genuinely American folk art is called santo art.

There are two predominant forms of santo art (*see* SANTOS AND SANTO ART). A *RETABLO* is a painting on gesso-covered wood panels. The wood panels are usually hand cut and shaped with an adze. A *bulto* is a carved wooden statue in the round. *BULTOS* are often fitted with articulated limbs and often appear unpainted. During the nineteenth century, most of the materials used were produced by the *santero*, or artisan. *Santeros* enjoyed an almost clerical status in the community.

The great folk artists in the first decades of the nineteenth century, the golden age of santo art, were Pedro Frequis, Molleno, José Rafael ARAGÓN, A. J. Santero, and the quill pen Santero. The great *santero* of the latter part of the nineteenth century was José Benito ORTEGA. In the twentieth century, José Dolores LÓPEZ and his son George were esteemed as great wood carvers. Toward the end of the twentieth century, *santeros*

Images used in early santo art continue to appear in contemporary art. (Cheryl Richter)

began to use commercial products in their artwork, though some traditional methods were still used.

Santo art often lacks signatures, indicating the lack of individuality. Idiosyncrasy was not as valued as faithfulness to tradition. The iconographic style of the religious subject matter was complemented by decorative and stylistic devices. Around the images, especially of the *retablos*, one finds flowers, curtains, and bold borders.

The content and form of the *retablos*, like Greek iconography, lack a perspectival dimension, depth, and tonal variation. The images are neither narrative in form nor realistic in style. The same cannot be said for *bultos*. Each santo is presented in abstraction from familiar earthly surroundings. There are no elements such as landscapes, towns, or houses. For example, St. Philip Neri, the patron saint of Albuquerque, is portrayed holding a rosary and a spray of lilies. These are not simply stylistic devices; they are symbols that identify this saint.

Such symbols are common in santo art. A dove may symbolize the Holy Spirit, and three flowers may symbolize the Holy Trinity. One *retablo* of St. Jerome depicts him as a New Mexican PENITENTE, beating his chest with a rock, clothed in a cardinal's robe. His attributes are a tonsured haircut and a trumpet. He is shown standing on Satan, who appears as a serpent with a man's head.

A typical *reredo* (altar screen) shows various saints, each one pictured in his or her own niche. The *reredo* from the Chapel of Our Lady of Talpa, painted by José Rafael ARAGÓN, shows the Immaculate Conception, Our Lady of Sorrows, the Holy Trinity, St. Francis, Our Lady of Sorrows, Nuestro Padre Jesus, and Our Lady of Solitude. Each stands isolated in his or her own niche.

Christ figures, the Virgin Mother, and saints dominated the content of santo art. Among the Christ images, the most popular deal with Jesus Nazareno (Jesus the Nazarene), the Cristo Crucifijo (the crucified Christ), and the Santo Entierro (the buried Christ). The Santo Niño of Atocha was also popular. Images of Our Lady proliferated in the form of Our Lady of Solitude, Our Lady of Sorrows, Our Lady of Guadalupe, Our Lady of Refuge of Sinners, and Our Lady of Mt. Carmel.

Popularly depicted saints include San Juan Nepomuceno, a Bohemian priest martyred for keeping secrets; San Ysidro Labrador, the patron saint of farmers; Santiago, the patron saint of Spain; San Antonio; San Ramon Nonantus, commonly invoked by pregnant women; St. Gertrude; St. Joseph; and St. Philip of Neri, the patron saint of Albuquerque, an Italian priest known for his ministry to the poor. A host of saints can be called on for every known ailment and human need. They provided a rich resource for santo art.

The function of santo images is essentially religious, and santos played a prominent role in family devotions and public rituals. The images were not necessarily ethical examples or role models but means of obtaining supernatural assistance. They were invoked for various reasons, including protection against lightning, help in securing lovers, and assistance in childbearing. *Bultos* in particular were highly valued for use in religious folk dramas, particularly in the re-enactment of the passion of Christ during Holy Week. For added realism, Christ figures were articulated at the limbs, were fitted with real human hair, had mica for eyeballs, and sometimes were equipped with real teeth. In public rituals, *bultos* were more commonly used than were RETABLOS because of their stark realism. Their ritual function probably accounts for their realism.

New Mexico was incorporated into the United States in the middle of the nineteenth century. Incoming Catholic clergy did not approve of santo art and replaced it with plaster cast statues and Currier and Ives lithographs. These were cheaper because they were mass produced, and they became more accessible after the coming of the railroads.

The *bultos* of Christ figures are sanguinary. They seem to drip with blood; streams of blood are painted flowing from the wounds and from underneath the loincloth. The blood is depicted in a highly stylized fashion. *Christ Crucified*, carved by José Rafael ARAGÓN for the Chapel of Our Lady of Talpa, is life-sized and articulated at the shoulders, indicating its ritualistic function. The Jesus Nazareno from Ojo Caliente reflects in its wounds and blood the preoccupation with the passion and suffering of Christ that New Mexican PENITENTES sought to imitate.

As mentioned above, *bultos* that were clothed, equipped with wigs, and sometimes fitted with real teeth exuded a stark realism that evoked horror among early Anglo observers. The realism of these *bultos* fit well with their role in the ritual re-enactments of the passion of Christ, which is the central feature of penitente faith.

Santo art did not die out in the twentieth century. The tradition was carried on by Mexican American artisans who saw in it both a means for preserving cultural identity and commercial value.

Mexican Muralism. Mexican American art owes a great historical and spiritual debt to Mexican muralists (*see* MURAL ART). Mexican muralists painted some of their greatest murals in the United States and undoubtedly provided Mexican American artists with some of their main themes and cultural symbols and icons. Diego RIVERA, David Alfaro SIQUEIROS, and José Clemente OROZCO are referred to as *los tres grandes*, or the three great ones. They profoundly influenced the development of Mexican American art. Rufino TAMAYO was also prolific in the United States, and some Mexican American artists claim him as an influence.

A renaissance of Mexican muralism was born from the Mexican Revolution. This resurgence from 1920 to 1925 was made possible in part by the support of José VASCONCELOS, the great Mexican educator, statesman, and philosopher. The Mexican muralists brought their epic form of socially realistic public art to the United States in the 1930's.

Rivera, Siqueiros, and Orozco were all in the United States (primarily in California) in the early 1930's. Orozco painted murals in Claremont, California, and also at the New School for Social Research in New York and at the Baker Library at Dartmouth College in Vermont. Siqueiros painted at the Chouniard School of Art. Rivera painted murals at the Stock Exchange Luncheon Club and at the California School of Fine Arts (later known as the San Francisco School of Fine Arts) in 1931. Later, he painted murals for Henry Ford in Detroit and for Nelson Rockefeller at the Rockefeller Center in New York. Tamayo produced murals at Smith College in Massachusetts as well as in Dallas and Houston, Texas. The Mexican muralists certainly influenced Mexican American artists, but they also influenced other American artists such as Jackson Pollock. The period from 1930 to 1934 was highly productive for the Mexican muralists.

Some of Orozco's greatest work was produced in the United States. In Mexico, his fame was eclipsed by that of his controversial contemporary Diego Rivera. Orozco made several trips to the United States. In 1927, he painted his Prometheus mural at Pomona College in Claremont, California. From 1932 to 1934, he was occupied with the Baker Library murals at Dartmouth, in which he depicted the angry Christ at the end of time, surrounded by the chaotic destroyed ruins of the weapons of war and the symbols of religion. Christ is portrayed here as a Promethean symbol. OROZCO drew on symbols of the pre-Columbian era and of the Mexican Revolution. His paintings were stark in their composition, bold in their lines, and strong in their colors.

Rufino TAMAYO lived primarily in New York from 1926 to 1948, with several years away from the city during that time. Many of his major works were produced in the United States. Unlike *los tres grandes*, he eschewed revolutionary themes. He was a master of chromatic color schemes, and his painting bordered on abstraction.

Mexican murals served a multitude of distinct but interrelated purposes. They promoted political consciousness and action. They were powerful vehicles of popular education in the sense that they informed the common people about their own history—the history of pre-Columbian Indians, the struggles for independence, and revolutionary Mexico. Murals were public art that addressed the visual needs of largely illiterate masses, much as the Greek icons in the Byzantine period had taught the illiterate the doctrines of Greek orthodoxy. Unlike the subject matter of the *RETABLOS* of the New Mexican *santeros*, the subject matter of the murals was necessarily realistic and narrative. In Mexico, murals were painted on government buildings accessible to the public. In effect, they gained the status of national art. The U.S. government also commissioned murals on government buildings, particularly during the Great Depression.

The themes of Mexican murals were vitally influenced by the indigenist movement. Indigenism attempted to revive interest in the history and aesthetics of the native peoples. It went further, however, and romanticized, idealized, and glorified the native peoples. According to the 1923 manifesto signed by *los tres grandes*, "The art of the Mexican people is the most important and vital spiritual manifestation in the world today, and its Indian traditions lie at its very heart."

The golden age of Indian civilization before the Spanish Conquest was a major theme for RIVERA. He tried to overcome the contempt that Mexican society held for Indians and mestizos by glorifying Indian cultures and vilifying the Spanish. He portrayed Spanish conquistador Hernán CORTÉS, for example, as a grotesque caricature of a man, with a crooked nose, and bowed legs. Rivera idealized the Indian past, portraying Mesoamerican cultures as harmonious, idyllic, and utopian. SIQUEIROS, like Rivera, used indigenous themes. He used Cuauhtémoc, the last Aztec emperor, executed by Cortés, to symbolize courage and the resistance of the downtrodden.

Orozco, on the other hand, opposed Indian glorification. Although he depicted QUETZALCÓATL as a states-

David Alfaro Siqueiros. (AP/Wide World Photos)

José Clemente Orozco at work on a mural titled Dive Bomber and Tank. *(AP/Wide World Photos)*

man, educator, and promoter of arts and civilization, he had Prometheus, the hero of Greek myth, as an archetype. He did not shy away from depicting the crueler and darker sides of Indian civilizations, including the inhumanity of Indian sacrifice.

Interest in the Indian past led to the idealization of MESTIZAJE, the blending of two cultures resulting in the creation of a third culture—mestizo culture. Mexico is largely a MESTIZO culture, produced by the intermingling of the Spanish and the Indians. *Mestizaje* became a symbol of the Mexican people and a theme of the Mexican muralists. Rufino Tamayo, in the mural *Birth of Our Nationality*, shows an Indian woman giving birth to a half-breed child. Orozco depicts the son of

Cortés and La MALINCHE as a mestizo. In the Palacio Nacional murals, Rivera presents the child of La Malinche as a brown-skinned Indian baby with the blue eyes of a Spaniard. Mexican American artists appropriated *mestizaje* as an icon in the form of a tripartite head to symbolize their cultural identity.

At the end of the Mexican Revolution, revolutionary history became a major theme of murals. This theme was appropriated by Mexican American muralists as well. Rivera's murals at the National Palace depict the history of Mexico, from the preconquest Indian civilizations, to the struggles for Mexican independence in 1810, to the Mexican Revolution. Rivera never tired of showing the ruling classes confronted by

Diego Rivera at work on the mural Detroit Industry *in 1932*. (AP/Wide World Photos)

the working classes. The revolution was also tied to the larger international picture. In the 1920's, Rivera and Siqueiros were members of the Communist Party. Rivera's mural *Man at the Crossroads* in Rockefeller Center was destroyed under the orders of Nelson Rockefeller because Rivera had included the heroic face of Vladimir Ilich Lenin. The mural showed the working class surrounded by capitalists as their oppressors and socialists as their liberators. Rivera reproduced the mural at the Palacio de Bellas Artes in Mexico City.

Mexican Graphic Art. Popular graphic art in Mexico influenced Mexican American graphic art, particularly POSTER ART. Jose Guadalupe Posada (1852-1913) set the standards for Mexican graphic art. Two periodicals, *Don Simplicio* (1845) and *El Calavera* (1847), contained illustrations of CALAVERAS (skulls) that became the signature motif in Posada's graphic art. Posada's *calaveras* became icons for Mexican American artists such as Luis Alfonso JIMÉNEZ, Jr., whose work almost equals in style and intensity the power of Posada's *calaveras*.

Posada's productive years were spent in León and Mexico City. He illustrated more than fifty different papers and did covers for romantic novels and collections of romantic songs. His work became popularized partly as a result of an increase in publication of inexpensive papers after the 1890's. His images had immediate relevance, spoke out against political corruption, and depicted the negative effects of modernization and social conflict.

The Taller de Gráfica Popular (People's Graphics Workshop), founded in 1937, carried on Posada's tradition. Politically and socially concerned artists used lithographs, woodcuts, and linocuts to publicize the exploitation of the poor. Woodcuts and linocuts were the preferred media because they were inexpensive and could be mass produced to reach the public. Public exposure was a major objective of Chicano artists in the latter part of the twentieth century.

Politicization of Art. Mexican American art of the twentieth century can be divided into pre-*movimiento* and *movimiento* art. The *movimiento* refers to the CHICANO MOVEMENT, a struggle for rights and recognition of Chicano culture. *Movimiento* art, better known as Chicano art, began to emerge in the 1960's as the artistic complement to the Chicano movement. From the beginning, Chicano art was highly politicized and community oriented.

In the first half of the twentieth century, Mexican American artists were more concerned with the aes-

thetics of art than with politics. One such artist was Octavio Medellín, a sculptor from Texas who worked in wood and stone. Born in Mexico, he studied art in San Antonio, Texas, and Chicago, Illinois. He also researched the art of the Mesoamerican civilizations. His work that most reflected the ideals of the Mexican muralist movement was a wood carving of a seven-foot column of mahogany, *History of Mexico* (1949). The carving on all four sides of the vertical rectangular column narrates the history of Mexico from the pre-Columbian world to the Mexican Revolution. Social realism is the motive force behind Medellín's poignant sculpture *The Hanged* (1942). His sensual sensibilities find expression in the graceful wood carving of an almost amorphous, flamelike female form, *The Bather* (1966).

Antonio García, another Texan, painted an oil on canvas called *Woman Before a Mirror* (1939). The vertical composition draws the viewer's attention to the woman's reflection in the mirror. The naturalistic depiction of the brown-skinned woman exudes a Mexican aesthetic. García also drew on popular religious symbolism in his fresco of the Virgin of Guadalupe in the Sacred Heart Church in Corpus Christi, Texas.

The Chicano art movement beginning at the end of the 1960's took a political turn as the artistic complement to *la causa*, or the Chicano movement. Artists were inspired by a confluence of events and movements that helped to rally, mobilize, and organize Mexican Americans along political, social, and economic lines. These events included the Cuban Revolution, the Civil Rights movement, the Vietnam War protest movement, and the farmworkers' struggles led by César Chávez. The *movimiento* crystallized into various groups and causes including Rodolfo "Corky" GONZÁLES' CRUSADE FOR JUSTICE in Denver, Colorado; Reies López TIJERINA's Alianza Federal de Mercedes in New Mexico; La RAZA UNIDA PARTY in Texas; and numerous Chicano student groups. The struggles were for concrete goals such as civil liberties, voter registration, an end to the Vietnam War, immigration rights, fair wages, decent housing, and bilingual education.

These struggles, movements, and causes provided rich themes for Mexican American art. For example, during the National Chicano Moratorium on Vietnam in 1970, Rubén SALAZAR, a Chicano journalist, was killed by a police tear gas canister. His death was memorialized by Frank ROMERO in his oil on canvas, *Death of Ruben Salazar*. The farmworker movement

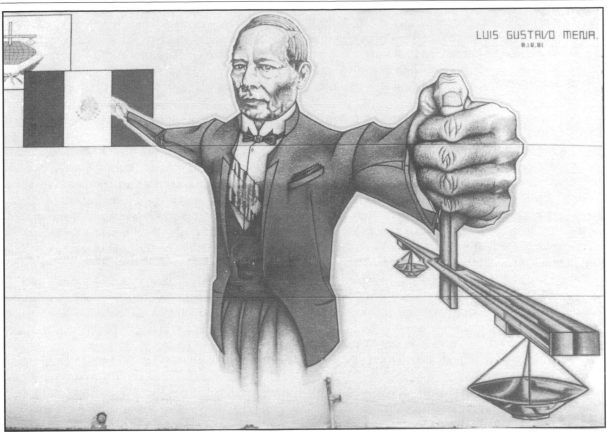

This mural of Mexican president Benito Juárez by Luis Gustavo Mena is an example of retrieval of cultural heroes. (Ruben G. Mendoza)

led by César Chávez provided key symbols that influenced the Chicano art movement—the red, white, and black eagle flag and the Virgin of Guadalupe. These symbols recur as principal Chicano icons in posters, murals, paintings, and sculptures.

The search for cultural identity revived indigenism, and Chicanos supported the struggles of Native American movements. *Movimiento* leaders such as playwright Luis VALDEZ stressed the Chicano-Indian identity and revived pre-Columbian imagery including AZTLÁN, the mythical homeland of the Aztecs. Cuauhtémoc, QUETZALCÓATL, and other Indian icons popularized by the Mexican muralists became essential symbols in Chicano art.

Our Lady of Guadalupe, Miguel Hidalgo, Emiliano Zapata, and Pancho Villa were retrieved as cultural heroes. As a result of the search for historical identity, Chicano art synthesized Indian culture, Hispanic Catholic culture, revolutionary themes, and urban images.

Feminism in Art. Feminism influenced Chicano art beginning in the 1970's. Chicanas began holding feminist caucuses at Chicano conventions, seminars, and conferences. Chicana artists were concerned with self-affirmation and empowerment, and they wanted to confront the MACHISMO evident in the *movimiento.* Chicana artists took to the female symbols and icons— the Virgin and La LLORONA (the weeping woman of Chicano folklore)—and reinterpreted them. Yolanda LÓPEZ, for example, painted a portrait of herself and other women as the Virgin of Guadalupe in 1978. Chicana artists also came to value the everyday woman's aesthetic in the home, expressed through home decorations and home altars.

In the search for positive images of womanhood, Chicana artists discovered Frida KAHLO, the Mexican surrealist painter and wife of Diego Rivera. She served as a powerful source of inspiration. Kahlo painted small paintings that in some respects resembled votive art, religious art narrating some healing or miracle, with an inscription of events at the bottom. Kahlo's favorite subject was herself. An example of her art is *Self Portrait on the Borderline Between Mexico and the U.S.* (1932). This oil on metal shows the artist standing on the border between Mexico and the United States. On the Mexican side are pre-Columbian images and symbols. On the United States side are symbols of capitalist industry. The painting clearly idealizes Indian Mexico and indicts the inhumanity of the United States.

Popularization of Chicano Art. The first forms of Chicano art to draw national attention were murals, posters, and performance art. In large U.S. cities with significant Chicano populations—Los Angeles, Houston, San Francisco, and Chicago—Chicano murals, akin to the Mexican murals, began to appear on public walls. Urban images became a new source of iconography. The barrio, CHOLOS, PACHUCOS, LOW RIDERS, bicycles, and tattoos served as icons expressing a unique cultural ethos.

Posters were lithographed for mass production. Malaquías MONTOYA, Rupert GARCÍA, Richard DUARDO, Amado PEÑA, Jr., and José MONTOYA produced artistic and politically critical silkscreen posters. Chicano photographers used the camera to depict Chicano urban life. Among the most prominent were José Galvez and Miguel GANDERT.

New tools and methods, products of urban life, were employed in new expressions of Chicano art. The spray can, used for graffiti, was used for more standard artistic purposes. Leo Limón used acrylic and spray paint on canvas to show a homeboy shooting another Chicano in *No Vale Homes* (1976).

Chicano art groups began to form in the 1970's. ASCO was an East Los Angeles performance group. It mixed cultural iconoclasm with political critique. Also in Los Angeles, Carlos Almaraz, Gilbert Sanchez Luján, Frank Romero, and Beto de la Rocha made up Los FOUR, a group that combined politics and visual arts. They were featured at the Los Angeles County Museum of Art in 1974. The Royal Chicano Air Force, formed by art professors at California State University, Sacramento, combined politics and art to raise political consciousness and to educate.

Chicano culture was distinguished from Mexican culture, but the CHICANO MOVEMENT insisted on a retrieval of Mexican Indian culture. Resistance against a dominant Anglo culture and affirmation of Chicano culture became the central themes of these urban art groups. A new term, *rasquachismo*, was coined to express the Chicano sensibility they so expertly exuded. It means an ironic and irreverent wit.

One Chicano artist who seemed to sum up the best of Mexican American art is Luis Alfonso JIMÉNEZ, Jr. Born in El Paso, Texas, the artist lived for a time in New York, and then in Hondo, New Mexico. His art is modern yet traditional. His art functions as social commentary and political critique, often satirizing U.S. culture. His *California Chick* (1968) shows a buxom blonde riding what appears to be a giant phallus. He is best known for his fiberglass sculptures, some of which are adorned with neon lights. His most famous sculpture is probably *American Dream*, which depicts the coupling of a female and an automobile, reminiscent of ancient archetypes including the pre-Columbian myth of a jaguar copulating with a human female to create a supernatural being. Jiménez is interested in the mechanization of society and its consequent dehumanization of people. Such destruction of personal and cultural identity is at the heart of modern Mexican American art. —*Michael Candelaria*

SUGGESTED READINGS:

• Ades, Dawn. *Art in Latin America: The Modern Era, 1820-1980*. New Haven, Conn.: Yale University Press, 1989. Catalog of an exhibition, with essays on various aspects of Latin American art.

• Cancel, Luis, et al. *The Latin American Spirit: Art and Artists in the United States, 1920-1970*. New York: Bronx Museum of the Arts, 1988. Catalog of the traveling exhibition, complete with essays on various aspects of Latin American art including constructivism and geometric abstraction.

• Griswold Del Cartillo, Richard, et al., eds. *Chicano Art: Resistance and Affirmation, 1965-1985*. Los Angeles: Wight Art Gallery, University of California, 1991. Catalog of an exhibition, with essays by Chicano art historians and critics.

• Quirarte, Jacinto. *Mexican American Artists*. Austin: University of Texas Press, 1973. One of the earliest books devoted to Mexican American artists. Lacks a synoptic approach.

• Steele, Thomas J. *Santos and Saints: Essays and Handbook*. Albuquerque, N.Mex.: Calvin Horn, 1974. A study on santo art from a Catholic priest's perspective.

• Weigle, Marta, et al., eds. *Hispanic Arts and Ethnohistory in the Southwest*. Santa Fe, N.Mex.: Ancient City Press, 1983. An ethnographic approach to various aspects of Hispanic arts including architecture, weaving, *retablo* painting, and *bulto* carving.

Art, Puerto Rican: The art of Puerto Ricans on the island and on the U.S. mainland reflects a varied heritage, from ancient Indian petroglyphs and Spanish colonial portrait painters to the social realism of Francisco Oller and the poster artists of the mid-twentieth century. Beginning in the 1960's, Puerto Ricans on the mainland rediscovered that heritage while experimenting in new art forms.

Taino Art. The original inhabitants of the Caribbean island of Borinquen (Puerto Rico) were the Taino Indians, who lived in large permanent villages. Christopher Columbus as well as other European explorers and settlers noted that the Taino were experienced woodworkers, potters, weavers, and carvers. Of particular interest to scholars are the fine Taino stone sculptures still found throughout the Caribbean basin. Some of the best examples of these *cemis* or *zemis* had gold or bone inlays. They were idols or fetishes believed to be inhabited by powerful spirits.

In addition to the *cemis*, there are fine circular stone belts, anthropomorphic masks, *guaycas* (seashell masks), and ceremonial spatulae used to induce vomiting during religious rituals. Another Taino artistic achievement was the use of huge carved stones to create what have been described as "baseball fields" for religious rituals. Ancient Taino pictograms (stone carvings) have been reproduced and disseminated in each of the national cultures of the Caribbean, becoming an intrinsic part of regional folklore. They have also been an inspiration to modern Puerto Rican artists on the island and the U.S. mainland.

Spanish Colonial Period. During the early part of the Spanish colonial period (sixteenth and seventeenth centuries), there were a few minor contributions to Puerto Rican art history. The first recognized Puerto Rican painter was Miguel García from San Germán, the second city established by the Spanish Crown in Puerto Rico. García painted the *Virgen de la Monserrate* and *The Adoration of the Three Kings* in the style of the Flemish engraver Martin Schongauer. Famous paintings produced on the island by unknown artists of the period include depictions of the Monserrate Virgin and Santa Barbara from the Church of Hormigueros; Our Lady of Valvanera from the Coamo Church; and The Virgin of the Rosary.

Eighteenth Century. In the eighteenth century, Puerto Rican painting flourished in the capital city of San Juan. The foremost painter of this period was José CAMPECHE y Jordán (1752-1809), a free mulatto. Campeche was mostly self-taught, although he studied for three years with Luis Paret y Alcázar (1749-1799), who came to the island after having been a Spanish court painter under King Charles III alongside the famed Francisco Goya. Campeche painted both religious and secular themes, but he excelled in portraiture. Among his best paintings are *El Jíbaro*, the first

graphic representation of the Puerto Rican peasant (campesino), and religious works such as *Santa Maria del Cervello* and *Our Lady of the Rosary*. His work reflects technical mastery of both figure line and color, as well as a refined insight. Although he produced an estimated five hundred pieces, less than one hundred have survived.

Nineteenth Century. In the nineteenth century, Joaquín J. Goyena (c. 1765-1834) specialized in miniature portraiture such as the *Canónico José Gutiérrez del Arroyo* and a series of depictions of uniforms worn by the island militia. Other major artists working in San Juan in the nineteenth century were Francisco Goyena O'Daly (c. 1758-1855), Juan Fagundo (d. 1847), Juan Cletos Noa and his artistic family, and Ramón Atiles Pérez (1804-1875), who painted government officials.

The first art school established in Puerto Rico was founded by the government in 1821 under the stewardship of José de Navarro. Many artists came from Spain, the United States, and Italy to settle in Puerto Rico. At the same time, several Puerto Rican artists went to Europe and were well received by the European courts. Among them were Adolfo Marín Molinas, José Cuchí y Arnau, and Pedro Pablo Pommayrac (1819-1880), who became a distinguished court painter under both Napoleon III and Empress Eugene of France and Queen Isabella II of Spain.

Francisco Oller. Puerto Rican art reached its fullest development at the end of the nineteenth century with painter Francisco OLLER y Cestero (1833-1917). Oller has been described as the first realist-impressionist painter of America since he borrowed both from the impressionist movement and the social realism of Jean Courbet, with whom he studied. He was the first artist to portray the Puerto Rican social reality of his day in portraits, landscapes, and depictions of local customs. He had a sensitive eye for drama, as well as a mastery of color, form, and chiaroscura (shading of light and dark). His extensive body of work includes *El Campesino*, *El Velorio* (the wake), *The Student*, *Master Teacher Cordero*, *El Guaraguao*, *El Trapiche* (the sugarcane mill), *Higüeras* (a fig tree), and a series of portraits of colonial governors.

Oller's work was highly acclaimed in both France and Spain, where he was appointed Royal Chamber Painter by King Amadeo I and later was invested as knight of the Royal Order of Charles III. In 1899, he established a modest art academy in San Juan, where he inspired many art enthusiasts to support social realism. He was also appointed the first drawing instructor

Some Puerto Rican artists create works celebrating national heroes, such as this portrait of Pedro Albizu Campos carried in a parade in New York City. (Hazel Hankin)

at both the University of Puerto Rico and the Puerto Rican Department of Education.

Early Twentieth Century Developments. During the first half of the twentieth century, many artists devoted themselves to capturing the Puerto Rican spirit, influenced by both Campeche and Oller. A noted impressionist painter was Miguel Pou (1880-1968), who often painted the historical buildings and local characters of his native town of Ponce. Another great figure was Ramón Frade (1875-1954), who had a reputation as an innovator despite his traditional style. Other notable early twentieth century landscape and portrait artists were Elías J. Levis, Juan Palacios, Fernando Díaz McKenna, Juan Rosado, José López de Victoria, and Julio Medina González.

During the first part of the century, sculptors such as Alejandro Sánchez Felipe, Cristobal Ruíz, Ángel Botello, Carlos Marichal, and Guillermo Sureda arrived in Puerto Rico. Their style and the schools they established influenced the development of Puerto Rican art later in the century.

Contemporary Art in Puerto Rico. The establishment of the Institute of Puerto Rican Culture in 1955 opened the door for the establishment of *centros culturales* (local popular art centers) throughout the island. The institute founded local museums for the preservation of local history and the cultivation of the arts. It supported the preservation and promotion of popular arts and crafts such as needlework, woodwork, ironwork, pottery, basketwork, tinplate, bobbin lace, and religious imagery (SANTOS), among others. It also established the first School of Plastic Arts, where masters have taught many distinguished artists.

Another major contribution to the development and appreciation of Puerto Rican fine art was the establishment in 1959 of the Ponce Museum of Fine Arts, which houses one of the best collections of nineteenth century pre-Raphaelite paintings in the Americas. The museum has committed part of its resources to the acquisition, preservation, and dissemination of Puerto Rican art.

The Institute of Puerto Rican Culture and the Ponce Museum encouraged many emerging and established artists to continue their work and experimentation. This led to the development of new schools of Puerto Rican art as well as the opening of art galleries, schools, and workshops. Most important, this new impetus generated an interest in and appreciation of fine art among Puerto Ricans.

The nostalgic and romantic past captured by Oller, Pou, José R. Oliver, Osiris Delgado, and others changed with the generation of 1950. This new group was interested in depicting the effects of the unresolved political status of the island. Antonio MARTORELL (b. 1939) and Carlos Raquel Cabrera (b. 1923) portrayed the poverty, social injustice, deplorable living conditions, and political repression that were common under the colonial regime. Their path was followed by Lorenzo HOMAR, Rafael Tufiño, Miguel Hernández Acevedo, Carlos Irizarry, and Carlos OSORIO.

Other schools of art represented by modern Puerto Rican artists include cubism (Luis Hernández Cruz), abstract art (Jóse R. Oliver), and expressionism (Olga ALBIZU and Julio Rosado del Valle). Primitivism was pioneered by Manuel Hernández Acevedo and Carlos Osorio and continued under Luis G. Cajigas (b. 1934) and Wilfred Labiosa (b. 1937). Although these artists were not formally trained in academia, their art received critical acclaim. Some of their favorite subjects are vignettes of Old San Juan, the *jíbaro*, traditional Puerto Rican folklore, and local political heroes.

Meanwhile, José Bucaglia (b. 1938) and Tomás Batista (b. 1935) represent the best of contemporary Puerto Rican sculpture.

Graphic Arts and Nuyorican Artists. Perhaps the most significant contribution Puerto Ricans have made to the international art world is in the area of poster art and woodcuts. In the late 1940's, the Puerto Rican government sponsored a graphics workshop that used bold silkscreen art to publicize social reforms. Participating artists such as Irene Delano and Lorenzo HOMAR helped draw world attention in the 1950's to the Puerto Rican graphic style, which became known for its forceful design, distinctive calligraphy, and political content. Like posters from revolutionary Cuba, Puerto Rican silkscreens and woodcuts were popular in the United States during the 1960's. The San Juan Biennial of Latin American Graphics in 1970 resulted in wider international acclaim.

By this time there were substantial numbers of Puerto Ricans in New York City who had migrated there for economic reasons. Ralph Ortiz and other politically active Nuyoricans, as the mainland Puerto Ricans were called, set up Taller Boricua in the Museo del Barrio in East Harlem in 1969. This workshop exhibited Puerto Rican art and exposed many young Nuyoricans to their cultural heritage. It also served to hone the skills and following of professionals such as abstract artist Raphael Colón Morales, surrealist Jorge Soto Sánchez, and ceramicist Nitza Tufiño. The latter was one of a number of Nuyorican artists who engaged young people in making murals and other public art projects. Although some Puerto Rican artists in the United States are mainly interested in formal concerns, many continue to pursue political issues in their work.

In 1973, the Museo del Barrio cosponsored an exhibition called "The Art Heritage of Puerto Rico: Pre-Columbian to the Present," with the Metropolitan Museum of Art. Another important exhibition of Puerto Rican art from the island was "Puerto Rican Painting," at the Museum of Modern Latin American Art in Washington, D.C., in 1987. The Museum of Contemporary Hispanic Art in New York frequently features the work of Puerto Rican artists.

—*Angel A. Amy Moreno de Toro*

SUGGESTED READINGS:

• Alegría, Ricardo. *El Instituto de Cultura Puertorriqueña, 1955-1973*. San Juan, Puerto Rico: Instituto de Cultura Puertorriqueña, 1973. A survey that traces the artistic contributions of the Institute of Puerto Rican Culture since its founding. Discusses folk arts, crafts, and fine arts.

• Benítez, Marimar. "The Special Case of Puerto Rico." In *The Latin American Spirit: Art and Artists in the United States, 1920-1970*, edited by Luis R. Cancel. New York: Harry N. Abrams, 1988. Describes the experience and development of Latin American art in the United States at a critical time.

• Cockroft, Eva. "The United States and Socially Concerned Latin American Art." In *The Latin American Spirit: Art and Artists in the United States, 1920-1970*, edited by Luis R. Cancel. New York: Harry N. Abrams, 1988. An excellent overview of both the development and the major contributions of Latin American and Puerto Rican artists in the continental United States.

• Delgado, Osiris. "Historia de la Pintura en Puerto Rico." In *La Gran Enciclopedia de Puerto Rico*, edited by Vicente Baéz. 8 vols. Madrid, Spain: R, 1976. A general survey of the history and development of fine arts in Puerto Rico to 1970. Contains many illustrations as well as insightful anecdotes about the artists and their work.

• Tío Fernández, Elsa. "Content and Context of the Puerto Rican Poster." In *The Poster in Puerto Rico, 1946-1985*. Rio Piedras, Puerto Rico: University of Puerto Rico Museum, 1985. An excellent overview of the historical development of the Puerto Rican poster both on the island and in the continental United States. Published in conjunction with a museum exhibition.

Art, Spanish American: Spanish American art represents the distinct Spanish colonial heritage in the United States. Religious, cultural, and economic needs motivated the establishment of Spanish American art industries including woodcarving, weaving, tinsmithing, and furniture making in the Southwest, principally in the state of New Mexico.

Spanish Heritage. From 1541 to 1846, explorers and settlers from Spain and New Spain (Mexico) settled and developed lands that after 1848 formed the Southwestern United States. Spanish styles of architecture and art influenced the ARCHITECTURE of churches and religious-based arts in this region. The ornate Baroque style was approved by the Catholic church's Council of Trent in 1563 and became predominant in the 1600's and 1700's. Spanish colonial architecture left a trace over a broad geographical area and a long period of time. The Spanish church design of a simple rectangle with two bell towers became common throughout the Southwest. In time, the native peoples of each distinct area added some forms of modification to Spanish style. Their use of color, cotton or wool, native wood types for carving, local plants for dyes, and adobe building materials altered Spanish tradition.

The Colonial Experience in New Mexico. European settlements began in the former Spanish colony of New Mexico in the late sixteenth century. The isolation and rough physical environment of the New Mexico colony produced a distinctive kind of Spanish colonial culture with its own unique forms of religious arts and domestic crafts. These were European in technology but often regional in style and materials. Settlers made their own carved and painted religious images or SANTOS, as well as furniture, household items, tools, textiles, clothing, and adornments.

From the time that "churro" sheep accompanied Juan de Oñate's entry into New Mexico in 1598, sheep, wool, and weaving have played an important part in the development of Spanish colonial culture in the American Southwest. New Mexican women wove and embroidered designs on woolen cloth to be used as wall hangings for the village churches. The dyes for the yarns were made from local plants, such as indigo for blue, logwood (mahogany) for brown, and the chamiso flower for yellow. Some villages were renowned for their fine weaver families, who relied on the craft for their income.

Radical changes affecting all aspects of the traditional social order in New Mexico came after 1846, when the Mexican American War began. Hispanic artists and craftspeople shifted from making objects that were an integral, necessary part of their daily lives to making luxury items to ensure their economic survival

The Casa del Prado Theater in San Diego, California, shows the Spanish colonial style. (Envision, Jean Higgins)

or, later, to affirm their cultural identity. New Mexicans were absorbed into the United States as a result of the TREATY OF GUADALUPE HIDALGO (1848). Many had to change their way of life in response to the Anglo culture that entered the area. Anglo culture was more commercial than cooperative. In addition, many Hispanos lost their land and had to rely on crafts as a means of making a living.

Art Industries. Cottage industries based on various colonial art forms became widespread in New Mexico. Many artists in northern New Mexico carried on Spanish American art traditions well into the mid-twentieth century, particularly weaving, the carving of santos, and the making of furniture in traditional eighteenth and nineteenth century styles.

In the 1960's and 1970's, New Mexican artists began to organize art groups with the intention of exploiting the traditional art forms of their Spanish colonial heritage. This new generation of artists used better tools and drew on their training in design to create more complex pieces as expensive art objects. This movement coincided with rising interest in ethnic cultures throughout the United States.

The need to establish an economic base prompted many artists to participate in this revival. One of the most popular forms of art was the religious woodcarvings, referred to as *BULTOS* or santos, made by artists called *santeros*. Another art form was the *RETABLO*, a painting on flat wood of saints or other religious images. Artists sought to recapture the traditional vivid colors used on these pieces and covered them with a coat of clear varnish. Saints were depicted in familiar, stylized fashion so that people would recognize them by their attributes, such as instruments of martyrdom or important events from their lives. New *santeros* also began to experiment with other styles, such as unpainted *bultos*.

Other Spanish American arts included tinwork and jewelry making. Hammered tin pieces were used to enhance mirrors, frame pictures, or decorate wall boxes holding santos. Spanish colonial skill in silversmithing mixed with southwestern Indian traditions to create a unique style that became much prized locally, nationally, and internationally.

The same Spanish colonial heritage found in New Mexican art and crafts can also be found in the literary

The Spanish colonial heritage in art survives in New Mexico as shown at the Martinez Trade Fair. (Elaine Querry)

arts. For example, New Mexican literature uses traditional *dichos* (proverbs), *adivinanzas* (riddles), and *leyendas* (legends) to create a regional flavor.

—*Santos C. Vega*

SUGGESTED READINGS: • Cali, Francois. *The Spanish Arts of Latin America*. New York: Viking Press, 1961. • Giffords, Gloria Fraser. *Mexican Folk Retablos: Masterpieces on Tin*. Tucson: University of Arizona Press, 1974. • Glubok, Shirley. *The Art of the Spanish in the United States and Puerto Rico*. New York: Macmillan, 1972. • Palmer, Gabrielle, and Donna Pierce. *Cambios: The Spirit of Transformation in Spanish Colonial Art*. Albuquerque: Santa Barbara Museum of Art and University of New Mexico Press, 1992. • *Spanish Textile Tradition of New Mexico and Colorado*. Santa Fe: Museum of New Mexico Press, 1979. • Steele, Thomas J. *Santos and Saints: The Religious Folk Art of Hispanic New Mexico*. Santa Fe, N.Mex.: Ancient City Press, 1982.

Arte Público (founded 1979): Nonprofit publisher. Arte Público provides a voice for authors of Hispanic descent. As of the early 1990's, it published twenty-five books per year and was the largest supplier of texts for courses in U.S. Hispanic literature. The press has received grants from the National Endowment for the Arts and the Rockefeller, Mellon, and Ford foundations.

Arte Público was conceived by Nicolás KANELLOS, who began a literary magazine titled *Chicano-Puerto Rican Review* for Hispanic writers unable to get their works published by major presses. This magazine, later retitled *The Americas Review*, precipitated the foundation of Arte Público. The University of Houston sponsors Arte Público. In 1994, the press had a staff of about twenty creative writers and literary scholars in addition to its advisory board.

Arte Público publishes most of its books in English for the purpose of satisfying the needs of Hispanic writers in America whose predominant language is English. Through *The Americas Review* and the publication of literary and reference books, Arte Público has presented Hispanic literary creativity, arts, and culture. Arte Público distributes books to the academic and library markets as well as to independent and chain bookstores.

Among Arte Público's major achievements has been the increased recognition of Hispanic authors. Among the authors that Arte Público has brought to increased prominence are Rolando HINOJOSA, creator of the Klail City Death Trip series of novels and recipient of the Casa de las Americas award; playwright Miguel PIÑERO, winner of the New York Drama Critics Award for best American play; and Nicolás Kanellos, recipient of the Whole House Heritage Award for Literature.

Arte Público has contributed considerably to the dissemination of Hispanic culture in the United States. In 1989, the Ford Foundation gave Arte Público a grant to publish collections of plays by Latino playwrights. As a result of this grant, Luis VALDEZ, the first Mexican American to create a Broadway play, produced *Zoot Suit and Other Plays* (1992). In 1991, the Rockefeller Foundation funded a project that collected documents written by Hispanics from the colonial period to 1960. A consortium of ten university presses in the United States, Mexico, Puerto Rico, and Spain published recovered material as individual works or in anthologies and textbooks. The heritage project's first contribution was *The Squatter and the Don* (1993) by María Amparo RUIZ DE BURTON, a fictional narrative about the clash of the Anglo and Hispanic cultures in California. The book was first published in 1885.

Arzola, Marina (July 12, 1939, Guayanilla, Puerto Rico—December, 1976, Puerto Rico): Poet. Arzola was an award-winning poet who published only one work in her lifetime but whose poems are widely anthologized. She received a degree in arts from the University of Puerto Rico, where she was a poet in "El grupo de Guajana" (The Guajana Group). The group, named for *Guajana*, a literary magazine founded in September of 1962, was notable for embracing a revolutionary literary aesthetic.

The turbulent decade of the 1960's shaped Arzola's work as well as the work of other Guajana poets, who wrote politicized, militant, and Marxist poetry focusing on the lives of common people. They looked to the work of Latin American poets Pablo NERUDA and César VALLEJO for inspiration, which they also found in the social rebellion of the period.

Arzola's early poetry volume *El niño de cristal y los olvidados* (1966) won the Primer Premio del Ateneo Puertorriqueño, and her only published work, *Palabras vivas* (1968), won the Premio de Club Cívico de Damas de San Juan. She left behind several unpublished manuscripts.

ASCO: Arts group. ASCO, formed in the early 1970's, consisted of four Chicano friends from East Los Angeles: Harry GAMBOA, Jr., GRONK (Glugio Nicandro), Willie Herron, and Patssi Valdez. Their murals incorporated styles that broke away from traditional Mexican forms. They drew inspiration both from the Chicano movement and from Anglo intellectual sources. *Asco* (meaning nausea or disgust) refers both to people's reported reactions to their work and also to the ugly, racist world the artists saw and tried to portray. Their murals and other works helped bring Chicano art to the public eye. They were performance artists as well as painters.

Asociación Nacional pro Personas Mayores (National Association of Hispanic Elderly): Advocacy group. This group was founded in 1975. As of the early 1990's, it had more than three thousand members, including about twenty-five hundred individuals and six hundred organizations. Its primary work concerns advocacy in favor of Hispanic and low-income elderly persons. It carries out its objectives through a variety of means, including a research center (National Hispanic Research Center); the *Legislative Bulletin*, a quarterly publication; a nationwide employment program (Senior Community Service Employment Program, funded by the Department of Labor); and technical assistance.

As of the early 1990's, the group had a staff of about thirty and maintained a library of approximately twenty-five hundred items. It directly aided more than nineteen hundred low-income people over fifty-five years of age in eleven states, providing them with employment. This organization reaches beyond the Hispanic community, conducting gerontological research through the Aging Network and the Hispanic Gerontological Traineeship Program.

The association sponsors publication of the quarterly *Legislative Bulletin*, the *Bibliographic Research and Resource Guide to the Hispanic Elderly*, a series of fact sheets (in Spanish) titled *A Nuestra Salud*, and many brochures. It also produces radio and television public service announcements as well as making filmstrips and videos available.

Asopao: Soupy Puerto Rican stew made with rice and peas. Asopao is a thick soup or thin stew, always containing rice and peas and usually featuring shellfish or chicken. In Puerto Rico, shellfish is the most common featured ingredient, while chicken is most common in New York City. *Asopao* without meat or fish also is eaten in both places. Although *asopao* is unique to Puerto Rican cuisine, it has a cousin in the jambalaya of New Orleans. This Portuguese-sounding word is a dialectal contraction of *asopado*.

Assimilation. *See* **Acculturation versus assimilation**

Astol, Lalo (Leonardo García Astol; b. 1906, Mexico): Radio personality. Astol was born to a theatrical family and as a child toured with his mother, a famous actress. Later, he toured with his father and brother in northern Mexico and in the Rio Grande Valley in the United States.

Astol began performing in the United States in 1921 and was associated with popular theatrical companies in San Antonio, Texas. During the Depression, he survived doing vaudeville. He is still remembered in communities of the Southwest for the role he created of Don Lalo, a comic hobo. In 1938, he began doing comic dialogues on Spanish-language radio. By 1940, he had become the emcee of a Mexican variety show on the radio, which later led to doing radio soap operas in the 1950's. His efforts were responsible for keeping plays and vaudeville routines alive in San Antonio after World War II—even if they had to be presented for free or at fund-raisers.

In the late 1950's and early 1960's, Astol broke into television. He wrote, directed, and acted in a serial titled *El Vampiro* (the vampire). Over the years, Astol has striven to keep Hispanic theater alive in the United States.

Astronomy: The world of the night sky was a precise and organized place to pre-Columbian civilizations on the American continents. The observation and study of the movement of stars and planets was significant to both practical and spiritual aspects of life in the great centers of the Mayan, Aztec, and Incan cultures, influencing many of the lesser-known communities throughout the region of South and Central America, and possibly the native communities of North America.

Pre-Columbian Astronomy. Several obstacles impede understanding of early astronomy in Latin America. First, European conquerors destroyed many of the manuscripts of the native civilizations. Epigraphers, who study the glyph or pictographic language of these classical American cultures, have established that many of the destroyed documents were family histories, community inventories, political histories, and extensively detailed and precise calendars.

In addition, the arriving explorers brought with them a European view of the world. Many scientific and technical achievements of the native peoples were overlooked because they did not conform to the current view of the world held by the conquering forces. Astronomical observation was particularly sensitive to this domination. European scientists were strongly influenced by Ptolemy's interpretation of the movement of stars and planets, as well as by the official position of the Roman Catholic church. Mayan astronomers were extraordinarily precise in their calculations of eclipses and other similar celestial phenomena and of lunar and solar movements for their calendars, but it would take hundreds of years for these achievements to be recognized.

For Incas, Maya, and Aztecs alike, developments in astronomical observation and of the computational skills to project celestial movement were rooted in religious practices. Aztecs and Incas observed all movements associated with the sun and moon, computing full and partial eclipses of both celestial bodies with great precision.

Aztec calendar stones are one example of the merger of science and art in the service of the gods and the proper calculation of religious celebration days. The Maya, who understood the numerical idea of zero, created a calendar more precise than any European calendar of that time. Calendars were created to establish the correct days for religious ceremonies and to calculate the proper days for the activities of the community related to agriculture, trade, and war.

Seventeenth and Eighteenth Centuries. Formal scientific study and research stagnated in the Americas until the seventeenth century, which saw the advent of larger urban areas with increased population and expanding economies. The university system was expanding throughout the Spanish Empire, as was the need for people with technical and scientific training. New World scientists were enthusiastic about the development of the telescope, and celestial observation was again at the center of interest.

Two scientists published noteworthy reports of their observations. Mexican scientist Diego Rodríguez (1596-1668) published *Observation of the New Comet*, a study of the 1652 comet that cites observations by Galileo. Carlos Sigüenza y Góngora (1645-1700), possibly a student of Rodríguez, published his observations of the 1680 comet. Sigüenza in particular was influenced by the *novatores*, Spanish scientists who were trying to understand and use new scientific ideas without openly breaking with official dogma and belief. Sigüenza himself used elements of the new cosmology of Copernicus without openly supporting it.

By the eighteenth century, the new science of Galileo, Copernicus, and Newton had percolated through the slowly changing institutions of education. At this time also, the Spanish Crown began to sponsor a broad range of expeditions throughout the North American continent with the purposes of studying and cataloging the natural history of its many regions. This coincidence of scientific activity and discussion helped compensate for the long delay in arrival of the latest advances in science in Europe.

Heliocentrism, the idea that the sun rather than the earth was the center of the solar system, was first being taught in the 1770's by José Celestino Mutis (1732-1808) at the Colegio Mayor del Rosario in Bogotá, Colombia. His disciple, Juan Eloy Valenzuela (d. 1834), began teaching Newtonian physics there in 1777. At the University of San Marcos in Lima, Peru, Cosme Bueno (1711-1798) taught Newton's doctrines beginning in 1758. The conflict between "new science" and "old view" forced progressive views outside the universities. Newtonian views were taught at the Real Convictorio de San Marcos in Lima, Peru, which was founded in 1774, but were not taught at the University of Mexico until the nineteenth century.

For the most part, astronomical studies during the

U.S. president Harry S Truman visits the Pyramid to the Moon at Teotihuacán, Mexico. (AP/Wide World Photos)

seventeenth and eighteenth centuries were applied to improving maps. The French expedition of 1735-1744, under the direction of Charles Marie La Condamine, is an example of this. Although organized by the French, the expedition was strictly supervised by the Spanish Crown, and Spanish researchers participated in the field work. The goal of this expedition was to measure the length of a degree in order to test Newton's assertions that the earth was not completely round. Jorge Juan (1713-1773), Antonio de Ullo (1716-1795), and Pedro Vicente Maldonado (b. 1704) accompanied La Condamine. The triangulation for this test was completed in 1739, when three degrees of latitude had been covered. During the time of this expedition, La Condamine exchanged astronomical data with Pedro Peralta (1663-1743), who was instrumental in diffusing the ideas of Newton and Copernicus among the intellectual community of Peru.

Many of the extensive expeditions of the era included astronomical observations. Noteworthy among these were the observations of the transit of Venus across the solar disk by Vicente Doz (c. 1736-1781) and Joaquín Velázquez de León (1732-1786) in Baja California (1789), and that of the transit of Mercury by Dionisio Alcalá Galiano (1762-1805) in Montevideo, Uruguay, in 1789.

By the eighteenth century, colonial science, which was by definition dependent on Europe, had managed to separate itself and establish collections of equipment and libraries that often competed with the best collections of the Old World. With the emergence of nationalism and the start of independence movements, scientific discussion fed into the political debate. The struggle for independence came at the expense of resources for research and investigation, and also at an incalculable cost in human life.

Twentieth Century Developments. The recuperation of scientific institutions and research was influenced by the French toward the end of the nineteenth century (in Colombia, Venezuela, and Brazil) and by Germans during the early part of the twentieth century (in Argentina). The Mexican Revolution invigorated that country's National Institute of Astronomy, as did the creation of new facilities for research.

Many Latin American scientists were educated in the United States after World War II and brought those educational influences home to invigorate national initiatives. Astronomical research in the twentieth century has been marked by a collaborative approach among universities in the United States, Europe, and Latin America. It also has been characterized by a balance between application and theory. For example, radio telescope time at Brazil's Instituto de Pesquisa Espaciais (Institute of Space Investigation) is divided among research for the improvement of cartography, study of the Antarctic, and the study of deep space phenomena.

In Chile, two facilities were noted for their collaborative activities in the 1990's. One was the Cerro Tololo Inter-American Observatory. Four hundred eighty kilometers north of Santiago, this facility had a fourteen-meter telescope that was considered to be one of the finest optical instruments in the world. This telescope allowed observation of the Magellanic Clouds, a formation not visible to observatories in the Northern Hemisphere. Far to the south, the Atacama desert was the site of Las Sillas Observatory, a collaborative facility with the European Space Agency. These were not merely geographical partnerships; 85 percent of the scientific staff at Cerro Tololo was Chilean.

The largest radio telescope in the world began operating in Arecibo, Puerto Rico, in 1960. This facility was administered by Cornell University of Ithaca, New York. In 1974, the Arecibo Interstellar Message was beamed to M-13, a globular star cluster twenty-five thousand light years away. In 1992, in celebration of the five hundredth anniversary of Christopher Columbus' historic first voyage, Arecibo sent another exploratory message, signaling the beginning of the National Aeronautics and Space Administration's survey known as the Search for Extraterrestrial Intelligence (SETI).

Latin American countries also joined in business ventures into space. French Guyana's Kourou Space Center, for example, launched an average of one satellite every month in the early 1990's, primarily for the purpose of communications but also for atmospheric and space studies. Argentina had plans to launch a telecommunications satellite.

As historical and anthropological studies of Latin America continue to expand understanding of its cultures and views of the world, understanding of astronomy and its role in the formation of these cultures also grows. Stargazing and the contemplation of the cosmos is woven through the scientific achievements of Latin America.   *—Marguerite Cotto*

SUGGESTED READINGS: • Berdan, Frances F. *The Aztecs of Central Mexico: An Imperial Society.* New York: Holt, Rinehart and Winston, 1982. • Berdan, Frances F. and Patricia Reiff Anawalt. *The Codex Mendoza.* Berkeley: University of California Press, 1992. • Engstrand, I. H. W. *Spanish Scientists in the New World: The Eighteenth-Century Expeditions.* Seattle: University of Washington Press, 1981. • Hilton, Ronald. *The Scientific Institutions of Latin America.* Stanford: California Institute of International Studies, 1970.

Asylum policies: Dictate criteria for allowing or disallowing refugees to stay in the country to which they have fled. (*See* REFUGEES AND REFUGEE STATUS.) Political asylum is a process that grants legal status to persons fleeing persecution in their home country. If asylum is granted in the United States, the refugee becomes a legal permanent resident, the first step toward obtaining citizenship.

To gain asylum in the United States, a person must prove refugee status. The REFUGEE ACT OF 1980 defines a refugee as a person who cannot return to his or her home country because of persecution or a reasonable fear of being persecuted because of race, religion, nationality, membership in a particular social group, or political opinion. After applying for asylum, a refugee has a chance to present his or her case at a hearing. If the case is denied, the refugee can appeal up to two times, each time at a progressively higher circuit of the court. If the case is still denied, the refugee can be deported legally. The State Department is responsible for determining asylum policy, and the IMMIGRATION AND NATURALIZATION SERVICE (INS) carries out this policy by handling refugees and their asylum applications.

Refugee Act of 1980. The Refugee Act of 1980 allowed for refugee admissions, the right to asylum, and resettlement assistance for refugees. It brought U.S. law into accord with the 1967 United Nations Protocol, which addressed refugees fleeing individualized persecution. The Cuban MARIEL BOAT LIFT, followed by civil strife in Nicaragua, El Salvador, and Guatemala, brought many Latinos into the United States and Canada to seek asylum; they accounted for about 85 percent of all U.S. asylum claims in the 1980's. Although the Refugee Act stipulated fair asylum policy and refugee admissions, it made no provisions for large influxes of asylum seekers; prior to the act, the number of asylum seekers had been small. Asylum policy thus adapted in response to pressures from foreign policy and from domestic and budgetary issues. The groups involved in creating and interpreting asylum policy, often at odds with one another, were the State Department, the INS and other refugee-related federal government groups; Congress and its appropriate committees; and interested public pressure groups.

Asylum policy often has varied depending on the refugee's country of origin. Refugees from El Salvador

NATIONALITY OF APPLICANTS GRANTED ASYLUM IN THE UNITED STATES, 1980-1992

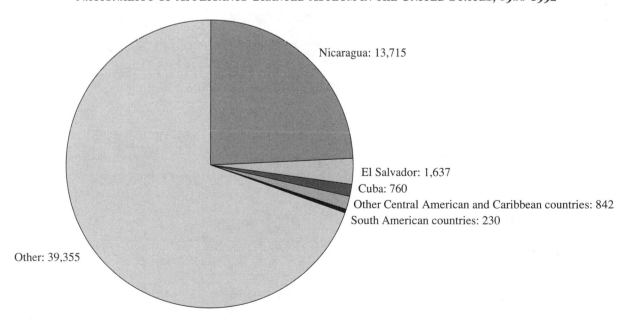

Nicaragua: 13,715

El Salvador: 1,637
Cuba: 760
Other Central American and Caribbean countries: 842
South American countries: 230

Other: 39,355

Source: Data are from Office of Refugee Resettlement, *Refugee Resettlement Program: Report to Congress, 1993* (Washington, D.C.: U.S. Department of Health and Human Services, 1993), Table 14.

Thousands of Cubans sought admission to the United States during the Mariel boat lift. (AP/Wide World Photos)

and Guatemala historically were granted few asylum claims. In El Salvador, civil war throughout most of the 1980's claimed many lives and brought ordinary citizens into danger. Executions of friends and families by death squads, torture, threats of death, and other atrocities were experienced by Salvadorans who fled; not all of them had strong political involvement. Despite these grim scenes and refugees' fear of returning home, only about 2.5 percent of all Salvadoran asylum cases were granted in the 1980's.

Guatelmalan refugees fleeing their country's unofficial civil war also seldom received asylum during the 1980's. In contrast, the proportions of asylum cases granted to Nicaraguans was more than 25 percent, and for refugees from Romania and the Soviet Union, the proportions granted were about 70 percent.

These numbers vary, in part, because of the United States' differing policies toward the governments of refugees' countries. The governments of Communist countries were not "legitimate" governments according to the United States, so refugees from those countries received a sympathetic response. The government of El Salvador, however, was dependent on large amounts of military aid from the United States, which supported the right-wing government. The U.S. government refused to acknowledge the persecution there

As many as six hundred people per night showed up at the Spanish Catholic Center in Washington, D.C., to apply for temporary protected status. (Impact Visuals, Donna DeCesare)

and denied asylum cases on the grounds that El Salvador was a democratic country and that any individual wishing to leave it sought better economic opportunity, was a guerrilla, or simply wanted to get away from generally violent conditions.

The rationale behind denying Guatemalans asylum was that because Guatemala had undergone governmental changes after the refugees had fled, they no longer needed to fear repression from the new government. Unfortunately, studies by human rights organizations found that in both countries, some of these individuals were persecuted after being returned; regardless of any changes in government, they were subject to such treatment as torture, "disappearance," or imprisonment.

With the immigration of Haitians and Cubans in the early 1980's, the United States revived the policy of holding asylum seekers in detention centers across the nation. The centers were run by the INS, which supplemented its own facilities by contracting with prisons and local jails and by converting other buildings. Refugees were held in these centers as "illegal aliens"; they were not given refugee status until they could prove they fit the refugee definition and thus were treated as illegals who could be deported at any time. These detention centers often were inadequately equipped to deal with long-term residents; they also sometimes forced refugees to live alongside hardened criminals. Many refugees had no legal assistance in detention centers, spoke no English, and had little or no knowledge of the U.S. legal system.

Refugee advocates were important in countering government pressures for deportation as being in the best interest of U.S. budget constraints and foreign policy. The SANCTUARY MOVEMENT, human rights organizations, and pro bono lawyers' groups all have worked to help asylum seekers through the process.

The Immigration Act of 1990. Asylum policy with respect to Latin American refugees changed with the IMMIGRATION ACT OF 1990, which allowed temporary refuge for Salvadoran asylum seekers under temporary protected status (TPS). It acknowledged the previously negated fact that persons fleeing generalized violence (in addition to individualized persecution) faced danger if deported back to El Salvador. It offered Salvadorans who had arrived in the United States before September 19, 1990, and had applied for the status during a certain period, an eighteen-month stay in the United States without fear of deportation. TPS was extended as delayed enforced departure (DED) until December, 1994. Negotiations continued in the mid-

1990's to provide future protection for these refugees. Guatemalans were not eligible for similar safe haven programs at that time, although efforts toward that goal were under way.

American Baptist Churches in the United States v. Thornburgh (1990) promised fairer asylum hearings for Salvadorans and Guatemalans. It resulted in a call for the readjudication of more than 150,000 asylum claims. In 1992, the percentages of asylum cases granted to Salvadorans and Guatemalans rose to 28 percent and 21 percent, respectively.

Canadian political asylum law is in accord with U.S. policy, also following the United Nations Protocol. Changes were made in Canada under amendments to the Immigration Act in 1992, which extended the definition of a refugee to include people fleeing civil strife and events seriously disturbing public order. Although their policies are based on similar criteria, Canada and the United States differ in their interpretations of asylum law, and Canada historically has granted more Salvadoran and Guatemalan asylum cases than has the United States. —*Michelle McKowen*

SUGGESTED READINGS: • Adelman, Howard, ed. *Refugee Policy: Canada and the United States.* Toronto: Centre for Refugee Studies, York University, 1991. • Bau, Ignatius. *This Ground Is Holy: Church Sanctuary and Central American Refugees.* New York: Paulist Press, 1985. • Coutin, Susan B. *The Culture of Protest: Religious Activism and the U.S. Sanctuary Movement.* Boulder, Colo.: Westview Press, 1993. • Keely, Charles B., and Sharon S. Russell. "Responses of Industrial Countries to Asylum Seekers." *Journal of International Affairs* 47 (Winter, 1994): 399-417. • Yarnold, Barbara M. *Refugees Without Refuge: Formation and Failed Implementation of U.S. Political Asylum Policy in the 1980's.* Lanham, Md.: University Press of America, 1990.

Ataque: Stress syndrome of some Puerto Ricans. *Ataque*, or *ataque de nervios* (attack of nerves), is a distressed state experienced by Puerto Rican people, mainly women. It is characterized by symptoms such as heart palpitations, trembling, faintness, nervousness, crying, hysterics, loss of consciousness, and seizures. *Ataque* usually occurs as a result of accidents, funerals, family arguments, or other emotionally trying situations. Although *ataque* crosses gender and class divisions, the majority of those who experience it are women above the age of forty-five. Unemployed single people with less than a high school education are more prone to *ataque*. Some medical practitioners see it is as a precursor of depression or more serious nervous disorders, although *ataque* is most commonly understood as a cultural way of expressing stress. *Ataque* is sometimes treated by an *ESPIRITISTA*.

Atole: Thick corn drink from Mexico. *Atole* is made by mixing corn dough (*masa*) into sweetened water and boiling it until it thickens to the consistency of an extremely thin sauce. It can be drunk hot or eaten cold, although most modern Mexicans prefer *atole* warm. Pre-Columbian Aztecs enjoyed *atole*, but modern *atole* recipes have been modified in the light of *HOR-CHATA*, a drink introduced by the Spanish in the sixteenth century. *Atole* can be flavored with fruit, cinnamon, almonds, vanilla, or chocolate; it can be diluted with milk; and the corn base can be replaced with rice. Some *atoles* are thick enough to support admixed pieces of cheese, corn on the cob, and pork.

August 29th Movement: Protest against the Vietnam War and police brutality. At its meeting in March, 1970, the Chicano Youth Conference called for a national protest rally on August 29 in Los Angeles to protest the high number of Latino casualties in the Vietnam War. This was part of the NATIONAL CHICANO MORATORIUM ON VIETNAM. Los Angeles Youth Conference leaders decided to combine the antiwar demonstration with a protest against police brutality after learning that six Mexican American prisoners had died in city jails in the previous five months.

On the day of the rally, thirty thousand people marched to City Hall chanting, "Aztlán: Love it or leave it," referring to the mythical home of the Aztecs before Europeans arrived. The march was peaceful and ended with a picnic in a local park. That evening, however, police arrested several Latinos at a liquor store, and a mob began throwing things at the officers. A large force of police responded by running into the park, swinging clubs and launching several canisters of tear gas into the picnickers. A fifteen-year-old boy and a reporter for a Spanish-language newspaper were killed in the chaos, but no police officers were ever charged with any crimes or excessive use of force. Protests against police brutality continued into 1971, but little changed. During a protest on January 31, 1971, police beat hundreds of marchers. The demonstrations ceased.

Autobiography: The early creators of autobiography presented cultural as well as personal significance in their works. The Romans, who provided the Latin root of the Spanish language, also gave the framework for autobiography by establishing it as an art form patterned as a cultural journey involving self-discovery. Saint Augustine's confessions, Petronius' picaresque elements, Lucius Apuleius' conversion drama, and Lucian's self-dissecting satirical works foreshadowed the novelistic and didactic elements common to Latino and U.S. autobiography.

The novelistic element of autobiography presents a series of events in a person's life, intertwined with cultural influences. Floyd Salas' *Buffalo Nickel* (1992), for example, presents his drama of becoming a man in a Latin American family under the conflicting influences of the values of the Catholic church, the bitter death of his loving mother, and the expectations of his father and brothers regarding appropriate male behavior. Salas portrays an authoritative Latin father who must control his family and maintain his public image as a person of honor and integrity. Salas' father has difficulty in relating emotionally to his sons. Salas' two older brothers, one a drug addict and petty thief and the other a bisexual scholar who commits suicide, serve as role models for the author. At first, Salas clings to his older brothers' influence in his character formation; however, he gradually becomes independent, thus completing his search for manhood. The novelistic element in Salas' autobiography gives the author's experiences a mythic overtone, thereby enabling his cultural identity to become more accessible to the reader.

The didactic element of modern Latino autobiography often concerns an author's portrayal of suppressed heritage. For example, in *Nepantla: Essays from the Land in the Middle* (1993), Pat MORA discusses education, the family and the female role in a Latin household, and the importance of her Mexican roots. Richard RODRIGUEZ analyzes the American educational system and shows the indestructible bonds of family love that survive the stressful changes of becoming Americanized. In *Hunger of Memory: The Education of Richard Rodriguez* (1981), he describes how education enabled him to overcome his feelings of public alienation, which were augmented by the intense cultural unity of his Spanish-speaking family. Rodriguez's difficult transition between his private and public identities provides insights on the problems of bilingual education and affirmative action.

Latino autobiography contains elements in common with most autobiography: the unique identity of the individual, time as a factor in self-development, chronology as the main structural element, and the life of the author recounted in a factual, retrospective manner. The major identifying element in Latino autobiography is its testimonial nature, with emphasis on cultural identity. Latino autobiography as a rule contains significant commentary on the author's cultural context.

Automobile industry: Latinos have been employed in the American automobile industry since the early part of the twentieth century. The development of the industry gained momentum when Detroit industrialist Henry Ford introduced the assembly line in 1913. Ford looked to Mexico, not only to recruit factory workers to offset the labor shortage created by World War I but also as a place to expand his industrial empire. Hundreds of Mexicans were on the Ford payroll before 1920, and other automakers followed the lead in employing Latinos.

Historian Dennis Valdes has described the Ford Service school, established by Henry Ford in 1917 to teach foreign students about the automotive industry. Ford's plan was to bring foreign students to his automotive operation in metropolitan Detroit and teach them all aspects of production, sales, and service. The training period varied in length, from a few months to a few years. Ford's intent was to send these students back to work in his operations in their countries of origin.

As the American economy faced the crisis of the Great DEPRESSION, Mexicans, and in some cases Mexican Americans, became part of a massive effort called "repatriation" that moved them back to Mexico. Valdes and others have documented the impact this had on such metropolitan areas as Detroit, which had lost about 80 percent of its Latino population by the end of 1932. The automobile industry began to employ Latino workers again in the late 1930's, as the nation watched war unfold in Europe.

In the 1990's, Latinos were working throughout the automotive industry. The American Federation of Labor-Congress of Industrial Organizations (AFL-CIO), which includes the United Autoworkers Union, reported a Hispanic membership of 1.2 million. Census figures indicate that the number of employees working at Hispanic-owned automobile dealerships, service stations, and automotive repair shops nearly doubled between 1982 and 1987. This figure grew from fewer than 10,000 in 1982 to 19,127 five years later. The publication *Hispanic Business* reported in 1992 that the top five Latino-owned dealerships, located in Colorado, Michigan, and Texas, recorded $955.55 million in combined sales in 1991.

Ávalos, David (b. 1947): Artist. As an activist artist in San Diego, California, where many undocumented Mexican workers cross into the United States, Ávalos has won recognition for public art projects that challenge racism and the treatment of immigrants.

To focus attention on the use of low-paid Mexican workers in San Diego's tourist industry, Avalos collaborated on a 1988 bus poster titled *Welcome to America's Finest Tourist Plantation*. The poster, which combined photographs of handcuffed Mexican men, hands scraping food off a plate, and a "Maid Service" sign, highlighted the gap between the tourist image of San Diego and the socioeconomic plight of Hispanic people who work in agricultural fields, hotels, and restaurants there.

A work with similar impact is Ávalos' *San Diego Donkey Cart* (1985), a sculptural work modeled on the donkey carts used as backdrops for tourist photographs. Instead of displaying colorful serapes, the wooden backboard of Ávalos' cart depicts a border guard frisking an undocumented worker. Ávalos placed the work strategically in front of San Diego's federal courthouse, where cases involving undocumented workers are tried.

Ávalos' art makes political statements on behalf of Latinos. He was the most controversial of the members of San Diego's Border Art Workshop, which also included Guillermo Gómez-Peña, Víctor OCHOA, and Isaac Artenstein.

Avila, Bobby (Roberto Francisco Avila y Gonzalez; b. Apr. 2, 1924, Veracruz, Mexico): Baseball player. The son of a prosperous lawyer, Avila was a star soccer player as a youth. He took up baseball at the urging of an older brother and as a teenager became a star in the Mexican League. In 1949, he was signed by the Cleveland Indians for $17,500. A line-drive-hitting second baseman, Avila went on to become one of the first Mexican players to have significant major league success.

In one 1951 game, Avila hit a single, a double, and three home runs; a year later, he led the American League with eleven triples. In 1954, he became the first Latino player to capture a major league batting title, leading the American League with a .341 average for the pennant-winning Indians despite playing half the season with a broken thumb. As a baserunner, he successfully used his soccer training to kick balls out of fielders' gloves when he was sliding.

Avila's batting helped him win all-star selections in 1952, 1954, and 1955. Late in his career, he changed

Bobby Avila was a star player for the Cleveland Indians. (AP/Wide World Photos)

teams three times between December, 1958, and July, 1959, playing for the Baltimore Orioles, Boston Red Sox, and Milwaukee Braves.

A national hero in Mexico, Avila returned to his homeland in 1960. He became a politician and later the president of the Mexican League.

Avila, Joaquín (b. 1948, Compton, Calif.): Attorney. After majoring in government at Yale University, Avila received his juris doctorate in law from Harvard Law School in 1973. After a year as a clerk for the Alaska Supreme Court, Avila became staff attorney in 1974 to the MEXICAN AMERICAN LEGAL DEFENSE AND EDUCATION FUND (MALDEF) in San Francisco. In 1976, he was promoted to associate counsel of MALDEF in Texas. In 1982, he was elected president of MALDEF, succeeding Vilma MARTÍNEZ.

During his three-year tenure, Avila focused on improving the political, economic, and community position of Latinos nationwide. Avila's earlier efforts in Texas, during a time of difficult challenges to civil rights progress, had resulted in significant civil rights victories, such as overturning discriminatory at-large election systems, that benefited Latinos and other groups. In 1980, he was responsible for invalidating a Texas reapportionment plan that violated Mexican American voting rights. Avila was a prominent force behind the extension of the federal Voting Rights Act of 1982.

Avocado: Buttery fruit of the avocado tree. Cultivated in Mexico and elsewhere in Latin America as a foodstuff, the avocado was one of the first plants domesticated in the Americas, and its cultivated remains in Mexico have been dated by archaeologists back to before 6000 B.C.E. The fruit was valued by the Aztecs, who called it *ahuacatl* ("fruit of the testicle tree") and believed that eating avocados increased male sexual potency. The fruit is eaten throughout Latin America, both raw and cooked. Cooked dishes range from avocado soups to stuffed avocados to avocado ice cream. Perhaps the best-known avocado dish is GUACAMOLE, a mashed and seasoned paste from Mexico.

Aylló, Lucas Vázques de. *See* **Vázquez de Ayllón, Lucas**

Ayuntamiento: Town council governing settlements in Spanish and Mexican territories. Members of the *ayuntamiento* were elected by the residents of the town. The *ayuntamiento* received its authority technically from the central government and through the viceroy, governor, and commander of the nearest presidio. The complicated delegation of power and the extreme geographic separation of pueblos from centers of authority allowed *ayuntamientos* much political autonomy in the northern frontiers of the Spanish/Mexican empire. People of the pueblos elected an *alcalde* (mayor) and *regidores* (council members) who represented this governing body. In the early years of Los Angeles, pueblo government also maintained a *comisionado*, appointed by the presidio commander. Some *ayuntamientos* also had a *sindico*, who functioned as a city attorney, tax collector, and treasurer.

Azaceta, Luis Cruz (b. Apr. 5, 1942, Havana, Cuba): Painter. Azaceta is noted for emotionally charged paintings that use violent imagery to express his fearful recollections of Cuba, the alienation of exiles and other outsiders, and the brutality of urban life.

Azaceta drew for pleasure as a youth, but art training in Cuba was at that time reserved for the wealthy. In 1960, he settled in the United States, joining relatives in New Jersey and working in factories. In 1966, he enrolled in New York's School of Visual Arts. He completed his studies in 1969, and after returning from a European trip that exposed him to the work of Francisco de Goya and other Spanish painters, Azaceta decided to start painting what he felt inside.

Azaceta's early work features bright, cartoonlike images outlined in black. Later, he used thick, multicolored layers of paint to portray figures that were pierced by nails, decapitated, or otherwise mutilated. Monsters, skulls, butcher knives, and self-portraits dominated Azaceta's work. By the 1980's, he had begun to focus on graphic scenes of urban ills.

Azaceta has taught art at universities in California, Louisiana, and New York. He has received fellowships from the Cintas Foundation, the Guggenheim Memorial Foundation, the National Endowment for the Arts, and the New York Foundation for the Arts.

Azpiazú, Don (Jan. 20, 1893, Cienfuegos, Cuba—Feb. 11, 1943, Havana, Cuba): Bandleader and pianist. During the 1920's, Azpiazú was the bandleader of the Havana Casino Orchestra. In 1930, his orchestra recorded "El manisero" ("The Peanut Vendor"). This recording became wildly successful and introduced the U.S. audience to authentic Latin music in the RUMBA style. A number of Cuban percussion instruments had not been heard by the American public prior to the release of "The Peanut Vendor."

After the success of this recording, Azpiazú recorded "Green Eyes" in 1931, with singer Chick Bullock. It is thought to be the first recording that mixed American popular song with Cuban music. In the early 1930's, Azpiazú was popular in both the United States and Europe. He returned to Cuba and, eventually, was overshadowed by other Latin bandleaders. By the time he died in 1943, Azpiazú had faded from the memory of the American public.

Aztec civilization: Most dominant civilization that existed in the Valley of Mexico on the eve of the Spanish Conquest. The myths and legends of the Aztecs tell of emergence from a land called AZTLÁN (place of the herons) in approximately A.D. 1168. Aztlán has never been positively identified. Historians believe that this place of origin is located somewhere northwest of the Valley of Mexico and would include the states of Jalisco, Colima, Nayarít, and Michoacán; it may extend north into the United States to present-day Arizona or New Mexico.

Aztec Migration. The Aztecs were one of many migrating tribes known as Chichimecas, a name taken from *chichi* (dog) and *mécatl* (rope or lineage); the pejorative phrase "dog people" was applied to these tribes by former Chichimecas living in city-states. The southward migrations of the Aztecs were inspired by their war god Huitzilopochtli (hummingbird wizard),

GEOGRAPHIC REGION OF THE AZTECS

UNITED STATES

MEXICO

Rio Lerma

Rio Tula

Teotihuacán

Tenochtitlán

Vera Cruz

Rio Balsas

La Venta

BELIZE

GUATEMALA

The meeting of Aztec ruler Moctezuma II and Hernán Cortés. (Library of Congress)

who instructed the Aztecs to do two things. They were to change their name to Mexíca, and they were to seek a place where a huge shallow lake was located. On this lake would be a number of islands; among them would be one small island covered with *tenóchtlis* (prickly pear cactus plants). One of these *tenóchtli* would be growing out of a rock, and perched upon it would be *quáuh* (eagle) devouring a *cóatl* (snake). It was upon that spot that the Mexícas (Aztecs) were to develop their city of TENOCHTITLÁN (place of the cactus on the stone, also known as place of the hard prickly pears).

The Mexícas expanded their island by using an ancient system of soil-building and cultivation known as *chinampas* (artificial islands). These *chinampas* were constructed by weaving reed baskets of enormous proportions, anchoring them to the shoreline of the island, tying them to one another and filling them with mud from the shallow lake bottom. When the mud dried, the Mexícas planted water-loving trees along the edges of the baskets so that their roots would hold these floating islands to the bottom of the lake. In the center

of the baskets, the Mexícas planted their crops and gardens. These so-called "floating gardens" expanded the island to a rough square measuring about two miles on each side. This island was laced through with canals and was connected to the mainland by three causeways.

Empire Building. It was in this setting that the founding of Tenochtitlán occurred in approximately 1325. From there the Mexícas developed a vigorous and vast social, religious, political, and economic empire. The political history of the Mexícas reveals a complex interplay of alliances as instruments for political consolidation in the Valley of Mexico.

The first alliance occurred when the Mexícas helped the city-state of Azcapotzalco conquer some territory early in the fifteenth century. In 1428, however, the king of Azcapotzalco ordered the execution of the Mexíca king, Chimalpópoca, along with the Tlatelólcan king, Tlacatéotl. Both were suspected of being disloyal. This act helped spark a rebellion, led by Itzcóatl and Nezahualcóyotl and supported by the

Tlaxcalans. The rebels defeated the Azcapotzalcans and elected to place Nezahualcóyotl as king of a new triple alliance made up of Tenochtitlán, Tlacópan, and Texcoco.

The confederacy, controlled by the Mexícas through force rather than mutual cooperation, became the instrument of imperial expansion. Imperialism started in the Valley of Mexico. Later, through the efforts of Moctezuma I, the empire expanded across central Mexico to reach both coasts, then reached southern Mexico.

The Mexícas controlled the city-states they conquered by using governors who acted under the direction of TENOCHTITLÁN. These governors extracted tribute from subjects in the form of such materials as feathers, jade, copper, gold, rubber, cotton, foodstuffs, and chocolate. These materials were also used to satiate the desires for luxury goods of the religious, aristocratic, and military elite. The most imposing tribute exacted on the city-states was the supply of people to be sacrificed to the enormous pantheon of Mexíca gods. People to be sacrificed were obtained through a system of *Xochiyaóyotl* (wars of the flowers). These wars were fought not for territorial or strategic advantage but only to take prisoners who would be sacrificed to Mexíca gods.

Religion. Religion dominated almost every aspect of Mexíca life. Huitzilopóchtli, the war and sun god, for example, demanded a daily diet of human hearts and blood to give him strength as he battled the lords of the darkness at the end of each day. This requirement was the foundation for imperial expansion.

Most other deities represented various aspects of natural forces. These gods were ancient by the time the Mexícas showed up in the Valley of Mexico; the Mexícas absorbed these gods within their religion. Some examples are Tláloc (water or rain god), Huehuetéotl (fire god), QUETZALCÓATL (feathered serpent, also known as the god of learning and of priesthood as well as the wind god) and Coatlicue (serpent skirt or earth goddess, the mother of Huitzilopóchtli).

These gods and others representing aspects of life such as corn, the maguey plant, death, life, cold, heat, and the seasons all revolved around the concept of duality, a balance between opposites. The balance needed to be maintained to guarantee the existence of humankind. The system of balances spawned complex rituals using human and other sacrifices. Generally, priests, soldiers, and aristocrats were concerned with the gods and goddesses that dealt with cycles of a cosmic and transcendental nature. The common people were more concerned with the "lesser" gods and goddesses dealing with cycles of everyday existence more closely associated with agriculture.

—*Moisés Roizen*

SUGGESTED READINGS: • Bernál, Ignacio. *Mexico Before Cortéz: Art, History, Legend.* Translated by Willis Barnstone. Garden City: N.Y.: Doubleday, 1963. • Caso, Alfonso. *The Aztecs: People of the Sun.* Translated by Lowell Dunham. Norman: University of Oklahoma Press, 1958. • Durán, Diego. *Books of the Gods and Rites and the Ancient Calendar.* Translated by Fernando Horcasitas and Doris Heyden. Norman: University of Oklahoma Press, 1971. • León-Portilla, Miguel. *Aztec Thought and Culture.* Translated by Jack Emory Davis. Norman: University of Oklahoma Press, 1963. • Sahagún, Bernardino de. *Florentine Codex: General History of the Things of New Spain.* Translated by Charles E. Dibble and Arthur J. O. Anderson. 12 vols. Santa Fe, N.Mex.: School of American Research, 1950-1963. • Velázquez, Primo Feliciano, trans. *Códice Chimalpópoca: Anales de Cuauhtitlan y leyenda de los soles.* Mexico City: Imprenta Universitaria, 1945.

Aztlán: Homeland of the Aztec people. During the Chicano movement, the term was revived as a symbol of unity among Chicanos. According to legend, Aztlán was the homeland of the Aztecs, which they left and later tried to relocate. Scholars have tried for years to define exactly the location of Aztlán. Some believe it to be in the southwestern United States, while others locate it in central to northeastern Mexico. In the 1960's, Chicanos adopted the term as a symbol of their movement, in a document called *El PLAN ESPIRITUAL DE AZTLÁN* (spiritual plan of Aztlán). The term is sometimes used to refer to the geographical area of the southwestern United States captured from Mexico during the Mexican American War (1846-1848). It symbolizes a union of Chicanos that gives them cultural and political independence from the mainstream Anglo culture, bringing to mind the image of a powerful indigenous culture before the arrival of Europeans in the Americas. In the 1960's and 1970's, as the Chicano movement gained strength, Aztlán served to unite Chicanos, regardless of class or economic standing, under one central concept. Through the concept of Aztlán, Chicanos recovered past history and sought to create their own new history.

Azuela, Mariano (Jan. 1, 1873, Lagos de Moreno, Jalisco, Mexico—Mar. 1, 1952, Mexico City, Mexico): Writer and physician. Azuela was one of Mexico's most prolific writers of the twentieth century. Writing more than twenty novels, he garnered the most critical acclaim for his five-novel chronicling of the Mexican Revolution. Educated as a physician, he wrote his first novel, *María Luisa* (1907), while working as a doctor in the slums of Mexico City. He received Mexico's National Prize for Literature in 1949.

A supporter of Francisco "Pancho" VILLA and a doctor in Villa's army during the revolution, Azuela fled with Villa's group to Texas when Venustiano Carranza seized control of the unstable government. Azuela wrote his highly acclaimed book *Los de abajo: Novela de la revolución mexicana* (serialized, 1915; book form, 1916; *The Underdogs: A Novel of the Mexican Revolution*, 1929) as a fugitive in the United States. The novel follows the life of a rural boy who joins Villa's army.

Azuela returned to Mexico to practice medicine and continue writing. His other highly acclaimed novels covering the Mexican Revolution are *Andrés Pérez, maderista* (1911), *Los caciques* (1917; *The Bosses*, 1956), *Las moscas* (1918; *The Flies*, 1956), and *Las tribulaciones de una familia decente* (1918; *The Trials of a Respectable Family*, 1963).

B

Babalâo: Priest of certain Afro-Brazilian and Afro-Caribbean cults. In Brazil, the *babalâo* is a priest in the *gêgé-nagó* cult, a sect with Sudanese roots. The chief role of this priest is to foretell the future. The divinatory method used by the Ifá priest involves insertion of mango seed halves or palm tree fruits through the links of a chain. The *babalâo* is also found in Cuba, where the term *ifá guensi* is sometimes used instead.

Baca, Elfego (1865, Socorro County, N.Mex.—Aug., 1945): Folk hero. Baca's Mexican American parents moved to Topeka, Kansas, shortly after his birth. He lived in Kansas until he was fifteen years old and therefore learned to speak English fluently. Upon returning to New Mexico as an adult, Baca resented the Texas cattlemen who had begun to overrun Socorro County after the Civil War. The Texans often used violence to intimidate Mexican sheepherders and drive them off the land.

Baca became a folk hero because of an incident that occurred in 1884. Shortly after several Texans had gone on a shooting spree in the small village of Frisco, Baca, who had volunteered to serve as a deputy sheriff, arrested a Texas cowboy and shot another Texan. Baca's actions angered the cattlemen, who then decided to "arrest" him for murder. In the meantime, Baca barricaded himself in a small shed. For the next thirty-six hours, Baca fought off eighty Texans. He finally surrendered, to a deputy sheriff he knew and trusted, on promise of a fair trial. He was subsequently acquitted.

Baca's heroic deeds propelled him into public life. He held various political offices beginning in the late 1880's. Baca also studied law. He gained admission to the New Mexico bar in 1894 and was later licensed to practice before the United States Supreme Court.

Baca, Jimmy Santiago (José Santiago Baca; b. Jan. 2, 1952, Santa Fe, N.Mex.): Writer. Award-winning poet Baca barely survived his tragic childhood. Abandoned by his divorced parents at the age of two, orphaned by the age of five, and living on the streets at the age of eleven, Baca was arrested and imprisoned for a drug

Jimmy Santiago Baca in 1993, outside his home in Albuquerque, New Mexico. (AP/Wide World Photos)

conviction when he was twenty years old. While incarcerated, Baca taught himself to read and write.

Baca began writing poetry in 1973 and soon began sending poems to *Mother Jones* magazine. Editor Denise Levertov not only printed his early work but also encouraged him to continue writing. Under her tutelage, Baca began collecting his poems. The collection resulted in *Immigrants in Our Own Land* (1979), a book for which Levertov secured a publisher.

All of Baca's writings are notable for their lyrical language and rich images, but his first book of poems received critical praise for its depiction of humanity triumphing over the despair of prison life. With the publication of his third book, *Martín; &, Meditations on the South Valley* (1986), Baca garnered international success, winning both the Before Columbus Foundation American Book Award and the Vogelstein Foundation Award. His other works include *What's Happening* (1982); *Black Mesa Poems* (1989), which won the Wallace Stevens Poetry Award; and several screenplays.

Baca, Judith F. (b. Sept. 20, 1946, Los Angeles, Calif.): Artist and community organizer. A pioneer of the Latino mural movement in Southern California, Baca has supervised the creation of numerous public murals in Los Angeles. She also, in 1976, helped found the Social and Public Art Resource Center, a nonprofit, multicultural organization dedicated to the promotion and cultivation of Latino artists.

Baca's early years were spent in a matriarchal household in Los Angeles. In 1969, she earned an art degree from California State University, Northridge.

As resident artist for the City of Los Angeles Cultural Affairs Division, Baca convinced youth from warring street gangs to work together painting community murals. The cooperative process is at the heart of all of Baca's public murals.

In 1973, Baca involved more than two hundred residents in creating a community mural in Venice, California. As director of the Citywide Mural Project, an innovative 1970's art program, she supervised the painting of more than 250 murals.

Baca's most ambitious project was directing the painting of a mural known as *The Great Wall of Los Angeles*, a visual history of Los Angeles begun in 1975 that shows the contributions of ethnic and immigrant groups to the city's culture. Incorporating the painting techniques Baca learned from Mexican muralist David Alfaro Siqueiros, the mural stretches across half a mile of a flood control channel.

Polly Baca-Barragán. (AP/Wide World Photos)

Baca-Barragán, Polly (b. Feb. 13, 1941, La Salle, Colo.): Legislator. Baca-Barragán attended Colorado State University, graduating in 1963. She became active in Democratic Party politics while in college. Her presidential campaign work included the national races of John F. Kennedy, Lyndon B. Johnson, and Robert F. Kennedy. Baca-Barragán served as director of Spanish-speaking affairs for the Democratic National Committee in 1971 and 1972.

Baca-Barragán's career as an elected public servant began in 1974 with her election to the Colorado state legislature. Four years later, her successful campaign for a seat in the Colorado State Senate earned for her the distinction of being the first Hispanic woman to serve in that capacity. Baca-Barragán was re-elected in 1982. Two years later, she served as vice chairwoman of the Democratic National Committee.

Baca Zinn, Maxine (b. June 11, 1942, Santa Fe, N.Mex.): Sociologist. A specialist in sex and gender roles, the sociology of the family, and race and ethnic relations, Baca Zinn has published more than a dozen articles in scholarly journals as well as serving as advisory editor to the journal *Gender and Society* and as associate editor of *The Social Science Journal* (1980-1983). Baca Zinn was elected president of the Western Social Science Association in 1985 and was part of the Committee on Women's Employment and Related Social Issues for the National Academy of Sciences. With D. Stanley Eitzen, Baca Zinn is coauthor of *Diversity in American Families* (1987) and coeditor of *The Reshaping of America: Social Consequences of the Changing Economy* (1989).

Baca Zinn earned her B.A. in sociology from California State College, Long Beach, in 1966. She began graduate studies at the University of New Mexico two years later, also teaching there. She earned her master's degree in sociology in 1970. She completed her doctorate at the University of Oregon in 1978, with the assistance of a Ford Foundation dissertation fellow-

ship (1973-1975). Baca Zinn began teaching at the University of Michigan at Flint in 1975, eventually becoming a professor in that school's sociology department. She later taught at the University of California, Berkeley, and at the University of Delaware.

Bacalaitos: Puerto Rican fritters made from dried cod. The widespread use of dried cod in Puerto Rico is a legacy of the Spanish. One the best-known dishes using it is *bacalaitos*, fritters usually eaten as snacks or appetizers, accompanied by beer or wine. Small chunks of reconstituted and desalted cod are fried in an ACHIOTE-colored batter flavored with sage and garlic.

A Puerto Rican cook fries bacalaitos. (Hazel Hankin)

Herman Badillo was elected president of the Bronx in 1966. (AP/Wide World Photos)

Badillo, Herman (b. Aug. 21, 1929, Caguas, Puerto Rico): Legislator. Badillo was orphaned at an early age. In 1940, he was sent to live with family members in New York City. Badillo was graduated with honors from the City College of New York and attended Brooklyn Law School at night.

Badillo's first political campaign in 1961 was unsuccessful. He performed public service through local appointed positions and was president of the borough of the Bronx from 1966 to 1969. His race for the office of New York City mayor was also unsuccessful but earned him name recognition and popularity vital in his historic election to the U.S. Congress in 1970. He was the first Puerto Rican to be elected as a voting member of Congress.

During his four terms in the U.S. House of Representatives, Badillo, a Democrat, represented the Twenty-fourth Congressional District of New York. He resigned in 1978 to join the administration of New York Mayor Edward Koch. He served as deputy mayor for management in 1978 and 1979.

Báez, Alberto Vinicio (b. Nov. 15, 1912, Puebla, Mexico): Physicist. Báez moved to the United States with his father, a methodist minister, when he was two years old. He married Joan Bridge, with whom he had three children: Pauline Thalia and noted folk singers Joan Chandos and Mimi Margharita. He received his B.S. in physics from Drew University in 1933, his M.A. from Syracuse University in 1935, and his Ph.D. from Stanford University in 1960. Báez has taught physics and mathematics and done research at Cornell University and Stanford University, among other schools. His main areas of research have been the uses of X rays in optical radiation, optics and microscopy, optical images and holography, and instrumentation for astronomy.

Báez, Joan Chandos (b. Jan. 9, 1941, Staten Island, N.Y.): Singer, songwriter, and civil rights activist. Báez is the daughter of Alberto Vinicio Báez, a physicist, and Joan Bridge Báez. At an early age, she showed musical talent, learning to play the guitar at

Singer Joan Báez appears at a 1986 concert for Amnesty International. (AP/Wide World Photos)

Braulio Baeza. (AP/Wide World Photos)

the age of twelve. While attending Palo Alto High School in California, she sang in the choir.

The family moved to Massachusetts after her father accepted a post at Harvard University in the late 1950's. Báez became interested in folk music and frequented the Boston coffee shops to listen to folksingers perform their music, which often contained social messages. Having been a victim of prejudice, she decided to become a folksinger in order to fight for equality for all people.

Báez made her professional debut as a folksinger at the 1959 Newport Folk Festival. The audience was impressed with her beautifully expressive soprano voice and her dynamic songs. In December, 1960, she released her first album, *Joan Baez.* The album included thirteen traditional folk songs. It was initially only moderately successful, but after the release of her popular second album, *Joan Baez, Vol. 2,* in 1961, her first album also became a huge success.

During the early 1960's, Báez's repertoire shifted from the traditional folk material toward more contemporary folk songs that expressed the turbulence of the period. Part of this change was influenced by her introduction to the work of songwriter Bob Dylan. Throughout the 1960's and 1970's, Báez was actively involved in a number of civil rights causes, including the plight of Hispanic farmworkers, the Civil Rights movement, and ending the Vietnam War.

In 1965, Báez founded the Institute for the Study of Nonviolence, and, in 1979, she co-founded Humanitas International. She released one of her most artistically and commercially successful albums, *Diamonds & Rust,* in 1975. Báez was able to blend her musical and social priorities into a positive force. In 1985, she performed at the Live Aid concert held in Philadelphia. Committing her life to worldwide human rights issues, Báez has done work for Amnesty International. In the 1990's, she remained committed to working for the betterment of all humankind and to producing poignant music.

Baeza, Braulio (b. Mar. 26, 1940, Panama City, Panama): Jockey. Baeza was born into a racing family, and he followed in the footsteps of his grandfather, father, and brothers to become a major figure in the sport of horse racing. Beginning his career as a walker at the age of eight, Baeza made his first race mount at fifteen. Four years later, his career took off; in 1959 and 1960, Baeza was the leading Panamanian jockey.

Baeza immigrated to the United States in 1960 and quickly met with success. He won the 1961 Belmont Stakes, and in the 1962 Kentucky Derby, he led the pack to the one-mile mark, but his horse lost its stamina and the pair finished ninth. Baeza later remarked that the incident had taught him an important lesson about pacing.

In 1963, Baeza won both the Kentucky Derby and Belmont Stakes. Other memorable moments in his career included a victory at the 1969 Belmont and a dramatic losing battle with Ángel Cordero for the 1976 Kentucky Derby.

Many racing insiders thought Baeza to be the sport's finest tactician. After a training session in 1963 when Baeza estimated a 49.2-second run to have lasted 49 seconds, he also became known as the jockey with "a clock in his head."

Baja California: Mexican peninsula extending south from the state of California. Historically, Baja California is one of the most arid, least accessible, and least developed regions of Mexico. The lowest population densities registered in Mexico (under one person per square mile) are found in the Baja Peninsula. In the late 1980's, however, as a result of the area's contiguity to Southern California's large population and industrial centers, transborder investment and development programs accelerated, along with migration into Baja California's vast underdeveloped space.

The first European contact occurred in 1533, when Fortún Jiménez, a pilot for Hernán Cortés, sailed into La Paz Bay on the southern tip of the peninsula. Fortresses were built to protect Jesuit and Franciscan missions by 1563. The first permanent settlement was a Jesuit mission established in 1697 in Loreto.

At various times, foreign troops attempted to seize control of Baja California and parts of Sonora. Ameri-

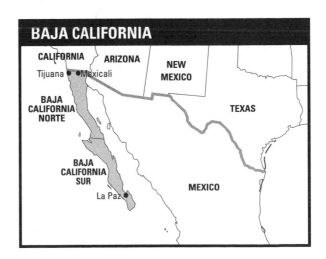

can forces occupied key ports during the Mexican American War (1846-1848). In 1853, an American adventurer, William Walker, invaded Baja California and proclaimed himself president of a new "republic." He was ejected the following year. In 1911, an army of adventurers invaded the northern part of the region in an unsuccessful try to set up a socialist regime.

Baja California of the late twentieth century was populated in large part by families with their first generations living near the border. They created a culture that is Mexican with substantial contributions from the United States. Commercial transactions were carried out in dollars as easily as in pesos.

The standard of living of northern Baja is exceeded in Mexico only in parts of the Federal District. Thousands of residents hold green cards allowing them to cross into the United States daily to work and shop. This region, so close to the United States and isolated from the Mexican mainland, became the most Americanized area of Mexico. TIJUANA, a border city with a population in excess of one million, was Baja California's largest employment and tourism center. Its industry was based largely on *MAQUILADORA* program (border industry) factories opened under a joint Mexican-United States agreement of 1965. Tourism was the most important economic activity in northwestern Baja. Ensenada, a popular tourist destination, became the center of the principal wine-growing region of Mexico and home of the country's finest wines.

The southern half of the peninsula is more closely influenced by the traditions and concerns of the Mexican mainland. Its climate, particularly at the southern end, differs from the north and center; its summers are hot and more humid, its winters delightfully tepid.

In winter months, the coast, with a wide array of fine beaches, excellent sport fishing, and whale watching opportunities, is another of Mexico's many tourist meccas. The Sea of Cortés (Gulf of California), which separates Baja California from the Mexican mainland, holds the widest diversity of marine life in the Northern Hemisphere. Development is focused on the Gulf of California and the tip of the peninsula. La Paz, with a 1990 population of about 100,000, is the capital of Baja California Sur and the only major city of the area.

Baldorioty de Castro, Román (1822—1889, Ponce, Puerto Rico): Writer and political figure. Baldorioty de Castro is recognized as one of nineteenth century Puerto Rico's leading political figures. He staunchly defended increased autonomy for Puerto Rico under Spanish colonial rule. He was appointed in 1870 as a deputy to the Cortes (the Spanish parliament), where he put his considerable oratory skills to work defending colonial rights. He founded the newspaper *El Derecho* in 1872. Through it, he addressed the issues of greater sovereignty and abolition of slavery.

In 1880, Baldorioty published a second newspaper, *La Crónica*. Seven years later, he founded the Partido Autonomista, which outlined a formula for Puerto Rico's self-rule. He was joined in this endeavor by such historic Puerto Rican figures as Luis MUÑOZ RIVERA and José Celso BARBOSA. Baldorioty's passion for Puerto Rican autonomy made him a target for Spanish persecution and ultimately imprisonment in Moro Castle.

Balseros: Literally "rafters," the term refers to Cuban refugees hoping to reach Florida in small boats. Although migration from Cuba to the United States has occurred since the Cuban Revolution in 1959, three major exoduses occurred between that time and the mid-1990's. (*See* CUBAN IMMIGRATION.) The first took place in 1960 and 1961, when thousands of people from Cuba's middle class fled to Miami following the ascent of President Fidel Castro in January, 1959. The second departure of refugees, the 1980 MARIEL BOAT LIFT, brought to South Florida a more representative sampling of the Cuban population. The 125,000 Cubans who arrived during five months were generally a younger, less educated, and more racially diverse group. In the summer of 1994, about 20,000 Cuban refugees fled Cuba. That group had an average age of twenty-eight and average education of ten years of school. Of those *balseros*, 80 percent were male and 60 percent were unmarried.

Bandini de Couts, Ysidora: Rancher. Bandini de Couts was one of three daughters of Juan Bandini, a Peruvian resident of San Diego and a prominent rancher who admired American government. Her father's attitude probably influenced Ysidora's conduct when United States forces occupied California in 1846. At that time, she and her two sisters welcomed the troops by making an American flag from white muslin sheets striped with red and blue silk from their gowns.

Bandini de Couts is also known for her work with the mission of San Luis Rey. The mission decayed rapidly after the departure of American troops who had protected the mission in 1852. Dams and embankments of irrigation ditches overflowed, and timbers and tile were carried away. Bandini de Couts, who lived at the nearby Guajome ranch, worked on the mission's restoration. She took the Stations of the Cross and one of the bells to her large adobe for safe-keeping. Her hopes began to be fulfilled on March 18, 1865. On that date, President Abraham Lincoln affixed his name to the title deed and returned the property to the Catholic church.

Bañuelos, Romana Acosta (b. Mar. 20, 1925, Miami, Ariz.): U.S. treasurer. Bañuelos was born to Mexican parents who were not U.S. citizens. When she was six years old, her parents were among those who were repatriated to Mexico during the Great Depression. She accompanied them to Mexico, where she spent her childhood. She returned to the United States at the age of nineteen, settling in Los Angeles, California.

With an initial investment of $400, Bañuelos opened a small tortilla factory in 1949. Her business, Romana's Mexican Food Products, grew into a $12 million concern over a twenty-year span, eventually employing hundreds of workers. Bañuelos also participated in the establishment of a Los Angeles financial institution. She was named Outstanding Businesswoman of the Year in Los Angeles in 1969. Her appointment as U.S. treasurer came in 1971, during the administration of President Richard M. Nixon. She was the first Mexican American woman and only the sixth woman ever to hold that position. She served until 1974, then returned to her entrepreneurial pursuits.

Barbacoa: Barbecue, or an animal's head cooked in an earth oven in northern Mexico. A *barbacoa* originally was a wooden frame erected over a fire pit, used to hold meat or fish during cooking. The word derived from an Arawak Indian word. In most parts of Latin America, *barbacoa* refers to grilling over an open fire, but in northern Mexico it denotes a special way of cooking the head of a cow, goat, or sheep (or sometimes other cuts of meat). The head is cleaned, wrapped in wet burlap, and placed onto hot coals in a pit. Earth is shoveled back over the head, which cooks slowly for several hours, often overnight. Edible parts of the head are eaten with tortillas and salsa. Restau-

The Senate Finance Committee questions Romana Acosta Bañuelos before approving her appointment as U.S. treasurer. (AP/Wide World Photos)

rants sometimes try to simulate this dish by steaming the head, but the results are unsatisfying.

Barbieri, Leandro J. "Gato" (b. Nov. 28, 1934, Rosario, Argentina): Saxophonist and composer. The first instruments that Barbieri played were the clarinet and the alto saxophone. In 1953, he joined the Lalo Schifrin band. During that year, he also started playing the tenor saxophone. In 1959, Barbieri moved to Brazil for six months and was influenced by a variety of Brazilian musical styles. He decided to expand his horizons even further by traveling to Europe during the early to mid-1960's. Barbieri met one of the leading free jazz (an avant-garde form) trumpet players, Don Cherry, in Paris in 1965. In the following year, the two of them made an album, *Complete Communion*, in New York City. Barbieri was heavily influenced by the free jazz tenor saxophone player Pharoah Sanders.

During the late 1960's, Barbieri mixed Latin American rhythms with free jazz. His 1969 album *Third World* was an exciting blend of various rhythms and included many frenetic tenor saxophone solos. In 1972, he altered his playing style for the soundtrack of the film *Last Tango in Paris*. The lush, romantic soundtrack earned Barbieri a Grammy Award. The recordings he made during the mid-1970's are considered some of his finest achievements. These recordings explored a large number of Latin styles. In 1988,

Saxophonist Gato Barbieri performs at the 1977 Newport Jazz Festival. (AP/Wide World Photos)

Barbieri released the album *Third World Revisited*, which proved that he had not lost his ability to produce driving, yet lush, tenor saxophone solos.

Barbosa, José Celso (1857-1921): Political leader. Barbosa was born into an impoverished black family and rose to a position of political influence. He attended the University of Michigan in 1880 as a medical student and returned to San Juan to practice medicine. Barbosa's political activities began in 1883, when he joined the Liberal Party, headed by Luis MUÑOZ RIVERA. Barbosa formed his own criteria for an autonomous government for Puerto Rico, causing him to split with Muñoz Rivera.

In 1898, the United States gained sovereignty over Puerto Rico as a result of the Spanish-American War. Barbosa and his followers, known as "Puros," then became advocates of federal statehood. Under the FORAKER ACT, enacted by the U.S. Congress in 1900, an executive council was established as part of the Puerto Rican government under American rule. Barbosa held many posts on the executive council. He also founded the Partido Republicano in 1900; it evolved into the PARTIDO ESTADISTA REPUBLICANO.

Barcelo, Gertrudes (1800, Sonora, Mexico—1852, Santa Fe, N.Mex.): Entrepreneur. Barcelo was born into a privileged Mexican household. Her family moved to Valencia, New Mexico, in the early 1820's. When Barcelo was married in 1823, she refused to relinquish to her husband, as custom dictated, either her right to make contracts or the deeds to her property. Barcelo and her husband relocated to Santa Fe, New Mexico. In 1825, she began operating a gambling house in the Ortiz Mountains, where she acquired the nickname "La Tules." As her fame and fortune increased (she became involved with trade and investing as well), Barcelo became a favorite in official Mexican circles. By the early 1840's, she was rumored to be Governor Manuel ARMIJO's mistress; at the least, she was his friend and political adviser.

Barcelo sided with the Americans during the United States military occupation of New Mexico in 1846. She relayed information about a conspiracy to American authorities and loaned a substantial amount of money to the United States forces for supplies.

Barcelo's financial acumen and feminist consciousness made her popular. She is one of the Southwest's most colorful characters, as evidenced by the fact that she arranged for her own funeral to be one of the most expensive and flamboyant in Santa Fe's history.

Barela, Casimiro (Mar. 4, 1847, Embudo, N.Mex.—Dec., 1920, Colorado): Politician. Barela received his early education from Father Jean Baptiste Salpointe, who later became archbishop. In 1867, Barela's family moved to Las Animas County in southern Colorado, where they became involved in stock raising and merchandising. Barela began his public life two years later. Between 1869 and 1874, he served as justice of the peace, county assessor and sheriff, and territorial legislator.

Barela championed the causes of his Hispanic constituents after his election to the state constitutional convention in 1875. He helped secure both a provision in the state charter for protection of the civil rights of the Spanish-speaking population and publication of all laws in Spanish and English, although that provision was limited to twenty-five years. A strong Democratic leader, Barela was elected to the first state senate in 1876. He served without a break for forty years, even though he switched to the Republican Party in 1900, and became known as Colorado's perpetual senator. He was twice elected president of the state senate. Barela was also elected and appointed to several national, state, and local offices. Barela retired from public life in 1916 after being defeated in an election for the state senate. He tended to his properties and cattle-raising operations until his death.

Barela, Patrocinio (1908, Bisbee, Ariz.—Oct. 24, 1964, Canon de Fernández, Mexico): Wood carver and sculptor. As a maker of sculptures and wood reliefs with religious themes, Barela helped sustain the Hispanic tradition of embracing religious objects—and the spiritual dimensions they represent—in daily life.

The descendant of early Spanish Americans, Barela never attended school. At a young age, he began tending goats, working in coal mines, hauling dirt, and doing other odd jobs. From 1936 to 1943, he was employed in the Federal Art Project of the United States government's Works Progress Administration.

His entry into the world of woodcarving began in the early 1930's when a priest asked Barela to repair a broken wooden figure of a saint. Soon after that, Barela was fashioning his own figures out of single pieces of cedar or pine that he found in local forests and woodpiles.

The subjects of Barela's works are saints, angels, madonnas, shepherds, animals, family groups, and figures of death. Sometimes sanded to smoothness and often rough hewn, the figures are stylized and primitive looking, and they range in size from a few inches to a few feet.

Barela's carvings abound in galleries and homes in New Mexico, and examples of his work can be found in museums from New York to California. His *Saint George* is in the National Museum of American Art in Washington, D.C.

Barraza, Santa (b. Apr. 7, 1951, Kingsville, Tex.): Artist. A descendant of Mexicans, Karankawa Indians, and Spanish colonials, Barraza has helped promote Latino culture by founding and advancing Chicano arts organizations, teaching in colleges and universities, and producing her own ethnic form of art.

Barraza earned bachelor's and master's degrees in fine art from the University of Texas at Austin. In 1976, she helped found Mujeres Artistas del Suroeste, one of the first nonprofit organizations aimed at promoting Chicana and Latina visual artists. In 1981, she opened Diseño Studio, the first Chicano art gallery in Austin, Texas. To cultivate stronger ties between Chicano and Mexican artists, she also helped organize the Conferencia Plastica Chicana, an international confer-ence held in 1979. In the 1980's, she began teaching in Pennsylvania schools, and by 1988, she had become an assistant professor at Pennsylvania State University.

Barraza's art blends symbols from her cultural heritage with Catholic imagery. Her mixed-media *retablos*, which have been exhibited in Mexico, Italy, England, Japan, and the United States, are modern versions of a sacred art form. Barraza paints brightly colored images of virgins, folk healers, Mexican revolutionary figures, and mythically powerful plants on sheets of galvanized steel.

Barrera, Lazaro Sosa (May 8, 1924, Marianao section of Cuba—Apr. 25, 1991, Downey, Calif.): Horse trainer. Born near the Oriental Park racetrack in Cuba, Barrera grew up around the sport of horse racing and went on to become the top prize-money-winning trainer in horse-racing history. Already well known throughout Mexico and the Caribbean, Barrera moved to the United States and entered racing circles in New York and California in the 1960's.

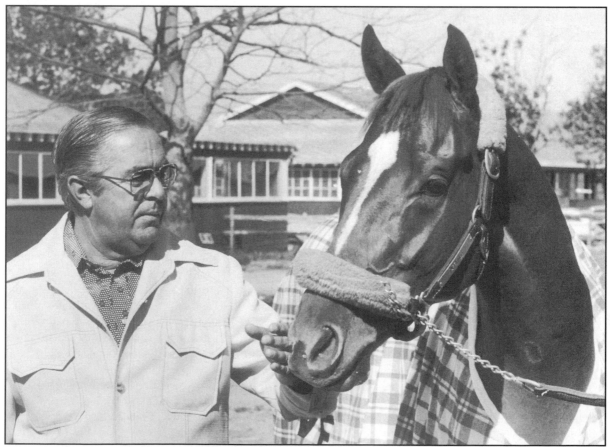

Lazaro Barrera with Affirmed, shortly before the horse won the Belmont Stakes to capture the Triple Crown. (AP/Wide World Photos)

In 1976, Rodriquez Tizol, a prominent thoroughbred owner from Puerto Rico, called on Barrera to train his spirited horse Bold Forbes. Taking this position moved Barrera to Harbor View Farm, one of the top stables in the United States. There, Barrera turned Bold Forbes, a horse with great natural speed but poor endurance, into a champion by running it through a series of long, slow gallops that gradually increased in tempo. Coached by Barrera and ridden by jockey Ángel CORDERO, Jr., Bold Forbes won the Kentucky Derby and the Belmont Stakes in 1976. Barrera gained even more prestige with Affirmed, the 1978 Triple Crown winner. The training of these two horses was considered among the best in racing history. The only trainer to win four Eclipse Awards as racing's outstanding trainer, Barrera was elected to the Racing Hall of Fame in 1979.

Barrera, Mario (b. Nov. 8, 1939, Mission, Tex.): Educator. Barrera is a scholar in ethnic studies. Among his publications is *Race and Class in the Southwest: A Theory of Racial Inequality* (1979). He earned his B.A. in geology at the University of Texas at Austin in 1961. His M.A. (1964) and Ph.D. (1970), both in political science, are from the University of California, Berkeley. Barrera worked as an associate professor at the University of California, La Jolla, from 1971 to 1976. In 1977, he joined the faculty of the University of California, Berkeley, teaching ethnic studies.

Barretto, Ray (b. Apr. 29, 1929, Brooklyn, N.Y.): Drummer, songwriter, and bandleader. While he was in the United States Army, stationed in West Germany, Barretto began playing the conga drums. After his tour of duty, he returned to New York City and frequently jammed with jazz musicians. Barretto decided to become a professional musician and joined Eddie Bonnemere's Latin Jazz Combo. During the 1950's, he also played with José Curbelo's and Tito PUENTE's bands. Having replaced the legendary Ramón "Mongo"

Ray Barretto. (Hazel Hankin)

SANTAMARÍA in Puente's band, Barretto remained with that influential group for four years. He did not limit himself to playing with jazz musicians; he also did session work on a number of rhythm and blues singles.

In the early 1960's, Barretto was asked by the jazz record company Riverside to make a Latin jazz album. With Barretto as bandleader, the album *Pachanga with Barretto* was recorded. Although the album was not a huge success, Barretto was inspired to form his own group, Charanga Moderna. Barretto was influential in introducing Latin rhythms to jazz music. Always willing to experiment and break through musical barriers, he added his special sound to such diverse musicians and groups as Freddie Hubbard, George Benson, the Rolling Stones, and the Average White Band. Through it all, Barretto remained true to his Latin roots. In the mid-1970's, *Latin NY* voted him best conga player on several occasions, once voting him musician of the year. Barretto is considered to be one of the most influential Latin drummers of all time.

Barrio, Raymond (b. Aug. 27, 1921, West Orange, N.J.): Writer and artist. An art instructor by profession, Barrio garnered critical and popular recognition for his first work of fiction, *The Plum Plum Pickers* (1969). Written during the height of the farmworkers movement, the drive to unionize California migrant farm laborers led by César CHÁVEZ, *The Plum Plum Pickers* became the favorite book of the movement and an underground hit.

At first, no major publishing house took interest in *The Plum Plum Pickers*, so Barrio published the book himself. The book sold extremely well in its initial printing. After being optioned by a major publishing house and widely anthologized, sales improved. Barrio's proletarian novel, depicting the demoralizing social and working conditions under which farm laborers live, is praised for its realism and for its language. Barrio skillfully used interior monologues, dialogues, and broadcasts to further the narrative.

Barrio founded Ventura Press, his own publishing house. He most often writes essays on art and culture. His other works, many self-illustrated, include *Art: Seen* (1968), *The Prism* (1968), *Mexico's Art and Chicano Artists* (1975), *A Political Portfolio* (1985), and the novel *Carib Blue* (1990).

Barrioization in California: The foothold that Mexicans had in California was lost in the mid-1800's as California became a state and as Los Angeles specifi-

cally was exploited as a new frontier for Anglo settlers and entrepreneurs. Californios, the Mexican people who had been living in the area, were systematically pushed to the east side of the Los Angeles River and into increasingly poor living conditions in an area that became known as the BARRIO. Stereotypes of the neighborhood soon gave the word "barrio" a negative connotation. The Los Angeles barrio was one of many created in cities of the Southwest and, to a lesser extent, across the United States.

Prior to 1848, a small population of Indians, Spaniards, and mestizos mixed fairly peacefully in California. After California officially became a state in 1850, it experienced a boom. Gold was discovered in the northern half of the state, attracting 100,000 Anglos. Many of them soon landed in Southern California. This effectively transformed the region's cultural and political situation.

A high percentage of Easterners who moved west of the Rockies eventually settled in the Los Angeles area. Cultural tensions sprung up immediately, and hostilities between 1850 and 1856 drove many Mexicans away from Los Angeles. Once the majority population, the remaining Mexican residents were pushed away from the city center to less desirable places, including the area east of the Los Angeles River. This area was not modernized or developed with the rest of the city, and Mexicans were excluded from the economic success experienced by the rest of Los Angeles.

By 1880, less than 10 percent of the Mexican population of Los Angeles had been there for more than one generation. Living conditions worsened with the demise of the traditional ranchero system. Few of the Latinos living near Los Angeles owned property, and the situation was little different elsewhere in the state. The Los Angeles barrio acted as an adobe enclave, a city within itself surrounded by Anglo American wood-framed suburbs.

Large numbers of Mexicans arrived in Los Angeles after 1910, escaping the violence of the Mexican Revolution. This made the already congested living conditions worse. The barrio was further hurt by newspapers in the post-World War II years. News accounts described the barrio as being infested by drugs, gangs, and crime. Public opinion of the Mexican American community remained unfavorable, and cases of police brutality rose. Barrio residents were hindered in their attempts to improve conditions by their lack of economic and political power. During the 1950's, only about one-fourth were registered to vote, and that proportion rose slowly during ensuing decades.

This home near a factory in East Los Angeles represents the barrio of the 1990's (David Bacon)

Barrios and barrio life: Barrios are densely populated neighborhoods with a predominantly Latino population. Barrios are associated, on one hand, with Latino cultural identity, family, and pride, and, on the other hand, with poverty, crime, substandard housing, and other social problems.

Barrio Characteristics. Barrios are generally poor urban neighborhoods within the confines or influence of a larger metropolitan area. Well-known examples are EAST LOS ANGELES (Mexican America) and East Harlem (Puerto Rican) in New York City. Latinos have tended to congregate in certain neighborhoods, like the European immigrants before them. Many had no choice but to live in barrios because of housing DISCRIMINATION and high rents in other areas. In the barrios, Latinos have historically been segregated from the rest of society in an insulated, isolated social environment.

The barrios provided a labor pool for employers, affordable housing for the poor and elderly, and a new beginning for new immigrants. Many immigrants faced unfamiliar legal, economic, and educational systems as well as social customs that relegated newcomers to the status of second-class citizens. The barrio,

with its familiar language, culture, and businesses, was a place to find work and housing as well as being a haven of cultural acceptance. Once barrio dwellers improved their status through education, vocational skills, or government aid, such as bills to help veterans purchase homes, they often moved out of the barrio to less dense urban or suburban areas.

Some aspects of the barrio give it the flavor of a close-knit small town or village in Latin America. Spanish is the language most commonly seen and heard on the streets, whether in San Jose, California; San Antonio, Texas; or Miami, Florida. Neighborhood businesses, usually small, cater to the needs of Latino residents, from groceries, check cashing, and immigration assistance to medicinal herbs, baptism outfits, and airplane tickets home. Catholic churches hold services in Spanish, as do storefront Protestant evangelical congregations. Social or athletic clubs often attract members from the same hometown in Mexico or Puerto Rico. Young Chicanos work on their cars and cruise the streets in low riding (*see* LOW RIDERS AND LOW RIDING), or otherwise altered, vehicles. Some barrios have cultural centers that promote the arts among Latino youth. Another sign of cultural vitality in many

Community members of this South Bronx barrio made special efforts to improve their environment. (Hazel Hankin)

barrios is the presence of MURALS, often depicting Mexican American or Puerto Rican heroes and heritage. This picture of positive community life is marred by signs of trouble, such as the GRAFFITI of rival GANGS.

Socioeconomic Conditions. Poor socioeconomic conditions have been entrenched in barrios for generations. With high birth rates and high rates of continuing immigration, more Latinos have been competing for fewer resources in the barrios since the 1970's. Housing tends to be older and more dilapidated than in other parts of the city, and to be managed by negligent absentee landlords. Schools have become increasingly segregated and overcrowded. There are rising numbers of female-headed households, especially among Puerto Ricans in the New York area.

Barrio crime worsened in the last three decades of the twentieth century. Petty crime and turf wars among gang members had always been commonplace, along with heroin use in the larger urban barrios. In the 1970's and 1980's, however, both street drugs (such as crack cocaine) and firearms became more widely available. Only a small percentage of barrio residents become gang members, drug addicts, or violent crimi-

nals, but the threat of crime pervades barrio life. Latinos are more likely than non-Latinos to be the victims of violent and household crime, according to a government study conducted in 1990.

Numerous barrios have been obliterated for industrial, commercial, or other forms of urban renewal and expansion in the twentieth century. Often barrios were cut in half by the building of highways, separating families and neighbors from one another and from their churches and stores as well as damaging the economic infrastructure. Barrio residents were usually no match for the combined forces of city boosters, municipal and federal governments, and corporations that intended to develop the land barrio residents called home. Although new construction created some new jobs, brought new money into the barrios, and may have made the barrios safer, many families were displaced. They often rented space from absentee owners and knew nothing about property transactions that affected them until eviction notices arrived.

Ties to the Barrio. Since the rise of the CHICANO MOVEMENT in the 1960's, many Latinos have chosen to stay in the barrio or revisit them frequently to help residents, especially youth, succeed. They have also expressed concern for women, prisoners, gang members, and the unemployed in the barrio. Chicano university faculty and students have tutored schoolchildren, staffed nonprofit community organizations, registered voters, promoted barrio arts, and worked toward finding solutions to socioeconomic problems. Some, such as Los Angeles County Supervisor Gloria MOLINA, have successfully run for office to protect the interests of Latinos in the barrio. The UNITED NEIGHBORHOODS ORGANIZATION (UNO) and other groups have been models for community empowerment.

In spite of their problems, the barrios have been and are the home of millions of Latinos. They are places where families relax and celebrate with favorite foods, drinks, and music, with fiestas and rituals interwoven into daily life. Chicano poet Abelardo "Lalo" Delgado explored the barrio in his poetry and has described the barrio as the life blood of CHICANISMO. Other writers have celebrated the barrio in autobiographical works, as Ernesto GALARZA did in *Barrio Boy* (1971).

—*Santos C. Vega*

SUGGESTED READINGS: • Blea, Irene I. *Bessemer: A Sociological Perspective of the Chicano Barrio*. New York: AMS Press, 1991. • Galarza, Ernesto. *Barrio Boy*. Notre Dame, Ind.: University of Notre Dame Press, 1971. • Gann, L. H., and Peter J. Duignan. *The Hispanics in the United States*. Boulder, Colo.: Westview Press, 1986. • Glazer, Nathan, and Daniel P. Moynihan. *Beyond the Melting Pot*. Cambridge, Mass.: MIT Press, 1963. • López, Arcadia H. *Barrio Teacher*. Houston, Tex.: Arte Público Press, 1992. • McWilliams, Carey. *North from Mexico: The Spanish-Speaking People of the United States*. Philadelphia, Pa.: J. B. Lippincott, 1949.

Baseball: *El béisbol* is a critical part of everyday life for many Latinos. In the Caribbean and in parts of Mexico, Central America, and South America, baseball is the principal sport and a continuing source of fascination. Latin American fans root for town teams, district teams, company teams, and national teams as well as for Latinos who play in the U.S. major and minor leagues.

Children throughout Latin America learn to enjoy baseball and organize their own informal games. (James Shaffer)

Latin American baseball is not merely an extension of the U.S. game; it has taken on a distinct character of its own. The culture of baseball has permeated every aspect of Latino life, both in the United States and in Latin America. The game is a frequent theme of music and radio, and it is reported in both the English and Spanish languages.

The Roots of Latin Baseball. Writers frequently comment on the presence of Latin American ballplayers in the United States in terms of an "influx," almost as if baseball were a uniquely U.S. sport being invaded by outsiders. In fact, Latin American baseball has a history nearly as lengthy as that of its northern counterpart. The first Latino to play modern major league baseball was Louis "Jud" Castro, an infielder from Colombia who played in forty-two games for the Philadelphia Athletics in 1902, the inaugural season of the American League.

Latin baseball in the early years was in some ways ahead of the U.S. sport, most notably in the relative racial tolerance that prevailed on Latin American fields. Decades before Jackie Robinson broke the major league color line in 1947, white players and black players were competing as equals in Mexico and throughout the Caribbean. For many years, Latin baseball gave African American players opportunities that they did not have in the United States, and many of the stars of the U.S. Negro Leagues also played in Latin America. Many white professionals from the United States also played Latin ball in the off-season; in a sense, therefore, baseball's color line was first crossed in Latin America.

Cuban Baseball. The saga of Latin baseball must begin in Cuba and the Caribbean, where *el béisbol* is as common as rum and palm trees. The early history of Cuban ball is murky, but the game in Cuba dates back at least to 1866, when a ship from the United States docked in Matanzas and the ship's crew invited the Cuban cargo handlers to join in a game. By 1878, when the Liga de Béisbol Profesional Cubana was founded, the game was firmly rooted in Cuban soil. Thirteen years later, there were seventy-five teams on the island; all these events antedate the Spanish-American War of 1898, when U.S. forces invaded Cuba.

The roots of Cuban baseball are tied to the efforts of three men, Nemesio Guillot, Esteban "Steve" Bellán, and Emilio Sabourín. Guillot popularized the sport in Cuba after he returned to the island from the United States, where he had learned the game while a student in the 1860's. Bellán, who played in the first profes-

sional league, the National Association, from 1871 to 1873, became the first Latino in organized U.S. ball. Sabourín, who fought for Cuba's independence from Spain, helped to found the island's first professional league; he used his baseball income to help fund the independence movement, incurring the hostility of the Spanish colonial government.

At the beginning of the twentieth century, visiting U.S. teams began to play off-season exhibition games on the island. The Cincinnati Reds, Detroit Tigers, and New York Giants were among the first major league teams to play against Cuban teams. U.S. professionals often competed against teams from Havana, Mariano, Almendares, and Cienfuegos.

Perhaps the most famous player of the early Cuban period was Martin DIHIGO, a gifted pitcher and hitter who starred in both Latin America and in the Negro Leagues from the 1920's into the 1940's. Other top Cuban players included José MENDEZ, a brilliant pitcher who often defeated visiting U.S. teams, Alejandro Oms, a star outfielder, and Luis TIANT, Sr., a pitcher whose son Luis, Jr., became a major league star of the 1960's and 1970's. Like many other top Latino players of the early century, Mendez, Oms, and Tiant also had successful careers in the Negro Leagues for such teams as the Cuban Stars and the New York Cubans.

Although dark-skinned Cubans were not allowed to play in the major leagues, lighter-skinned players such as Adolfo "Dolf" LUQUE were able to forge successful major league careers. Luque, nicknamed "The Pride of Havana," pitched for four major league teams from 1914 through 1935, winning 193 games and leading the National League with 27 victories in 1923.

During World War II, when talent was scarce in the United States, many Cuban players were signed by major league teams, most notably the Washington Senators. Such recruiting, though, was largely informal, based on scouting reports of winter league play. After the war, a more formal talent pipeline was laid when the Havana Cubans began play as a Washington affiliate in the Florida International League, a Class B minor league. In 1954, the Havana franchise was renamed the Sugar Kings and promoted to the International League, a top-level minor league. Cuba's standing as the leading Latin baseball power was further evidenced by the results of the Caribbean World Series, a tournament for the champions of the Latin American leagues. From 1949 to 1960, Cuban teams won seven of twelve titles.

The Cuban Revolution of 1959 changed the character of baseball on the island. Links with the U.S. pro-

Dolf Luque pitched for the New York Giants in 1933. (AP/Wide World Photos)

fessional leagues were severed, and top players were no longer permitted to seek fame and wealth abroad. Instead, prompted by the urgings of Fidel Castro, a dedicated fan and former amateur pitcher, Cuba became the world's leading amateur baseball power. Cuban teams have since achieved consistent success at every level of international amateur play, including the Pan American Games, the Goodwill Games, and the World Series of Amateur Baseball. In 1992, Cuba took the gold medal in baseball at the Barcelona Olympics.

The revolution, however, put a virtual stop to the flow of Cuban talent to the big leagues. From the 1950's through the 1970's, such talented Cubans as Orestes "Minnie" MINOSO, Luis Tiant, Jr., Tony OLIVA, Bert CAMPANERIS, Mike Cuellar, and Tony PEREZ were among the major leagues' leading stars; all, however, had left Cuba before Castro clamped down on emigration. Subsequent major leaguers of Cuban ancestry, such as José CANSECO and Rafael Palmeiro, were reared in the United States. After the 1991 season, however, René Arocha, a star of the Cuban national team, defected to the United States and became a starting pitcher for the St. Louis Cardinals.

Baseball in Mexico. The origins of Mexican baseball also are cloudy. Some historians believe that the game was brought to Mexico by railroad workers from the southwestern United States in the 1880's. Semi-professional leagues have existed in Mexico since the 1920's. Baseball has been especially popular in northern Mexico, the Pacific coastal regions, and the Yucatán-Caribbean area. Professional leagues operate year-round, and the winter league champion participates in the Caribbean World Series.

In the 1940's, the Pasquel family, the owners of the Veracruz franchise in the Mexican League, began a celebrated effort to recruit U.S. players for Mexican clubs. At first, the Pasquels made overtures only to Negro Leagues stars and to Latin Americans with U.S. experience. Many players accepted the relatively high salaries the Mexican League offered. In 1946, however, the Pasquels began offering large sums to white major leaguers to induce them to abandon the U.S. leagues for Mexico. Such stars as Mickey Owen, Sal Maglie, and Vern Stephens accepted, prompting outraged major league club owners to threaten defectors with five-year suspensions. Most quickly returned to their former teams, and the Mexican League, which had experienced large financial losses, was forced to reduce the scale of its operations. In 1955, the league became part of the U.S. minor league system.

The first Mexican to play major league ball was Baldomero Melo "Mel" Almada, an outfielder who made his debut with the Boston Red Sox in 1933. By far the most famous of the many Mexican major leaguers is Fernando VALENZUELA, a lefthanded pitcher who in 1981 won the National League Rookie of the Year and Cy Young Awards and led the Los Angeles Dodgers to a World Series title. Also notable among Mexican professionals is Hector Espino, a star slugger of the 1960's and 1970's who refused repeated offers from major league teams in order to remain in Mexico.

Baseball in Puerto Rico. Baseball was introduced into Puerto Rico from Cuba in the 1890's. After the occupation of the island by U.S. troops in 1898, the game spread rapidly, and professional leagues sprang up shortly after the turn of the century. The major cities of the island, such as Bayamón, Arecibo, Ponce, Santurce, Caguas, and San Juan, have amateur and professional teams. The Federación de Béisbol Aficionado de Puerto Rico is the leading amateur organization, and the Asociación de Peloteros Profesionales de Puerto Rico organizes the island's professionals.

Roberto CLEMENTE, a Puerto Rican who starred for the Pittsburgh Pirates from 1955 to 1972, became the first Latino to be inducted into the U.S. National Baseball Hall of Fame. A four-time batting champion and a superb outfielder, Clemente was named the National League's most valuable player in 1966. His death in a 1972 plane crash occasioned mourning throughout the Caribbean; in Puerto Rico, he is regarded as a national hero. Other notable Puerto Rican major leaguers include Orlando CEPEDA, a leading National League slugger of the 1960's; José Cruz, a versatile outfielder of the 1970's and 1980's; and 1990's stars Roberto ALOMAR, Carlos Baerga, Juan GONZÁLEZ, and Rubén SIERRA.

Baseball in the Dominican Republic. Baseball was brought to the Dominican Republic from Cuba in the 1890's. The island's first professional teams, Licey and Nuevo Club, played each other in 1907. Between 1911 and 1920, amateur teams also sprang up across the island, in small towns as well as in the capital, Santo Domingo.

The history of Dominican baseball is tied to economics and agriculture, especially to the growing of bananas and sugarcane. Company teams were organized in the banana-growing regions of the island and in many Dominican sugarcane mill towns. Dominican professional teams are organized by the Federación Nacional de Peloteros Profesionales. The finalists from the winter league play go on to the Caribbean

Roberto Clemente. (AP/Wide World Photos)

Juan Marichal pitches a shutout victory in 1965. (AP/Wide World Photos)

series, which Dominican teams have won many times. Amateur ball on the island is played mostly in the provinces and small towns.

In the 1930's, Dominican dictator Rafael Trujillo combined two of the island's strongest teams, Licey and Escogido, into a single franchise to play for Santo Domingo, which he had rechristened Ciudad Trujillo. He also recruited top foreign players, including DIHIGO and Negro Leagues stars Satchel Paige, Josh Gibson, and Cool Papa Bell, to play for his personal team. Other foreign players were paid high salaries to bolster the competition. As a result, Dominican baseball of the late 1930's was among the world's best. Before long, however, Trujillo's heavyhanded tactics—his soldiers reportedly threatened his players after losses—and generally repressive regime caused the imported stars to flee the country.

Dominican baseball experienced another renaissance in the mid-1950's, when the country's professional league switched from summer to winter play. U.S. pro-

fessionals began to play off-season ball on the island, and Trujillo, who had previously embargoed local talent, began allowing top Dominican players to compete in the U.S. in the summer months. Dominicans including Juan MARICHAL, an outstanding pitcher, Manny MOTA, a skilled pinch hitter, and Felipe, Matty, and Jesus ALOU, brothers who at one time played together in the San Francisco Giants' outfield, soon became major league stars.

After Trujillo's assassination in 1961, the flow of Dominican talent to the majors increased. Such stars as Rico CARTY, César CEDEÑO, Pedro GUERRERO, Mario Soto, Joaquín ANDUJAR, George BELL, Tony FERNANDEZ, Juan Samuel, Tony PEÑA, and Julio FRANCO have been among the dozens of Dominicans to play major league ball in recent decades. In particular, San Pedro de Macorís, a city of less than one hundred thousand residents, has produced a remarkable number of big-league stars. The development of such talent has been stimulated by the founding of Dominican baseball

Lefty Gomez as he pitches the opening game of the 1937 World Series. (AP/Wide World Photos)

academies by major league teams, notably the Los Angeles Dodgers and Toronto Blue Jays.

Other Latin American Baseball. Baseball has been played in Venezuela, Panama, and Nicaragua since the turn of the century. Each of these countries has its own professional leagues, and each has sent distinguished players to the majors. Venezuela has been especially noted for producing outstanding shortstops, among them Alfonso "Chico" Carrasquel, Luis APARICIO, Jr., Dave CONCEPCIÓN, Ozzie Guillén, and Omar Vizquel. Other star players from Venezuela have included outfielder Tony Armas, catcher Bo Díaz, and pitcher Wilson Alvarez. Top Panamanian major leaguers have included Ben OGILVIE, a slugging outfielder of the 1970's and 1980's; Manny Sanguillen, a top catcher of the 1970's; and Rod CAREW, an infielder who won seven American League batting titles from 1969 to 1978. Nicaragua's most famous baseball expatriate is Dennis MARTINEZ, who left his war-torn country to star for the Baltimore Orioles in the 1970's and who in 1991 became only the twelfth player in major league history to pitch a perfect game.

U.S.-born Latino stars have included Vernon "Lefty" GOMEZ, a leading pitcher of the 1930's and 1940's; Keith HERNANDEZ, a batting champion and perennial Gold Glove first baseman of the 1970's and 1980's; Edgar Martinez, the 1992 American League batting champion; and Robin Ventura, a top third baseman of the 1990's.   —*Rafael Chabrán*

SUGGESTED READINGS:

- Kanellos, Nicolás. "Baseball." In *The Hispanic-American Almanac.* Detroit: Gale Research, 1993. A short but useful article on Latinos and baseball from a Latino perspective. Contains good information on Latinos in both the Negro and Cuban leagues.
- Klein, Alan M. *Sugarball: The American Game, the Dominican Dream.* New Haven, Conn.: Yale University Press, 1991. Outlines the history of baseball in the Dominican Republic. An anthropological treatment that includes socioeconomic and political information on the development of the sport on the island.
- Krich, John. *El Béisbol: Travels Through the Pan-American Pastime.* New York: Atlantic Monthly Press, 1989. Examines baseball culture in Mexico, Puerto Rico, the Dominican Republic, Nicaragua, and Venezuela. A mix of travel literature and journalism offering more commentary than history.
- Minoso, Orestes, with Herb Fegan. *Just Call Me Minnie: My Six Decades in Baseball.* Champaign, Ill.: Sagamore, 1994. An autobiographical look at a top Latino player's life in baseball. Minoso narrates sixty

years of baseball, from his early career in the Cuban Leagues to his later years in the majors.

- Oleksak, Michael M., and Mary Adams Oleksak. *Béisbol: Latin Americans and the Grand Old Game.* Grand Rapids, Mich.: Masters Press, 1991. Surveys the importance of baseball in several Latin American countries (Cuba, Mexico, the Dominican Republic, and Puerto Rico) by tracing the history of professional and amateur leagues and players, as well as contacts with U.S. teams. The single most useful book on the topic.
- Ruck, Rob. "Baseball in the Caribbean." In *Total Baseball*, edited by John Thorn, Pete Palmer, and David Reuther. New York: Warner Books, 1989. Although brief, this is one of the best sources for the history of Latinos in baseball. Focuses on Caribbean ball from a historical perspective.

Battered women: Women who are abused emotionally, psychologically, physically, or sexually by their husbands or partners. The battering of women by their male partners or husbands has been recognized since ancient times. Greek and Roman laws included provisions for a man to use physical punishment of his wife if she engaged in "inappropriate behavior" such as adultery or even drinking wine.

Societal acceptance of wife battering is not limited to ancient times. Anthropologists have found that wife beating is common in many societies throughout the world. Wife abuse occurs more often in societies in which cruelty and aggression are common and in cultures in which the status of women is lower than that of men. There may be as many as two million women battered in the United States each year. Statistics compiled by the Federal Bureau of Investigation for the early 1990's indicate that about 25 percent of all murders in the United States happen within the family. About 28 percent of all families in the United States have experienced marital violence, with the female partner overwhelmingly the victim.

Wife battering is a profound and complex social problem. Although unemployed and lower-income men are reported as wife abusers more frequently than are higher-income men, spouse abuse happens at all levels of American society and in every ethnic and racial group. There appear to be no clear and effective explanations for and solutions to this problem. Social factors such as a general acceptance of violence, devaluation of women, and acceptance of men's right to dominate women may contribute to the occurrence of wife battering. Children who have seen their father abuse their mother, for example, may use this model of conflict resolution in their own adult relationships. Unequal power distribution between men and women within a partnership may also contribute to the likelihood of wife battering. If marriage is seen as a hierarchical relationship in which dominance of one (the male) partner over another (the female) is sanctioned by society, men may see it as more appropriate to settle disputes using verbal, physical, or sexual force against their wives. At the same time, women may believe that they have no recourse other than to accept the abusive situation. In addition, life stressors such as poverty, lack of education, unemployment, illness, and citizenship status may contribute to the incidence of abuse. All these stressors are more common among Latinos than among the American population as a whole.

Latino culture has a traditional family structure in which gender and marital roles are clearly and rigidly defined. The MACHISMO ideals held by some segments of the Latino population decree that a man must be the dominant authority figure in a family, the key decision maker, and the protector and provider. Many Latinas have to work outside the home to help support their families. In this situation, a Latino man may see his traditional role being threatened, as he is no longer the sole provider for his family. He may abuse his wife in an attempt to reassert his masculine role.

For some Latino subgroups, machismo ideas also condone and even encourage a man's heavy drinking. Alcohol abuse on the part of men is another factor closely associated with wife battering and is a strong contributing factor in the incidence of abuse in Latino households. Although the mechanisms surrounding wife battering are not always apparent, it is clear that some traditional beliefs and values in the Latino culture, coupled with specific social factors, provide an environment in which domestic violence is more likely to take place.

Bay of Pigs invasion (Apr. 17, 1961): The successful Cuban Revolution under the leadership of Fidel CAS-TRO eventually led to the Bay of Pigs invasion, an

Castro's military forced the U.S. withdrawal from the Bay of Pigs. (AP/Wide World Photos)

ill-fated attempt by the Central Intelligence Agency (CIA) to overthrow the new regime.

During 1960, conversations with Castro led Vice President Richard Nixon to conclude that Castro would not have free elections or fair trials in Cuba: Cuba's new leader claimed that the Cuban people did not want them. Nixon was also disturbed by Castro's pro-Communist posture. Moreover, President Dwight D. Eisenhower was concerned about the close ties Castro had developed with Nikita Khrushchev and the Soviet Union.

After the 1960 presidential election and Nixon's close defeat, president-elect John F. Kennedy was persuaded that planned actions against Castro should be carried out, something that he later regretted. Originally, the strategy was to conduct a modest guerilla action, using mostly anti-Castro Cubans. The concept developed into an all-out paramilitary action, planned by the CIA, using some Americans who attempted to disguise their nationality. The involvement of American pilots was not discovered by President Kennedy until two years after the invasion, when it was announced by Senator Everett Dirksen that four American fliers had died in the Bay of Pigs battle.

The invasion force consisted of a navy, including a five-vessel merchant fleet; a paratrooper unit; Brigade 1506, consisting of about fourteen hundred Cuban exiles; and various air units. The defense against the invasion was orchestrated by Castro himself. Castro's defenses included a number of C-33 aircraft and several Russian-made tanks.

One of the major battles at the Bay of Pigs (Bahía de Cochinos) was fought on the northern outskirts of Playa Larga. The battle pitted the invading Cuban exiles against Castro's forces. Although the Cuban exiles scored an impressive victory at the rotunda of Playa Larga, they knew it was only temporary because they were out of ammunition, hungry, and exhausted.

Badly outnumbered, the invading Cuban exiles were bombarded by Castro's air force, tanks, and artillery. The hoped-for overthrow of Castro never materialized. After withdrawal of the invasion forces and victory at the Bay of Pigs, Castro spoke on television for almost four hours. He claimed that the Cuban planes that were bombed at Campo Libertad were merely dummy targets. He chided the CIA for misjudging the resolve of his military units and even pointed out basic military errors in the invasion strategy.

During the invasion, 1,189 members of Brigade 2506 were captured, and about 110 died; approximately 150 did not land for various reasons. Eventu-ally, the United States was able to exchange the prisoners for $53 million worth of food and drugs.

President Kennedy regretted his decision to allow the CIA to carry out the Bay of Pigs invasion. He lamented the loss of life and deplored his decision to let it happen.

Bayfest (Corpus Christi, Tex.): Annual festival held the last weekend in September. Bayfest, sponsored by Bayfest, Inc., is one of the largest international festivals held in the United States. Begun in 1976 and styled as a family festival, it features music, folk dancing, games, foods, arts, and crafts. It is held in a seaside six-block area of North Shoreline Boulevard. The area is closed to private vehicles. The waterside site allows raft races, a comic anything-that-floats-but-a-boat race, fireworks over the bay, and Coast Guard sea-air rescue demonstrations.

Although Bayfest is not exclusively Hispanic, more than half of the festival's performers are Mexican American, and Mexican and Tejano folk culture is prevalent. Bayfest draws more than 350,000 visitors annually.

Beans: Native American foodstuff. Beans are a mainstay of folk cooking throughout Latin America. Mexican Indians were eating beans before 5000 B.C.E., and beans remained an important foodstuff through Aztec times, when four species were grown and used. Today, common beans in their great variety dominate bean usage in Latin America, though lima beans are used to a lesser extent. Garbanzos, an Old World food, are not true beans. Beans are especially critical to the diet of the poor because they are a good source of protein and key amino acids. They are eaten many ways, including boiled and mashed, admixed with rice and seasonings, added to soups and stews, and made into fritters. Most beans are dried before use in Latin America.

Bear Flag Revolt (1846): The Bear Flag Revolt of 1846 marked the beginning of military efforts to wrest California from Mexican rule and align it with the United States instead.

In 1846, American settlers in northern California were anxious over unfounded rumors that the Mexican government was instigating Indian uprisings. Rumors also predicted the settlers' imminent expulsion from California.

In early June, a Mexican force transporting a large number of horses to General José Castro stopped overnight at Sutter's Fort. Castro apparently was outfitting

A performer at Bayfest. (Cheryl Richter)

himself for civil war with Pío Pico (*see* PICO FAMILY), his political rival in Los Angeles; however, local settlers mistook his intentions and hastily raised a ragtag band of about one dozen men. Led by Ezekiel Merritt, they set out to protect their interests by following and capturing the troops and confiscating their horses. The Mexican soldiers were set free and instructed to warn Castro that American settlers were ready to fight to protect their lands.

The insurrectionists—a mix of homesteaders and adventure seekers—then went to Sonoma, a small former military garrison and home of the wealthy General Mariano G. Vallejo. No soldiers were stationed at the pueblo, but it still held a few arms. At dawn, the settlers took over the garrison and took Vallejo prisoner. They confiscated nine old cannons and a large quantity of Vallejo's liquor, which they immediately began consuming. Even though Vallejo supported the peaceful annexation of California by the United States, he was taken to Sutter's Fort and imprisoned.

One settler at Sonoma, William B. Ide, wrote a long, rambling proclamation spelling out grievances, calling for the overthrow of Mexican rule, declaring California a republic, and pledging the new republic to the protection of all of its peaceful citizens. The men sewed a flag sporting a red star, a grizzly bear, and the words "California Republic." They thus came to be know as "Bear Flaggers," or simply Bears.

Meanwhile, insurrectionists began occupying Sutter's Fort, the civilian fortification of John Augustus Sutter. Sutter, who had carefully maintained neutrality through years of disputes between the Mexicans and the settlers, was coerced into joining the rebels' cause.

The revolt might never have begun without the sympathy of U.S. Captain John C. Frémont, who was encamped nearby. Frémont seemed anxious to protect the settlers and willing to take military action if necessary, but had not yet committed his troops to the Bears' cause.

On June 24, Castro sent troops under the command of Captain Joaquin de la Torre to expel the settlers from Sonoma. The Bears—now about forty men—routed de la Torre's force. The next day, Frémont answered the settlers' appeals and led a company of his men in pursuit of the retreating Mexican forces.

When he returned, Frémont organized the Bear Flaggers into a battalion made up of settlers and men from his troops. Frémont made himself their commander, began rigorously drilling them, and declared that he would begin a conquest of California in the name of the United States. Because Frémont's actions predated official word of the Mexican American War in the territory, he resigned his military command to lead this unsanctioned revolution. Within days, word of the war arrived. The Bear Flaggers, now legitimately the California Battalion, became local heroes and went on to fight in the Mexican American War.

Becerra, Xavier (b. Jan. 26, 1958, Sacramento, Calif.): Legislator. Becerra completed his undergraduate studies in economics in 1980 at Stanford University and was awarded his J.D. from Stanford Law School four years later. Becerra's legal career began in a legal services office, representing the mentally ill. He worked with State Senator Art Torres before joining the California Department of Justice as a deputy attorney general.

In 1990, Becerra left Sacramento for Los Angeles and a successful race for the state assembly. Choosing to take advantage of new opportunities for higher office offered by federal redistricting, Becerra did not complete his first term in the California State Assembly. He won the right to represent California's Thirtieth Congressional District in a decisive victory in 1992. He quickly was appointed to committees on education and labor, judiciary and science, and space and technology.

Belizean Americans: Located on the Caribbean coast of Central America between Mexico and Guatemala, Belize has an area of 8,800 square miles and had a population estimated at 189,000 in 1992. Hispanics account for about 45 percent of the population and *CRIOLLOS* (mulattoes) for 40 percent.

Belize was part of the heartland of the classic Mayan civilization. Buccaneers used the country as a safe haven and a source of logwood after 1600. Civil wars in the Yucatán during the nineteenth century sent large numbers of Mayan Indians and MESTIZOS to Belize. Independence from Great Britain was granted in 1981.

Migration to North America increased after World War II because of poor economic conditions and greater ease of access to the United States and Canada. Two factors precipitated an even larger wave of Belizeans going to the United States beginning in the 1960's: the devastating hurricane of 1961 and a sense of disaffection among Creoles as the right to vote was extended during the pre-independence era.

U.S. census data combine Belizeans with "other Central Americans." Estimates in the 1990's range to

STATISTICAL PROFILE OF BELIZEAN AMERICANS, 1990

Total population based on sample: 21,205

Percentage foreign-born: 75%

Median age: 29 years

Percentage 25+ years old with at least a high school diploma or equivalent: 69%

Occupation (employed persons 16+ years old)

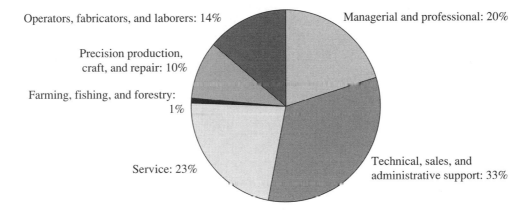

Operators, fabricators, and laborers: 14%

Precision production, craft, and repair: 10%

Farming, fishing, and forestry: 1%

Service: 23%

Managerial and professional: 20%

Technical, sales, and administrative support: 33%

Percentage unemployed: 11.3%

Median household income, 1989: $27,449

Percentage of families in poverty, 1989: 15%

Source: Data are from Bureau of the Census, *Census of 1990: Ancestry of the Population in the United States* (Washington, D.C.: Bureau of the Census, 1993), Tables 1, 3, 4, and 5. Figures for occupations are rounded to the nearest 1%.

more than 100,000 people of Belizean descent living in the United States, with the largest concentrations in Los Angeles, the New York City area, and the Chicago area. Each of these areas claimed about thirty thousand Belizeans. The Miami, New Orleans, Houston, and Detroit/Windsor, Ontario, communities were significantly smaller. At least three of Belize's ethnic groups were represented in these major population centers; Creoles, mestizos, and GARIFUNA (Black Caribs). In New York, the Belizean community appears to be settled primarily in Brooklyn, with few ethnic enclaves. In the Chicago area, ethnic patterns are more apparent. In Chicago proper, Creoles and Garifuna predominate, but the Evanston area is mixed Creole and HISPANIC.

Belizean Americans organize themselves into associations for three major reasons: to celebrate traditional holidays, to provide aid for Belize, and to explain themselves to their neighbors. In New York, Chicago, Los Angeles, Detroit, and Miami, organi-

zations sponsor festivities for St. George's Caye Day and Independence Day, on September 10 and 21, respectively. The Consortium for Belize Development works with American foundations and the government of Belize on economic aid projects. The Chicago-Belize Sporting Association raises money to support sports in Belize. Belizean Americans exhibit little interest in politics outside their community, although both Evanston, Illinois, and New York City have had aldermen from Belize.

The New York, Chicago, and Los Angeles communities have summer festivals to celebrate Belize. These fairs include Belizean traditional music, modern *soka* and *punta rock*, artists, food, and crafts. Los Angeles had about ten Belizean restaurants by the early 1990's as well as a Belizean radio program.

By the early 1990's, more than half of all Belizeans had either traveled to the United States or had an immediate relative living there. Consular officials in-

George Bell rounds third base after hitting a home run in his one thousandth game in the major leagues. (AP/Wide World Photos)

dicated that a considerable number who visit the United States do not return to Belize. Belizean Americans without a doubt figure among the undocumented residents of the United States.

Bell, George (Jorge Antonio Bell y Mathey; b. Oct. 21, 1959, San Pedro de Macoris, Dominican Republic): Baseball player. Signed in 1978 by the Philadelphia Phillies, Bell spent three seasons in the Philadelphia minor league system before he was acquired by the Toronto Blue Jays in 1980. He made his major league debut with Toronto in 1981 and established himself as a regular in 1984, when he hit twenty-six home runs and batted .292.

A powerful outfielder who hit right-handed, Bell had his best season with the Blue Jays in 1987. That year, he set team records for home runs (47), runs batted in (134), and slugging percentage (.605); led the American League in runs batted in; and was named the American League's Most Valuable Player. A two-time American League All-Star, Bell signed with the Chicago Cubs after the 1990 season and made the National League All-Star Team in 1991. Nevertheless, the Cubs traded Bell to the Chicago White Sox, for which he drove in 112 runs in 1992. After struggling with injuries for much of the 1993 season, Bell was released by the White Sox.

Beltrán, Lola (b. Sinaloa, Mexico): Singer. The daughter of a mine manager and a housewife, Beltrán grew up in northwestern Mexico amid a strong tradition of folk music. In 1953, while still a teenager, she went to Mexico City to seek her fortune. She begged her way into a rehearsal of the Mariachi Vargas group, the music of which she had known and admired for years on the radio, and pleaded for an opportunity to sing. She impressed the group and songwriter Tomás Mendez, and in a year she was on her way to becoming an international MARIACHI star.

Over the next four decades, Beltrán established herself as *La Reina* (the queen), touring throughout Latin America, the United States, and Europe and recording more than one hundred albums. Among her most popular songs are "Black Dove," "Bed of Stone," "Three Days," "To the Four Winds," and "If You Should Return." Beltrán combines her powerful voice and regal bearing with a passionate and sensitive delivery suited to the diverse songs and ballads of the mariachi genre. Once established as a singer, Beltrán went on to work in the Mexican cinema, where she has been featured in more than fifty film musicals.

Benavides, Santos (1823, Laredo, Tex.—Nov. 9, 1891): Politician and soldier. Born to a Mexican captain stationed in Laredo, Texas, Benavides obtained an excellent education during his youth. He learned about cattle raising and acquired a basic knowledge of merchandising. Benavides aided the Mexican border separatist movement in the late 1830's and became active in Texas politics during the 1850's. He was elected mayor of Laredo and chief justice of Webb County.

During the Civil War, Benavides recruited Mexican American soldiers for the South and protected the cotton trade with Mexico from attacks by bandits, Indians, and Juan Cortina's followers. His efforts earned him a promotion to colonel, the highest military rank earned by any Mexican American in that conflict.

Benavides developed an extensive wholesale and retail business on both sides of the border after the Civil War. His commercial interests led him to oppose Porfirio Díaz's attempts to depose Mexican President Sebastián Lerdo de Tejada. Díaz succeeded in 1876.

Benavides also actively participated in Texas politics after the Civil War. He was twice elected alderman in Laredo and served three terms in the state legislature. In 1884, he represented Texas at the World's Cotton Exposition in New Orleans, Louisiana.

Bencomo, Mario (b. July 26, 1953, Pinar del Río, Cuba): Bencomo is famous for semi-abstract paintings full of bright, swirling forms. His maternal ancestors were Jewish, and his father was from the Canary Islands. Although Bencomo disliked the political fervor that was widespread in his native land when he was growing up, his positive memories of Cuba's colorful natural environment have enriched his paintings. The dramatic swirling forms of deep red, purple, yellow, and blue that are the hallmarks of his works—some of which he creates by twirling a paintbrush between the palms of his hands—suggest natural forces such as wind and fire, as well as change, chaos, and emotional intensity.

One group of Bencomo's acrylic-on-canvas paintings deals with natural or mythical environments. This group includes *Starry Night* (1986) and *Paradiso Lontano* (1986). Other works, such as *Extasis de Santa Teresa* (1993), are based on historical people and ideas.

Bencomo's work has been included in individual and collective exhibitions in Michigan, Massachusetts, New York, Florida, and the District of Columbia, as well as Mexico, Switzerland, and Canada. He left

Cuba with his family in 1968 to live in the United States.

Bendito: Common Puerto Rican interjection. "*Bendito*," or "*Ay, bendito*," is a common Puerto Rican interjection with a variety of meanings ranging from exhaustion, commiseration, and sufferance to empathy. Literally, *bendito* is Spanish for blessed. Its connotative meaning depends on the intonation given to it by the speaker. The interjection is so prevalent in Puerto Rican speech that it has been identified throughout Latin America and Europe as one of the telling linguistic idiosyncrasies of the islanders.

Bent's Fort: Trading post. When Mexico seceded from Spain in 1821, trade began between this newly created nation and the United States. In 1833-1834, brothers William and Charles Bent and Ceran St. Vrain completed a trading post along the Arkansas River in southeastern Colorado. It quickly became one of the most important hubs for U.S. trade with Mexico and the western territories all the way to the Pacific Ocean. Bent's Fort was an immensely profitable venture that thrived until the late 1840's. Charles was killed in the Taos revolt of 1848. William Bent abandoned the fort after a cholera epidemic swept into the area from Missouri a few years later.

Bernal, Vicente J. (Dec. 15, 1888, Costilla, N.Mex.—Apr. 28, 1915, Dubuque, Iowa): Poet. Bernal is one of the earliest Hispanic writers from the American Southwest to publish in English. His only printed work is a collection of poems, ten brief pieces of prose, and oratory published posthumously by the *Telegraph-Herald* of Dubuque in 1916. Bernal also wrote in Spanish. Half of his collection is in Spanish.

Born in a small isolated mountain village, Bernal lived and worked on his grandfather's farm. His education came from Presbyterian parochial schools. Bernal's Protestant faith led him to the Midwest to continue his studies. Accepted by his European American peers at Dubuque German College and Academy (now the University of Dubuque) in Dubuque, Iowa, Bernal wrote poetry in English from 1913 to 1915. One of the thirty-four English-language poems he wrote, dedicated to the college, was set to music and became the college's alma mater. What scholars know of the poet's life comes from faculty members of the college.

Bernal died of a brain hemorrhage a year before completing his studies. His brother, Luis E. Bernal,

and Dubuque faculty member Robert N. McLean collected and edited his poems and prose.

Betances, Ramón Emeterio (Apr. 8, 1827, Cabo Rojo, Puerto Rico—Sept. 18, 1898, Paris, France): Revolutionary. A physician trained in France, Betances gained notoriety by ministering to the poor and needy in the Mayagüez area of Puerto Rico during the 1855 cholera epidemic. He also established himself as an active abolitionist and as a leader of the independence movement in Puerto Rico.

Spanish authorities banished Betances from the island on several occasions. After his June, 1867, expulsion, Betances traveled widely to promote the overthrow of Spanish rule in Puerto Rico. Betances' efforts, which produced the ill-fated revolt at the town of Lares on September 23, 1868, were plagued by misfortune. Betances lost his munitions in the Dominican Republic and his ship in Saint Thomas. Meanwhile, Puerto Rican patriots had their share of troubles. They had to advance the starting date for their revolution by a week when Spanish authorities accidentally learned about the conspiracy. Some supporters wavered, unsure of having either the will or the military supplies to defeat the Spanish army. As a result, Spanish authorities crushed the uprising swiftly.

Although the Spanish government declared an amnesty, Betances exiled himself to France, never to return to the island. He crusaded for Puerto Rico's independence until his death.

Bethlehem, Pennsylvania (incorporated as borough, 1845): Home of a Mexican labor colony developed from 1923 to 1930. Nearly one thousand Mexicans were brought to Bethlehem, Pennsylvania, in the spring of 1923 to work in the steel industry. Labor shortages caused by World War I led steel industrialists to recruit workers in Mexico and transport them by railroad to Pennsylvania.

Newspaper accounts described the arrival of the Mexicans as "a veritable invasion." Previous labor unrest in the area lay behind a somewhat hostile reception for the new arrivals. Labor strikes in 1919 and 1920 suggested to residents of Bethlehem that the Mexicans could be used as strikebreakers in the event of further labor unrest. The fact that the overwhelming majority of Mexicans who came to Bethlehem during this period were men could also have been unsettling.

Like their contemporaries in such industrial centers as Detroit, Michigan, and Homestead, Pennsylvania, the Mexican immigrants in Bethlehem were for the most part single men who depended upon the few Mexican families in the colony for meals. This situation enabled Mexican women, in particular, to earn money by providing meals. The Bethlehem Steel Corporation provided barracks for the men and two-family frame housing in the labor camp adjacent to its Coke Works facility. According to company records, in May of 1923, 790 Mexicans were employed by Bethlehem Steel. This number steadily declined until 1930, when only 125 Mexicans were listed on company records. As many as thirty-three Mexican families, in addition to a large number of single men, lived in the labor camp in 1923 and 1924. By 1929, seventeen families (including fifty-six children) and only thirty-four single men remained in the labor camp.

A *corrido* (folk ballad) from that era titled "El Corrido Pensilvanio" describes both the anticipation Mexicans felt in leaving behind the cotton fields of Texas and the anxiety they experienced when faced with the unfamiliar machinery in the steel mills. It also captures the loneliness of the men who had to live in the foreign environment without their families. Many men saved enough money to return to Mexico to bring their families back with them to Pennsylvania. There is also evidence that once established, Mexicans sent for family members to join them, as also happened in such places as Detroit and Homestead.

As the American economy began its decline toward the Great Depression, the steel industry lost the capacity to employ large numbers of people. The Mexican population in Bethlehem declined as people either returned to Mexico or sought employment opportunities elsewhere.

Biculturalism: Ability to function in two different cultures. Reflecting a growing appreciation for ethnic pride and cultural diversity, biculturalism increasingly is viewed as a valuable and important skill. Biculturalism helps members of ethnic minorities to achieve higher levels of social, educational, and economic success. It also contributes to a more stable society.

Development of Biculturalism. As attitudes toward ethnic minorities have shifted in the United States, so too has understanding of biculturalism. Earlier regarded as confused and disturbed, bicultural individuals have become recognized as proficient and capable communicators.

A person who is bicultural is socially and institutionally skillful in two different cultures, demonstrating fluency in language, mastery of interpersonal situations, and sensitivity to cultural norms and values. There are two paths to becoming bicultural: One can

be born into a family in which the parents or close relatives are of differing cultural or ethnic backgrounds, or one can be a member of a community with a culture different and distinct from that of the larger population. Ethnic communities offer immigrants and members of minority groups an opportunity to preserve and reinforce cultural ties that would otherwise fade in deference to the dominant culture.

The value of this type of preservation has not always been recognized. For many years, those supporting the process known as assimilation (*see* ACCULTURATION VERSUS ASSIMILATION) argued that immigrants should strive to strip away their culture of origin in order to become fully "American." More recently, however, an emphasis on pluralism, or MULTICULTURALISM, has suggested the image of America as a mosaic of cultures existing independently, complementing one another and forming a whole different from any of the parts but influenced by all of them.

Negative Views of Biculturalism. That biculturalism in the United States has been associated with psycho-

Bicultural people form relationships with others both inside and outside their culture. (Jim Whitmer)

Spectators cheer the Mexican and Mexican American runners in the New York City Marathon. (Odette Lupis)

logical problems, emotional disorders, and other negative characteristics is probably representative of prejudices against minority groups rather than fact. Assumptions that bicultural individuals have dual identities and divided loyalties that lead to internal conflicts date to the 1930's, when the preference for assimilation was strong and the tolerance for diversity low. Around this time, the concept of marginality was introduced as a way of characterizing individuals who live between two cultures, belonging fully to neither. Marginalized individuals experience psychological conflict and an inability to resolve differences in status between their two cultures. Biculturalism, it was believed, causes this imbalance. More recent evidence suggests that it is not biculturalism per se that leads to feelings of marginality, but instead rejection by the dominant culture.

Acceptance of Biculturalism. During the closing years of the twentieth century, with a shift in U.S. policy toward endorsing multiculturalism, biculturalism began to receive more objective investigation. Research from the 1980's suggests not only that it is possible for individuals to manage simultaneous participation in two cultures but also that those who do so may actually be mentally and emotionally healthier than those who do not. Similarly, individuals who have attained bicultural status are more stable than those who attempt to minimize their ethnicity through assimilating. Those individuals from minority groups who have effective bicultural skills are better equipped to compete with members of the dominant culture, and they achieve greater degrees of educational, social, and economic success than do their monocultural counterparts.

The benefits experienced by bicultural individuals vary according to the degree of bicultural competence they achieve, which appears to be based on a number of factors. These factors include the level of familiarity an individual has with the two cultures, a positive attitude toward both cultures, and a sense of groundedness. Being familiar with a culture includes knowing, appreciating, and accepting its basic beliefs and values, enabling an individual to make appropriate conversational and behavioral choices. If two cultures have conflicting values, such as the Latino emphasis on family versus the dominant American emphasis on the individual, the bicultural person may experience stress until he or she fuses the two preferences and arrives at a resolution. Having a positive attitude toward both cultures is another important part of bicultural success. It includes recognizing the value of

biculturalism and removes the external pressure to prefer one culture over another. Finally, bicultural individuals who have established stable social networks in both cultures, a concept also known as groundedness, experience high degrees of bicultural success. It is important to note that these factors matter little if the dominant culture is not receptive to the individual's participation.

As various U.S. minority populations grow in size, the value of biculturalism appears to be indisputable. Social scientists agree that the stability of a society depends on how successfully its cultures communicate. Bicultural individuals are especially well equipped to meet this challenge. Biculturalism is a valuable attribute not only for members of minorities but for all Americans, because it helps build community strength and participation. —*Regina Howard Yaroch*

Suggested Readings: • Bernal, Martha E., and George P. Knight, eds. *Ethnic Identity: Formation and Transmission Among Hispanics and Other Minorities.* Albany: State University of New York Press, 1993. • Katz, Phyllis A. "Developmental and Social Processes in Ethnic Attitudes and Self-Identification." In *Children's Ethnic Socialization: Pluralism and Development,* edited by Jean S. Phinney and Mary Jane Rotheram. Newbury Park, Calif.: Sage, 1987. • LaFromboise, Teresa, L. K. Hardin, and Jennifer Gerton. "Psychological Impact of Biculturalism: Evidence and Theory." *Psychological Bulletin* 114 (November, 1993): 395-412. • Van Den Bergh, Nan. "Managing Biculturalism at the Workplace: A Group Approach." *Social Work with Groups* 13, no. 4 (1990): 71-84. • Van Oudenhoven, Jan Pieter, and Tineke M. Willemsen, eds. *Ethnic Minorities: Social Psychological Perspectives.* Berwyn, Pa.: Swets North America, 1989.

Bigotry. *See* **Discrimination, bigotry, and prejudice against Latinos**

Bilingual education: Bilingual education is the practice of giving lessons to students in more than one language on an ongoing basis. The steady growth of Hispanic and other minority populations in the United States has generated much public controversy over the advantages and disadvantages of bilingual education.

History of Bilingual Education. In 1968, Congress passed the BILINGUAL EDUCATION ACT. Although bilingual education had already existed in the United States for decades, this act was the first piece of legislation to formally recognize that non-English speakers in the United States were at a severe educational disad-

LATINO CITIZENS' ATTITUDES TOWARD BILINGUAL EDUCATION, 1989-1990

Support or strongly support bilingual education

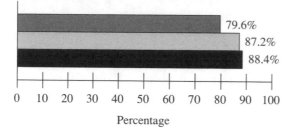

Willing to pay more taxes for bilingual education

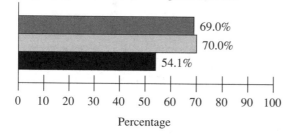

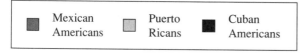

Source: Data are from the Latino National Political Survey, which polled a representative sample of 1,546 Mexican Americans, 589 Puerto Ricans, and 682 Cuban Americans in forty metropolitan areas in 1989-1990. See Rodolfo O. de la Garza et al., *Latino Voices: Mexican, Puerto Rican, and Cuban Perspectives on American Politics* (Boulder, Colo.: Westview Press, 1992), Tables 7.19 and 7.21.

vantage and needed programs designed specifically for their needs. Shortly thereafter, the case *LAU V. NICHOLS* (1974) went before the Supreme Court, which ruled that laws requiring English-only school instruction violated the civil rights of Chinese American students in San Francisco, California. This court decision thus reaffirmed the sentiments expressed in the Bilingual Education Act.

Those in favor of bilingual education were encouraged by the act and the subsequent court case, but some steps were also taken in the opposite direction. In 1986, voters in California passed a measure that made English their official state language; Florida passed a similar law in 1988. Some proponents of bilingual education view these laws as symbolically racial in nature and argue that they demonstrate voter fear that

allowing other languages to be taught in U.S. schools may result in the loss of English as the common American language.

Nevertheless, some bilingual education programs have been instituted in the United States, including Chinese-English instruction in San Francisco, French-English instruction in some areas of Maine, and Spanish-English instruction in several Southwestern states. These programs have been studied closely to determine whether they are ultimately beneficial to students. Some critics, however, have pointed out that studies of bilingual programs are often flawed. In *Attitudes Toward Bilingual Education: A View from the Border* (1984), for example, Harmon M. Hosch observed that many evaluations of bilingual education programs lacked sufficient sampling procedures or sample size and failed to take into account such variables as socioeconomic status and students' initial language skills. Hosch also noted that such studies were often conducted by people involved in the programs, possibly resulting in biased evaluations.

Debate over Bilingual Education. Opponents of bilingual education cite many reasons for their position. On a practical level, they argue that the lack of trained teachers, community support, and effective teaching materials limits the effectiveness of bilingual programs. These critics also argue that if programs are instituted on a widespread basis, Hispanic activists may demand more such programs, encouraging separatist feelings and loyalty to the ethnic community rather than to the United States. Critics point to Canada as proof of this assertion and attribute many of Canada's domestic problems to the nation's official French-English bilingual policy, which, they assert, has caused many people in the French-speaking province of Quebec to consider secession from Canada.

On a more individual level, critics of bilingual education claim that providing lessons in both English and other languages prevents students from mastering English as quickly as they would if they were simply immersed in it. In addition, some argue that children who grow up with two languages—and therefore, two cultures—will experience identity crises that could hinder their intellectual and emotional development. Critics also assert that use of a second language slows the teaching process, reducing the quality of education for native English speakers.

Proponents of bilingual education, on the other hand, argue that such programs encourage students to retain pride in their ethnic identity while simultaneously learning English. This, they claim, will allow

Students in bilingual classes learn a second language through primary instruction in their primary language.
(Impact Visuals, Mark Ludak)

Hispanic and other minorities to play a greater role in U.S. economic, political, and social life. Proponents point to evaluations of existing programs that show that students taught bilingually perform as well as those taught in English and become skilled in their mother tongues at the same time. Some proponents even claim that these students score higher than their English-only counterparts in areas such as math and vocabulary. Proponents also argue that bilingual education will result in higher high school graduation rates for Latinos and other minorities.

In addition, proponents of bilingual education argue that ENGLISH-ONLY legislation could have broad detrimental effects. Such laws, they claim, could breed antagonism between Hispanics and non-Hispanics and might adversely affect tourism and foreign investment in the United States. Further, if laws require information to be dispersed solely in English, people may not be able to get important medical or emergency information. Moreover, proponents of bilingual education argue that the cost of enforcing English-only legislation must be taken into account and assert that interpreting such laws could be both difficult and time-consuming. *—Amy Sisson*

SUGGESTED READINGS: • Adams, Karen L., and Daniel T. Brink, eds. *Perspectives on Official English: The Campaign for English as the Official Language of the USA*. New York: Mouton de Gruyter, 1990. • Alatis, James E., ed. *Current Issues in Bilingual Education*. Washington, D.C.: Georgetown University Press, 1980. • Cordasco, Francesco, with George Bernstein. *Bilingual Education in American Schools: A Guide to Information Sources*. Detroit: Gale Research, 1979. • Garcia, Ofelía, ed. *Bilingual Education*. Philadelphia: J. Benjamins, 1991. • Hosch, Harmon M. *Attitudes Toward Bilingual Education: A View from the Border*. El Paso: Texas Western Press, University of Texas at El Paso, 1984. • Paulston, Christina Bratt. *Bilingual Education: Theories and Issues*. Rowley, Mass.: Newbury House, 1980. • Turner, Paul R., ed. *Bilingualism in the Southwest*. 2d rev. ed. Tucson: University of Arizona Press, 1982.

Bilingual Education Act (1968): Federal education law. This legislation was designed to assist children who were non-native speakers to learn English more easily. The law was designed to help "Americanize" and assimilate these children, but it was used more generally to provide programs to improve access to better education. Many school districts were encouraged to upgrade the standards to which Spanish-speaking students were held; most districts were also instructed to integrate and improve the ethnic balance in areas where Spanish-speaking students were a distinct majority. The act had its largest impact in states in the Southwest as well as states such as New York and Florida, where large Spanish-speaking populations existed. Although many in the Latino community approved of the intent of this legislation, there was concern that the negative images of educational disadvantage and cultural deprivation implied by this act were damaging to the pride that Latino youngsters were being encouraged to take in their heritage and language.

Bilingual Foundation for the Arts (Los Angeles, Calif.): Producer of Latino theater. Founded in 1973 by actress/director Carmen ZAPATA, the Bilingual Foundation for the Arts produces and performs professional-quality English- and Spanish-language Latino theater. The group's bilingual actors perform both classic and contemporary pieces for Latino and non-Latino audiences in Los Angeles and on tour. The foundation also offers training for actors and technicians, offers residencies for directors and playwrights, sponsors a children's theater program called Teatro Para los Niños, creates new translations of plays, and presents the annual El Angel Award to one Latino artist and two corporations that have significantly contributed to Latino arts.

Bilingual Review Press (founded 1974): Publisher. The press publishes a journal, *The Bilingual Review*, dedicated to the linguistics and literature of BILINGUALISM and Hispanic culture in the United States.

Bilingual Review Press is a part of the Hispanic Research Center at Arizona State University. In addition to *The Bilingual Review*, it publishes Hispanic creative literature and scholarly works on such topics as linguistics, contemporary literary criticism, and Chicano studies. It accepts unsolicited manuscripts and, as of 1994, distributed more than fourteen hundred titles from other publishers. In addition, it joined in a partnership with Bantam Doubleday Dell's Anchor line to publish many Bilingual Review Press titles in paperback editions, making them available in national bookstores and academic markets.

Bilingual Review Press is at the forefront of the presses specializing in Hispanic literature and scholarly writing. The press adds approximately twelve new titles to its catalog each year. As of 1993, it listed more than one hundred books. Among the award-winning titles it has published are *The Ultraviolet Sky* (1988) by Alma Luz Villanueva and *The Devil in Texas* (1990, a translation of Aristeo BRITO's *El diablo en Texas*, 1976). The press has helped to increase the publication of works by female Hispanic writers.

Bilingualism: The alternate or habitual use of two languages. Bilingualism is a multifaceted phenomenon that has been given a spectrum of definitions. At one end, researchers define bilingualism as "the native-like control of two languages." At the other end, researchers define it as the ability of a speaker of one language to produce complete, meaningful utterances in another language. In other words, determining whether a person is indeed bilingual is no easy task. Research into bilingualism is also interdisciplinary. Researchers from different fields of study such as linguistics, sociology, anthropology, communications, psychology, and education use different methods, criteria, and theories in their investigations of bilingualism.

Some of these linguists define bilingualism in terms of "degree." Linguists speak of "passive" or "receptive" bilingualism. For example, a person may have no "productive control" (the ability to speak, read, or write) over one of the languages but may be able to understand utterances in it. Researchers have also addressed various questions that can help to determine an individual's bilingualism. By determining the degree, function, alternation, and interference of each language, bilingualism can be defined. In other words, one should ask: How well does the bilingual person know each of the languages? What uses does a bilingual speaker have for each of the languages? To what extent does the individual alternate between the languages? To what extent does the person manage to keep both languages separate, or to what extent does the individual fuse the two languages?

Although researchers vary in how they address, define, and study the topic of bilingualism, most take the following factors into account: the age of the bilingual speaker when he or she acquired each language, the context around the speaker, the way the speaker "mentally organizes" his or her speech, the individual's competence in each language, the use or function of each language, and the speaker's attitude toward each

Young students can begin to learn a second vocabulary while still learning a primary language. (Impact Visuals, Cindy Reiman)

of the two languages. In short, in defining bilingualism, any researcher must examine the origin of each of the speaker's languages, the speaker's competence in both languages, the function of each language, and the speaker's language attitudes. These criteria allow for a comprehensive overview of an individual's degree of bilingualism.

Researchers have also discovered the need to examine the possible effects of bilingualism. Bilingual speakers view their ability to speak, read, write, or understand two languages differently. For some speakers, especially minority group members, bilingualism is a necessary means of preserving their own language and identity while also maintaining political and economic links with the majority. To a certain extent, therefore, studies of bilingualism and related issues are a product of the coexistence of majority and minority groups in a society.

Birria: West Mexican manner of slow-cooking goat meat. *Birria* resembles BARBACOA, since a large chunk of meat is cooked slowly to retain its juices and make it very tender. The traditional meat is goat, although lamb is often used. In the most traditional manner, the meat is marinated for a period of hours (at least overnight) in a mixture of chiles, garlic, vinegar, and other seasonings. The marinated meat is then wrapped in maguey leaves and roasted in a covered pit. Modern adaptations have done away with the maguey leaves, placed the meat in a closed pot, and replaced the earth oven with an above-ground version. *Birria* is eaten for an informal meal and often accompanied with beer. *Birrirías*, restaurants specializing in *birria*, are common in Southern California, an area to which many West Mexicans have immigrated.

Birth control and family planning: Latinos had the highest fertility rate and largest family size of any major population group in the United States as of the early 1990's. Several factors contributed to relatively low use of birth control among Latinos. These included lack of information about and access to contraception as well as traditional cultural and religious beliefs that were biased against family planning.

Population Growth and Fertility. From 1980 to 1990, the Latino population grew by 53 percent—five times as fast as the total U.S. population and eight times as fast as the non-Latino population. Half of this growth came through natural increase and half through immigration. At the current rate of growth, Latinos were projected in the early 1990's to become the largest ethnic minority in the United States by about the year 2000.

A major reason for rapid Latino population growth, in comparison to growth of other groups, was the fact that the Latino population was younger than the non-Latino population, with a higher proportion of women of child-bearing age. Latinos had a median age of 26.2 years as of 1991, compared to 33.8 for non-Latinos. Mexican Americans were the youngest Latino subgroup, with a median age of 24.3 years, compared to 26.7 for Puerto Ricans, 27.9 for Central and South Americans, and 39.3 for Cuban Americans. Only 19 percent of Latinos were age forty-five or older, compared to 32.1 percent of non-Latinos.

The fertility rate (births per thousand women) for Latinas was exceptionally high, particularly among recent immigrants. In 1990, the fertility rate per thousand American women aged fifteen to forty-four was 93.2 for Latinas, compared to 67 for the overall U.S. population, 65.2 for white women, 78.4 for black women, and 58.1 for Asian American women.

The fertility rate of Latinas in the labor force was 67.6, compared to 132.3 for Latinas not in the labor force. This is similar to the patterns among Anglos and African Americans, although the overall rates for Latinas were higher. Latinas in professional and managerial jobs have fewer children than those in lower-paid occupations, as in other population groups. Fertility rates for Latinas were not predictable from income group, but Latinas from higher-income families were more likely than other Latinas to be childless.

High fertility rates mean a higher proportion of children in the Latino population as well as larger families. Nearly 40 percent of Latinos were under twenty years of age in 1990, compared with 28 percent of non-Latinos. About 38 percent of Latino families had four or more people, compared to 29 percent of non-Latino whites.

Population pressure creates certain economic and social pressures for Latinos. Data from birth certificates reveal that Latina mothers are more likely to be at risk for poor birth outcomes. They are more likely to be teenaged, unmarried, and economically disadvantaged, and they are more likely to have less than a high school education and to lack adequate prenatal care. In 1991, 24 percent of Latino families were headed by females, according to census figures, and these families were more likely than others to live in poverty.

Teenage Pregnancy. The problem of adolescent pregnancy among Latinas swelled to crisis proportions in the late twentieth century. Although the impact of un-

Birth control of all forms, particularly abortion, has met opposition in the Latino community. (Odette Lupis)

planned pregnancies is greatest on teenage mothers, the consequences of teenage pregnancy reach throughout the entire Latino community. In some states, Latinos are tremendously overrepresented among adolescent parents. In California and New Mexico, for example, about half of all teen births in 1990 were to LATINAS. An alarming issue for the Latino community is that the majority of teenage parents do not marry. This contributed to the increase in single-mother families from 13 percent of Latino families in 1970 to 19 percent in 1990.

Latina adolescents become pregnant before they are ready to become parents primarily because of lack of knowledge about and access to birth control. Other causal factors relate to low educational attainment and

socioeconomic status as well as their outlook for the future. Latino youth are less likely to complete high school and enter college than are white and black teenagers. Latino children are also more likely than non-Latino white children to live in families that are poor. This is particularly true of Puerto Rican children, who have the highest POVERTY rate of all Latinos. As a result of limited educational opportunities and low socioeconomic status, Latino youth tend to have low expectations for the future. Many youth view childbirth and parenting as a sign of adulthood and an opportunity to feel loved.

Attitudes About Family Planning. Beliefs about birth control and family planning are influenced by an individual's family background, religion, and culture,

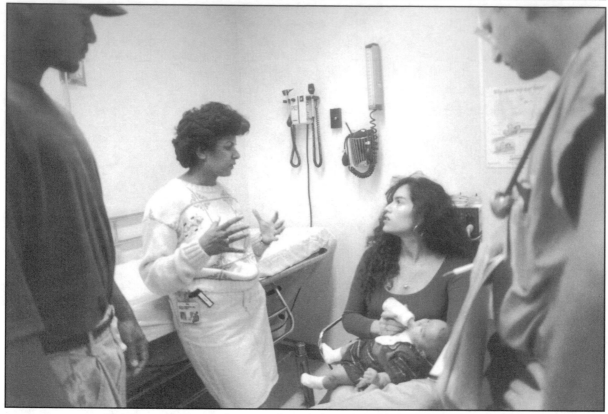

Many young Latinas make a conscious choice to begin families. (Hazel Hankin)

as well as education and economic status. Traditionally, Latinos believe that the family is the central and most important institution in life. The family supports each of its members, and individuals are expected to put the interests of the family before their own concerns. The Latino idea of *la familia* goes beyond the nuclear family household of a man, his wife, and their children to include both maternal and paternal relatives in the extended family. A family's strength is thought to lie in its large size, a view that can be traced to a heritage of family members working together for mutual economic gain.

The concept of *la familia* also implies the ideal roles and behaviors of family members. The traditional Latino family is a patriarchy that revolves around a strong male figure who is ultimately responsible for the well-being of all individuals under his roof. Part of this ideal is the concept of MACHISMO, in which masculine pride is closely linked to family honor and duty. In reality, however, women are strong contributors to decision making and are often the internal authority figures in the family. This is contrary to the STEREOTYPES in which the woman is viewed as subservient to the man.

One of the greatest changes in the Latino family has been expansion of the woman's role beyond child rearing and household chores. LATINAS have been increasingly influenced by the Latina feminist movement to break out of the cocoon of their traditional culture. Many are challenging church and cultural conventions concerning patriarchy, birth control, and family size.

The Catholic religion has had a strong influence on institutions of *la familia*. The high birth rates in the Latino community are partly a result of this influence, as birth control is stigmatized by the church and many families fear the authority of the church. Some Latinas believe that the conditioning of the CATHOLIC CHURCH and ignorance about sex and birth control are obstacles that must be overcome if the issue of POVERTY in the Latino community is to be fully addressed.

Changing attitudes toward early and frequent pregnancies are particularly important for young Latinas. Although education concerning sex and birth control was rare in the past, it is becoming more openly presented and more accepted by Latina women. More young Latinas are also challenging the assumption that women should take sole responsibility for preventing pregnancy and are asking their partners to assist with birth control.

Knowledge about and access to birth control methods are important factors in changing the high fertility patterns of Latinos. Improved opportunities with respect to education and employment will also help change attitudes regarding family planning and family size. As Latinos become more educated and enjoy higher economic status, they will be more likely to take advantage of birth control and family planning.

—*Maria Wilson-Figueroa*

SUGGESTED READINGS: • Griswold del Castillo, Richard. *La Familia: Chicano Families in the Urban Southwest, 1848 to the Present*. Notre Dame, Ind.: University of Notre Dame Press, 1984. • Jaffe, Abram J., Ruth M. Cullen, and Thomas D. Boswell. *The Changing Demography of Spanish Americans*. New York: Academic Press, 1980. • Jencks, Christopher, and Paul Peterson, eds. *The Urban Underclass*. Washington, D.C.: Brookings Institution, 1991. • Moore, Joan. *Going Down to the Barrio: Homeboys and Homegirls in Charge*. Philadelphia: Temple University Press, 1991. • Moore, Joan, and Raquel Pinderhughes, eds. *In the Barrios: Latinos and the Underclass Debate*. New York: Russell Sage Foundation, 1993. • Morales, Rebecca, and Frank Bonilla, eds. *Latinos in a Changing U.S. Economy*. Newbury Park, Calif.: Sage, 1993.

Bisbee deportations (July 12, 1917—August, 1917): Deportations of striking workers. In response to a strike in the copper-mining town of Bisbee, Arizona, 1,186 men were arrested, sent by train to New Mexico, and abandoned in the desert.

On June 27, 1917, three thousand copper miners in and around Bisbee, Arizona, went on strike under the leadership of the INDUSTRIAL WORKERS OF THE WORLD (IWW). Like miners striking elsewhere in Arizona that year, the strikers wanted a share of the increased profits that MINING companies were making as a result of World War I.

Shortly after the strike began, Cochise County Sheriff Harry Wheeler requested the aid of troops from the governor, Thomas Campbell. Campbell sought federal troops, asking the secretary of war to investigate the situation in Bisbee. On June 30 and July 2, an army officer reported that everything was peaceful and that no troops were needed.

On the morning of July 11, Walter Douglas of the Phelps Dodge Company, which owned some of the

Members of the Industrial Workers of the World were forced to leave in July, 1917. (AP/Wide World Photos)

mines in Bisbee, announced that he would not compromise with the miners. That evening, managers of the mining companies held a public meeting at which they revealed Douglas' plan to end the strike. The decision was made to deport the striking miners and their supporters. The organizers censored telephone and telegraph lines in order to prevent news of the deportation from reaching the outside world.

Early on the morning of July 12, Sheriff Wheeler assembled a force of more than two thousand deputies. He accused the strikers of threatening and beating nonunion workers. The deputies arrested strikers and their sympathizers on charges of vagrancy, treason, and disturbing the peace. Some men were beaten during the arrests; one miner and one deputy were killed. The arrestees were forced to march to a local ballpark.

Mine managers gave the strikers one more chance to return to work. Many of them accepted. The remaining 1,186 prisoners were forced aboard boxcars and taken by train to Hermanas, New Mexico. The deputies abandoned the deportees there, leaving them in the desert without adequate food, water, or shelter.

On July 14, federal troops rescued the men and took most of them to Columbus, New Mexico, where they were cared for until September. Deportations continued until late August, when Governor Campbell requested that the practice end.

Most of the deportees were foreign; about one-fourth of them were Mexicans. Many of the deportees were never able to return to Bisbee. Company managers and local officials had used fear of violence and the lack of state or federal troops as excuses to deport striking workers. Both federal and state charges of kidnapping were brought against those responsible for the deportations. None of those charged was ever convicted.

The deportations were criticized at both the state and federal levels, but they effectively ended the influence of the IWW in Arizona. Organized labor was severely weakened and would never again have much influence in the state. With the weakening of the union, Bisbee became increasingly a one-company town, dominated by Phelps Dodge. Underground mining became less important, and more mining was done in open pits, which required less skilled labor.

Bishop's Committee for the Spanish-Speaking Peoples: Religious organization. Founded in 1945, this group was later renamed the Secretariat for the Spanish Speaking. It was formed on the initiative of the National Conference of Catholic Bishops of the United States. As of the early 1990's, it consisted of 140 diocesan directors providing consultation services to the Catholic dioceses with significant Hispanic populations. (*See* CATHOLIC CHURCH AND CATHOLICISM.)

The group's goal is better service to Hispanic church members. It was founded with the intent of improving the physical and spiritual lives of parishioners. Specific goals revolve around employment, education, leadership training, health, and civil rights.

The secretariat now encompasses the former Bishop's Committee for Migrant Workers. It operates as an information and concept center dealing with pastoral ministry research. The group also serves as a liaison linking other churches and agencies (private and governmental) and coordinating their common efforts in favor of Hispanics in a particular community. The secretariat publishes the quarterly *En Marcha* and the *Hispanic Apostolate Diocesan Directors* (an annual publication).

The secretariat became a division of the United States Catholic Conference in 1968. In 1975, it was made an agency of the National Conference of Catholic Bishops.

Bithorn, Hiram (Hiram Gabriel Bithorn y Sosa; Mar. 18, 1916, Santurce, Puerto Rico—Jan. 1, 1952, El Mante, Mexico): Baseball player. The first major league player from Puerto Rico, Bithorn debuted with the Chicago Cubs in 1942. A right-handed pitcher, Bithorn had a losing 9-14 record as a rookie but returned to post impressive numbers in his second year. In 1943, Bithorn had an excellent 2.60 earned-run average (ERA) while leading the National League with seven shutouts and compiling a good 18-12 record.

Military service in 1944 and 1945 took Bithorn out of the game. He returned to the Cubs in 1946 and posted a 6-5 record, but he was traded to the Chicago White Sox in 1947. He pitched only two innings for the White Sox before a sore arm ended his major league career. During his short career, he won thirty-four games with eight shutouts and a respectable 3.16 ERA. Bithorn attempted to make a comeback in the Mexican leagues, but he was fatally shot on New Year's Day, 1952.

Black Legend: Anti-Spanish sentiment regarding activities in the New World. The Black Legend is a twentieth century term referring to the systematic denigration of the character and the achievements of Spain since the Spanish Conquest. Its source lies in the

Hiram Bithorn, shortly after being signed by the Chicago Cubs. (AP/Wide World Photos)

Rubén Blades marks his ballot in the 1994 Panamanian elections, in which he is a candidate for president; he placed third in the balloting. (AP/Wide World Photos)

atrocities the Spanish committed against the native population of the Americas and the extermination of entire native civilizations. Many religious figures reported these atrocities, but the protests of Fray Bartolomé DE LAS CASAS had the most impact. He defended the natives of America by stating that they were full human beings with sophisticated cultures.

Blades, Rubén (b. July 16, 1948, Panama City, Panama): Singer, songwriter, actor, and attorney. Blades is the son of Rubén Dario Blades, a police officer, and Anoland Blades, a singer and radio actress. In the 1950's, Blades listened to American rock and roll and doo-wop music on the radio, using the radio to teach himself to sing and play the guitar. He practiced singing in English, even when he did not understand all the words. In 1963, Blades joined his brother's band, in which he also sang in English. Blades was so outraged by a 1964 attack by U.S. troops on Panamanian student demonstrators, however, that he turned his back on anything American, including singing in English.

During the late 1960's, Blades sang in a number of Latin bands. He first recorded with Los Magnificos in 1968. In addition to pursuing a singing career, he studied law and political science at the University of Panama. His studies were interrupted when the Panamanian military closed the university because of student unrest. Blades decided to go to New York City to concentrate on his singing career. He recorded the album *De Panama a Nueva York* with the Pete Rodriguez band in 1970. The University of Panama reopened, so Blades returned to finish his studies. He was graduated from the university in 1974 with a degree in law and political science. For a short time, he served as an attorney for the Banco Nacional de Panama.

Blades returned to New York in 1974 to advance his singing career. He found a job working for Fania Records, which specialized in Latin American music. Although he began working for Fania in the mailroom, he eventually got the opportunity to record and to be the company's legal representative. During the late 1970's, Blades recorded with the Ray Barretto band and with the Willie Colón Combo. He remained with the combo until 1982, when he became a solo artist. In 1984, he signed with Elektra and released the SALSA album *Buscando América*, which combined various rhythms. Blades then took a break from recording and enrolled at Harvard University. In 1985, he received a master's degree in international law. Blades released his first English-language album, *Nothing but the Truth*, in 1988. In addition to having an extremely

successful recording career, he has appeared in several films, including *The Last Fight* (1982), *Crossover Dreams* (1985), and *The Milagro Beanfield War* (1988). He also has remained active in Panamanian politics.

Bloody Christmas case (December 24, 1951): Police brutality incident. On Christmas Eve of 1951, seven Chicano youths were arrested following a run-in with police officers in Los Angeles, California. They were charged with battery and interfering with the officers.

The youths were taken to the Lincoln Heights police station in Los Angeles, where they allegedly were beaten during a drinking party at the station. Early the following year, a Los Angeles grand jury indicted eight police officers in connection with the alleged beatings. All eight officers were reprimanded and disciplined by the Los Angeles Police Department, and several of the officers were convicted and received prison sentences.

Blowout (March, 1968): Student protest. "Blowout" was the term used by Latino students to describe their boycott of classes in Los Angeles, California, and other cities in the Southwest. Early in March, 1968, more than ten thousand Latino students at five Los Angeles high schools walked out of classes and demanded better education, courses in Latino history, bilingual education, more teachers and counselors of Hispanic descent, and more sensitivity on the part of white teachers and administrators to the needs of students from the BARRIOS. Led by high school teacher Salvador B. CASTRO, the students remained away from classes for several days. At the same time, activist Rodolfo "Corky" GONZÁLES inspired mass demonstrations and protests in Denver, Colorado, calling the school administration to expand its curriculum by including subjects of interest to Spanish-speaking Americans.

In Los Angeles, school officials called for the police, who ended the boycott by beating hundreds of students with billy clubs and forcing them back into schools. Dozens of protesters were arrested, and many were jailed, including Castro. After weeks of bitter negotiation, school administrators agreed to meet some of the students' demands. Change occurred slowly.

Boarding schools: Federal, private, and church-sponsored educational institutions located away from students' homes and communities. They were established for the purpose of molding all aspects of a child's life. Boarding schools for American Indians emphasized ACCULTURATION, religious conversion, and formal Western education.

The Americanization of Indian tribes was judged to be extremely important to the U.S. government as the West became more populated with Europeans. Provisions for schools and boarding schools were often included in treaties made with Indians between 1788 and 1871. President Ulysses S. Grant believed that Indians should be educated for the two purposes of civilization and citizenship. By 1900, there were twenty-five off-reservation boarding schools in the United States.

Federal boarding schools were established in the 1870's. They were located off the reservations because it was believed that students could be Americanized more easily when away from their homes. Sometimes students were forcibly removed from home to attend the schools.

Education among Indian tribes was informal, traditional, and both ceremonial and practical. Indian students attending boarding schools were mixed without regard to social or tribal relationships, different languages, or customs. Academic subjects usually were taught in the morning. In the afternoon, students were put to work learning practical skills. Boys were taught vocations including farming; girls were taught homemaking and crafts.

None of the schools encouraged tribal customs. They suppressed and discouraged the practice of tribal ceremonies and forbade students from speaking in their tribal languages. It was not until 1929 that policies were changed so that students were not punished for talking in their native languages, wearing customary hairstyles and dress, or practicing Indian religion.

Boarding schools were a centerpiece of Indian education off reservations from 1890 to 1920. They were very expensive to operate, however, and some boarding schools were converted to day schools, with students returning home after classes. Many were improved, offering more academic subjects and up-to-date vocational training. Less emphasis was placed on regimented behavior. Student care improved in the areas of medical and food services.

It was not until the late 1940's that the Bureau of Indian Affairs changed its rules about sending Indian children to boarding schools. Students were then directed to go to public schools unless they had social or educational problems. In the 1970's, policies were revised again to give Indian parents and tribes more choice.

Although they often did a creditable job of achieving the short-term goals of teaching English and practical skills, boarding schools failed the Indians at a more social and personal level. Indians held onto their traditions despite assimilation efforts, but they suffered in the process. The schools were another example of the government exercising pervasive control but not living up to its obligations.

Boarding schools of a voluntary nature continue, but on a limited basis. They offer the opportunity for students to experience life away from home, perhaps in a social environment above that of the home community.

Bodega: Small retail store or tavern where food is served. The *bodega*, or grocery store, is both an important commercial center and a social center in Latin America. It provides a variety of products and a place for the exchange of information affecting the community. In the United States, the *bodega* usually offers a variety of Latin American and Caribbean staple foods, beverages, and publications not usually marketed by larger commercial establishments. *Bodegas*, usually identified with a Latino community, also serve as social centers. In Cuba, a *bodega* is a tavern that serves inexpensive meals. In Mexico, *bodegas* are sometimes called *tienda de abarrotes* (grocery stores).

A bodega *offers products unavailable elsewhere, often in an informal atmosphere.* (Frances M. Roberts)

Bogardus, Emory Stephen (Feb. 21, 1882, near Belvidere, Ill.—Aug. 21, 1973, Los Angeles, Calif.): Sociologist. Bogardus' work focused on race relations and the role of leadership among Mexican Americans. In one of his many important studies, concerning the zoot-suit riots of the 1940's, he discovered, contrary to stereotypes, that only about 3 percent of Mexican American youths were in zoot-suit gangs and that only a few more wore the distinctive clothing. Bogardus was the author of numerous books in the fields of sociology and literature, and he was a registered social worker.

Bogardus held bachelor's (1908) and master's (1909) degrees from Northwestern University and a Ph.D. (1911) from the University of Chicago. He also held Litt.D. degrees from the University of Southern California (1945) and the University of Arizona (1960) and an LL.D. from Boston University (1950). He began his long teaching career at the University of Southern California in 1911 as an assistant professor of sociology and economics. Within four years, he had risen to the rank of professor of sociology. He was the organizer and the first chair of his school's sociology department and was director of the division of social work within that department from 1920 to 1937. Bogardus also worked as regional research director for Southern California for the Pacific Coast Race Relations Survey (1923-1925), was president of the Los Angeles Social Service Commission (1916-1918), and edited the *Journal of Sociology and Social Research* (1916-1961).

Bolero: Cuban dance and musical form. A slow to moderate song in duple meter, accompanied by BON-GOS, conga drums, and claves, the bolero is characterized by sentimental texts; long, flowing melodies; two contrasting periods of sixteen or thirty-two measures each, often in the AABA form; and a complex rhythm derived from the use of the *cinguillo* and *tresillo*. Boleros originated in the nineteenth century, developing from Afro-Cuban forms such as the CONGA, DANZÓN, and CONTRADANZA. The Cuban bolero reached the repertory of MARIMBA bands in Central America and Mexico, where two types of bolero developed: the *romántico*, danced and/or sung, and the *ranchero*, only sung.

Bolillo: Pejorative term for an assimilated Latino. *Bolillo*, literally translated as "roll," originally was a Mexican pejorative term for Anglos, so named because they ate rolls rather than tortillas. The term came to refer to assimilated Latinos who, like rolls, are brown on the outside and white on the inside. It can also refer to a light-skinned Latino. The term is perceived as an insult.

Bomba: Puerto Rican music and dance form. Bombas are four-line recitations of poetic and satirical content alternated with dance and performed by a leader who,

with the cry of "bomba," designates a chorus of participants to respond with improvised verse. It is played typically by two bombas (drums made of kegs or barrels with goatskin heads), one pitched higher than the other. The *burlador* is the larger one, and the *requinto* is the smaller one. Other instruments include *palillos*, two sticks played on the side of a drum or on a wooden surface, and a single MARACA. Characteristic of the bomba is that dancers direct the drums rather than vice versa.

Bongos: Pair of small, single-headed drums of Afro-Cuban origin. Bongos first appeared in Cuba around 1900. They come in pairs of two either cylindrical or conical hardwood shells of the same height but of different diameters, created from hollowed tree trunks. Their heads, made of a membrane or plastic material, are either nailed or screw-tensioned. Players hold bongos between the knees, usually with the larger drum to their left, and play them with their bare hands, rapidly striking the heads with their finger tips, flat fingers, and the butts of their hands.

Bonilla, Frank (b. New York, N.Y.): Scholar. In 1993, Bonilla became executive director of the Inter-University Program for Latino Research (IUP) at Hunter College of the City University of New York (CUNY). The IUP is a consortium of university-based research centers focusing on the situation of Latinos in the United States. Prior to 1993, Bonilla was the first director of CUNY's Center for Puerto Rican Studies, founded in 1973, and taught political science and sociology.

Before joining the CUNY faculty, Bonilla taught political science at Stanford University (1969-1972) and was a program adviser in social science to a Ford Foundation project in Brazil (1967-1972). He taught political science at the Massachusetts Institute of Technology from 1963 to 1967 and was a member of the American Universities Field Staff from 1960 to 1963. In the latter position, he collaborated on a research program carried out on behalf of the United Nations Educational, Scientific, and Cultural Organization (UNESCO) and the Economic Commission for Latin America, surveying various Latin American countries to investigate the relation between social development and education.

Bonilla holds a bachelor's degree in business administration (1949) from the College of the City of New York, an M.A. in sociology (1954) from New York University, and a Ph.D. in sociology (1959) from

Tony Bonilla addresses a gathering in Austin, Texas, in 1986. (AP/Wide World Photos)

Harvard University. He is the author of numerous books on economic and social issues as well as articles focusing on Puerto Rico and its people. Particular concerns of his research are the general welfare and civil rights of the large Puerto Rican community of New York City. He participated in the formation of ASPIRA, the Puerto Rican Forum, and the Puerto Rican Development Project.

Bonilla, Rubén "Tony" (b. Mar. 3, 1936, Calvert, Tex.): Attorney. After graduating from Del Mar College in 1955 with a bachelor's degree in education, Bonilla obtained a B.A. from Baylor University in 1958 and was graduated from the University of Houston in 1960.

Bonilla's career began in 1960 with the law offices of Read, Bonilla and Berlanga. From 1964 to 1967, he was a member of the Texas state legislature, and he served on the board of directors of the LEAGUE OF UNITED LATIN AMERICAN CITIZENS (LULAC) in Washington, D.C. From 1972 to 1975, he was president of LULAC. Bonilla was also chairman of the National Hispanic Leadership Conference. He was a member of the Texas' Bilingual Task Force and the Task Force on Public Education. In 1986, he was a representative on the United States Information Agency (USIA) tour of South America to discuss drug issues. In 1987, Bonilla participated in a conference on enhancing cooperation between Hispanic Americans and Spain in celebrating the 1992 quincentennial.

From 1973 to 1978, Bonilla was chairman of the board of directors of the Corpus Christi Chamber of Commerce. He was a member of the coordinating board of the Texas college and university system from 1973 to 1979 and was chairman of the Corpus Christi, Texas, quincentenary committee.

Bootlegging: Smuggling of alcoholic beverages. During Prohibition (1919-1933), the United States government attempted to outlaw alcoholic beverages. The attempt was unsuccessful. Manufacturing of alcoholic beverages continued despite the law, and smugglers brought liquor from countries that did not enact prohibition laws.

In 1919, after a long debate by those who spoke of the evils of "demon rum" and those who considered alcoholic beverages to be a regular part of American life, the United States government outlawed the distribution, sale, and importation of all alcoholic beverages. The Eighteenth Amendment, establishing Prohibition, was ratified on January 16, 1919. The Volstead Act, providing enforcement guidelines, was passed on October 28.

Although many people before and since Prohibition have thought that the elimination of alcohol would be beneficial, most historians agree that the attempt to enforce such an elimination was futile. People did not stop drinking; they merely stopped buying drinks in legal establishments. A new criminal class was born during this period in response to the demand for alcoholic beverages in a country that would not permit their legal sale.

The term "bootlegging" originated from the practice of hiding liquor in one's boots to bring it across the U.S. border, or simply to take it to places outside the home. Smuggling of this type was, by its nature, on a small scale. A much larger amount of alcohol was imported into the United States by Caribbean merchants, many of whom became rich in the process. The most important import from Latin America was West Indian rum; the term "rum runner," referring to a smuggler, originates from this trade.

The Coast Guard was helpless beyond the three-mile limit of American territory in the Atlantic Ocean, and the Mexican and Canadian borders proved impossible to control completely. In addition, many Americans opposed Prohibition. Many border guards were less than stringent in their patrols and checks, either not wanting to enforce an unpopular law too strenuously or personally opposed to the law.

Although it is impossible to find reliable data, it is clear that the economies of a number of Latin American countries, particularly the Caribbean nations, benefited from exporting alcoholic beverages to the United States. The effect on Latinos living in the United States is difficult to determine. Many Mexicans who came to the United States illegally brought alcoholic beverages with them, as they were a ready source of income.

Prohibition was repealed in 1933, for several reasons. Chief among them was the fact that although alcohol consumption had not declined to any large extent, the profits from liquor sales had fallen into the hands of the criminal class rather than legitimate business people, with a resultant decline in tax revenues. Al Capone, one of the most famous Chicago gangsters of the time, was finally indicted for tax evasion rather than for other forms of criminal activity.

Bootlegging of a different sort continued long after the United States legalized alcohol. A number of drugs, particularly cocaine and marijuana, are imported into the United States in large quantities from Latin America. Researchers into the DRUG TRADE often compare bootlegging to this more recent counterpart.

Border conflicts: Conflicts along the U.S.-Mexico border have played a pivotal role in relations between the countries and the lives of Mexican Americans. Border disputes have stirred nationalism and anti-Mexican sentiment in the United States.

Alienation. The two centuries between 1680, when European competition for control of the North American continent began in earnest, and 1880, when tension subsided in the borderlands, constituted a period of acute alienation between Anglos/Anglo-Americans and Spaniards/Mexicans. In colonial days, the British, and to some extent the French as well, constantly challenged the Spanish presence in the farthest reaches of northern New Spain, creating zones of tension from Texas to Louisiana to Florida. In time, the Spanish and French frontiers receded, while the British, and later the Anglo-Americans, advanced southward and westward. Continuous confrontations over territory kept the borderlands in a state of turmoil.

The controversy over the limits of the Louisiana Territory became one of the most contentious issues of the early nineteenth century. The United States, which acquired Louisiana in 1803, claimed Texas as part of its purchase from the French, but the Spaniards strongly disagreed. After years of acrimony, the United States and Spain signed the ADAMS-ONÍS TREATY in 1819, establishing definite borders for Louisiana and recognizing Texas as Spanish territory. American expansionists, however, remained adamant about the "legitimacy" of the U.S. claim to Texas.

Between the 1820's and the 1840's, Texas figured prominently in the border conflicts between the United States and Mexico. In 1836, Anglos, who had moved into Texas en masse in preceding years, led an insurrection against the Mexican government. By 1845, that province became part of the United States through annexation. To Mexico, the U.S. annexation of Texas amounted to an act of grievous aggression. The conflict over Texas comprised a major issue in the deterioration of relations between the two nations.

War broke out in 1846, leading to further U.S. absorption of Mexican territories. In 1848, at the conclusion of the MEXICAN AMERICAN WAR, the new borderlands, which were dissected by the Rio Grande and an irregular line from El Paso to the Pacific Ocean, remained a tension-filled environment. Indian raiders, filibusters, bandits, and other lawless elements capitalized on the isolation and lack of governmental controls

of the area to carry on their illicit activities. The area remained sparsely populated and undeveloped well into the late nineteenth century.

Coexistence. The climate of alienation began to lessen significantly around 1880. By that date, several major controversies had been resolved, including border location disputes, claims of aggrieved citizens, Indian raiding, and frontier lawlessness. In addition, the railroads reached the borderlands, bringing more residents, spreading modernization, and stimulating the economy. Governmental institutions began to function more effectively in the region, leading to greater stability. In the 1910's, however, the borderlands temporarily regressed to a condition of alienation when the MEXICAN REVOLUTION engendered violent confrontations.

Interdependence. By the 1920's, major political, economic, and social restructuring in Mexico ushered in a new peace, growth, and prosperity that led to improved conditions throughout the nation, including the northern border region. Meanwhile, anti-Mexican sentiments subsided sufficiently in the United States to allow the two nations to construct a more harmonious relationship. Extreme nationalism and militarily driven violations of sovereignty along the border were relegated to history; disagreements henceforth would be resolved diplomatically.

Since the 1930's major border-related diplomatic breakthroughs achieved in the spirit of "good neighborliness" have included border rectification agreements, water treaties, the BRACERO PROGRAM, and the TREATY OF EL CHAMIZAL. Changes in Mexican law have permitted greater foreign investment, leading to substantial increases in binational trade.

The welcome climate of greater cooperation initiated after the Mexican Revolution facilitated increased interactions across the border, heralding the age of interdependence. Economic growth engendered prosperity, population expansion, and new problems. Undocumented migration took center stage in the new diplomatic agenda, followed by drug trafficking, trade competition, and environmental pollution. By the early 1990's these problems frequently produced friction on the border. —*Oscar J. Martínez*

SUGGESTED READINGS: • Fernández, Raúl A. *The Mexican-American Border Region: Issues and Trends.* Notre Dame, Ind.: University of Notre Dame Press, 1989. • Hall, Linda B., and Don M. Coerver. *Revolution on the Border: The United States and Mexico, 1910-1920.* Albuquerque: University of New Mexico Press, 1988. • Martínez, Oscar J. *Troublesome Border.*

Guards at the U.S.-Mexico border at Brownsville, Texas, around 1915. (Library of Congress)

Tucson: University of Arizona Press, 1988. • Paredes, Américo. *"With His Pistol in His Hand" : A Border Ballad and Its Hero.* Austin: University of Texas Press, 1958. • Reisler, Mark. *By the Sweat of Their Brow: Mexican Immigrant Labor in the United States, 1900-1940.* Westport, Conn.: Greenwood Press, 1976. • Rippy, J. Fred *The United States and Mexico.* New York: Knopf, 1926.

Border Folk Festival (El Paso, Tex.): The annual Border Folk Festival, begun in 1973, is held at the Chamizal National Memorial, which commemorates the peaceful settlement of a boundary dispute between the United States and Mexico. The fifty-five-acre site annually hosts about fifty thousand visitors during the several days of the festival. Included are traditional food, folk arts and crafts, concerts, and workshops and special programs for children. The primary focus is on music and dance. About one-fourth of the performers are Mexicans or Mexican Americans. Although it is on a less impressive scale than Corpus Christi's BAYFEST, San Antonio's TEXAS FOLKLIFE FESTIVAL, or Brownsville's CHARRO DAYS, the Border Folk Festival is one of the best known of its sort.

Border Industrialization Program: Mexico's industrial revolution reached its peak after the end of World War II. The country's Border Industrialization Program was an attempt to relieve the unemployment problem in northern Mexico.

Following World War II, industrialization in Mexico transformed the economic and social structure of the country. It became a new permanent and dynamic feature of national life. The country has considerable coal deposits, offering a tremendous advantage for the nation's industrialization interests. It also has substantial oil reserves. These and other factors helped the nation to expand its industrialization efforts in order to compete more aggressively in the international marketplace.

An "era of good feeling" between the United States and Mexico was partially responsible for the increased industrialization of northern Mexico after World War II. On December 23, 1942, the United States and Mexico signed a wartime reciprocal trade treaty that lowered duties on a number of manufactured items entering Mexico from the United States. Reduced duties encouraged industrial production, particularly near the border. The increased industrialization of northern Mexico included a number of important economic developments that changed the financial future of the country. Cement plants were erected in Hermosilla, Sonora, in order to meet the increasing cement needs of the northwest zone. During 1947, a cement plant was also established by the Vallina banking interests in Nombre de Dios, Chihuahua. California Cement was established in 1958 in Ensenada, Baja California. Other new industrial enterprises in northern Mexico were in the textiles industry. The MINING and metallurgy industries also showed gains in northern Mexico after World War II, as did pleasure industries, such as the Tecate Brewery in Baja California.

In 1965, Mexico established the MAQUILADORA (assembly plant) program in order to relieve a major unemployment problem. By 1983, *maquiladoras* employed some 130,000 workers near the border. Nearly six hundred factories generated about two billion dollars annually.

The Border Industrialization Program was controversial. Its proponents argued that it allowed Mexico to benefit from infusions of U.S. capital and created Mexican jobs. Opponents complained that it diminished the number of available jobs in the United States. The North American Free Trade Agreement (NAFTA) helped accelerate the creation of trade arrangements that gave U.S. companies more latitude in establishing plants in northern Mexico, where labor was relatively inexpensive. Opponents of the *maquiladora* program and NAFTA complained of the loss of U.S. jobs to "cheap foreign labor."

One part of the Mexican industrialization effort has centered on the automobile industry. Since 1950, the Mexican government has stressed the sale of cars assembled with a maximum proportion of parts made in Mexico, particularly in the northern part of the country. During 1952, the Diesel Nacional was created in order to construct diesel trucks and small cars under Fiat patents.

Border region and culture: The two thousand-mile international boundary between the United States and Mexico divides two countries with very different histories and socioeconomic conditions. The border has become much more than a political line. It is a broad international zone that has evolved since the mid-1800's to link adjoining communities of two countries with increasingly common binational concerns. Commonalities in the border region relate to culture, economics, political change, natural resource use, environmental concerns, communications, tourism, and migration. All these concerns assumed greater importance in the 1990's with the passage of the NORTH

AMERICAN FREE TRADE AGREEMENT (NAFTA).

History. The twentieth century border between the United States and Mexico did not exist prior to 1845. In that year, the annexation of Texas by the United States resulted in a shared border along most of the Rio Grande (Rio Bravo del Norte, in Mexico), with most of its bordering territory jointly claimed. The war between the United States and Mexico that began in 1846 was concluded militarily in 1847 with the American occupation of Mexico City, the territories of California and New Mexico, and several cities in the Mexican states of Chihuahua and Coahuila. The war was concluded politically by the TREATY OF GUADALUPE HIDALGO (1848), which ceded more than one million square miles of former Mexican territory to the United States and established most of the current border. The portion of the border between Mexico and Texas was drawn as the mid-channel of the Rio Grande. The border with California was drawn as a surveyed line from the Tijuana River at latitude 32° 32' north on the Pacific Coast, to a point on the Colorado River west of what later became the town of Yuma, Arizona. Except for a short distance along the Colorado River, the border separating Arizona and southwestern New Mexico from Mexico was established by surveyed lines after the GADSDEN PURCHASE in 1854.

A Changing Border. The United States acquired no further territory from Mexico after 1854, nor were there major boundary disputes between the two nations after that date. The chief source of political friction related to the border treaty was the unreliability of using the dynamic Rio Grande as a dividing line. It soon became evident that the Rio Grande was prone to changing its course during major floods. A major southward shift of the river occurred in 1864, placing tracts of Mexican territory on the Texas side of the river. These tracts of land, called *bancos*, were increasingly isolated by swings of the Rio Grande during the next forty years. Repeated Mexican calls for redress led to the signing of the Banco Treaty in 1905, in which the United States and Mexico agreed to exchange *bancos* in equal amounts from time to time in an attempt to compensate for shifts in the river's course.

One large *banco*, named El Chamizal for the scrubby bush that grew on it, had been isolated north of the river in 1864 between the cities of El Paso, Texas, and

San Antonio, Texas, celebrates a fiesta in the Mexican tradition. (James Shaffer)

Ciudad Juarez, Chihuahua. The disposition of this parcel had not been clarified in the 1905 treaty; thus, in 1910, the United States agreed to arbitration by a joint Mexican-American commission that was appointed by both governments to settle the dispute. The commission decided that El Chamizal should be returned to Mexico; however, the United States refused to accept the ruling, although it had agreed initially to accept the commission's decision. The matter continued as a political irritant between the two countries until 1963, when the TREATY OF EL CHAMIZAL was signed by presidents John F. Kennedy and Adolfo López Mateos. As a result of this act, 4.3 miles of new concrete riverbed was laid and a new bridge, the Free Bridge, was constructed. On December 13, 1968, presidents Lyndon Johnson and Gustavo Díaz Ordaz met at this bridge and diverted the Rio Grande into its new course, thereby returning the 437 acres of El Chamizal to Mexico.

The International Boundary and Water Commission of the United States and Mexico was established by treaty in 1944 as a binational commission with the fundamental responsibilities of boundary demarcation, division of water resources, flood control, and other water-related political issues of concern to both nations. It followed an active course in physically rectifying the channel of the Rio Grande after the 1930's. By 1992, a total of 6,920 acres of land had been exchanged by the two countries as a consequence of the straightening and shortening of the river's course by engineering projects. As an example, one stretch of the boundary east of El Paso was shortened from 155 to 86 miles. The consequence of such projects along the full length of the Rio Grande was to relocate the border by placing the river within an engineered channel rather than allowing river flooding to dictate the placement of the international boundary.

Geography and Climate. The United States-Mexico border adjoins four U.S. states—California, Arizona, New Mexico, and Texas—and six Mexican states—Baja California, Sonora, Chihuahua, Coahuila, Nuevo Leon, and Tamaulipas. Within these states, there are twenty-three United States border counties and thirty-eight Mexican border *municipios* (counties). Among governmental units immediately along the border are eleven major pairs of "twin cities" and several other scattered towns.

Climatic conditions in the border region range from semi-arid to true desert. The average annual rainfall along the delta of the Rio Grande in the Texas-Tamaulipas area is 20 to 25 inches, which decreases to less than 10 inches in northern Chihuahua-southern New Mexico. To the south is the Chihuahua-Coahuila Desert, which is even drier. The border from eastern Arizona to northern Baja California extends through the Sonoran Desert, the driest region of North America. That desert extends into California and Arizona to the north and Baja California and Sonora to the south. Rainfall totals there average less than 2 inches per year. The average rainfall in San Diego and Tijuana, on the Pacific Ocean terminus of the border, is about 11 inches. The availability of water is the crucial limiting factor for the ecosystems and human communities of the entire border region.

The air masses that prevail across most of the border region are generally dry but bring seasonal extremes of temperature. The cold, dry air that dominates the higher elevations from southern Arizona to northern Nuevo Leon brings frequent freezes from November to April. These invasions of cold air often create blizzards across this region. During the summer, hot, dry air masses dominate, and temperatures from southwestern Texas to northeastern Baja California can exceed 100 degrees Fahrenheit. Only near San Diego-Tijuana at the extreme west and near Brownsville-Matamoros at the extreme east of the border are temperatures moderated by bodies of water.

The natural environment of the border region has not served as a politically or economically unifying factor. The sparsely inhabited dry country on both sides of the border historically has served as a wide buffer zone separating the distant centers of power of both the United States and Mexico. The emergence after World War II of a border region suturing two nations together socioeconomically resulted in spite of physical geography.

The economies of the border states have had a common feature in their abundant mineral resources. Sonora has been the leading producer of copper in Mexico from its mines around Cananea. Arizona produces almost 65 percent of the copper in the United States from its mines in the southern part of the state. California produces oil, natural gas, and evaporite minerals; New Mexico produces coal and natural gas; and Texas produces natural gas, sulfur, and more than one-third of the United States' oil. Tamaulipas is a major producer of natural gas and oil. Chihuahua produces silver, lead, zinc, and gold. Coahuila has produced nearly all the high-quality coal in Mexico, as well as barite and fluorite. Nuevo Leon produces iron ore and limestone. This mineral diversity on both sides of the border has allowed most of the border states to develop

Small stands selling Mexican and American food serve patrons of a San Antonio, Texas, carnival. (James Shaffer)

diversified economies incorporating mining, agriculture, and livestock grazing. Trading of mineral resources across the border has served to strengthen economic ties between the two countries.

Population. Computation of the human population of the border region necessarily depends on how the area is defined. Many border scholars consider the border region to be a band roughly one hundred miles wide centered on the international boundary.

Estimates of the human population on the border itself in 1900 range from 70,000 to 100,000, with half living in San Diego, California. The official 1990 census figures for Mexico and the United Sates show that the population for the border region had increased to more than 11 million, a growth rate considerably higher than for any other regions in the two countries.

In 1990, about 16 percent of the Mexican population lived in the six border states, a figure of 13.3 million people. Nearly 4 million lived in *municipios* along the border. In the same year, 21 percent of the United States' population, nearly 52 million people, lived in the four border states. About 7.5 million of those people lived in counties along the border.

The rate of increase in population in border states and municipalities also was high between 1980 and 1990. The general rates of population increase for Mexican border states and *municipios* between 1986 and 1990 were 6.5 percent and 9 percent, respectively; the rate of increase for Mexico as a whole was about 2.1 percent. The high rates of increase for the border political units were largely a result of in-migration of people from southern and central Mexico. The 6.5 percent rate of increase for the six Mexican states consisted of a 2 percent rate of natural increase added to a 4.5 percent rate of in-migration. Similarly, the Mexican border municipalities' growth rate of 9 percent resulted from 1.8 percent natural increase added to a rate of in-migration of 7.1 percent. Some Mexican border cities had growth rates exceeding 10 percent.

The U.S. states and counties along the border showed a similar trend. The population growth for the entire country averaged 1.2 percent from 1986 to 1990, but the rates of increase for border states and counties averaged 2.8 percent and 2.1 percent, respectively. (San Diego County showed a 3.5 to 3.7 percent annual increase.) These rates consisted of a 1.1 percent rate of natural increase for the states added to an in-migration rate of 1.7 percent, and a natural rate of increase of 1.2 percent for the counties added to a 0.9 percent rate of in-migration. Population growth rates along both sides of the border region were above national averages, largely as a result of in-migration.

The border population of Mexico was very young in comparison with that of the United Sates—35 percent of Mexico's border population was younger than fifteen years of age, compared to 23 percent in the United States. The percentage of older people in the Mexican border population is considerably smaller than in the U.S. border population.

Another important dynamic in the border region has been the heavy increase in urban populations on both sides of the boundary. In the 1990 census, more than 90 percent of the total population of the border region lived in the twenty-two major urban centers. These cities grew after 1950 because of historical transborder connections, connections to the hinterland of each country, and recent economic developments.

Socioeconomic Conditions. Between 1848 and the 1940's the U.S.-Mexico borderlands were economically and socially marginal to both counties. After World War II, there were dramatic changes in the border region. They occurred for several major reasons: a Mexican national development program aimed specifically at the border cities, illegal and legal migrants choosing to settle permanently in border cities, the economic boom in the states of northern Mexico, and the growth of population and economic activity of the Sun Belt states of the United States.

The binational BORDER INDUSTRIALIZATION PROGRAM (BIP), approved in 1965, transformed the townscapes of the Mexican border cities. This program, known as the MAQUILADORA program, was intended to boost economic activity in Mexican border cities by establishing *maquiladoras* (industrial parks) for products of American corporations. The program began slowly but expanded rapidly between 1980 and 1992. The Mexican government estimated that nearly all the net growth or employment in Mexico during those years, almost 600,000 jobs, was in the *maquiladora* program. By 1993, nearly twenty-two hundred *maquilas* (individual assembly factories) were functioning, and 92 percent were located in cities in the six border states of Mexico. By 1993, the BIP provided 81 percent of Mexico's manufactured exports and almost 40 percent of Mexico's total exports to the United States. This program was responsible for the bulk of the nonpetroleum, nonagricultural foreign exchange earnings

of Mexico between 1982 and 1993, an amount that reached nearly $3.75 billion per year by 1990.

The Lower Rio Grande Valley. This subregion is dominated by the contiguous twin cities of Brownsville, Texas (1990 population 105,000), and Matamoros, Tamaulipas (population 310,000). It has been common in the border region for the Mexican city to have a larger population. Brownsville had a Mexican American population of 81 percent and an economy based heavily on commerce with Mexico. The port of Brownsville served the entire lower Rio Grande Valley of Texas as well as Matamoros and Monterrey, Mexico. Both Brownsville and Matamoros were agricultural supply centers, and Matamoros has received many winter tourists from the United States. After 1970, this portion of the border was the most heavily used by illegal immigrants from Central American countries, with more than 90 percent attempting to cross in this area.

McAllen, Texas (1990 population 75,000), and Reynosa, Tamaulipas (population 320,000), lie sixty miles to the west. Reynosa has benefited economically from a major Pemex petrochemical complex and is a tourist and agricultural center. McAllen's economy was based on the oil and natural gas industry but also depends heavily on retail sales to Mexican shoppers. In the early 1990's, Reynosa and Matamoros had 8 percent of the total *maquilas* in the BIP.

The Central Rio Grande Valley. This subregion had three sets of twin cities: Laredo, Texas (1990 population 124,000), and Nuevo Laredo, Tamaulipas (325,000); Eagle Pass, Texas (26,000), and Piedras Negras, Coahuila (108,000); and Del Rio, Texas (35,000), and Ciudad Acuna, Coahuila (58,000). The two Laredos are integrated, contiguous border cities that sit astride the main highway connecting Monterrey and San Antonio. They have been important border crossings connecting the industrial centers of both nations. Laredo, with a purchasing region of more than 500,000 people, mostly living in Mexico, in the early 1990's had the highest per capita retail sales in the United States. Laredo was also 94 percent Mexican American. Three bridges were built across the Rio Grande at Laredo, including one that opened to serve increased truck traffic in 1991. The three Mexican cities in this subregion had about 8 percent of the MAQUILADORAS along the border. Cultural integration was shown by the Nuevo Laredo professional baseball team, which played one-third of its home games in Laredo. Binational cooperation has been demonstrated by the joint decision by the United States and Mexico in 1989 to construct a sewage disposal plant in Nuevo Laredo.

El Paso, Texas, and Ciudad Juárez, Mexico. El Paso (1990 population 592,000) and Ciudad Juárez (1.5 million) are located at the far western terminus of the Rio Grande as a border river. The two cities are contiguous and have been increasingly integrated economically and socially. El Paso was second only to San Diego in the early 1990's for the number of border crossings occasioned by commerce and tourism. El Paso's economy depended on retail trade with Mexico, light industry, the military, and the transportation industry. The economy of Ciudad Juárez was based on tourism, agriculture, and U.S. trade. More than four hundred *maquilas* (19 percent of the total) were located in Ciudad Juárez, placing it second only to Tijuana. Nearly 130,000 people worked in these *maquilas*. A major concern of these twin cities has been the condition of the air basins and water supplies they share. Air and water pollution on one side of the border affect the other, stimulating joint concerns for common use of water supplies and air quality.

Nogales, Arizona, and Nogales, Sonora. Nogales, Arizona, had a 1990 population of 30,000, which was more than 82 percent Mexican American. Nogales, Sonora (population 180,000), is contiguous with its neighbor to the north, and their economies have been heavily linked. During the early 1990's, Nogales, Sonora, had more than eighty *maquilas*, with a total employment in excess of twenty-two thousand. The border crossing was the largest port of entry for fresh vegetables from the irrigated river valleys along the Sonora-Sinaloa coasts of Mexico. More than one million tons of vegetables per year were exported to the United States, and the trade was especially heavy during the winter months. Air pollution, border crime, flood control, and sewage disposal are important binational issues.

Imperial-Mexicali Valley/Rio Colorado. Two population clusters occur in this subregion: One consists of Yuma, Arizona (1990 population 55,000), and San Luis Rio Colorado, Sonora (150,000 to 200,000 estimated). The other is Mexicali, Baja California (800,000), and Calexico, California (92,000). This sector of the border region has been dominated by the irrigated agriculture practiced along the lower Colorado River and in the adjoining Mexicali and Imperial valleys. Water supply and quality have been the most important binational

San Diego's Old Town features a cluster of international shops and restaurants. (Justine Hill)

issues: The quality of water delivered to Mexico, as the last user of Colorado River water, has been one issue; the quality of water in streams such as the "New River," which carries polluted drainage water across the border into the United States, has been another. San Luis Rio Colorado was the fourth-largest city in Sonora by the mid-1990's; its growth was mainly fueled by agricultural expansion after 1970. Mexicali, which is the only Mexican state capital situated on the border, also grew rapidly with an economy that depended on agriculture and the BIP. More than 160 plants, nearly 8 percent of the total, were located around Mexicali in 1993.

San Diego and Tijuana. This subregion had the highest population in the border region. San Diego County had a population of 2.5 million in 1990; the city of San Diego had a population of 1.2 million, of which 15 percent was Mexican American. Tijuana, Baja California, which lies directly on the border, had a population estimated at between 750,000 and 1.1 million. The city of Tecate, thirty-five miles east of Tijuana, had a population of approximately 44,000.

San Diego is located twelve miles north of Tijuana. Much of San Diego's growth occurred for reasons other than its location within the border region, including the military, the aerospace and electronics industries, tourism, and the favorable subtropical climate. Only after World War II did significant transborder tourism and commercial trade develop and expand the city's linkage to Tijuana.

Tijuana developed primarily as a border city, and its growth after 1950 was rapid and largely unplanned. The economic growth was fueled by tourism—here were more than forty million legal border crossings per year—and the BIP. In 1993, there were 638 *maquilas* in Tijuana, about 29 percent of the total, employing nearly 40 percent of all workers in the border region. Tecate had more than 105 maquilas, about 5 percent of the total. In response to the heavy transborder commercial traffic stimulated by the BIP, a major border crossing was opened at Otay Mesa, east of Tijuana's downtown area. This border sector also had the largest number of illegal border crossings per year, with more than 600,000 apprehensions in the San Ysidro office of the Immigration and Naturalization Service (INS) in 1991. In the 1990's, flooding of the Tijuana River and sewage disposal were serious problems that remained to be solved by binational cooperation.

Problems and Challenges. By the 1990's, the primary economic and social linkages between the United States and Mexico were well established across the border region. The NORTH AMERICAN FREE TRADE AGREEMENT (NAFTA), passed in 1993, was scheduled to abolish all tariffs on goods and services within ten years. Tourism between the United States and Mexico increased by 55 percent between 1986 and 1992, from 11.4 million to 18 million visitors heading south. The *MAQUILADORA* program boosted employment in border cities and enabled U.S. corporations to remain competitive in global markets. Commercial trade increased between border cities, although the direction and amount of trade remained dependent on such factors as the dollar-peso exchange rate and the price of oil. Mexican consumers on several occasions either threatened or carried out a boycott of U.S. merchants to bring attention to treatment of legal border crossers that they believed was unfair.

Export-import trade between the two nations burgeoned; Mexico became the United States' second most important trading partner in 1991. Petroleum and natural gas have become important commodities in transborder trade. In 1993, more than $4 billion worth of petroleum was exported to the United States, which re-exported 91 billion cubic feet of natural gas to Mexico as well as large quantities of refined petroleum products such as gasoline. Trade of agricultural products from the linked areas of the Rio Grande Valley and the Mexicali-Rio Colorado-Imperial Valley region was expected to increase in both directions because of NAFTA.

Social linkages are shown by the percentages of the populations of U.S. border municipalities and states that are Hispanic. In 1993, approximately 25 percent of California's population was Hispanic (90 percent of which was Mexican American), and this ethnic group was the most rapidly increasing group in all four border states. Hispanic populations ranged from 15 percent to 91 percent in the twelve major U.S. border cities. The movement of workers from Mexico into the United States allowed the harvesting of agricultural crops and provided a large pool of laborers for the U.S. domestic and commercial sectors. This socioeconomic process began with the bracero program of 1942 to 1964 and was continued with the provisions of the IMMIGRATION REFORM AND CONTROL ACT OF 1986.

Along with these positive factors, there were several areas of concern to government planners in both countries. The *maquiladoras*, although beneficial to U.S. business, were increasingly viewed in Mexico as counterproductive to the needed industrial development of the nation. *Maquilas* primarily employed women, their pay was low, and their rate of turnover was high. Urban

Border Patrol agents escort five young men back across the U.S.-Mexico border after their illegal crossing. (AP/Wide World Photos)

infrastructure, such as schools, electricity, water, fire protection, and sewage, were lacking for workers who clustered near industrial parks in slumlike conditions. According to Mexico's environmental protection ministry (SEDUE), more than half of the MAQUILADORAS produced toxic waste, and many discharged it untreated as wastewater or into drainage ditches. In sites from California to Texas, these toxic wastes were blamed for environmental contamination and suspected human illnesses. Another concern was the estimated eight million tons of hazardous materials shipped into Mexico from the United States each year by businesses trying to avoid disposing of them under expensive Environmental Protection Agency guidelines.

Air pollution has been a growing concern in the border region. Residents of El Paso and Ciudad Juárez share an air basin that was seriously polluted by emissions on twelve to sixteen days per year between 1988

and 1992. These emissions were especially noxious at border crossings, where long lines of vehicles wait to cross with engines idling—each day there were more than 1.5 million such crossings. In addition, clouds of toxic gases have been released inadvertently by *maquilas* and chemical plants in Ciudad Juárez, Nogales, and Matamoros.

Water quality was the most critical concern throughout the border region through the early 1990's. On the Texas side of the Rio Grande, numerous *colonias* (unregulated settlements) used water contaminated by sewage or industrial runoff. Sewage outfall from the Tijuana River flowed northward to contaminate beaches in the southern part of San Diego County. In the Imperial Valley, the New River brought so much toxic contamination in its flow that it could not be used to irrigate crops. Ciudad Juárez had no municipal sewage treatment facilities and pumped fifty-five million gallons of untreated waste into ditches that drained into the Rio Grande.

Two large aquifers supplied the cities of El Paso and Ciudad Juárez with fresh water; however, the cities pumped 200,000 acre-feet of water per year from the underground reservoirs, which have a recharge rate only about 10 percent of that figure. As the twentieth century came to a close, massive binational cooperation was needed to treat sewage and protect fresh water supplies along the border.

Crossborder illegal migration from Mexico was an "off-the-table" topic in the NAFTA agreements. This issue was prominent politically in California in 1992 and 1994, as the governor sought to force the costs of providing border protection and social services for undocumented immigrants onto the federal government. The construction of border fences and walls at Ciudad Juárez and Tijuana in the early 1990's served more to create social tensions than to curb illegal immigration.

In Mexico, a new political awareness of the border region evolved after 1982. The strength of political parties opposing the ruling Partido Revolucionario Institucional (PRI) in the border states demonstrated the increasing political alienation of northern Mexico from other areas of the country. Luis Donaldo Colosio was chosen as the PRI candidate in 1994, the first time a resident of the border region was so honored. Colosio was from a ranching family in Magdalena, Sonora, about sixty-five miles south of Nogales. Following his assassination in Tijuana in March, 1994, Ernesto Zedillo was chosen as the new candidate. Although Zedillo was born in Mexico City, he spent most of his life in the Mexicali Valley. The election of Zedillo meant that for the first time a representative from the border region was at the head of the Mexican government.

—*Richard L. Haiman*

SUGGESTED READINGS:

• Arreola, Daniel, and James Curtis. *The Mexican Border Cities: Landscape Anatomy and Place Personality*. Tucson: University of Arizona Press, 1993. An extensive work by two geographers examining the urban dynamics of border cities.

• Fernandez, Raul A. *The Mexican-American Border Region: Issues and Trends.* Notre Dame, Ind.: University of Notre Dame Press, 1989. A useful synthesis of all major cultural, historical, economic, and environmental factors in the study of the border region.

• Hall, Douglas K. *The Border: Life on the Line*. New York: Abbeville Press, 1988. A sensitive synthesis of prose and photography that tells the human story of life in the border region.

• Herzog, Lawrence A. *Where North Meets South: Cities, Space, and Politics on the U.S.-Mexico Border*. Austin: University of Texas of Austin, 1990. Surveys the important aspects of the evolution of urban space and morphology along the border.

• Jamail, Milton H., and Margo Gutierrez. *The Border Guide: Institutions and Organizations of the United States-Mexico Borderlands*. Austin: University of Texas of Austin, 1992. A comprehensive compendium of all major sources and agencies that provide analyses of and data on the border region.

Boricua: Puerto Rican people. Boricua is the collective name Puerto Rican people sometimes use to refer to themselves. In pre-Hispanic times, the Taino Indians called the island of Puerto Rico "BORINQUEN," and during the country's fight for independence from Spain, the name resurfaced. In the 1960's and 1970's, Borinquen became an important symbol of cultural nationalism to mainland Puerto Ricans, some of whom wanted independence for the island. Labeling themselves Boricua acknowledged the importance of indigenous roots to Puerto Ricans' identity. Puerto Ricans in the United States continue to use Boricua as a term of pride and identification with their roots.

Borinquen: Taino Indian name for the island of Puerto Rico. After Christopher Columbus landed on the island, he renamed it San Juan Bautista. In Puerto Rico's struggle for independence from Spain in the late 1800's, the name was revived by Puerto Ricans. Immigrants from Puerto Rico to the United States often referred to their homeland as "Borinquen *querido*," or beloved Borinquen.

Bossa nova: Brazilian style of jazz samba and dance form. A combination of North American jazz and South American SAMBA, the bossa nova was designed to be listened to and played. The basic step associated with the dance (step on one foot and touch with the other) originated later. Characteristic of this musical style are the basic duple meter of the samba (with more harmonic and melodic complexity), less emphasis on percussion, a soloist accompanied primarily by the guitar (both for harmonic and percussive support), and subdued, almost spoken singing. It originated in the late 1950's and became popular in the 1960's, affecting other popular music forms.

Botánicas: Stores selling medicinal plants and herbs. Also called *yerberías*, *botánicas* sell HERBAL MEDI-

This botánica *displays religious figurines in its front window.* (City Lore, Martha Cooper)

CINE and a variety of other magico-religious products in Latino communities. These plants and herbs are sold and recommended by *curanderos*, Latino folk practitioners, spiritualists, and faith healers. (*See* CURANDERISMO and SPIRITISM AND SPIRITUALISM.)

Botánicas have their roots in the European apothecary tradition and in Native American herbal markets. Aztecs developed botanical gardens and did research on medicinal plants. They had a highly developed botanical taxonomy and vast empirical knowledge of medicinal plants and herbs.

Hernán Cortés reported to King Charles V of Spain that he had seen vast open-air Aztec herbal markets and that Aztec apothecaries sold medicinal herbs and plants from their homes. Aztecs esteemed their medicinal plants and herbs both for their medicinal qualities and for their religious significance. The Spanish quickly became aware of the importance of the native herbal tradition. They were interested in herbs and medicinal plants not only for scientific reasons but also because of economic considerations related to the trade in herbs and spices that was so important during the age of exploration. Philip II sent his personal physician, Francisco Hernández, to New Spain in 1570 and charged him with making a full account of all medicinal herbs, trees, plants, and seeds, as well as their uses in the New World.

In a *botánica*, one can meet with *herbolarios* and *YERBEROS*, herb specialists who know the medicinal qualities and therapeutic uses of plants and herbs. These herb shops sell to *curanderos*, people with some knowledge of herbal remedies, and those who have been recommended by *curanderos*. *Curanderos* make decoctions and infusions from leaves, bark, roots, seeds, and flowers they have purchased in the herb stores. Occasionally they mix powdered forms of plants with oils, which can also be bought in *botánicas*. Salves, ointments, and materials for poultices can also be found in these shops.

In a *botánica*, one might find such products as *aceite de vibora* (rattlesnake oil), *alamo sauco* (cottonwood), *hueso de albaricoque* (apricot seed), *alcanfor* (camphor), *yerba del lobo* (licorice), *yerba buena* (spearmint), and *ajenjo* (absinthe). These products are touted as cures for snakebites, infertility, arthritis, and kidney disease as well as folk illnesses such as *mal de ojo* (evil eye), *susto* (fright), and *empacho* (stomach obstruction). *Botánicas* may also sell other magico-religious products, including traditional Catholic religious iconography, such as images of Christ, the Blessed Mother, and the saints; incense, candles, and holy water; and magic potions and amulets.

Botero, Fernando (b. Apr. 19, 1932, Medellín, Colombia): Artist. As a figurative painter and sculptor, Botero has specialized in depicting plump, exaggerated figures that convey humor or satire. The painting style that has earned him an international reputation combines the primitive features of Colombian folk art, the satirical worldview and meticulous painting techniques of leading Spanish painters, and the influences of Mexican muralists and Italian Renaissance masters.

Botero began his artistic career as a newspaper illustrator. After graduating from college in Medellín in 1950, he moved to Bogotá and presented his first solo exhibits. In 1952, Botero won a national prize for painting. Soon after that, he traveled throughout Europe and Mexico to study art.

Botero moved to the United States in 1960, and before the artist had turned thirty, one of his paintings had been purchased for New York City's famous Museum of Modern Art. Eventually, Botero's work was exhibited worldwide and added to museum collections in Puerto Rico, the Dominican Republic, France, Italy, Germany, Finland, Spain, Venezuela, and Colombia.

Botero's paintings often feature Latin American generals, politicians, kings, and families with pets that resemble their owners—all rotund, and almost all with large heads and hands out of proportion to their bodies. He has also created parodies of well-known paintings. In the 1970's, Botero began adding giant bronze sculptures of humans and animals to his repertoire.

Box bill (1926): Legislation proposed by Texas congressman John C. Box as an amendment to the Immigration Act of 1924. The Box bill proposed that countries in the Western Hemisphere be included as part of the quota system imposed in the 1924 act, thus limiting the total number of immigrants to be admitted from Mexico to two thousand per year.

In response to concerns arising from the growing number of Mexican immigrants who were entering the United States during the early 1920's, the House Immigration and Naturalization Committee held various hearings throughout the country regarding the impact of the proposed bill. At these hearings, agricultural interests (cattle ranchers and farmers) and railroad owners were among the employers who were worried that a lowered quota would drive their businesses into bankruptcy. These employers clearly favored a policy of unrestricted migration because it would result in a large pool of easily exploited laborers from Mexico who would work for lower wages than American workers were willing to accept.

These commercial interests were opposed by labor organizers and union representatives, who were concerned about protecting the rights of workers already in the United States, and by State Department officials, who were anxious that the bill not negate the department's efforts to improve relations between the United States and Mexico through the Good Neighbor Policy. The lobbying efforts of the commercial interests succeeded in preventing passage of the bill.

Boxing: Boxing was integrated into Latin American culture by the early 1900's. The sport has provided a source of inspiration and role models for Latinos, many of whom have become world champions and helped to make boxing a major and popular sport.

Boxing's Introduction. Boxing was introduced into Latin American culture in the late 1800's as a result of contact with the British (the inventors of modern boxing) and Americans. Boxing was introduced into Chile, for example, in the late nineteenth century by British sailors in the port of Valparaiso. From there, it spread to Santiago. The close geographic ties between North and South America also facilitated the introduction of boxing into Latin American culture.

Following the American and British models, Latin Americans began to organize sports and athletic clubs around the turn of the century, changed school curricula to put greater emphasis on sports, and established national associations and physical education facilities. Latin Americans likewise affiliated themselves with emerging international sports associations and events, including the Olympic and Pan American Games.

Many Latin Americans were early participants in the Olympics, and several were successful in boxing. For example, Argentina fielded its first full team in 1924, and in the four sets of Olympic Games between 1924 and 1936, it won sixteen medals in boxing.

As sports became increasingly institutionalized and commercialized, the professional sports in the United States with the greatest mass appeal (among which was boxing) were also professionalized among Latinos and Latin Americans. Chile held its first professional bout in 1905, and professional boxing began in Venezuela in 1922.

Boxing's Virtues. In both the United States and Latin American countries, boxing and other sports were perceived by some government officials and many people in society at large as activities that would confer physical and spiritual growth, teach discipline, forge a sense of national identity, and earn international respect and prestige. In addition, they could be economically profitable. Cesar Vicale, former president of the Argentine Olympic Committee and Argentine Boxing Federation, optimistically pronounced in 1922 that Argentina was on the threshold of perfecting its people. Andres Olan Santandreu of Mexico in 1950 conceded that injuries and physical damage were integral parts of boxing but argued that boxing was justified by the fact that it improved health and protected the vigor of society. Roberto Riviero and Leo Benitex wrote in 1981 of Venezuela's success in professional boxing. At that time, several of its boxers were world ranked, and boxing provided a source of employment and income to an otherwise underdeveloped land.

The 1923 heavyweight championship bout between Jack Dempsey and Argentinean Luis Angel Firpo was an important event in developing a sense of identity for Argentine sport. Firpo was the first Argentine athlete to attract worldwide attention.

Boxing has obtained added luster and status among Latin Americans through its use in literature. Noted regional writers such as Nicolás Guillén, Roberto Arlt, Maria Ester Gilio, Fernando Alegría, and Julio Cortázar have used boxing in their writing. American novelist Jack London's short story "The Mexican" (1913) told of eighteen-year-old Felipe Rivera, who took up boxing in exile in America in order to raise money to help finance a revolution against Mexican dictator Porfirio Díaz.

Other writers, however, have attacked, denounced, and condemned boxing as a barbaric blood sport. Elio Menendez, Victor Joaquin Ortega, Esteban Navajos, Rafael Ramirez Heredia, Carlos Perozzo, and Alfonso Rojas Sucre, among others, have characterized boxing as anti-sport and anti-culture. Boxers inflict and suffer excessive physical damage, and the sport's brutality and violence, they argue, stimulate primitive instincts in the spectator. Boxing, they contend, improperly glorifies brute force and hinders moral growth. Additionally, boxing is to be condemned for its corrupt aspects, including use of drugs, fixed fights, and ties to organized crime.

Boxing has survived these repeated attacks in Latin American countries as well as in the United States. In the Western Hemisphere, it is a permanently established, high-profile, popular sport.

Latin American Champions. The emphasis placed on boxing by Latin American countries has resulted in pronounced success. The first Latin American champions appeared in the 1920's and 1930's; they included Pancho Villa, Young Perez, and Kid Chocolate. By the

Roberto Duran lands a hard shot on Mexico's Juan Medina on the way to a technical knockout. (AP/Wide World Photos)

1990's, Latin American countries had produced more than 150 world champions.

The United States is the center of world boxing in terms of resources, training facilities, competition, and opportunity to achieve recognition and wealth. Many Latin American fighters traveled to the United States, either to live and train there or to promote their careers by fighting frequently there. U.S. fights offered more media exposure and larger purses.

Latin American boxers have attained widespread media exposure. *Sports Illustrated*, for example, has carried feature articles on Panamanian champions Eusebio Pedroza and Roberto DURAN, Nicaraguan champion Alexis ARGUELLO, and Mexican champion Julio César CHÁVEZ. Articles on Latin American fighters regularly appear in specialized boxing magazines such as *KO* and *The Ring*. Additionally, *Sports Illustrated* has published articles on the place of boxing in Latin American society, including articles on a ritualistic traditional festival of fist-fighting among two Indian tribes in Bolivia and on Palenque de San Basilio in Colombia, a town of three thousand people that has produced three world champions and in which boxing is a community fixation. Additionally, Latin American fighters receive exposure in the United States through cable and network television appearances.

The long, established history of boxing in the United States and the role of Latin Americans and Latinos in it have been a source of inspiration and pride. Boxers become role models, encouraging careers in boxing among the large population of Latinos. As a result, professional boxing has become a major sport venue for Latinos.

The Rewards of Boxing. The motivations for Latinos to become boxers are the same as for Latin Americans and non-Latinos. Part of boxing's appeal is that it offers a way out of poverty and isolation. It provides the opportunity to obtain wealth, power, fame, and heroic status. Underprivileged youth with limited opportunities view boxing as a means to a better life. The odds are heavily against success at any more than a local level, but the many Latin American and Latino champions show the possibilities.

Young Latinos and Latin Americans turn to boxing for additional reasons. One is that boxing provides a strong sense of identity and pride. It evokes strong emotions of respect and admiration. As one example, after Mexican American Bobby Chacón was defeated by Nicaraguan Alexis Arguello, out of respect for Arguello's skills and compassion he named his next child Alexis.

Another reason for boxing's popularity is appreciation of the atmosphere of brutality and violence. It is perceived as a "blood sport," offering the opportunity to display MACHISMO and to vent feelings of hatred and contempt. Writer Hugh McIlvanney observed that no fighters anywhere are more dedicated to the raw violence of the business than are Mexicans. He mentions a gym in Mexico City where more than a hundred boxers work out regularly and others come for a chance to show that they can transfer their fighting skills from the alleys to the boxing ring.

A symbiotic atmosphere of violence can develop between fighter and fan. McIlvanney observed on one occasion that Latino fight fans in Los Angeles were a screaming mob whose lust for blood gave the Olympic Auditorium the atmosphere of a Guadalajara cockfight, but a hundred times more intense.

The gentlemanly Alexis ARGUELLO once approached Panamanian Roberto DURAN to shake his hand. Duran, famous for his intense hatred of opponents, backed away, screaming at Arguello, "Get away from me! I'm not your friend! Get away from me!" Duran remarked after beating an opponent that if he had been in condition, the opponent would have been sent to the morgue rather than the hospital. On another occasion, Duran made an obscene gesture to opponent Sugar Ray Leonard's wife and called her a *puta* (whore). At the end of their first fight, Duran spat in Leonard's face.

Prominent Latino Fighters. A number of Latino fighters have achieved varying degrees of prominence and fame. Art Aragon was a popular local fighter in the Los Angeles area in the 1950's and was one of the early Latinos to gain national exposure. Champions include Carlos PALOMINO, welterweight, 1976-1979; Arturo Frias, lightweight, 1981-1982; Bobby Chacón, featherweight, 1974-1975, and junior lightweight, 1982-1983; Paul Gonzalez, light flyweight, 1984 Olympic gold medalist; Richard Sandoval, bantamweight, 1984-1986; Tony Lopez, junior lightweight, 1989-1990; Orlando Canizales, bantamweight champion beginning in 1988; and Michael CARBAJAL, silver medalist in the 1988 Olympics and light flyweight champion from 1990 to 1994.

Particular attention has been paid to Oscar DE LA HOYA, an outstanding example of a young Latino fighter who has risen above modest circumstances to attain international recognition, wealth, and admiration. He provides an ideal role model and advertisement for what boxing has to offer to talented Latinos.

De la Hoya was born to Mexican American parents on February 4, 1973, in the barrio of East Los Angeles.

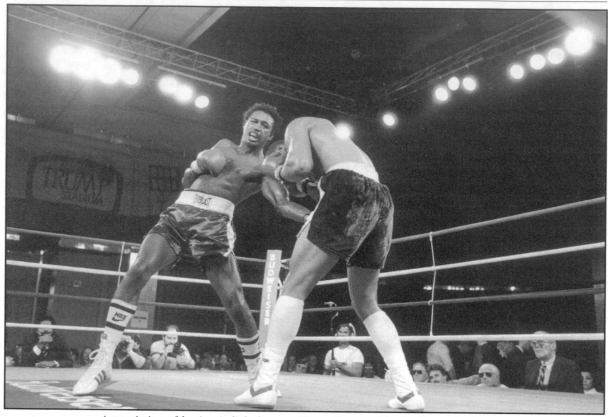

Appreciation of boxing is linked to machismo. (Impact Visuals, Donna DeCesare)

He was a national Golden Gloves champion at the age of fifteen and accumulated a remarkable amateur record of more than two hundred wins against only five losses. He was the only gold medal winner (lightweight) on the American boxing team at the 1992 Olympics.

As a professional, de la Hoya accumulated eleven straight wins, ten by knockout. Most of these fights were televised. He won the World Boxing Organization (WBO) junior lightweight title by a knockout in 1994 in only his twelfth fight. His appeal is enhanced by his being an American citizen of Mexican descent, which gives him a crossover appeal generally unattainable by Latin American fighters. Fight promoter Bob Arum said of de la Hoya that he is an Olympic star who is American but who carries a Mexican flag into the ring. Arum believed that de la Hoya had the potential to be more successful than Sugar Ray Leonard and Marvin Hagler, perhaps even rivaling Muhammad Ali.

—Laurence Miller

SUGGESTED READINGS:

• Arbena, Joseph L., ed. *Sport and Society in Latin America: Diffusion, Dependency, and the Rise of Mass Culture.* New York: Greenwood Press, 1988. De-scribes the interrelationships between sports and various Latin American societies. Contains interesting data about boxing.

• Farhood, Steve. "The Damaged Image of Oscar de la Hoya." *The Ring* 73 (April, 1994): 22-23, 58-59. Discusses the pressures and decisions confronting the "Golden Boy" of professional boxing and issues of wealth and control of his career.

• Fernandez, Bernard. "He Wants It All and He Wants It Now." *KO*, May, 1994, 28-31, 55. Chronicles Oscar de la Hoya's career, beginning in the East Los Angeles barrio. Discusses the special problems and concerns that fame entails.

• Meserole, Mike, ed. *The 1994 Information Please Sports Almanac.* Boston: Houghton Mifflin, 1994. Issued yearly. Contains a thorough discussion and analysis of the year's major fights as well as a comprehensive list of past and present champions in each weight division.

• Oates, Joyce Carol, and Daniel Halpern, eds. *Reading the Fights.* New York: Henry Holt, 1988. A series of essays on various aspects of and concerns related to boxing in America. Contains a number of references to Latin American fighters.

Boyle Heights (East Los Angeles, Calif.): Residential area. In the 1930's and 1940's, Mexican Americans and African Americans began settling or resettling in the area east of the Los Angeles River. Boyle Heights, originally a Jewish neighborhood, became the focal point of this activity.

Inspired by the Watts riots, Boyle Heights residents began mass protests over civil rights issues in the late 1960's. Beginning in 1969, students at Roosevelt High School staged a series of walkouts, demanding improvements in education, which up to that time had stressed vocational studies over academic subjects. By 1994, the neighborhood was overwhelmingly Chicano, though recent arrivals included many Salvadorans, Puerto Ricans, and Vietnamese.

Boza, Juan (May 6, 1941, Camagüey, Cuba—Mar. 7, 1991): Artist. Boza is celebrated for mixed-media altars that combine images of African deities and Christian saints with jungle foliage, draped cloth, and objects associated with the practice of magic.

The son of a shoemaker and a housewife, Boza grew up in a family devoted to ancestry, religion, and storytelling. These influences and the Afro-Cuban altars of worship surrounding him as a youth are reflected in the art he created as an adult.

In 1959, Boza was awarded a scholarship to study at the Academia de Bellas Artes de San Alejandro in Havana, Cuba. After being expelled from the school over political issues, Boza became an award-winning lithographer and was hired as a designer for the National Council of Culture. He was fired from that position in 1971. Devastated, Boza continued to paint but had to earn a living by restoring religious statues. In 1980, he left Cuba for New York, New York.

Boza's work in Cuba was dominated by abstract images. His art as an exile incorporated obvious images of plants, animals, and people into sites designed to inspire prayer. In the 1980's, he earned several fellowships and awards, and his art was exhibited in New York, Florida, New Jersey, and Louisiana, as well as in Japan, Germany, England, and Mexico.

Bracero Program (1942-1964): Agreement between the United States and Mexico to contract guest workers. The agreement allowed nearly five million Mexican braceros into the United States during its twenty-two-year existence. The program had widespread ramifications, benefiting agricultural businesses but damaging labor relations and the civil rights of Latinos throughout the nation, particularly in the Southwest.

History. The 1930's saw a labor glut, but the entry of the United States into World War II ended the Depression's severe unemployment. Fourteen million Americans had entered the armed forces by 1942, and ten million workers became employed in the labor-hungry war effort. This led to a labor shortage in the nation's agricultural areas and railroads. Field hands were needed to harvest crops in the Southwest, California, and the Midwest. Agribusiness leaders petitioned the government to provide them with temporary workers. In early 1941, Texas farmers petitioned for lifting of restrictions in the IMMIGRATION ACT OF 1917 so that Mexican workers could more easily enter the United States. This was followed by official requests from the Midwest and California. By the beginning of 1942, Mexican workers were entering the United States. Organized labor protested the importation of Mexican workers, as did Mexican American organizations such as the National Spanish-Speaking People's Congress and the Federation of Spanish-American Voters of California. Both organized labor and Mexican American groups feared that braceros would be used as pawns to weaken the position of organized labor and the Mexican American worker.

Mexican American groups as well as the government of Mexico were apprehensive over the treatment of Mexican and Mexican-descended peoples in the United States. Mass deportations during the Great Depression were still fresh in public memory, as were current racist practices in the Southwest and California. The Mexican government insisted that any labor agreement with the United States uphold the provisions of the Mexican Constitution, which required that labor contracts be approved by the government, that wages be agreed upon in advance, and that transportation costs be borne by employers. Many growers were opposed to these demands and advocated unilaterally opening the border, but the Franklin Roosevelt Administration opposed this aggressive action because of the damage it would do to the GOOD NEIGHBOR POLICY.

On August 14, 1943, Roosevelt and Mexican president Manuel Ávila Camacho formally agreed to a guest-worker program to be overseen by both governments. Their agreement, which served as the basis for the bracero program until 1947, called for the Mexican government to supply U.S. growers with as many field workers as needed for the duration of the war. The agreement gave the Mexican government the right to select the workers so as not to harm the Mexican economy. Braceros were to be used only in agriculture and only in the event of a shortage of domestic workers.

The agreement also provided several safeguards for Mexican nationals working in the United States. The U.S. government promised that guest workers would be treated equitably with American workers, would receive a preagreed minimum wage, would be provided with sanitary and adequate habitation and with round-trip transportation, and would receive equal protection before the law.

The number of Mexican workers in the United States rose dramatically. By July of 1945, there were more than 120,000 braceros working in the United States. In 1950, there were 430,000 braceros entering the country through the three central recruitment centers in Mexico: Hermosillo, Chihuahua, and Monterrey. While importing thousands of braceros, however, the IMMIGRATION AND NATURALIZATION SERVICE (INS) was deporting hundreds of thousands of "illegal" aliens, peaking at 1.1 million deportations in 1954. From 1944 to 1953, the INS deported nearly 5 million undocumented workers. This paradoxical phenomenon, known as the "revolving door policy," supplied a steady flow of both "legal" and "illegal" workers, used strategically to keep wages low and the labor market glutted. The "illegal" work force was used to undercut wages, while braceros were used to impress upon the undocumented workers that their positions were tenuous because braceros could always be brought in.

In 1948, control of the bracero program was given to the U.S. secretary of labor. Critics charge that collusion between the growers and the secretary resulted in further lowering of the wage scale, with the importation of large numbers of "illegals" during harvest time. A common practice of deporting workers shortly after the harvest kept wages in the growers' pockets. Powerful growers' interest groups formed to keep the profitable system from being reformed. Groups such as the Imperial Valley Farmers Association and the San Joaquin Farm Production Association convinced the government that they could not abide by the stipulations of the bracero agreement, claiming that it favored the braceros' interests above their own.

The Birth of Public Law 78. By 1951, the Mexican government, tired of the widespread exploitation of braceros, insisted that the U.S. government take tighter control over the growers and supervise recruitment directly. The government responded in 1951 with the institution of PUBLIC LAW 78, which gave the secretary of labor the right to recruit Mexican workers and "illegals" who had lived in the United States for at least five years; according to the law, the secretary of labor could also set their wage levels unilaterally. The legislation resulted in an increase in the migratory flow from Mexico, thus enlarging the labor pool, eroding wages even further, and giving growers even more

BRACEROS CONTRACTED IN THE UNITED STATES, 1951-1964

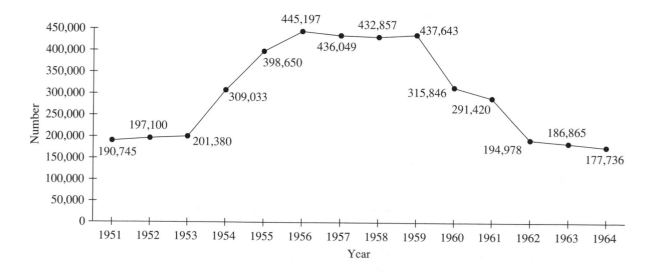

Source: Data are from Juan Ramon García, *Operation Wetback: The Mass Deportation of Mexican Undocumented Workers in 1954* (Westport, Conn.: Greenwood Press, 1980), p. 237, Table 10.

Note: The number for 1951 includes 46,076 workers contracted under a 1949 agreement.

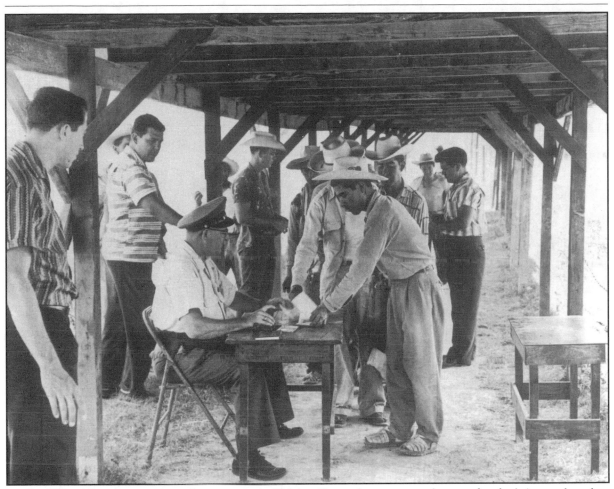

Mexican farm laborers are processed at a center in Hidalgo, Texas, that saw more than one hundred thousand workers in 1958. (AP/Wide World Photos)

power to hire workers on their own terms. At the same time, the new law stripped Mexico of its remaining power to regulate the flow of labor from its own work force.

The passing of the IMMIGRATION AND NATIONALITY ACT OF 1952 (McCarran-Walter Act) made the importation or harboring of "illegal" aliens a federal crime but did not make it a crime to hire an "illegal alien." This became known as the "TEXAS PROVISO" and made the undocumented worker even more powerless while giving growers de facto authorization to hire and import as many undocumented workers as they needed to harvest crops cheaply. This undermined the position of the hapless braceros even further, giving them no legal recourse.

In 1953, the Mexican government protested the gross exploitation and mistreatment of the braceros and unauthorized workers in the United States. The Dwight D. Eisenhower Administration responded by opening the border starting in January of 1954. This led to an even larger labor pool, lower wages, and an increased number of immigrants. Mexico was forced to accept guarantees by the U.S. government that these workers would be treated fairly, promises that had been broken for more than a decade. Although growers overwhelmingly approved of the open border, there was a national outcry, mostly by nativists and labor organizations, against the ever-growing numbers of Mexican workers coming across. This outcry resulted in the infamous OPERATION WETBACK (1954), which sent almost two million Mexican immigrants to jails, detention centers, and border crossings for deportation.

The contradiction between importing workers and deporting workers at the same time has been explained as an attempt by the growers to control labor, lower wages, and guarantee a large labor supply. The growers were successful in all three principal aims. In 1959,

Braceros work on a tomato crop in the Rio Grande Valley. (AP/Wide World Photos)

the American Federation of Labor-Congress of Industrial Organizations (AFL-CIO) began to lobby for termination of the Bracero Program. This growing protest, coupled with César CHÁVEZ's labor organization activities in California and Texas, led to the program's termination. Public Law 78 was terminated on May 29, 1963. The Bracero Program had lasted eighteen years longer than originally agreed upon.

Impact on Labor Relations. Because agricultural businesses depend upon the timely harvest of crops, the threat of work stoppages, strikes, or worker agitation in the form of unionization poses a threat to a grower's investment. For this reason, growers prefer a labor glut, many more workers than there are jobs. In such a situation, a strike or demand for higher wages can be circumvented by bringing in other, more desperate, workers. If there is no risk of a strike, the grower has the advantage of contracting a large number of workers to pick the crop quickly. In these cases, the workers do not benefit; the same total wage payment is spread among more workers, who must find

new jobs sooner than otherwise. The bracero program provided growers with an abundance of laborers, who not only worked very hard but had no real protection and no legal recourse when treated unfairly.

The Great DEPRESSION, while providing employers with a surplus of labor, also brought about unrest in the ranks of industrial workers. Unionization and strikes had resulted in higher wages and employer concessions in industry. This was seen as a threat to farmers and large growers, labor being the only economic factor under the direct control of the agricultural employer. The Bracero Program was seen as a way of circumventing labor unrest in the fields.

The braceros were used by agribusiness interests to weaken the positions of labor unions, undocumented workers, and Latino field workers. Because braceros were virtually slave labor once delivered to a grower, growers did not need to pay fair wages, give labor concessions, or compete in the labor market. Consequently wages dropped, abuses became commonplace, and unionization attempts failed. The profits from bracero and "illegal" labor put the large agribusiness growers at a distinct advantage over one-family farms, which did not have the same access to braceros. During the period of the Bracero Program, American agribusiness became a global power that acquired investments and properties throughout the world.

The 1947 LABOR-MANAGEMENT RELATIONS ACT (Taft-Hartley Act) limited labor's rights. This led to a conservative turn in LABOR UNIONISM, influenced by an era of intense fear of communism. To escape the charge of communist sympathy, the AFL-CIO did not attempt to intervene in anti-Mexican worker discrimination or abuse, nor even to organize farmworkers, until 1959.

The overflowing labor pools that resulted from PUBLIC LAW 78 gave rise to further exploitation of farmworkers. Even as wages fell, growers routinely took as much as half of a bracero's paycheck for "food allocation," serving extremely cheap meals whether the worker wanted them or not. Through provisions of the McCarran-Hartley Acts of 1950 and 1952, the deportation of braceros and undocumented workers became even easier. They could be deported on the grounds of being suspected "communists" or "subversives." The fear of deportation or detention made it difficult for farmworkers to unionize or even demonstrate for better working conditions and wages. Protesting was dangerous and opened the worker to being labeled as an "agitator" or "communist," subject to arrest and deportation. Labor historians commonly interpret the Bracero Program, the McCarran-Walter Act, the Taft-Hartley Act, and other legislation of the era as attempts to curtail U.S. labor activism. The Bracero Program therefore can be seen in a broader context than simply the importation of Mexican workers during a period of labor shortage.

The 1960's saw the organization of farmworkers under leaders such as César CHÁVEZ. Improvement of working conditions came, slowly and painfully, but inexorably. The plight of the bracero in the United States directly affected the lives of undocumented Mexican workers, Latino field workers, and American workers in general. It served to enrich American agribusiness; bring millions of Mexicans to the United States, many of them eventually becoming citizens; and influence the cultural and political climate of the Midwest, the Southwest, and the West Coast.

—*Manuel Luis Martinez*

SUGGESTED READINGS:

• Acuna, Rodolfo. *Occupied America: A History of Chicanos.* 2d ed. New York: Harper & Row, 1981.

Acuna gives an in-depth analysis of the place of the Chicano in American history. Recommended for an understanding of the ramifications of the Bracero Program on the Mexican and Chicano community.

• Anderson, Henry P. *The Bracero Program in California.* New York: Arno Press, 1976. A rigorous study of the Bracero Program's institutionalization in California. Predominantly a statistical and ethnographic study of Mexican immigrant workers.

• Cockroft, James D. *Outlaws in the Promised Land: Mexican Immigrant Workers and America's Future.* New York: Grove Press, 1986. Extensive analysis of the history of Mexican labor in the United States. Cockroft's in-depth analysis of the Bracero Program demonstrates the uses of Mexican labor to benefit U.S. agribusiness and weaken the position of American labor activism.

• Craig, Richard B. *The Bracero Program: Interest Groups and Foreign Policy.* Austin: University of Texas Press, 1971. Concentrates on the conflict between American corporate interests and the Mexican economy.

• Galarza, Ernesto. *Merchants of Labor: The Mexican Bracero Story.* Charlotte, N.C.: McNally & Loftin, 1964. The classic text on the subject. Galarza was himself a migrant worker who later became leader of the National Farm Labor Union. This book brought the plight of the bracero to the public and was influential in ending the program. Carefully documented and researched. Analysis centers on the California bracero.

• Kiser, George C. *The Bracero Program: A Case Study of Its Development, Termination, and Political Aftermath.* Ann Arbor, Mich.: University Microfilms International, 1982. Kiser's doctoral thesis is an extensive treatment of the bracero with an emphasis on the experience of the bracero in the Midwest. Well documented and easy to read. Kiser also gives extensive coverage of congressional battles and debates over Public Law 78.

• Sosnick, Stephen H. *Hired Hands: Seasonal Farm Workers in the United States.* Santa Barbara, Calif.: McNally & Loftin, 1978. Sosnick examines the psychological, cultural, and social profile of the migrant worker. Recommended for the researcher who needs a wide knowledge of migrant labor, past and present.

Bracetti, Mariana (b. c. 1840): Revolutionary figure. Bracetti earned her place in Puerto Rican history by playing a unique role in El GRITO DE LARES, Puerto Rico's 1868 proclamation of independence from Spain. Bracetti sewed the flag raised by the rebel forces.

On September 23, 1868, four hundred people in the town of Lares rose against Spanish rule. The rebellion lasted one day. Historians have pointed to a lack of military training and sufficient arms, as well as prior knowledge of the revolt by the Spanish forces, as factors in its brevity.

Because the Spanish knew of their plans, rebel forces struck earlier than planned. Their leader, Ramón Emeterio BETANCES, was not yet back in Puerto Rico from his travels outside the country when the revolt began. Puerto Rican independence groups hold annual commemorations on the anniversary of El Grito de Lares, and it has evolved into a semi-official holiday.

Brazilian Americans: The number of people of Brazilian background in the United States was relatively insignificant until the second half of the twentieth century. By the 1990's, one could not yet speak of many Brazilian Americans as native U.S. citizens descended from Brazilian citizens. Most were people from Brazil newly resident in the United States.

History. The history of Brazilians in the United States is sparse, going back only to the nineteenth century. On the occasion of the centenary of the United States (1876), the last emperor of Brazil, Dom Pedro II, made an extensive tour of the United States, curious about its republican government and democratic culture. After his deposition in 1889, the newly formed Republic of Brazil sent the first Brazilian ambassador to the United States. On the eve of and during World War II, a Brazilian cultural presence was welcomed in the United States in order to strengthen the pan-American alliance.

As part of a cultural interchange, the popular figure of Carmen MIRANDA appeared in American films and on records. Renowned classical musician Heitor Villa-Lobos gave concerts throughout the United States. Noted painter Cándido Portinari did mural paintings for the Hispanic Division of the Library of Congress and the headquarters of the United Nations.

An international projection of Brazilian popular music began in the postwar period. Tom Jobim, one of the leading figures of BOSSA NOVA (the "new beat"), came to the United States, collaborating with Frank Sinatra. At this time a Brazilian colony, resulting from growing diplomatic and business ties between the two countries, began to emerge in the United States. It was focused primarily in New York City and Washington, D.C.

The Late Twentieth Century. Brazilians increasingly migrated to the United States as refugees, occasionally political but primarily economic. Although the Brazil-

ian community remained small in relation to those of other Latin American groups, in the span of about one generation the number of Brazilians in the United States grew to an estimated half million.

The Brazilian coup of 1964 began a military regime marked by torture and repression. The military government, which retained power until 1985, produced a large number of political refugees, some of whom sought asylum in the established Brazilian community in New York City or in the intellectual and cultural environs of Boston. One of the few Brazilian presidents ever to go in exile, Juscelino Kubitschek (the builder of Brasilia), spent time in the United States.

Opportunity, as well as hardship in their homeland, attracted Brazilians to the United States. The growing worldwide popularity of Brazilian music attracted numerous Brazilian musicians, including Chico Buarque and Milton Nascimento, to the recording industry in Southern California. In addition, Brazilian cinema figures such as actress Sonia Braga went to Hollywood. Another nucleus of the Brazilian community in the United States thus was established in Southern California.

The overwhelming force creating the flood of Brazilians to the United States was the economic crisis in Brazil that began in the mid-1980's. The rate of inflation rose to more than 1,000 percent per year, and extensive unemployment occurred in all levels of society. Anecdotal evidence indicates that the number of Brazilians in the New York-New Jersey area doubled or tripled in the late 1980's, and early 1990's. Brazilians formed another nucleus of their American community in MIAMI, FLORIDA, becoming as significant in real estate acquisition as were Cubans, Venezuelans, and Colombians.

Population Characteristics. For the most part, Brazilian immigrants cannot be characterized as poor, desperate refugees. New York City has the largest, oldest, and most active concentration of Brazilians. They are primarily lower- to middle-class, trying to make a living and save something to send back to families in Brazil. The shoeshine business in Manhattan became dominated by Brazilians. Forty-sixth Street, between Fifth Avenue and the Avenue of the Americas, has been designated "Little Brazil" because of the dominance of Brazilian businesses along it. A city in the interior of Brazil, Governador Valadares, thrives on income sent by its emigrant natives working in New England. In Miami, Brazilians are primarily members of the upper and upper-middle classes, having left Brazil to save their sometimes considerable fortunes.

STATISTICAL PROFILE OF BRAZILIAN AMERICANS, 1990

Total population based on sample: 57,108

Percentage foreign-born: 72%

Median age: 27.7 years

Percentage 25+ years old with at least a high school diploma or equivalent: 78%

Occupation (employed persons 16+ years old)

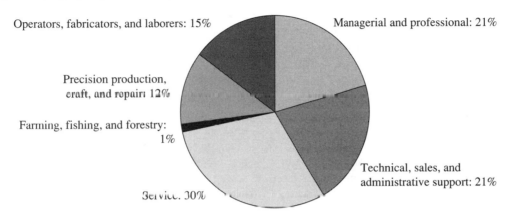

Operators, fabricators, and laborers: 15%

Managerial and professional: 21%

Precision production, craft, and repair: 12%

Farming, fishing, and forestry: 1%

Technical, sales, and administrative support: 21%

Service: 30%

Percentage unemployed: 6.2%

Median household income, 1989: $27,309

Percentage of families in poverty, 1989: 12.3%

Source: Data are from Bureau of the Census, *Census of 1990: Ancestry of the Population in the United States* (Washington, D.C.: Bureau of the Census, 1993), Tables 1, 3, 4, and 5.

Brazilians in the United States generally are settled along the East Coast, concentrating around the New York metropolitan region up to Boston and down to Washington, D.C. Another concentration occurs in the Los Angeles metropolitan area. The rapid, extensive population increase in the Miami area occurred later.

As new immigrants, most Brazilians think—like many of their predecessor immigrants—that they will one day return, richer and more secure, whence they came. Like most of those immigrant forebears, many, probably most, will not return. It is thus from the generation of immigrants of the late twentieth century that a significant community of Americans born of Brazilian descent will emerge.

SUGGESTED READINGS: • Avila, Fernando Bastos de. *Economic Impacts of Immigration: The Brazilian Immigration Problem*. The Hague: Martinus Nijhoff, 1954. • Azevedo, Fernando de. *Brazilian Culture: An Introduction to the Study of Culture in Brazil*. New York: Macmillan, 1950. • "Brazilians Abroad." *Brazil Watch* 10 (March 29–April 12, 1993): 11-17. • Holloway, Thomas H. *Immigrants on the Land: Coffee and Society in Sao Paulo, 1886-1934*. Chapel Hill: University of North Carolina Press, 1980. • Margolis, Maxine L. *Little Brazil: An Ethnography of Brazilian Immigrants in New York City*. Princeton, N.J.: Princeton University Press, 1994. • Skidmore, Thomas E. *The Politics of Military Rule in Brazil, 1964-85*. New York: Oxford University Press, 1988.

Brinson-Pineda, Barbara (b. 1956, San Francisco, Calif.): Poet. Brinson-Pineda has taught creative writing at the University of California, Santa Cruz. A bilingual writer, she often incorporates both Spanish and English in her poems. Her volumes of poetry include *Nocturno* (1978), *Vocabulary of the Dead* (1984), and *Speak to Me from Dreams* (1989). Her first two poetry collections are chapbooks, volumes of poetry printed in limited quantities by small presses to introduce new writers to readers and literary critics.

Brinson-Pineda's poems are seemingly uncomplicated verses constructed with short lines and clear, direct language. Her work has garnered praise for capturing the natural poetic qualities of everyday speech.

Speak to Me from Dreams, Brinson-Pineda's best-known work, was published by Norma ALARCÓN's Third Woman Press, based at the University of California, Berkeley. Brinson-Pineda's work, as is most of the creative work published by Third Woman Press, concentrates on analyzing gender issues through the voices and perspectives of women. *Speak to Me from Dreams* is divided into three sections, each depicting a different historical period; each section is narrated by three different personas, each named María and each depicting her social-historical constraints.

Brito, Aristeo (b. Oct. 20, 1942, Ojinaga, Mexico): Writer. One of the few Mexican American writers who writes almost exclusively in Spanish, Brito traveled back and forth across the United States-Mexican border as a farmworker until becoming a United States citizen in 1967. A professor of Spanish literature, Brito has focused on redefining the American literary canon through the traditional venues of academia. He worked to establish Chicano literature as a permanent section of the Modern Language Association, an important academic organization in the humanities, when he was a delegate to that association in the 1970's.

Brito's first publication, *Fomento literario: Cuentos; poemas* (1974) is just what the title indicates: a collection consisting of eight stories and seventeen poems. Like many of the Chicano poets writing during the Chicano movement, Brito worked with Aztec mythology. *El Diablo en Texas* (1976; *The Devil in Texas*, 1990), a folk-based fantasy divided into three chronological periods, is Brito's first published novel. The novel's sections examine aspects of Mexican American and European American relations during different historical periods: Anglo settlement and Mexican displacement in Texas (1883), zoot suiters and World War II (1942), and self-awareness in the midst of the Chicano movement (1970).

Broadcast journalism: Broadcast news sources exist for the Latino community on both radio and television and in both English and Spanish. Most communities are served by local radio and television stations that produce their own news broadcasts. In addition, sev-

eral national news programs and services target Latino audiences.

Radio. Spanish-language radio began in the 1920's, soon after radio broadcasting developed in North America, when English-language station owners began renting time slots to Latino brokers. During the unpopular early-morning time slots, these brokers would play popular Latino music and provide news from Mexico and other parts of Latin America as well as news about local Latino communities. By 1946, Spanish-language radio programming was popular enough for the first full-time station to be established. KCOR-AM in San Antonio, Texas, the first full-time Spanish-language radio station in the United States, was founded by Raúl Cortez, a former broker.

U.S. Spanish-language radio has since expanded to more than 150 full-time stations, more than 200 part-time stations, several Latino commercial and public radio owners' associations, and various specialized news services. Many radio stations produce their own news broadcasts by gathering information from international wire services and supplementing these reports with news of local events. Many others, however, subscribe to news services. There are three major news services: Spanish Information Systems, RADIO NOTICIAS, and Noticiero Latino. All three produce and distribute five- to ten-minute news programs that subscribers broadcast directly. The services also produce sports specials, news magazines, and public-affairs programs.

Many commercial and public English-language radio stations provide programming targeted to Latinos. Much of this programming is music, but news and public-affairs programs are also aired. One such program of note is *Latino USA*. Launched in 1993 at the University of Texas at Austin, *Latino USA* is an English-language radio journal of news and culture. It is a weekly programming service that provides Latino perspectives on many of the most important news events of the week, as well as interviews, commentaries, and feature stories on a variety of topics related to Latinos.

Television. Three major Spanish-language television networks serve Latinos across the United States and Canada: Univisión, Telemundo, and Galavisión.

Univisión. The Univisión network began with the establishment of KWEX-TV in San Antonio and KMEX-TV in Los Angeles in 1961 and 1962. These stations were owned principally by Emilio Azcárraga Vidaurreta, a Mexican media magnate who saw the United States as a great export market for programming produced in Mexico. Under his direction from 1961 to 1988, the organization expanded from two stations to more than ten directly owned and operated stations, twenty affiliate stations, and a programming network that was originally called SPANISH INTERNATIONAL NETWORK (SIN).

Programming on SIN consisted mainly of films, telenovelas (soap operas), variety shows, sporting events, and news from Mexico. An important program produced at the U.S. headquarters was *Noticiero SIN*, the national nightly newscast, which was originally designed to provide viewers with news focusing on events and people related to the Latino and Latin American communities.

In 1988, after a legal battle, the network and its stations were sold to Hallmark Industries. *Noticiero Univisión* (as the newscast became known) continued to provide important information to the Latino commu-

nity, including coverage of U.S. and Latin American political events. Local news organizations were also expanded. In 1992, the Univisión network and its stations were sold again, this time to a group of investors with interests in Latin America. The group consisted of A. Jerrold Perenchio, a Latino businessman with an interest in media; Televisa, the Mexican television organization owned by the Azcárraga family; and Venevision, the largest media organization in Venezuela.

The two major news programs produced by Univisión are *Noticiero Univisión* and *Primer Impacto*. *Noticiero Univisión* continues the tradition of *Noticiero SIN*, providing a half-hour nightly news recap. The style of the program is much like that of major English-language network newscasts, but there is an emphasis on the needs and interest of the Latino audience. *Primer Impacto* provides news stories as well as information on Latin America's most-wanted criminals and unsolved mysteries.

Both programs are produced at the Univisión headquarters in Miami, and both are served by a large team of correspondents based at Univisión's news bureaus around the world. These correspondents are able to provide up-to-date coverage on breaking news anywhere in the world.

The Univisión news department also supports local affiliate news organizations. In much the same way the English-language networks do, Univisión provides a news service. On a daily basis, news footage and stories put together by the national news team are sent via satellite to affiliates for use on local newscasts.

Telemundo. The Telemundo network was established in May, 1986, by a group of investors called Reliance Capital Group. Reliance, headed by Saul Steinberg and Henry Silverman, purchased several stations in New York, Puerto Rico, and Miami and began producing programming for the new network. Much of the initial programming was produced with partners. Telemundo coproduced a national newscast with the Cable News Network (CNN) from 1988 through 1993 and a music video program with Music Television (MTV) called *MTV Internacional*. From the beginning, the philosophy behind Telemundo's programming has been to target North American Latinos and their experience in the United States and Canada.

Noticiero Telemundo and *Ocurrió Así* are the two major news programs produced by Telemundo at its Miami headquarters. *Noticiero Telemundo* is a nightly half-hour newscast that recaps important news around the world. *Ocurrió Así* covers more sensational news stories, with a particular focus on Latin America and

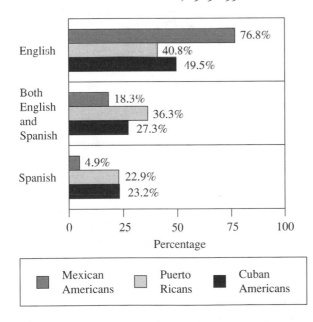

LANGUAGE OF NEWS SOURCES MOST COMMONLY USED BY LATINO CITIZENS, 1989-1990

English
- 76.8%
- 40.8%
- 49.5%

Both English and Spanish
- 18.3%
- 36.3%
- 27.3%

Spanish
- 4.9%
- 22.9%
- 23.2%

Percentage

■ Mexican Americans   ■ Puerto Ricans   ■ Cuban Americans

Source: Data are from the Latino National Political Survey, which polled a representative sample of 1,546 Mexican Americans, 589 Puerto Ricans, and 682 Cuban Americans in forty metropolitan areas in 1989-1990. See Rodolfo O. de la Garza et al., *Latino Voices: Mexican, Puerto Rican, and Cuban Perspectives on American Politics* (Boulder, Colo.: Westview Press, 1992), p. 72, Table 5.2.

Note: Respondents selected their two most commonly used news sources from the choices of television, newspapers, magazines, and radio.

Telemundo provides news from around the world. (James Shaffer)

the Latino Community. Like Univisión, Telemundo has correspondents around the world who provide up-to-the-minute coverage for its viewers. *Noticiero Telemundo* was broadcast to nineteen Latin American countries as of the early 1990's.

In a move toward the future, telemundo launched *Telenoticias*, a twenty-four-hour news service, in partnership with Reuters in June, 1994. *Telenoticias* is broadcast to Latin American countries, the United States and Canada. It is designed as a half-hour "wheel" format that provides major headlines and sports and financial news.

Galavisión. Galavisión was established in 1979 as a premium cable service by Univisa, a subsidiary of Televisa also owned by the Azcárraga family. Programming is largely from Mexico and includes recent Mexican movies, Mexican sporting events, and special programming. Galavisión was also the launching pad for a Spanish-language news service based in Mexico City called Empresas de Comunicaciones Orbitales (ECO). ECO programming was broadcast directly on Galavisión as well as distributed around the world to such organizations as CNN, ABC, and CBS. In 1986,

Galavisión was converted to a basic cable service, increasing its potential market to two million Latin viewers.

From the beginning, new programming on Galavisión originated in Mexico. Mexico's most popular national news program, *24 Horas*, was broadcast directly on Galavisión. With the establishment of ECO, news coverage increased on the network. The focus continued to be on Mexico and surrounding areas. Through ECO, Galavisión viewers have access to a twenty-four-hour-a-day news channel serving Europe, Latin America, and North America.

English-language Television. In general, little English-language news produced in the United States and Canada is targeted at Latinos, although local markets that have large Latino populations often tailor their coverage to include news about Latin America and the Latino community. In an effort to court the growing Latino market, however, some large English-language media organizations have established their own Spanish-language news services. In March, 1993, for example, NBC launched *Canal de Noticias de NBC*, a twenty-four-hour-a-day news service.

Journalists. The journalists who work in the Latino broadcast news industry must be fully bilingual—able to speak English well enough to function in the U.S. news industry and able to speak Spanish well enough to write for and communicate with the Latino audience. Many of the correspondents and reporters who work in Spanish-language television news are from Latin America and have had extensive news experience in their native countries. They bring a wealth of knowledge about Latin American politics, culture, and experience to their positions in the industry. Others are Latinos who have been reared and educated in the United States or Canada. They understand the life of the Latino as a minority outside Latin America, and they understand U.S. and Canadian political and social systems. The combination results in coverage that is in line with the needs and interests of the Latino audience. —*Patricia Constantakis-Valdés*

SUGGESTED READINGS:

• Subervi-Vélez, Federico A., with Charles Ramírez Berg, Patricia Constantakis-Valdés, Chon Noriega, Diana I. Ríos, and Kenton T. Wilkinson. "Mass Communication and Hispanics." In *Handbook of Hispanic Cultures in the United States: Sociology*, edited by Félix Padilla. Houston: Arte Público Press, 1994. This chapter is an extensive survey of Latino-oriented media in the United States and of media portrayals of Latinos in English-language mainstream media.

• Veciana-Suarez, Ana. *Hispanic Media: Impact and Influence*. Washington, D.C.: Media Institute, 1990. Explores the impact of the Latino media on U.S. business and politics.

• Veciana-Suarez, Ana. *Hispanic Media, USA*. Washington, D.C.: Media Institute, 1987. Presents a general survey of the Latino media sources in the United States, including television networks, newspapers, radio, and magazines.

• Wilson, Clint, Jr., and Felix F. Gutiérrez. *Minorities and Media*. Beverly Hills, Calif.: Sage, 1985. Describes the relationship between minorities and the mass media in the United States. Covers broadcast media, print media, and the advertising industry.

Brown Berets: Chicano paramilitary youth organizations in existence from 1968 to 1972. The group's primary objectives were to improve conditions in the Mexican American community and to defend it from police brutality. As a paramilitary organization, the Brown Berets were often compared to the African American Black Panthers, who were active during the same period. Unlike the Marxist Black Panthers, however, the Brown Berets were cultural nationalists.

The founder of the Brown Berets was David Sánchez, then a college student in Los Angeles. In 1967, Sánchez formed the Young Chicanos for Community Action, a group that evolved from a church-sponsored service club into the paramilitary Brown Berets. The Brown Berets officially organized around the time of the BLOWOUT, the East Los Angeles high school walkouts, in 1968. They had chapters in more than a dozen states, mostly in the Southwest, West, and parts of the Midwest. Both men and women were members.

The Brown Berets worked to improve health care, housing, and education in Mexican American BARRIOS. They fought against police harassment and brutality, standing as a peaceful force between civilians and police at political and cultural events. They also sought to reclaim land taken from Mexico by U.S. forces before the TREATY OF GUADALUPE HIDALGO (1848). Their most notorious action in this effort was the occupation of Santa Catalina Island off the coast of Southern California in 1972.

After supporting high school walkouts, the Brown Berets worked with other Chicano organizations such as MOVIMIENTO ESTUDIANTIL CHICANO DE AZTLÁN (MECHA) in 1969 to organize the NATIONAL CHICANO MORATORIUM ON VIETNAM. They started a free medical clinic in East Los Angeles, printed a newspaper called *La Causa*, worked with prison youths, and educated Mexican Americans through lectures, books, and films.

The Brown Berets saw militarism as the most effective and efficient way to organize and coordinate Chicanos on a large scale. Unlike other Chicano organization, they recruited street youths, some of whom were former prison inmates and gang members, as well as some high school and college students. In general, they distrusted other Chicano and Anglo leaders, many of whom they saw as *vendidos* (sell-outs) or manipulators. This attitude prevented them from taking advantage of established community activists and liberal patrons who could have helped the group secure funding, legal aid, and possibly better treatment. The Brown Berets' uncompromising stance may have strengthened their will from within and given them greater legitimacy in the barrio.

Because of their active role in exposing social injustice in the Chicano community, their distrust of nonmembers, and their quasi-military appearance, the police saw the Brown Berets as a threat, and they became the target of police infiltration, harassment, slander, and raids. During the Los Angeles walkouts, the police falsely named the Brown Berets as the event organizers. Thirteen Chicanos including seven Brown Berets, were indicted on conspiracy charges, drawing media attention away from the real concerns behind the protest.

The Brown Berets continued to be stereotyped, misrepresented, and sometimes romanticized in the press. This, combined with police infiltration and internal struggles, kept the organization from solidifying as a national group and caused Sánchez to disband all chapters in 1972.

Brown Scare (1913-1918): Period of hysteria in which Mexicans in the Southwest were labeled as agitators and discriminated against. In the 1910's, American manufacturing and industry increased tremendously in volume and drew many job seekers, among them large numbers of Mexicans fleeing the Mexican Revolution. Cities such as Los Angeles experienced rapid population growth and changing demographics as these im-

migrants moved into existing communities and established neighborhoods of their own. After a spurt of prosperity, however, the United States faced an economic depression, organized labor disputes, border conflicts, and the advent of World War I. These factors combined to produce nativism among some non-Hispanics, who blamed Mexicans and Mexican Americans for the troubles of U.S. society. Unfortunately, nativist attitudes were mirrored by those in political power.

Nativist Anglos feared that Mexican immigrants were linked to organized labor and radical political movements. Nativists incorrectly blamed Mexicans for the violent labor disputes of the period, arguing that because they "could not assimilate" into American society, they were prone to such disruption. This repressed Mexicans' legitimate labor complaints. If they were treated unfairly on the job, they became afraid to strike for fear of harsh reprisals.

The political activities of Mexican immigrants were highly publicized, causing nativists to fan the flames

Some refugees from the Mexican Revolution went to the detention camp at Fort Bliss, near El Paso, Texas. (Institute of Texan Cultures)

of the Brown Scare. Exiled members of Mexico's PAR-
TIDO LIBERAL MEXICANO (PLM), a party in opposition
to Porfirio Díaz, had headquarters in Los Angeles and
were active during the early years of the Mexican
Revolution, attempting an invasion of Baja California
in 1911. The PLM's leader, Ricardo FLORES MAGÓN,
organized in Southern California and called on fellow
Mexicans and Mexican Americans to put an end to
discrimination against them in the United States. Flores was imprisoned after a long trial for breaching
neutrality laws during the Baja incident.

Along the U.S.-Mexico border, tensions were high.
The media played up nativist fears that the Mexican
Revolution would spread to the United States. In
1913, a *Los Angeles Times* editorial proclaimed that
border communities were surely fated for capture by
Pancho VILLA. City police began intensifying their
watch over Mexican communities and began arresting
Mexicans.

In 1916, the border town of Columbus, New Mexico, was raided by Mexicans. As a result, Los Angeles
prohibited liquor and gun sales to Mexicans and tripled police personnel in their communities. City officials discussed deporting or detaining Mexicans who
had immigrated to the United States in the previous
three years and also warned of the dangers of allowing
further Mexican immigration. In Texas, thousands of
Mexican Americans were killed by Texas Rangers,
vigilantes, and police. Authorities excused this by say-
ing that the revolution caused border troubles and police were defending American interests.

Another contributor to the Brown Scare was the
Germany-Mexico connection during World War I.
Various events led to rumors that Germans were recruiting Mexicans in the United States to serve as
spies and provoke a war. In 1917, President Woodrow
Wilson publicized an intercepted message from Germany to Mexico in which Germany offered Mexico
support in the event of war with the United States; if
Mexico agreed to the alliance, Germany would help it
regain land in the American Southwest. Anti-German
sentiment was rampant, and any association of Germany with Mexicans fueled existing prejudice against
them.

Mexican American communities were the scape-
goats of the hysteria of the 1910's. Mexican *MUTUALIS-
TAS* and individuals spoke out against the outrages, but
the U.S. government supported the hysteria. After
1918, American anti-German sentiment was redirected
toward political radicals, causing a Red Scare similar
to the Brown Scare.

Brown v. Board of Education (May 17, 1954): Court
ruling on segregation in education. In *Oliver Brown et
al. v. Board of Education of Topeka et al.* (347 U.S.
483), usually cited as *Brown v. Board of Education*, the
plaintiffs were African American children. The case
challenged state laws that denied these students admission to schools attended primarily or exclusively by
white children. The Supreme Court, in a unanimous
decision, struck down the "separate but equal" doctrine, established in *Plessy v. Ferguson* (1896), that had
allowed segregated schools to exist.

During the mid-1940's, the National Association for
the Advancement of Colored People (NAACP) accelerated its campaign against segregation in public education. A first step came in the *Sweatt v. Paint* decision
(1950). Marion Sweatt, an African American, had been
denied admission to the University of Texas Law
School because of his race. He sued the university on
the grounds that he was denied equal protection of the
laws as guaranteed by the Fourteenth Amendment. At
the time the suit was filed, there was no law school in
the state for African American students, but during the
proceedings one was established.

The state court upheld the "separate but equal"
clause, ruling that Sweatt could attend the new school,
but on appeal the Supreme Court ruled that the education received there would not be substantially equal to
that received at the University of Texas Law School.
Sweatt's right to attend the University of Texas Law
School was confirmed.

With this foundation, NAACP attorneys filed suit
attacking segregation in public education. Four cases,
from Kansas, South Carolina, Virginia, and Delaware,
were consolidated in *Brown v. Board of Education*.
Although local conditions in the four cases varied,
each involved African American children seeking admission to public schools in their community on a
nonsegregated basis. Each of the schools in question
was attended only by white students. The plaintiffs
argued that segregated public schools were not, and
could not be made, equal; therefore, African American
students were deprived of the equal protection of the
law.

In its ruling, the Court stated that intangible factors
could contribute to inequality in education. The factors
included the ability to study with and to engage in
discussion with other students. Because of their different student populations, segregated schools were
therefore inherently unequal. The Court also stated
that to separate children from others of similar age and
qualifications solely on the basis of their race would

generate a feeling of inferiority as to status in the community.

This case resulted in rapid changes in favor of African American students. Little headway was made, however, in ending the discrimination and segregation experienced by Latinos. Legally, Latinos were not distinguished from whites, so school districts were allowed to continue segregation of Latino students. Many Latinos lived in less wealthy neighborhoods, and because many school districts were funded by property taxes, schools for Latino children were often underfunded. In addition, undocumented Latinos faced difficulties in pursuing their civil rights as a result of their residency status.

Decades passed before the right of Latinos to equal education became encoded in law and protected by the judicial system. *PLYLER V. DOE* (1982), for example, established that undocumented residents of Texas had the right to education in public schools. In *SAN ANTONIO INDEPENDENT SCHOOL DISTRICT V. RODRÍGUEZ* (1973), the

Brown v. Board of Education helped to integrate schooling, making the scene in this school computer lab possible. (Hazel Hankin)

Supreme Court ruled that school districts could base funding for education on property taxes. The ruling stated that an education was being provided in the less wealthy districts (with predominantly Latino populations) and that no discrimination against an identifiable class of persons had been proved. In *Edgewood v. Kirby* (1989), however, the Court ruled that Texas' method of funding education through property taxes was not efficient and ordered redesign of the system to allow school districts relatively equal access to funds.

Brownsville, Texas: County seat of Cameron County. The population of the Brownsville-Harlingen metropolitan area, according to the 1990 census, was 260,120. Brownsville is located on the Rio Grande opposite Matamoros, Mexico.

General Zachary Taylor founded Fort Brown on March 28, 1846, opposite Matamoros, Mexico. The fort was in a region of Texas claimed by both Mexico and the United States. Founding of the fort helped provoke the Mexican American War.

The town of Brownsville grew around the fort. In 1859, Juan CORTINA and his supporters raided and captured Brownsville, provoking the six-month Cortina War.

Meat prices dropped in 1869, but the price of a cowhide did not, bringing about skinning raids from both sides of the border. The South Texas Anglos organized vigilance committees for protection from the Mexican raiders. Overzealous committee members raided Mexican ranches, killing every adult male, burning ranch buildings and stores, and taking over the Mexican ranches. In 1876, the TEXAS RANGERS brought peace to the area.

The Matamoros-Monterrey railroad was completed in 1905, as was the first international bridge in the area. This bridge linked Brownsville and Matamoros, fostering social and commercial interaction.

The Mexican Revolution, beginning in 1910, and civil strife brought many upper-class Mexicans into Brownsville. The city's population reached twenty thousand by 1930. As the agricultural industry grew, so did the need for Mexican laborers. Mexican immigration was perceived by the United States government as a serious problem. Immigration reform laws were passed in 1924, and the Border Patrol was created. By the late 1920's and early 1930's, a ruthless and indiscriminate policy of deportation was implemented, and entire neighborhoods of Mexicans were deported. These laws led to the establishment of categories of

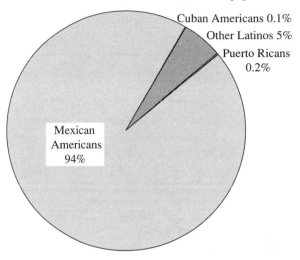

LATINO POPULATION OF BROWNSVILLE, TEXAS, 1990

Total number of Latinos = 212,995; 82% of population

Cuban Americans 0.1%
Other Latinos 5%
Puerto Ricans 0.2%
Mexican Americans 94%

Source: Data are from Marlita A. Reddy, ed., *Statistical Record of Hispanic Americans* (Detroit: Gale Research, 1993), Table 110.
Note: Figures represent the population of the Brownsville-Harlingen, Texas, Metropolitan Statistical Area as delineated by the U.S. Bureau of the Census. Percentages are rounded to the nearest whole number except for Cuban Americans and Puerto Ricans, for whom rounding is to the nearest 0.1%.

legal resident aliens, commuters (people who live in Mexico and commute to jobs in the United States), and crosser/shoppers.

In 1942, Mexico entered into an agreement with the United States, the BRACERO PROGRAM, to provide contract labor. This agreement guaranteed transportation for the Mexican braceros, specified working conditions and pay scales, and provided subsidies to American farmers who hired braceros. In the 1950's, it was cheaper to hire unregistered Mexican workers rather than formally contract Mexican labor; therefore, the number of legal braceros decreased and the number of illegal border crossers increased.

Mexico established the BORDER INDUSTRIALIZATION PROGRAM in 1965, in cooperation with the American government. This program was designed to attract American labor-intensive industrial interests to the border region of Mexico. The agreement led to a large increase in population in Brownsville and Matamoros, along with much of the rest of the border region. The area prospered in the 1960's and 1970's. The Mexican government devalued the peso in 1982, bringing an abrupt end to the economic prosperity in Brownsville.

Undocumented residents and lower-income people were hurt the most.

Brownsville's population continued to grow, but the percentage of poor people grew faster than the city as a whole. Latinos accounted for 82 percent of the population of the Brownsville-Harlingen area according to the 1990 census. The largest foreign trade zone-enterprise zones in the United States are at the Port of Brownsville and the Brownsville International Airport.

Bruce-Novoa, Juan D. (b. June 20, 1944, San José, Costa Rica): Scholar. Bruce-Novoa is a leading cultural critic and scholar in the field of Mexican American studies. His father, James H. Bruce, worked as a coffee importer in Costa Rica, and he is Chicano on his mother's side. The family emigrated to the United States a year after his birth. Bruce-Novoa is a professor of Spanish and has taught at several universities across the United States and in Germany.

One of the most provocative and renowned critics working in Chicano criticism, Bruce-Novoa seeks in his work to find a broad-based approach to the whole of Chicano literature. Bruce-Novoa's published interviews with important Mexican American writers such as Rudolfo ANAYA, Tomás RIVERA, and many others are invaluable resources for readers wanting to understand a particular author's aesthetics. As a writer himself, Bruce-Novoa believes in writing from the "space" created by dual Mexican and American identities.

Bruce-Novoa's *Chicano Authors: Inquiry by Interview* (1980) and *Chicano Poetry: A Response to Chaos* (1982) are seminal surveys of Chicano literature. His other works include *La literatura chicana a través de sus autores* (1983; editor, with José Guillermo Saaverdar), *Antología retrospectiva del cuento chicano* (1988), and *RetroSpace: Collected Essays on Chicano Literature* (1990).

Brujo: Person who practices witchcraft. In Peru, a *brujo* is simply a person who practices witchcraft. In Guatemala, the term also designates a healer, or *curandero*. For Mexican Americans, a *brujo* is a person who practices witchcraft with intent to harm. Illnesses attributed to their work are diagnosed and attended to by a *curandero*. Both the *brujo* and the *curandero* are key figures of CURANDERISMO, a system of folk healing based on the premise that illness can have both natural and supernatural sources.

Bucareli, Antonio María (Jan. 24, 1717, Seville, Spain—Apr. 9, 1779, Mexico City, Mexico): Soldier and administrator. Spanish noble Bucareli rose from a cadet at the age of fifteen to lieutenant-general of the royal armies in Spain through his ability and service in many military campaigns. He next became captain-general and governor of Cuba, again serving ably. Bucareli later became viceroy, captain-general, and governor of New Spain (1771-1779). He is deemed to be one of the most able Spanish viceroys. According to Mexican historians, the entire period of Bucareli's rule was graced by uninterrupted peace, promoted by a man of integrity and intelligence.

Bucareli's achievements include a "Spanish Monroe Doctrine" that kept England and Russia out of New Spain. He also authorized many successful enterprises, including establishment of means to transport artillery from the Atlantic to the Pacific coast (1773), finding a land route to Alta California (1774), exploration of San Francisco Bay (1775), and the founding of San Francisco (1776). His informed efforts, somewhat compromised by appointment of a separate commandant-general of the frontier provinces, continued until his death in 1779. The respect of Bucareli's subjects was shown by his burial in Mexico City's Church of Guadalupe, an honor accorded to no other Spanish colonial official.

Bueno, María Ester Audion (b. Oct. 11, 1939, São Paulo, Brazil): Tennis player. The graceful beauty of Maria Bueno hid the powerful abilities of this tennis star. Primarily self-taught, Bueno started playing tennis at the age of six and quickly developed her trademark speed and power serve that stemmed from a long backswing.

In 1959, at the prestigious Wimbledon tournament, she shocked officials and fans with her bright pink "panties" designed by tennis couturier Ted Tinling. (Her colorful clothing was in strong contrast to the traditional white worn by other players.) Bueno won the singles title, making her the first South American to do so. That same year, she won the U.S. National Championship. A year later, she successfully defended her Wimbledon title.

A severe case of hepatitis handicapped her game from May, 1961, to September, 1963. Bueno returned strong, winning the U.S. National Championship in 1963, 1964, and 1966 and recapturing the Wimbledon title in 1964. As a doubles player, she won twelve Grand Slam crowns with six different partners, including Darlene Hard and Nancy Ritchey.

Her tremendous start led the Associated Press to name her the Female Athlete of the Year in 1959.

María Bueno playing in the 1962 U.S. National Championships. (AP/Wide World Photos)

Bueno was ranked number one in the world that year and again in 1960.

Buitron, Robert (b. 1953): Photographer. Arizona photographer Buitron has earned acclaim with photographs presenting contemporary views of Mexican American and Mexican families and culture. His photographic series "Family and Photography: A Portrait of a Family in Two Cultures" is characteristic of his work. Completed during the late 1970's and early 1980's, the series presents Latinos with a common heritage and divergent lifestyles. It includes a photograph of a wrinkle-faced man from Guanajuato, Mexico, cradling individual and group photos of his ancestors, as well as a suburban Texas couple posed beside their lawnmower and modern home.

Buitron was one of ten photographers commissioned to produce the officially sanctioned photographic interpretation of the Olympic Games held in Los Angeles, California, in 1984. Buitron's black-and-white photos focus on the ceremony and ritual of the Olympics.

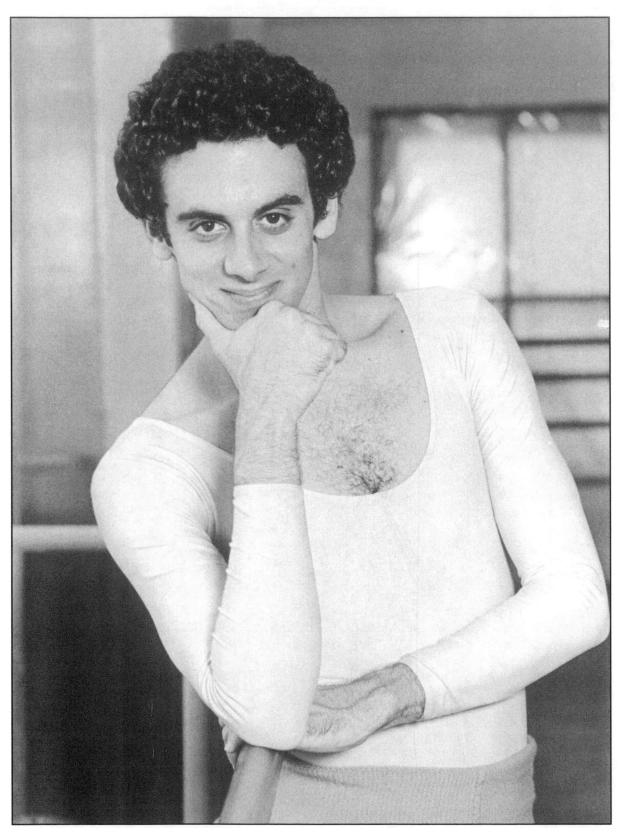

Fernando Bujones in 1979. (AP/Wide World Photos)

Buitron's work has been widely exhibited in museums in the American Southwest, as well as in Mexico, and it has been published in art books and newsletters. Buitron is an active member of the arts organization Movimiento Artistico del Rio Salado.

Bujones, Fernando (b. Mar. 9, 1955, Miami, Fla.): Ballet dancer. Bujones' parents separated when he was five years old. His mother, a former dancer and theatrical stage manager, took him to Havana, Cuba. There he began his study of ballet with Fernando and Alicia Alonso at the Ballet de Cuba. Bujones and his mother returned to the United States in 1965, and he entered the New York School of American Ballet at the age of twelve. Two years later, he was invited by George Balanchine to join the New York City Ballet.

His professional debut came in 1960, dancing the pas-de-deux duet from *Don Quijote* at Carnegie Hall. He became a soloist with American Ballet Theater in 1973 and was its principal dancer from 1974 to 1985. In 1974, he was awarded the gold medal at the Seventh International Ballet Competition in Varna, Bulgaria. Bujones has been a guest artist with ballet and opera companies all over the world, including La Scala Milano, the Royal Swedish Ballet, and the Paris Opera. His choreographies include *Grand Pas Romantique* (1984) and *Raymondal* (1988). Internationally recognized for his midair turns, precise leg beats, and high elevation, Bujones received a *Dance* Magazine Award in 1982 and a *New York Times* Artistic Award in 1985. He was named a permanent international guest artist with the Boston Ballet in 1987. The governor of Massachusetts proclaimed May 4, 1990, to be "Bujones Day."

Bultos: Statues. *Bultos* are carved wooden statues of a religious nature. They feature religious personages and figures, often with movable limbs. *Bultos* are sometimes used in religious ceremonies.

Bulto has a number of meanings, among them the volume of an object, a protuberance on a surface, a parcel or package, and the mass of an object of imprecise shape or form. In Mexico, it is a measure equivalent to that of a sack containing five hectoliters of seeds or dry goods. The term is also used in the expression *a bulto*, meaning to make an imprecise measurement of an object or quantity: "Contamos a bulto unas cien casas" would translate as "We counted approximately one hundred houses."

Buñuelo: Fritters or deep-fat fried dough. *Buñuelos* originated in Spain and have proliferated throughout Latin America. All *buñuelos* are made by frying wheat-flour dough in deep fat, but they may be shaped like balls, cakes, or even thin sheets. Some are sweet, but some are not. Most Latin American countries have *buñuelos* made of rice, mashed potatoes, and bread crumbs bound with egg. There are national specialties such as Colombia's bean *buñuelos*, Cuba's apple *buñuelos*, and the Dominican Republic's mamey *buñuelos*. Mexico alone has more than forty types of *buñuelos*. Some are eaten only during particular fiestas.

Burciaga, José Antonio (b. Aug. 23, 1940, El Chuco, Tex.): Writer and artist. Burciaga is both a successful writer and a muralist. A journalist and freelance writer in the early 1970's, he contributed to the syndicated column "Hispanic Link" and the Pacific News Service. Branching out from journalism, Burciaga founded Diseños Literarios, a publishing company in Menlo Park, California. The company published *Restless Serpents* (1976), his first collection of poems and drawings, bound together with work by poet Bernice Zamora. His poetry collection *Undocumented Love* (1992) won the Before Columbus American Book Award.

The most memorable aspect of Burciaga's writing is his use of humor. A skillful satirist, he writes about Chicano experiences and cultural issues. His essay collection *Weedee Peepo* (1988) takes a comical yet critical look at issues affecting Mexican Americans. His humor is not limited to written forms. He is a founding member of the comedy group Culture Clash. His published works include *Drink Cultura: Chicanismo* (1993) and (with Emy Lopez) *Versos para Centroamerica* (1981; verses for Central America). As a muralist, Burciaga has had solo showings across the United States and in several cities in Mexico. In 1985, he became a resident fellow at Stanford University.

Burgos, Julia de (Feb. 17, 1914, Carolina, Puerto Rico—July, 1953, New York, N.Y.): Poet. Burgos was one of Puerto Rico's finest writers. Her widely anthologized poems are noteworthy for their cultural nationalism and natural imagery. Burgos was a member of the Nationalist Party and fought all her life for independence. As a biracial woman who never escaped poverty, she suffered class, racial, sexual, and cultural oppression. All these struggles shaped her literary vision, with feminism and nationalism standing out as key issues.

Her writings were published in her native Puerto Rico, Cuba, and the United States. No copies of her first volume of poetry, *Poemas exactos a mí misma* (1937), are known to exist. As a young writer, she caught the attention of notable Puerto Rican writers and critics. Burgos' second collection of poems, *Poemas en veinte surcos* (1938), contains some of her finest work and shows the influence of Chilean poet Pablo NERUDA. Her next volume, *Canción de la verdad sencilla* (1939), won the Premio de Instituto de Literatura Puertorriqueña.

Suffering from depression and alcoholism, Burgos died homeless in New York City. She was later identified and buried in Puerto Rico. Her other works include *El mar y tú, otros poemas* (1954) and *Antología Poética* (1967), both published posthumously.

Burrito: Filling wrapped in a wheat-flour TORTILLA. Burritos are popular in northern Mexico and the adjacent United States. They are made by wrapping a filling, usually BEANS and cheese or shredded meat, with a large wheat flour tortilla. SALSA can be added at the diner's discretion. Burritos are from northern Mexico, especially Sonora, where they are a prominent food for snacks and light meals. Burritos are common as take-out food in the United States, particularly along the Mexican border.

Business and corporate enterprise: Latino businesses in the United States and Canada are usually small, family-owned and -managed, and successful within Latino communities of urban areas. There has been significant growth in the number of these businesses in the United States since the 1980's, but Latino businesses and corporations in Canada remain a minuscule part of that country's economy. The most successful Latino group as entrepreneurs are Cubans and Cuban Americans in Miami, Florida.

Latino businesses and corporations in the United States and Canada have developed only to the extent

MINORITY-OWNED FIRMS, 1987		
Racial/Ethnic Group	1987 Revenue (billions of dollars)	Number of Firms
Hispanic	24.7	422,373
Black	19.8	424,165
Asian/Pacific Islander	33.1	355,331
American Indian/Alaskan	0.9	21,380

Source: Data are from Marlita A. Reddy, ed., *Statistical Record of Hispanic Americans* (Detroit: Gale Research, 1993), Table 723. Original data are from 1987 Economic Census, as printed in *USA Today*, June 17, 1992, p. 4B.

that Latinos in general have progressed economically. Most Latinos in these two countries are wage earners rather than business owners, and a majority of the wage earners are employed by non-Latino businesses. Analyses of Latino-owned businesses mainly refer to entrepreneurs, who are a small minority of the community's economic participants. Even established, profitable businesses are seldom patronized by members of other ethnic communities. The exceptions, Latino businesses that have an impact on the larger economy, are localized, such as Cuban businesses in and around Miami, Florida. One of the few Latino-owned national corporations that has been competitive with comparable businesses is Bacardi, a large corporation that makes liquor products. Nevertheless, as the numbers of Latinos grow and more reach middle-class status as employees and consumers, the trend toward ownership of more successful businesses that appeal to a broader, interethnic clientele is expected to grow.

Historical Development of Businesses. A majority of the Latinos who have emigrated to the United States or Canada have been employed in menial jobs. They have not had the financial resources or business skills to establish businesses. The two major exceptions to this have been Cubans in Miami and immigrants to Canada from South and Central America.

The earliest Cuban exile groups arrived in southern Florida between 1959 and 1980. They included middle-class and lower-upper-class professionals and business leaders. Many continued their careers as doctors, lawyers, and corporate executives. Exile groups from the 1980 MARIEL BOAT LIFT and later, however, consisted of lower-income persons without professional or corporate backgrounds. After 1980, Cuban immigrants did not provide the business leadership of earlier groups.

In Canada, Latino immigration after the 1980's included a high proportion of formally educated persons from South and Central America. Nearly one-third of the immigrants had doctoral degrees or terminal degrees in their fields of expertise. Because of their class backgrounds and their business and other skills, they constituted a potential business and professional leadership group. In the 1990's, the unemployment rate among Latinos in Canada was nearly 33 percent, however, and many of the jobless were Latinos with business ownership backgrounds. By the early 1990's, Latinos in Canada had not established large, competitive corporations with an effect on the national economy.

Latino Businesses in the United States. The largest Latino immigrant group in North America has been

Many Latino entrepreneurs get their start in small businesses catering to an ethnic clientele, like this East Los Angeles gas station of the 1960's. (AP/Wide World Photos)

Mexicans in the United States. Large numbers of Mexicans were recruited in the late eighteenth and early nineteenth centuries for railroad construction or as employees of farms, meat-packing plants, brickyards, and canneries. They tended to be from lower economic classes and without ownership skills. Later immigrants were hired as agricultural laborers or were undocumented employees in manufacturing. The exceptions have been mostly small, Mexican-owned businesses in Mexican American enclaves in cities in southwestern and western states. Although business ownership for this group has been modest and unemployment high, Mexicans have enjoyed more business success than the second-largest Latino group in the United States and Canada, Puerto Ricans.

Puerto Ricans immigrated to the mainland of the United States in large numbers following World War II. This surge of immigration was directly related to the attempted industrialization of Puerto Rico. The attempts stalled, industrialization was only sporadically successful, and employment was difficult to obtain. Most Puerto Ricans settled in the large urban centers of the East Coast of the United States and attempted to work in manufacturing trades; however, many lacked transferable skills. The results have been the worst UNEMPLOYMENT and poverty rates of any major Latino group in the United States or Canada. Although some Puerto Ricans have had limited business successes as owners of small groceries and community-serving stores, they have been the Latino group least likely to achieve business ownership. The difficulties of obtaining capital and developing business executive skills affected Puerto Ricans on the mainland and on the island. Cubans have had far greater success on the island of Puerto Rico than Puerto Ricans have, becoming prominent in industries such as communications. That success has made Cuban-Puerto Rican relationships abrasive, with some Puerto Ricans resenting the roles of Cuban entrepreneurs on the island.

The Cuban business history in the United States has

been distinctive. Unlike other Latino groups, Cubans have considered themselves political rather than economic refugees. They have largely succeeded in the local economies where they were concentrated. These population concentrations have been limited to Miami, Florida; parts of New York City and New Jersey; and the southern section of Broward County, including Fort Lauderdale, Florida. Cuban business acumen has resulted in the growth of local chains, such as Sedano's Supermarkets in Dade County, Florida, which was one of the three largest Latino-owned corporations in the United States and Canada in the early 1990's.

There has been a competitive spirit among Cuban-owned banks, grocery chains, insurance agencies, car franchises, private school systems, and personnel agencies. Most of these businesses cater to Latino clientele but affect the local economy because Latinos are a majority of the population of Dade County.

After 1980 and the Mariel boat lift, few Cuban exiles brought with them business executive backgrounds and skills, although many have been trained and educated in the United States for employment levels that are higher than their Mexican or Puerto Rican counterparts. This was partly a result of special federal assistance that Cuban exiles received but other Latino groups did not. Another factor was that earlier exiles who were entrepreneurs tended to hire new Cuban arrivals rather than employing persons from other ethnic communities.

In addition to the major groups noted above, increasing numbers of Latino immigrants came to the United States from the Caribbean and Central America beginning in the early 1980's. They have had a high incidence of UNEMPLOYMENT AND UNDEREMPLOYMENT. The economically displaced from these groups often are among the lowest wage earners in urban industries that are not Latino-owned; a few elites among them, by contrast, have established successful businesses that cater largely to other Latinos.

Latino Businesses in Canada. In Canada, there have been three waves of Latino immigration: Ecuadorans and Colombians were the main arrivals in the 1950's; other South Americans, such as Argentineans and Chileans, predominated in the 1960's; and Central Americans, such as Salvadorans, were numerous in the 1980's. Canada's strict laws regarding the employment of noncitizens have affected these groups. It is easier to determine who is a nonlegal immigrant in Canada than in the United States because of the small number of Latinos in Canada. Although many Central and South Americans in Canada have professional and business

MAJOR INDUSTRY GROUPS WITH THE LARGEST RECEIPTS BY LATINO-OWNED FIRMS, 1987	
Industry Group	*Receipts (billions of dollars)*
Special trade contractors	2.266
Automotive dealers and service stations	2.100
Food stores	1.836
Eating and drinking places	1.645
Business services	1.420
Wholesale trade—nondurable goods	1.388
Health services	1.326
Miscellaneous retail	1.267
Wholesale trade—durable goods	1.057
Trucking and warehousing	.907

Source: Data are from Carol D. Foster et al., *Minorities: A Changing Role in American Society* (Wylie, Tex.: Information Plus, 1992), p. 29, Table 3.5. Original data are from Bureau of the Census, *1987 Survey of Minority-Owned Business Enterprises, Hispanic* (Washington, D.C.: Bureau of the Census, 1990).

backgrounds, many have been prevented from practicing their skills because of their immigrant status. There are no nationally competitive Latino-owned corporations in Canada, with the exception of the Bacardi headquarters in Toronto. It is unlikely that this situation will change unless far larger numbers of Latinos immigrate to Canada; more relaxed laws regulating business employment and ownership by noncitizens will also be required before Latino entrepreneurship has large effects on the national economy.

Specific Latino Business Effects. In spite of immigration problems, lack of investment funds, linguistic barriers, and modest skills for business ownership, Latinos as a group began advancing economically in the 1980's and 1990's in two ways: They were becoming the fastest-growing work force in the United States and were establishing increasing numbers of businesses in the United States and Canada.

By 1990, the five hundred largest Latino-owned businesses in the United States had sales of $9 billion. These companies, each of which was at least 5 percent Latino-owned, had an average revenue growth of 8.1 percent.

The number one performer among Latino-owned businesses in 1990 was Bacardi Imports, Inc., of Miami, which had sales of $602 million. Bacardi was followed by Goya Foods, Inc., of New Jersey, with sales of $330 million. The success of Bacardi and Goya Foods, however, hides a persistent problem with most Latino-oriented businesses, the appeal to a limited market. Although Bacardi has appealed to a broad spectrum of consumers in the United States and Canada, Goya has not; its strong sales have resulted from saturating the Latino market in the United States. Its attempts to sell its products to non-Latinos had little success by 1988, although it penetrated some non-Latino markets after that. Sedano's Supermarkets of Miami, another successful Latino-owned business, also developed its clientele nearly exclusively in Latino ethnic enclaves. Furthermore, by the 1990's, non-Latino corporations had begun to target the Latino market: For example, Campbell's soups was outselling Goya in Puerto Rico by marketing products similar to Goya's under the brand name Casera.

Latino entrepreneurs who attempt to expand their businesses still function largely within Latino communities. In 1988, four of the top ten Latino businesses sold food or liquor; three were car dealerships, two were real estate agencies, and one was a bank. There was a geographic concentration of the top businesses: one half of the top ten were located in Dade County, Florida. The largest businesses that operated outside of Latino ethnic enclaves were ranked eighteenth, twentieth, and twenty-sixth on the list of the top businesses in 1988; they were a container distributor, an auto parts manufacturer, and an asphalt manufacturer.

Although Cubans and Cuban Americans in Miami continue to lead Latino businesses economically, they are hardly representative of the Latino population. The approximately one million Cuban Americans are a small proportion of the nearly thirty million Latinos estimated to live in the United States. In Miami, thirty-five of every one thousand Latinos owned their own business in 1990; in New York, where the Latino population was predominantly Puerto Rican, only eight of every one thousand Latinos owned their own business. Therefore, although Latino businesses have been growing in number, the increases have been disproportionately among one nationality and in a few locales.

The increase in business ownership occurred especially between 1982 and 1987. The overall increase during those years was 14.3 percent among all Latinos, Cubans led in firms owned, followed by "other Hispanics," Mexicans, and Puerto Ricans. By 1987, African Americans owned 424,000 businesses and Latinos 422,000, in spite of the fact that many Latinos did not arrive in the United States until after World War II.

In Canada, Latino business expansion was less visible. Fewer than 300,000 Latinos were estimated to be living in Canada in 1990. Approximately 60 to 70 percent of Canada's Latinos lived in the Toronto, Ontario, metropolitan area, in which there were approximately 750 Latino-owned businesses in 1994. Most

INDUSTRY CLASSIFICATION OF LATINO-OWNED BUSINESSES, 1987

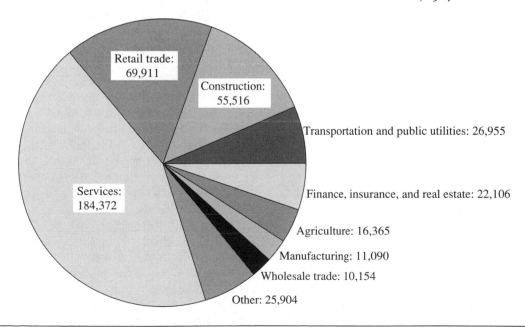

Retail trade: 69,911

Construction: 55,516

Transportation and public utilities: 26,955

Finance, insurance, and real estate: 22,106

Services: 184,372

Agriculture: 16,365

Manufacturing: 11,090

Wholesale trade: 10,154

Other: 25,904

Source: Data are from Marlita A. Reddy, ed., *Statistical Record of Hispanic Americans* (Detroit: Gale Research, 1993), Table 843.

were restaurants or were engaged in food production, importing, and distribution. One-fourth of the Latino population lived in Montreal; the rest were scattered mostly in western Canadian urban centers. Latino-owned businesses in Canada are mostly small, family-run organizations. This trend, however, may be modified by the development of several food cooperatives established by Central American immigrants. These have the potential for market expansion and the hiring of larger numbers of employees.

Latino-owned businesses and corporations in the United States and Canada will affect national economies more as they are able to sell to non-Latinos. In 1993, Latinos were ranked as the third-largest group of workers in the United States. The United States Department of Labor estimated that 8.8 million Latinos would join the U.S. work force by the year 2005. More Latinos could also expect to hold professional and managerial positions, gaining experience that could transfer to business ownership. Latino businesses, in order to grow to a significant size, have had to appeal to a broad, interethnic clientele. With expansion beyond Latino enclaves, they have the opportunity to directly affect the larger U.S. and Canadian markets. Even though the Latino market is growing, the most successful businesses will reach beyond it. The future of Latino-owned businesses lies in their capacity to sell broadly to diverse ethnic populations and to remain competitive with businesses owned by members of other ethnic communities.

—Max Orezzoli and William Osborne

SUGGESTED READINGS:
• Cafferty, Pastora San Juan, and William C. McCready. *Hispanics in the United States.* New Brunswick, N.J. Transaction Books, 1985. A demographic portrait of Hispanics in the United States and a rationale for their having new social agendas. Chapter 7 is a serious review of job and employment opportunities and disappointments faced by Hispanics in the labor markets.
• Morales, Rebecca, and Frank Bonilla, eds. *Latinos in a Changing U.S. Economy.* Newbury Park, Calif.: Sage, 1993. A critical assessment of the relation of ethnic interdependence and ethnic inequality. The authors perceive Latinos' economic and social positions to be generally declining in the United States within this environment of diversity.
• O'Hare, William. "Reaching for the Dream." *American Demographics* 14 (January, 1992): 32-36. This article, with specific data, emphasizes that the mid-1980's were good years for most minority entre-

preneurs but that the varying ethnic groups build businesses at different speeds. Hispanic Americans surpassed most other minority communities except Asian Americans.
• Shorris, Earl. *Latinos: A Biography of the People.* New York: W. W. Norton, 1992. One of the few volumes to concentrate on personal histories from a large variety of Latino national groups in order to assess perspectives on economic and social participation in the United States.

Busing: In the context of education, busing refers to transporting students from one school in a particular district to another school in the same district for the purpose of alleviating racial SEGREGATION. The history of busing is tied to the history of segregation. To understand whether busing is the only legal and practical means to end segregation, as argued in 1980 with the Helms-Johnson Amendment, an understanding of segregation as practiced in the United States in the twentieth century is helpful.

For twenty-five years after the BROWN V. BOARD OF EDUCATION ruling in 1954, federal courts heard cases involving the problem of finding appropriate remedies for school segregation. The primary significance of *Brown* was that it struck down the longstanding "separate but equal" doctrine maintained in districts and legalized in the *Plessy v. Ferguson* (1896) case.

Schools have maintained many types of systems to accomplish segregation. One type isolated Hispanics in "Mexican schools" on the basis of gerrymandered school districts. In another, practiced primarily in California, migrant Hispanic workers were put in "Mexican schools." This practice was challenged in MÉNDEZ V. WESTMINSTER SCHOOL DISTRICT (1947). The school district had refused to allow the Méndez children and other Hispanic children to attend the local school, which had a predominantly white student body. The judge stated that "the paramount requisite in the American system of public education is social equality. It must be open to all children by unified school association regardless of lineage."

The case raised the issue of appropriate remedies for segregation. Redrawing attendance zones to form neighborhood schools was struck down in *Swann v. Charlotte-Mecklenburg Board of Education.* (1971). The Supreme Court approved busing in this case, ruling that desegregation could not be limited to walk-in schools. Houston, Texas, and its suburban areas formed a unitary school district, and further forced busing was ruled unnecessary. Many formerly white

Busing can help create diverse sets of schoolmates. (James Shaffer)

districts, however, had long ago become dominated by Hispanics, who were not counted as nonwhites on census records before 1970. Hispanic group leaders said the ruling was not satisfactory.

The Helms-Johnson Amendment (1980) was introduced in Congress to limit the ways by which courts could impose the remedy of busing to correct legally recognized segregation. At the heart of the argument was whether legislation could identify "reasonable" student transportation in school districts and, more important, whether the legislation had the right to say that busing was only one of several remedies to correct segregation. Busing was finally decided to be "nothing less than a constitutional requirement," with no other remedy available to secure the rights guaranteed by the Fourteenth Amendment to the Constitution. Most desegregation plans needed some kind of transportation in order to carry out the orders. For example, redrawing of school districts usually caused some neighborhoods to be far enough from their school to require busing of students.

Busing has been judged by the Supreme Court to be a valid and necessary means to ensure an integrated school system. Challenges to the Helms-Johnson Amendment have been upheld by the Justice Department on the basis that Congress does not have the authority to contract or withdraw constitutional rights and cannot use powers against the courts.

C

Caballeros de Labor (Knights of Labor): Labor union. This organization was founded in the early 1880's in the Southwest and was modeled after the Nobel Order of the Knights of Labor, a labor union in Philadelphia, Pennsylvania. The Mexican American order never received recognition by the Philadelphia order. The Caballeros de Labor, headed by Juan José Herrera, concerned themselves with protecting their farmlands from Anglos who wanted to steal their land. They were less interested in the issue of the eight-hour workday than were the nationwide Knights of Labor.

trary to the FOURTEENTH AMENDMENT's equal protection clause. The district court ruled in their favor, but the U.S. Supreme Court reversed the lower court's decision, declaring that restrictions enacted primarily for a political (as opposed to economic) function were acceptable.

California law stipulated that persons who sought employment as state, county, or city "peace officers" must be citizens of the United States. In this case, José Chavez-Salido and others had unsuccessfully sought employment as deputy probation officers in Los Ange-

Cabell v. Chavez-Salido *allowed requirements of citizenship for peace officers.* (Robert Fried)

Cabell v. Chavez-Salido (Jan. 12, 1982): Employment discrimination lawsuit. In this case, cited as 454 U.S. 432, Hispanic permanent resident aliens living in California had applied unsuccessfully for employment as deputy parole officers. They brought suit in a federal district court, charging that California's law stipulating that all peace officers must be U.S. citizens was con-

les County. All were lawfully admitted permanent resident aliens. Chavez-Salido and the others argued in federal district court that California's requirement that peace officers be citizens was unconstitutional, under the Fourteenth Amendment's equal protection clause. The district court agreed with the plaintiffs, declaring the California statute invalid.

The United States Supreme Court, however, reversed the lower court decision on a 5-4 vote. The Court admitted that laws affecting noncitizens in a primarily economic way were subject to strict judicial scrutiny. In this case, however, the justices ruled that the restrictions were primarily political, not economic. The *Cabell* decision echoed earlier calls for a two-step process in evaluating whether any restriction by a state upon aliens served economic or political ends. First, the court must find that the restriction is properly specific: If a restriction is too broad or too narrow, the state's claim to a legitimate political function is weakened. Second, restrictions for political ends could be applied only to "state elective or important nonelective executive, legislative, and judicial positions." In the case at hand, the justices ruled that the restriction was properly specific and was applied to an important nonelective position. The restrictive law, therefore, was proper and was not contrary to provisions of the Fourteenth Amendment.

In summing up its decision, the five justices constituting the majority explained that probation officers and their deputies "partake of sovereign's power" and are called upon to exercise power over individuals in the community. Therefore, a requirement of citizenship was appropriate for those who "symbolize this power of the political community over those who fall within its jurisdiction."

This case limited the efforts of community activists in Latino neighborhoods who hoped to make the law enforcement, judicial, and penal systems more responsive to the needs of immigrants and aliens. Although the courts were willing to take some steps to limit economic discrimination against noncitizens, they would not allow noncitizens full and equal participation in government.

Cabello, Domingo (1725, Castile, Spain—1801, Nicaragua): Soldier and administrator. Cabello joined the Spanish army in 1741. He served as an officer in the province of Toledo and in Portugal and Cuba. Cabello's bravery during the siege of Havana (1762) earned for him the governorship of Nicaragua, which he held until becoming governor of Texas in 1778. During his eight years in Texas, Cabello, now a colonel, introduced laws among the Spanish colonists that led to more orderly living. He was also reportedly instrumental in pacification of the fierce Indians of Texas, mostly Apaches and Comanches, through fair treatment and sound trade practices.

Cabello's success with the Indians was noteworthy because, had battle been necessary, he had fewer than two hundred troops to pit against nearly ten thousand Indian warriors. The peace Cabello secured with the Indians lasted thirty years. Another of his notable actions was the stimulation of Antonio Gily Barbo's settlement of Nacogdoches. This settlement soon became Texas' main center of Indian trade and a major force in continuing peacekeeping efforts. Cabello also commissioned Pedro VIAL's search for a route from San Antonio, Texas, to Santa Fe, New Mexico. He did not see the fruits of his efforts, as he left Texas in 1886 upon promotion to subinspector of troops of Cuba. Later, he became a brigadier general and commandant general of Nicaragua.

Cabeza de Baca family: New Mexico politicians and civic leaders. The Cabeza de Baca family is descended from Cristóbal Baca, who took part in the 1598 expedition into New Mexico led by Juan de OÑATE. The family name was changed from Baca by Luis María Baca in 1803.

Politician and journalist Ezequiel Cabeza de Baca was born in 1864 in Las Vegas, New Mexico. He would later rival his father, Tomás, who was himself a judge and territorial legislator. He received his primary education in Las Vegas and attended the Jesuit Las Vegas College from 1878 to 1882. In 1891, Ezequiel took the position of associate editor of the Las Vegas weekly newspaper *La Voz del Pueblo*; in 1900, he became editor. In 1893, he was appointed deputy clerk to Félix Martínez upon the latter's election to the Fourth District Court in San Miguel County.

In succeeding years, as a result of his editorship and involvement in statewide affairs in advocacy for Latino rights, he rose to the position of county chairman of the Democratic Party and became a prominent political leader. Although he opposed ratification of the 1910 New Mexico constitution because of its failure to address Latino education and land issues, he was nominated and elected as the state's first lieutenant governor in 1911 and narrowly missed election to the U.S. Senate in 1913. In 1916, despite ill health, he was elected as New Mexico's second governor. On February 18, 1917, only a month and a half into his term as governor, he died of pernicious anemia in Santa Fe. He was buried in Las Vegas.

Educator and writer Fabiola Cabeza de Baca Gilbert was born in 1898 in Las Vegas, New Mexico. She is a second cousin to Ezequiel. In 1921, after acquiring an extensive knowledge of folk diet and customs, she received a college degree from New Mexico Normal

School (later called New Mexico Highlands University). In 1929, she was awarded a B.S. from New Mexico State University at Las Cruces. After more than three decades of teaching and learning among Pueblo Indians of New Mexico, in 1951 she established United Nations nutrition centers serving the Tarascan Indians of Lake Pátzcuaro, Mexico, and in the 1960's she organized Peace Corps training programs in the same region. During these years, while living in Santa Fe, she hosted a radio program on culture and nutrition and wrote a weekly column in the Spanish-language newspaper *El Nuevo Mexicano*. As a writer, she is best known for *We Fed Them Cactus* (1954), a personal history of the Cabeza de Baca family, but she is also noted for her work on New Mexican food, customs, and folklore. She left public service in 1959, and in 1970 she retired to Las Vegas, New Mexico.

Fernando E. Cabeza de Baca, born in 1937, is a businessman and public servant. He was born and educated in Albuquerque and received both a B.A. in public administration and his legal training from the University of New Mexico. He then served with the U.S. Army Intelligence Airborne Corps in Vietnam, earning military decoration.

During the 1960's and 1970's, he served in various public service positions, including commissioner of the New Mexico department of transportation and western regional director for the federal Department of Health, Education, and Welfare. He was appointed special assistant to the president by Gerald Ford in 1974.

Fernando E. Cabeza de Baca is known for his involvement in veterans' service and civil rights organizations, including the American Legion and the League of United Latin American Citizens. He has worked prominently to promote minority business interests. Along with running his own business, he has lectured widely on the free enterprise system and was a visiting lecturer at Harvard University.

Cabeza de Vaca, Álvar Núñez (1490, Extremadura, Spain—c. 1560, Seville, Spain): Explorer. Cabeza de Vaca was the treasurer of the Crown for an expedition led by Pánfilo de NARVÁEZ to settle Florida. The expedition reached the Tampa Bay area in 1528 and traveled inland. Following an Indian attack, the expedition returned to the coast and fled west in makeshift barges. Only fifteen men remained of an expedition of more than five hundred.

Cabeza de Vaca spent eight years in the areas north of the Gulf of Mexico. Often he was no more than a slave to Indians, but later he was praised as a medicine man. He met with three other survivors and in 1536 finally found Spaniards in the town of San Miguel in northern Mexico. Although his entire journey was one of hardship, his accounts inspired future expeditions by Francisco Vázquez de CORONADO and Hernando DE SOTO.

After his experience in North America, Cabeza de Vaca went back to Spain. In 1540, he went to South America with a capitulation for Rio de la Plata. He was betrayed and returned to Spain as a prisoner. He died in Seville around 1560, after he wrote a narrative of his adventures in the New World.

Cabinet Committee on Opportunities for Spanish Speaking People (CCOSSP): U.S. government committee. This committee replaced the INTER-AGENCY COMMITTEE ON MEXICAN AMERICAN AFFAIRS established during the Lyndon B. Johnson Administration. The CCOSSP was established in December, 1969, for a five-year term.

The CCOSSP's goals were similar to those of the previous committee but broader, including all Spanish-speaking people in the United States. It sought to reach Spanish-speaking people through federal programs, increase Latino appointments to federal posts, and develop new programs as needed. The first chair was Martin Castillo, who devised a program to increase Latino representation in federal government. Castillo resigned and was replaced by Henry M. RAMÍREZ. Ramírez administered small business aid but did not establish new programs. He claimed success for the CCOSSP, but many believed that he spent considerable energy on Richard Nixon's reelection campaign and failed to uphold the CCOSSP's legislative mandate. After the initial five-year term, funding was not renewed. The CCOSSP was dissolved in December, 1974.

Cabrera, Lydia (May 20, 1900, Havana, Cuba—Sept. 19, 1991, Miami, Fla.): Ethnologist. Cabrera's collections of Afro-Cuban folklore constituted a major contribution to the anthropological study of Cuba. Her interest in Afro-Caribbean culture began when she left Cuba in 1927 to study Asian religions at L'École du Louvre in Paris, France. She published the first of her more than twenty books in 1936. Her best-known work is probably *El Monte* (1954), a seminal work in Spanish on SANTERÍA religious practices.

Cabrera lived in Cuba from 1938 to 1960, then settled in Miami, Florida, after a brief period in Spain.

This statue of Juan Rodríguez Cabrillo looks toward San Diego, California. (Envision, Michael J. Howell)

Students of Afro-Cuban culture traveled to her home, as did artists and writers interested in that culture. She continued to collect folk tales while living in Miami.

Cabrillo, Juan Rodríguez (c. 1500, Portugal or Spain—Jan. 3, 1543, San Miguel Island, Calif.): Explorer. Cabrillo led the first expedition to the Pacific coast of the United States. Little is known about his background. Until late in the twentieth century, scholars believed that Cabrillo was Portuguese, but later evidence indicated that he was Spanish.

Cabrillo came to the New World at a young age. He served with Pánfilo de NARVÁEZ in Cuba and probably went with him to Mexico when Narváez tried to arrest Hernán CORTÉS for failing to return to Santo Domingo on the order of Diego VELÁZQUEZ DE CUÉLLAR. Like many of Narváez's men, Cabrillo stayed with Cortés.

After the conquest of Mexico, Cortés organized several expeditions on the Pacific coast. Cabrillo was the leader of one such expedition in 1542. He sailed farther north than had any previous expedition. He entered San Diego Bay and visited many islands located off the coast of California. He made notes of the flora and fauna of the region and visited many Indian villages while searching for places to settle. In January of 1543, while still traveling along the coast, Cabrillo died of complications from a wound incurred when he broke his arm.

Cacique: Indian chieftain or political leader of a region. The term *cacique* derives from the Caribbean Taino language and designates the chief of a tribe. Among Central and South American tribes, the term is used to identify a chieftain. Since the nineteenth century, the term has also been used to designate a person who imposes his or her authority over a community in an abusive fashion. The *cacique* is thus a person who uses wealth and intimidation to achieve control of the political and economic life of a community or region and views its members as extensions of his or her private property. This political phenomenon is called *caciquismo*.

Cadena Radio Centro (founded 1986): Radio network. As the largest Spanish-language radio network in the United States, Cadena Radio Centro covers North, Central, and South America as well as the Caribbean region. As of 1994, it had ninety-two affiliates established in seventy-five cities in five countries.

Grupo Radio Centro, the largest radio company in Mexico, established Cadena Radio Centro in Hollywood, California. The network sells programming and services to Spanish-language stations throughout the Americas. Its programming includes newscasts, entertainment programs, sports specials, informative capsules, and music programs. Its audience as of 1994 included more than twenty-two million listeners. The network received the 1994 Golden Mike Award for the Best Radio Network News Service.

Cadena Radio Centro offers a service providing new reports every hour, twenty-four hours a day, to sixty affiliated Spanish-language stations linked via satellite. Its programming service operates seven days a week and has two information lines. One transmits its five-minute news reports every hour. Three of these transmissions each day originate from Mexico City, and another three focus on Latin American news. The other line transmits a variety of programs, including *En Concierto* (prominent Hispanic artists introducing their music), *Cristina Opina* (opinions by Cristina Saralegui on a wide range of subjects), *Tribuna Deportiva* (a live sports call-in talk show), and news of special events. Affiliates purchase all or only some of these programs, depending on local or regional interests.

Calaveras: Candy skulls for the celebration of the Mexican Day of the Dead. The Day of the Dead (DÍA DE LOS MUERTOS), November 2, is an important festival in Mexico. Families conduct all-night celebrations at cemeteries, home altars are made, and special foods are prepared or purchased. Among those foods are *calaveras*, representations of skulls made from spun sugar. These skulls are often given to children, with the recipient's name across the forehead, as a reminder that all children someday will join their ancestors in death. Neither the *calaveras* nor the Day of the Dead, is grim, however; the holiday is a time to commune with dead loved ones.

California: Both historically and because of its large Latino community, California has played a role second only to Texas among U.S. states for its importance to Mexican American issues.

Spanish California. During most of the Spanish colonial period, settlement in California depended mainly on two factors: military security forces and religious missionary activities. Although a Spanish presence was established by several explorers early in the sixteenth century, it was not until the voyages of Sebastian Vizcaino (1600 and 1602) that California's major seaports—San Francisco, Monterey, and San Diego—were placed on detailed maps. Permanent military control of these areas did not come until the next century.

José de Galvez occupied San Diego and Monterey in 1769, when Spain began to fear the advance of Russian traders southward from Alaska. By that date the second, more penetrating force of Catholic missionaries (first Jesuits, then Franciscans) was determined to spread Christianity into areas that had never been explored, let alone settled.

After Father Junípero SERRA's arrival in San Diego in 1769, missionary activity placed most of California's first Latino communities on the map. In the 1770's, these included San Juan Capistrano, Santa Barbara, San Luis Obispo, Monterey, San Jose, and San Francisco. Eventually twenty-three main missions were founded.

By the time the twenty-second mission was founded in San Rafael in 1817, a split had appeared between missionaries and Spanish authorities, who had other priorities for colonial development. Father José Altimira, a Franciscan, hoped to extend explorations and missions inland to Santa Rosa, but his goal was cut short. The dedication of Sonoma Mission in 1823, shortly after Mexico became independent from Spain, marked the end of the mission era. In fifteen years' time, secularization laws passed by Mexico reduced the landholding and tax privileges of the richest missions, opening the way for new forms of colonization.

Mexican Colonial Ranchos and Pueblos. After 1822, the pueblo, or colonial village, and the rancho land grant (*see* RANCHOS AND RANCHO LIFE) helped shape California before it became a state in 1850. Mexico's 1824 Colonization Law was designed to attract private parties to California by offering grants of land as ranchos to petitioners who proposed economic development plans. Only thirty ranchos were granted by the Spaniards, whereas the Mexicans granted almost eight hundred in twenty-five years.

CALIFORNIA'S LATINO POPULATION, BY COUNTY, 1990

NORTHERN CALIFORNIA COUNTIES

1. Del Norte
   2,414 (10.3%)
2. Siskiyou
   2,549 (5.9%)
3. Modoc
   701 (7.2%)
4. Humboldt
   4,989 (4.2%)
5. Trinity
   431 (3.3%)
6. Shasta
   5,652 (3.8%)
7. Lassen
   2,883 (10.4%)
8. Mendocino
   8,248 (10.3%)
9. Tehama
   5,124 (10.3%)
10. Plumas
    907 (4.6%)
11. Butte
    13,606 (7.5%)
12. Glenn
    4,958 (20.0%)
13. Lake
    3,633 (7.2%)

14. Colusa
    5,424 (33.3%)
15. Sutter
    10,592 (16.4%)
16. Yuba
    6,728 (11.6%)
17. Sierra
    184 (5.5%)
18. Nevada
    3,269 (4.2%)
19. Placer
    13,871 (8.0%)
20. El Dorado
    8,777 (7.0%)
21. Sacramento
    121,544 (11.7%)
22. Yolo
    28,182 (20.0%)
23. Napa
    15,941 (14.4%)
24. Sonoma
    41,223 (10.6%)
25. Marin
    17,930 (7.8%)
26. Solano
    45,517 (13.4%)
27. Contra Costa
    91,282 (11.4%)
28. San Joaquin
    112,673 (23.4%)
29. Alameda
    181,805 (14.2%)

30. San Mateo
    114,627 (17.6%)
31. SantaCruz
    46,797 (20.4%)
32. Santa Clara
    314,564 (21.0%)
33. Stanislaus
    80,897 (21.8%)
34. Calaveras
    1,714 (5.4%)
35. Amador
    2,520 (8.4%)
36. Alpine
    74 (6.6%)
37. Mono
    1,126 (11.3%)
38. Tuolumne
    3,726 (7.7%)
39. Mariposa
    697 (4.9%)
40. Merced
    58,107 (32.6%)
41. Madera
    30,400 (34.5%)
42. San Benito
    16,800 (45.8%)
43. Monterey
    119,570 (33.6%)
44. Fresno
    236,634 (35.5%)
45. Kings
    34,551 (34.1%)
46. Tulare
    120,893 (38.8%)
47. Inyo
    1,536 (8.4%)
48. San Francisco
    100,717 (13.9%)

SOUTHERN CALIFORNIA COUNTIES

49. San Luis Obispo
    28,923 (13.3%)
50. Kern
    151,995 (28.0%)
51. Santa Barbara
    98,199 (26.6%)
52. Ventura
    176,952 (26.4%)
53. Los Angeles
    3,351,242 (37.8%)
54. San Bernardino
    378,582 (26.7%)
55. Riverside
    307,514 (26.3%)
56. Orange
    564,828 (23.4%)
57. San Diego
    510,781 (20.4%)
58. Imperial
    71,935 (65.8%)

Source: Data are from *California Statistical Abstract 1993* (Sacramento: California Department of Finance, 1993), Table B-5; and Marlita A. Reddy, ed., *Statistical Record of Hispanic Americans* (Detroit: Gale Research, 1993), Table 109.

Note: The numbers below each county name are the county's Latino population and the percentage of the county's population that is Latino. Figures for cities represent Metropolitan Statistical Areas (MSAs) as determined by the Bureau of the Census.

Olvera Street was an important social and economic center for Mexican Americans in Los Angeles. (Security Pacific Bank Collection, Los Angeles Public Library)

Ranchos could be as large as eleven leagues (approximately forty thousand acres), but most were five or fewer leagues. In a little more than two decades, 672 ranchos were granted; some were given to influential families from the pre-Mexican period who constituted the Hispanic Californio elites who continued to play an important role even after California was acquired by the United States. Among the ranchos of major families were Rancho San Antonio (now Oakland, Alameda, and Berkeley), granted to the Peralta family; and Rancho San José de Gracia de Simi (100,000 acres in Ventura County), granted to the PICO FAMILY, one of whose members, Pío Pico, was the last Mexican governor of California. Lesser known early rancho sites were Rancho San Miguel, 4,443 acres granted to José Noé in 1845 around what is now the Twin Peaks district of San Francisco, and more than 2,000 acres granted near the San Francisco Presidio to Henry Fitch, a non-Hispanic settler.

Several influential rancho families began lobbying for higher degrees of Californio autonomy from Mexico City's control. In 1836, "radicals" Juan Bautista ALVARADO and José Castro led a revolt against the governor in Monterey, winning some of their autonomy goals. Castro also was involved in a revolt against Governor Pío Pico in 1846, when the Mexican American War was under way.

The first two Spanish pueblos under a 1781 *reglamento* (regulation) sent to California's administrative center at Monterey were El Pueblo de Nuestra Señora la Reina de Los Angeles de Porciúncula (now Los Angeles) and Santa Barbara, both of which received settlers, or *pobladores*, recruited in Mexico. Other pueblos of note were San Fernando (founded in 1797) and Agua Mansa and La Placita in the San Bernardino Valley (directly beside which a non-Hispanic settlement called Riverside was later established).

Los Angeles, with its expanding Hispanic population, was increasingly important in the late nineteenth century and throughout the twentieth century. This pueblo, with 140 settlers in 1790, was meant to be a self-supporting agricultural settlement, part of whose labor was "contracted" with nearby Gabrielino Indians. At least sixty ranchos were granted in Los Angeles' vicinity. An early example were José Verdugo's Rancho San Rafael, covering what became Glendale and Burbank.

Expansion of settlement activity after the Colonization Law of 1824 called for a revision in the status of LOS ANGELES. In 1836, Los Angeles—then peopled by more than 1,600 settlers—became a *ciudad*, or formal city, with political and economic responsibilities covering the entire southern zone of Alta California, including San Diego. By the end of the Mexican period, it had replaced Monterey as the primary colonial city and was one of several district capitals to elect Alta California's deputy to the Mexican Congress. All of this changed once the Mexican American War separated California from Mexico. Los Angeles' Mexican population, like those of other key pueblos such as San Jose, Sacramento, and Santa Ana, was reduced from majority to minority status.

During the first fifteen years of California's statehood, Los Angeles' Mexican population increased fourfold, constituting 47.1 percent of the population. Many newcomers may have been immigrants who stayed after the gold rush. More than 25,000 Mexicans crossed the Sonora border in only four years. By 1900,

CALIFORNIA'S PROJECTED POPULATION BY RACIAL/ETHNIC GROUP *(percentages)*				
Year	Hispanic	Caucasian	Black	Asian and Other
1970	12	78	7	3
1980	19	67	8	7
1990	25	58	7	10
2000	29	52	7	12
2010	34	46	7	13
2020	38	41	7	14

Source: Data are from California Department of Finance, Population Research Unit, *Report 88P-4.*

the percentage of Mexicans in Los Angeles had declined to 19.3 percent. In addition to changes in relative numbers resulting from lower levels of Mexican immigration and greater numbers of non-Hispanics moving westward in the last quarter of the nineteenth century, the socioeconomic profile of Mexicans in Los Angeles and other former pueblos took on new patterns.

From Pueblos to Barrios. The position of CALIFORNIOS was substantially reduced during the first fifty years of U.S. statehood. Despite Californio presence in the first legislatures (eight of forty-eight delegates elected to California's Constitutional Convention in 1849 were Californios), politics began to undermine the position of what was soon to become an influential but declining minority. As the gold rush developed, approximately 100,000 non-Hispanics overwhelmed the 13,000 Spanish speakers who remained in California. After the discriminatory FOREIGN MINERS' TAX LAW was imposed (not only on resident Hispanics, but on the wave of European immigrants as well), other laws were passed that forced a land-owning elite (some two hundred families holding fourteen million acres) to defend their rancho titles. Many ranchos had to be sold to U.S. settlers who filed claims, and some titles were canceled. Some rancho owners received patents (as late as the 1870's) for portions of their original holdings. A case in point was the Peralta family's loss of Rancho San Antonio, which was worth an estimated $3 million, to a triad of lawyers headed by Horace Carpentier, the first mayor of Oakland.

Barrioization began to occur around 1900. The process that had led to the decline of nineteenth century ranchos was accompanied by significant changes in vocational prospects for Latinos in California. The transfer of domination of the ranching sector to non-

LATINO POPULATION OF CALIFORNIA, 1990

Total number of Latinos = 7,687,938; 26% of population

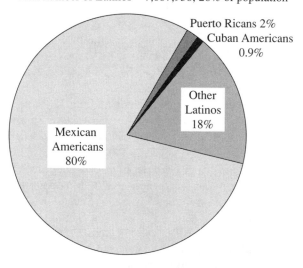

Puerto Ricans 2%
Cuban Americans 0.9%
Other Latinos 18%
Mexican Americans 80%

Source: Data are from Marlita A. Reddy, ed., *Statistical Record of Hispanic Americans* (Detroit: Gale Research, 1993), Table 106.
Note: Percentages are rounded to the nearest whole number except for Cuban Americans, for whom rounding is to the nearest 0.1%.

Hispanics and the rise of major farming concerns before World War II combined to make employment possibilities for Mexican Americans and new immigrants concentrated in the unskilled labor sector, especially where new manufacturing concerns were growing. Where this was the case, pueblo communities remained population centers for Mexican American descendants of the Californios, while new locations grew up (often on towns' outskirts) nearer job sites. In time, these locations became BARRIOS filled with workers and their families, many of whom were new immigrants. During World War II, California, which rapidly became a center for armaments and aviation companies, attracted another tide of Mexican immigrants with promises of factory work in addition to the expanding agricultural employment in the Imperial, San Joaquin, and Salinas valleys.

Farmworkers and Postwar Urban Patterns. A shortage of agricultural workers during World War II prompted the U.S. government to enter into the BRACERO PROGRAM, an arrangement with Mexico. Overnight, thousands of Mexican workers came to the fields of the Southwest, particularly to California's Central Valley.

The postwar future of these legal migrant workers, along with thousands of others who came without papers, became a major social and political issue in California, continuing for several decades. As certain agricultural areas witnessed a growth in the numbers of Mexican American farmworkers, labor activists became concerned over their exploitation by farm owners. Although efforts to involve Mexican workers in farm labor organizations began in the 1930's, the best-known movement was led by César CHÁVEZ and the

The United Farm Workers played an important role in securing the rights of field workers in California. (David Bacon)

UNITED FARM WORKERS, beginning in 1965 with the DELANO GRAPE STRIKE.

By the 1970's, the importance of growing urban communities had overshadowed the situation of Mexican Americans in rural farm settings. The major example of urban Hispanic growth is Los Angeles, the Spanish-surnamed population of which went from 9 percent in 1960, to approximately 28 percent by 1980, and to nearly 38 percent (3.35 million) in 1990. It is estimated that between 1970 and 1973, more than three-quarters of a million immigrants entered Southern California from Mexico, most coming without legal authorization. Two-thirds of these tried to settle in the Los Angeles area; others spread to barrios of medium-sized cities throughout the state.

Given these large numbers of arrivals, traditional Mexican American "downtown" neighborhoods (such as La Placita, near Union Station in Los Angeles) proved inadequate to house legal and illegal immigrant families. In Los Angeles, an enormous barrio formed in EAST LOS ANGELES and major sections of the San Gabriel Valley. Statistics from the 1980's show that although the number of Latinos in such sprawling barrios remained constant, many families in low-income, slum-ridden, urban environments relocated as quickly as possible. Owner-occupied housing in East Los Angeles had been as low as 7.2 percent by the early 1990's, while middle-class neighborhoods that were predominantly Hispanic, such as Pacoima and areas near the harbor, had attracted home buyers.

One positive side of the concentrations of Latinos in major California cities has been political representation, through the electoral process, in local and state government. This had seemed impossible as late as the 1960's, when only one Mexican American, Edward Roybal, had succeeded in winning an elected post (on the Los Angeles City Council, between 1949 and 1962). After Roybal advanced to a congressional seat in 1962, activists from Mexican American communities in California began to realize the political potential that could serve the barrios' interests. At the end of the 1960's, Julian Nava became the first Mexican American to be elected to the Los Angeles School Board. By the 1980's and 1990's, not only had the city of Los Angeles and the San Gabriel Valley elected Mexican Americans to Congress, but California had sent several congressmen and congresswomen, as well as high-ranking appointed officials, of Mexican heritage to the federal government in Washington.

—*Byron D. Cannon*

SUGGESTED READINGS:
- Haas, Mary L. *The Barrios of Santa Ana: Community, Class, and Urbanization, 1850-1947*. Irvine: University of California Microfilm, 1985. A thesis, one of several studies that focus on former Mexican pueblos (such as Sacramento and San Jose) that would find themselves incorporated into twentieth century urban centers.
- Hijar, Carlos, Eulalia Perez, and Agustin Escobar. *Three Memoirs of Mexican California*. Berkeley: Friends of the Bancroft Library, University of California at Berkeley, 1988. Valuable transcriptions of manuscript diaries kept by ordinary Californios. One is by a woman who witnessed the passing of California from Spanish to Mexican to American control.
- Pitt, Leonard. *The Decline of the Californios: A Social History of the Spanish-Speaking Californians, 1846-1890*. Berkeley: University of California Press, 1966. Traces the growth and decline in social position and property ownership of Mexican rancho families before and after U.S. statehood.
- Priestley, Herbert I. *Franciscan Explorations in California*. Glendale, Calif.: Arthur H. Clark, 1946. A classic covering the colonial politics behind the founding of California's missions.
- Skerry, Peter. *Mexican Americans: The Ambivalent Minority*. New York: Free Press, 1993. Although focused on political organizations of Mexican Americans, this book contains up-to-date information on key Chicano communities, especially in Los Angeles and San Antonio.

Californios: People of Mexican and Spanish descent who were in California prior to conquest by the United States. Californios originally comprised many races and classes of people, although over time the term became associated with Californians of Spanish descent. Most of the first settlers in Los Angeles were mixed-race people, but once haciendas developed and a rigid social hierarchy became established among the *POBLADORES* (town settlers), upper-class Mexicans took an increasing interest in their own *pureza de sangre* (purity of blood).

During the Spanish period, the GENTE DE RAZON (landed, Catholic, speakers of Castilian Spanish) began to draw racial as well as class distinctions between themselves and both the Indians living in and around the missions and the lower-class VAQUEROS (cowboys) employed at the haciendas. By the time of Mexican independence from Spain in 1821, Californios had established a nominal caste system dividing people on the basis of land ownership. Although mostly mestizo, many of the *gente de razon* identified themselves as Spanish to distinguish themselves racially from the mostly Native American landless people.

The term "Californio" again changed meaning following the introduction of non-Hispanic white people into California and the imposition of U.S. racial categories. New settlers seeking to share or possess Mexican land in California assigned a higher racial status to mestiza Californianas (female Californios of mixed race); however, lower-class mestizas and all Mexican men continued to be regarded as mixed race.

This division of Californio society along gender and racial lines justified the subsequent American conquest. Anglo Americans saw higher-class, "white" Californianas in need of salvation from the lower-class, racially inferior Mexican men and women who predominated in California. Prior to the outbreak of the Mexican American War in 1846, some Anglo policymakers advanced the idea that a conquest of California would save the Californio inhabitants from their own inabilities to govern and develop the region.

In the wake of the conquest, both Anglos and Californio elites increasingly reserved the term "Californio" for upper-class, "Spanish" descendants of the original Mexican settlers. Former Mexican nationals who were granted the luxury of calling themselves Californios accepted this classification to avoid the rampant discrimination many Anglos directed against mestizos living in California. Non-Hispanic whites chose to glorify the Californios and the days of Spanish California rather than acknowledge the severe conditions many Mexican Americans lived under during the second half of the nineteenth century. This romanticization of the past permitted many whites to imagine themselves as the heirs to an Edenic Californio world while conveniently erasing a quarter century of Mexican rule in California. In the late nineteenth century, Anglo Californians restored missions, mimicked mission style architecture, and held immense fiestas and parades in honor of "Spanish" California. The old Californios and their descendants participated in these festivals to validate the myth perpetuated by these events.

Calle Ocho (Miami, Fla.): Neighborhood. Literally translated as Eighth Street, Calle Ocho is a center of

The Little Havana Community Center on Calle Ocho is a social center for Cuban Americans. (Impact Visuals, Julio Etchart)

life in the LITTLE HAVANA section of Miami. It is the site of an annual block party featuring Latin music, culture, and food.

In 1978, the Kiwanis of Little Havana invited the rest of Miami to a thirteen-block party. More than 100,000 people attended, and Calle Ocho instantly became a major event. Known as the largest block party in the world, the Calle Ocho celebration has been televised nationally and internationally. By 1993, the party had expanded from thirteen to twenty-three city blocks. Attendance has exceeded one million.

Calle Ocho Open House—Carnaval Miami (Miami, Fla.): The annual Carnaval Miami celebration is held from early February through the middle of March. Begun in 1977, the festivities offer an imposing array of events that includes Carnaval Night in the Orange Bowl, the *paseo* (parade), and the CALLE OCHO Festival, which occurs in Little Havana, an area of SW Eighth Street featuring Latino shops and restaurants.

In addition to traditional foods, games, dances, and folk arts and crafts, the festival includes the largest street party in the United States, a golf tournament, a cooking contest, live music and entertainment, a beauty contest, and an eight-kilometer foot race. Many events raise money for charitable organizations.

Although other Latinos participate, the festival is principally Cuban in flavor because of the large Cuban American population of Miami. About a million and a half visitors each year, as of the early 1990's, make Carnaval Miami the largest Latino festival in the United States.

Calleros, Cleofas (1896—1973, El Paso, Tex.): Writer Calleros, a Texas writer, was a journalist and chronicler of history and religion in the American Southwest. A devout Catholic and lifelong member of the Knights of Columbus, Calleros wrote primarily about the Catholic missions in and around El Paso. He also recorded mission histories from throughout Texas as well as from the mission in Juárez, Mexico. He wrote sixteen books about Texas' early inhabitants and missionaries, most in collaboration with Marjorie F. Graham.

Calleros also wrote a regular column titled "Then and Now" in an El Paso newspaper. These columns were collected in the volume *El Paso-Then and Now* (1954). Like his books, his journalism was concerned with historical narratives of Texas missions. Calleros wrote some books in Spanish, several about Nuestra Señora de Guadalupe Mission.

When not writing about Texas history, Calleros worked within his church and the Knights of Columbus. His other works include *El Paso's Missions and Indians* (1951), *The Mother Mission: Our Lady of Mount Carmel* (1952), *Queen of the Missions* (1952), *Tigua Indians: Oldest Permanent Settlers in Texas* (1953), and his final book, *Seventieth Anniversary of Columbianism in Texas* (1972).

Caló: Dialect used by urban Mexican American youths. Caló is a dialect that combines Spanish, English, and neologisms. Also known as *Caló pachuco* or *Caló pocho*, this dialect varies according to the geographical area where it is spoken. Caló has been used by Mexican American poets and novelists for its linguistic richness and as a reflection of bilingual code switching. One of the first novelists to use Caló was Daniel VENEGAS.

Camarillo, Albert Michael (Alberto Camarillo; b. Feb. 9, 1948, Compton, Calif.): Historian. Camarillo has devoted much of his research effort to uncovering the history of Americans of Mexican descent, and other racial minorities, in U.S. cities. His best-known work is *Chicanos in a Changing Society: From Mexican Pueblos to American Barrios in Santa Barbara and Southern California, 1848-1930* (1979). He is also the author of *Chicanos in California* (1984), written for a more general audience, and several books on family and labor issues. Camarillo's extensive bibliographical research resulted in several volumes, including *Latinos in the United States: A Historical Bibliography* (1986) and *Mexican Americans in Urban Society: A Selected Bibliography* (1986).

Camarillo has served as executive director of the Inter-University Program for Latino Research (1983-1988) and as director of the Stanford Center for Chicano Research (1980-1985). He began teaching history at Stanford University in 1975, eventually attaining the rank of professor. Aided by a scholarship from the Mexican American Political Association, he earned a B.A. in history at UCLA in 1970. His Ph.D. in history, focusing on the Mexican American experience, came in 1975.

Camarón: Shrimp. *Camarónes* are the most commonly eaten shellfish in Latin America, consumed in every country with local access to them. They are prepared variously in soups, TACOS, casseroles, AL-BÓNDIGAS, sauced dishes, and salads. They are commonly pickled in Puerto Rico and dried in Mexico,

This Mexican dish is camarónes rancheros, *jumbo prawns sautéed in tomato sauce and served with rice, salad, and guacamole.* (Robert Fried)

each method altering the basic taste. Shrimp are eaten regularly mostly in coastal zones, where they are inexpensive.

Camino Real, El: Highway. Literally translated as "the royal road," El Camino Real is a pathway stretching from the upper Baja Peninsula to the San Francisco Bay area, linking California's missions. Other roads called El Camino Real exist, but California's is the best known.

California's missions were established at distances approximating a day's ride on horseback. The trail between them, El Camino Real, later became California's Highway 101. Reproductions of mission bells mark the trail, appearing every ten miles along the highway. The El Camino Real Association was established in 1904 to revive the route and promote restoration of the missions. The first of the mission bells along the route was placed in 1906.

Campa, Arthur León (Arturo Campa; Feb. 20, 1905, Guaymas, Sonora, Mexico—1978): Folklorist. Campa wrote about the legends of the American Southwest and on differences between Anglo and Mexican Americans. His publications include *A Bibliography of Spanish Folklore in New Mexico* (1930), *Treasures of the Sangre de Cristos* (1962), and *Hispanic Culture in the Southwest* (1979).

Campa grew up on a ranch near El Paso, Texas, where his family moved after his father was killed by followers of Pancho VILLA. He earned a degree at the University of New Mexico at Albuquerque in 1928, then taught at Albuquerque High School. He returned to the university and earned his master's degree in 1930. Campa worked on his doctorate at Columbia University for the next ten years during the summers, teaching in the modern language department at the University of New Mexico during the academic year. He earned his Ph.D. in 1940 and continued to teach at

Shortstop Bert Campaneris throws to first base for an attempted double play after forcing out Junior Moore. (AP/Wide World Photos)

the University of New Mexico. In 1946, he accepted a position as chair of the modern languages department at the University of Denver. He stayed at that university until his retirement in 1972.

Campaneris, Bert (Dagoberto Campaneris y Blanco; b. Mar. 9, 1942, Pueblo Nuevo, Cuba): Baseball player. Campaneris entered the major leagues in 1964 by hitting a home run on the first pitch thrown to him (making him the third player in baseball history to do so). The right-handed shortstop's major league career spanned nineteen years and included seasons with the Kansas City-Oakland Athletics, the Texas Rangers, the California Angels, and the New York Yankees.

Campaneris proved to be a well-rounded player. In a 1965 publicity stunt, he played every position in a nine-inning game for Kansas City. He led the American League in triples in 1965, in hits in 1968, and in stolen bases in 1965, 1966, 1967, 1968, 1970, and 1972. He was named to the American League All-Star Team in 1965, 1972, 1973, 1974, 1975, and 1977.

In the 1972 American League playoffs between Oakland and Detroit, a pitch from Lerrin LaGrow hit Campaneris in the ankle. Campaneris threw his bat at LaGrow, and a fight ensued as Detroit manager Billy Martin came after Campaneris. Both were ejected, and Campaneris was suspended for the remainder of the playoffs and the first seven games of the 1973 season. Reinstated for the World Series, he was hit by three more pitches. Oakland went on to win that series as well as the 1973 and 1974 world championships. Campaneris, ironically, finished his major league career in 1983 as a utility infielder for Martin's New York Yankees, batting a career-high .322 in sixty games.

Campechanas: Mexican sweet rolls. *Campechanas* are a type of PAN DULCE made in Mexican *panaderías* (bakeries). They are oval pastries with a shiny, sugar-glazed topping. Rich in shortening, they are very flaky, almost shattering at the first bite. *Campechanas* are one of the many *panes dulces* that are the province of the *panaderías*, almost never made at home. Their name derives from Campeche, where the recipe reputedly was created.

Campeche, José (Jan. 6, 1752, San Juan Puerto Rico—Nov. 7, 1809, Puerto Rico): Painter, sculptor, architect, and musician. Considered to be Puerto Rico's first great artist, Campeche is best known as a portraitist of Puerto Rico's upper-class society. He was also a prolific painter of religious images and founder of Puerto Rico's school of painting.

The son of a freed black slave and a Spanish woman, Campeche showed an early fondness for drawing. He helped his father make carvings and decorative paintings for churches. While young, he learned drawing by copying pictures of saints.

In his twenties, Campeche learned about technique, color, and European painting conventions from exiled Spanish painter Luis Paret y Alcalzar. Although he never studied anatomy or mastered perspective, Campeche excelled in composition and detail, and he earned commissions across the island and beyond.

Completed primarily between 1785 and 1801, Campeche's portraits depict Puerto Rican governors, bishops, military officers, and their ladies in formal, full-length poses. In addition to portraits and religious images, Campeche's work includes paintings that catalog eighteenth and nineteenth century Puerto Rican life. He painted the first paving of San Juan's streets, recorded the invasion of Puerto Rico by British forces, and completed a panoramic view of the city. Campeche completed more than four hundred paintings.

Campesino: Literally, "country person." The definition of a *campesino* varies regionally and by time period. It consistently applies to Mexicanos or other Latinos who work in agriculture. In the nineteenth

In common North American usage, campesino *refers generally to Latino farmworkers.* (Library of Congress)

century, the term applied to those who worked on large farms, participated in the sharecropping system, or maintained subsistence farms. During the twentieth century, the term increasingly became identified with fieldworkers working long hours, with dangerous pesticides, for low wages. César CHÁVEZ and the UNITED FARM WORKERS union raised the plight of the *campesino* to national attention during the late 1960's and early 1970's through highly publicized labor strikes, protest marches, boycotts, and hunger strikes.

Campusano, Jesús "Chuy" (b. 1944): Painter. As one of three artists who painted the first recognized outdoor mural in San Francisco's MISSION DISTRICT, Campusano is considered one of the forerunners of the Chicano mural movement in California. The outdoor mural was painted in 1971 on the storefront of Horizons Unlimited, a job training center frequented by Latinos. Campusano and painter Ruben Guzmán made the lettering and decorations for the mural, which depicts four scenes of local Latino life as drawn by cartoonist Spain Rodríguez.

That first mural is especially significant because it drew attention to the positive ways Latinos were beginning to view themselves—as carriers of a rich cultural heritage instead of as Spanish-speaking outsiders to Anglo culture. Because the Mission District was becoming home to increasing numbers of Mexicans, Nicaraguans, and immigrants from El Salvador, assimilation and cultural identity were critical issues in the neighborhood.

Subsequently, Campusano organized a team of muralists to paint a Mission District community center and designed a mural for the Mission District Bank of America. After returning from study in Mexico during the mid-1970's, he completed additional murals for a library and a police station.

Canada: The world's second largest country in area, Canada had a 1991 population of 26,994,045. Canada increasingly is becoming multicultural, with a relatively small but growing number of Latinos.

Immigration and Ethnicity. Until the late nineteenth century, most Canadian immigrants came from France or the British Isles; beginning about 1880, large numbers of other European groups began to enter the country, especially from Germany, Italy, The Netherlands, Poland, and the Ukraine. A large influx of non-Europeans became noticeable after the Immigration Act of 1967 ended legal discrimination based on race or culture, allowing immigrants to come based on a

CANADA'S IMMIGRANT POPULATION BY PLACE OF BIRTH			
	1967	1986	1991
Mexico	1,262	13,845	19,395
El Salvador	N.A.	11,245	38,300
Haiti	N.A.	31,951	39,880
Jamaica	N.A.	87,600	102,440
Spain	8,162	12,760	11,170
Portugal	57,427	139,640	161,180
Argentina	5,336	8,365	11,110
Chile	N.A.	17,800	22,875
Guyana	N.A.	50,820	66,060
Other South American countries	N.A.	36,525	50,525
Total immigrant population	N.A.	3,908,150	4,342,890

Source: Data are from the 20 percent sample data of the 1991 census of Canada and other Canadian census documents. Data appear in Statistics Canada, *Immigration and Citizenship* (Ottawa: Statistics Canada, 1992).

Note: N.A. = not available.

merit-point system that emphasized job skills.

Between 1981 and 1991, almost half of all immigrants were born in Asian countries, 25 percent in Europe, 10 percent in Central or South America, and 6 percent in the Caribbean. In the 1991 census, 31 percent of Canadians reported origins other than English or French, with 532,060 reporting Aboriginal origins. Regarding language, 67 percent of Canadians said they most often spoke English at home, 24 percent most often spoke French, and 8 percent (2.1 million people) most often spoke another language, including 145,000 who spoke Spanish and 153,000 who spoke Portuguese.

Canada's first significant Spanish-speaking settlements began in 1913-1914, when two thousand immigrants came from Spain. Few more immigrated during the interwar years, but from 1945 to 1991 approximately twenty-six thousand Spaniards arrived in Canada. The majority settled in the provinces of Ontario and Quebec, and they were overwhelmingly located in cities such as Toronto, Montreal, and Vancouver. In the census of 1991, 158,010 Canadians said they were of European-Spanish origin. Immigrants from Spain have tended to assimilate rapidly, especially in the French-speaking parts of Canada. They usually have not spoken the Spanish language beyond the second generation.

Between the end of World War II and 1967, about thirty-five thousand Latin Americans entered Canada, mostly from Argentina, Mexico, and Brazil. This number increased in the early 1970's because of liberal immigration laws combined with a large demand for unskilled and semiskilled workers in manufacturing. After the overthrow of the regime of Salvador Allende in 1973, the Canadian government sponsored a special program that allowed sixty-nine hundred Chilean refugees to enter the country. Military conflicts in Central America in the 1980's sent several thousand refugees to Canada from El Salvador, Guatemala, and Nicaragua. In the 1991 census, 119,980 Canadians indicated they were of Central or South American origin.

Settlement and Employment. Many Latin American immigrants found positions in the manufacturing sectors of Toronto and Montreal, while others were attracted to the agricultural jobs of Alberta and western Canada. By the late 1980's, Latin Americans were found in all provinces and were entering the fields of real estate, insurance, and travel. In employment and educational attainment, Latinos in Canada have faced many of the same problems as those in the United States. To promote success and maintain a sense of cultural identity, they have formed numerous organizations throughout Canada. Such groups include the Center for Spanish-Speaking Peoples in Toronto and the Confédération des Associations Latino-Americaines in Quebec City. Chileans have formed cultural and financial groups such as the Winnipeg Chilean Association, and an Ecuadoran-Canadian soccer league holds weekly matches in Toronto and Montreal. Several Spanish-language newspapers are published in the larger urban areas of the country.

It is estimated that about 35,800 people came to Canada from the West Indies before 1967, mostly from the English-speaking islands of Barbados, Jamaica, and Trinidad. Approximately one-third of these people were of African ancestry. The number of West Indians increased significantly after 1967, with a significant influx of Haitians into the French-speaking province of Quebec. West Indians tended to settle in the cities of Toronto and Montreal, where there have been numerous instances of racial discrimination and conflict. In the 1991 census, 96,620 Canadians said they were of West Indian origin, with less than two thousand from Cuba and the Dominican Republic.

Ethnic Politics. Until the early 1970's, Canada's ethnicity was usually defined in terms of "two found-

A band of South American street musicians performs in Toronto. (Dick Hemingway)

CANADA'S LATINO POPULATION, BY PROVINCE

Arctic Ocean

UNITED STATES

Yukon Territory
25

Pacific
Ocean

Northwest Territories
15

British
Columbia
8,140

Alberta
7,230

Saskatchewan
1,135

Manitoba
2,905

Hudson
Bay

Ontario
37,685

Quebec
28,460

Newfoundland
675

Prince Edward Island
85

New
Brunswick
100

Nova Scotia
355

UNITED STATES

Atlantic
Ocean

Source: Data are from *Statistics Canada* (Cat. No. 93-315), Table 1A.

Note: Numbers represent estimates from a 20 percent sample. Categories of ethnic origin included in the totals are "Latin, Central, and South American origin" and "Cuban origin." Note that the numbers exclude an estimated 22,885 people of Haitian origin.

ing nations," the French and English. Since that time, the role of other ethnic groups has emerged, especially in the English-speaking parts of the country. In 1971, Canada's official policy became "multiculturalism within a bilingual framework." Not all Canadians supported the policy of multiculturalism, and hostility was especially strong in the province of Quebec, where many French Canadians believed that the policy diminished their position in the country. The multicultu-

ral policy meant that all cultural identities should have equal respect, but it did not supplant the bilingual policy, which recognized French and English as the two official languages.

Despite many ethnic disputes, Canada is one of the most democratic and liberal countries of the world. Its human rights traditions were enhanced with the addition of the Charter of Rights and Freedoms of 1982. Article 15 of the charter proclaims that all persons have "the right to the equal protection and equal benefit of the law without discrimination." The province of Quebec, however, has not approved the constitutional changes of 1982, and the most basic ethnic question is whether Quebec will remain a part of the Canadian federation. Although a majority of Quebecers voted against independence in the referendum of 1980, they were bitterly disappointed in 1990 and 1992 when the rest of Canada failed to agree to a special status for Quebec. —*Thomas T. Lewis*

SUGGESTED READINGS:

• Brunet, Jean, with Howard Palmer. *Coming Canadians: An Introduction to a History of Canada's Peoples*. Toronto: McClelland & Stewart, 1988. • Driedger, Leo, ed. *Ethnic Canada: Identities and Inequalities*. Toronto: Copp Clark Pitman, 1987. • Elliott, Jean, ed. *Two Nations, Many Cultures: Ethnic Groups in Canada*. Scarborough, Ontario: Prentice Hall of Canada, 1979. • Hawkins, Freda. *Canada and Immigration: Public Policy and Public Concern*. 2d ed. Kingston: McGill-Queen's University Press, 1988. • Statistics Canada. *Immigration and Citizenship*. Ottawa: Statistics Canada, 1992. • Watkins, Mel, ed. *Canada*. New York: Facts on File, 1993. • Wood, Dean, and Robert Remnant. *The People We Are: Canada's Multicultural Society*. Toronto: Gage, 1980.

Cancel Miranda, Rafael (b. 1929, Mayagüez, Puerto Rico): Revolutionary figure. Cancel Miranda refused to serve in the U.S. Army in the early 1950's and was sentenced to two years in prison. After completing his sentence, he lived for a while in Cuba. From there he went to New York.

Cancel Miranda joined fellow nationalists Lolita LEBRÓN SOTO, Andrés FIGUEROA CORDERO, and Irving Flores in New York. In an effort to focus national attention in the United States on the movement to make Puerto Rico an independent nation, the four

Demonstrators at a 1976 Puerto Rican parade in New York City carry photos of imprisoned nationalists. (Hazel Hankin)

staged an armed attack on the U.S. House of Representatives on March 1, 1954. Five congressmen were wounded.

For his actions, Cancel Miranda was sentenced to serve twenty-five to seventy-five years in prison. He and his fellow nationalists were pardoned by President Jimmy Carter in 1979. Their return to Puerto Rico was widely celebrated.

Canción: Musical form meant exclusively to be sung. The *canción* is a type of refrain song or *villancico* popular in the fifteenth and sixteenth centuries. Characteristic of the *canción* is an introspective rather than narrative mood, contrapuntal style, the ABBA musical form, a serious and poetic theme, and a romantic and sentimental text, often concerning love. After about 1630, the term referred to a type of Spanish poem characterized by seven- and eleven-syllable lines with freely invented rhyme, along with musical accompaniment to such poems. Some types of *canción* include *canción habanera*, *bambuco*, and bolero, each with a distinctive rhythm.

Candelaria, Nash (b. May 7, 1928, Los Angeles, Calif.): Novelist. Although he was born in Los Angeles, Candelaria has a New Mexican heritage often displayed in his writing. He is a descendant of some of the first settlers of New Mexico and one of Albuquerque's founding families. Candelaria's writing often depicts the history of that state's Mexican American population. Like his ancestor Juan Candelaria, who wrote a history of New Mexico in 1776, Nash Candelaria is notable for his historical contribution. His first three novels are a historical trilogy of New Mexico.

His first publication, the semiautobiographical quest novel *Memories of the Alhambra* (1977), garnered positive reviews. Candelaria's novel, about protagonist José Rafa's search through his family's genealogy in a quest for identity, suffered from inevitable comparisons with another, bigger selling, quest novel, Alex Haley's *Roots* (1976). Candelaria's second novel, *Not by the Sword* (1982), won the Before Columbus Foundation American Book Award for 1983. The novel examines the impact of the Mexican American War on the lives of New Mexicans who later became Americans through annexation. Candelaria's other works include *Inheritance of Strangers* (1984, a sequel to *Not by the Sword*) and the short-story collection *The Day Cisco Kid Shot John Wayne* (1988).

Canosa, Jorge L. Mas. *See* **Mas Canosa, Jorge L.**

Canseco, José (José Canseco y Capas; b. July 2, 1964, Havana, Cuba): Baseball player. Canseco, a powerhouse outfielder known for both his home runs and his off-the-field antics, did not play baseball until he was thirteen. He did not make his high school varsity squad until his senior year, and he struck out on his first major league at-bat. When Canseco found his swing, however, he became one of the best power hitters in baseball.

Named the Minor League Player of the Year for 1985 by *The Sporting News*, Canseco was brought up to the Oakland Athletics in 1986. After hitting 33 home runs and driving in 117 runs in his first season, he was named American League Rookie of the Year. An intensive weight-training program had made him one of the strongest players in baseball, and opposing pitchers soon came to fear his enormous power.

In 1988, Canseco hit and ran his way into the record books with a league-leading 42 home runs and 40 stolen bases, making him the first player in the "40/40 Club." Also in 1988, he led the American League in slugging percentage (.569), hit three home runs in one game, and knocked in 124 runs. He was the easy winner of the league's Most Valuable Player Award, becoming the first unanimous selection since 1973.

Oakland's "Bash Brothers," Mark McGwire and Canseco, led the team to 1988, 1989, and 1990 American League championships as well as the 1989 World Series title. Canseco again led the league in home runs (44) in 1991 and became the first Oakland player with consecutive seasons of more than one hundred runs batted in. All-Star selections came in 1986, 1988-1990, and 1992. In August, 1992, Canseco was traded to the Texas Rangers.

Cantinflas (Mario Moreno Reyes; Aug. 12, 1911, Mexico City, Mexico—April 20, 1993, Mexico City, Mexico): Actor. The sixth of fifteen children, Moreno ran away from agricultural school to join a *carpa*, or traveling tent show. As a nervous stand-in during a performance, he created the garbled, stuttering character that charmed audiences and soon became his stock stage persona. He took the name "Cantinflas" from a nonsense word shouted out by a heckler.

An example of the *peladito*, or "little naked one," Cantinflas was a sympathetic, inventive Everyman who improvised dialogue filled with gibberish and non sequiturs. Soon regarded as the Mexican Charlie Chaplin, he became one of the biggest Spanish-language film stars and a reliable box-office draw. His Mexican films include *No te engañes, corazón* (1936),

José Canseco hits a home run in the second game of the 1990 World Series. (AP/Wide World Photos)

Cantinflas appears in a bullfight fantasy in the film Pepe. (AP/Wide World Photos)

Allí está el detalle (1941), and *El circo* (1944). His *Ni sangre ni arena* (1941), a satire of the popular 1941 bullfighting film *Blood and Sand*, was a smash hit that outgrossed *Gone with the Wind* (1939) in Mexico. In the 1950's, he had his own production company and was active in film-industry unions. Cantinflas played glorified servants in two Hollywood films, *Around the World in Eighty Days* (1956) and *Pepe* (1960).

Capablanca, José Raúl (Nov. 19, 1888, Havana, Cuba—Mar. 8, 1942, New York, N.Y.): Chess champion. Capablanca, one of the greatest natural talents in chess history, learned the game by watching his father play. A child prodigy, he was soon beating master-level players; at the age of thirteen, he defeated the champion of Cuba.

In 1904, Capablanca moved to New York City to attend school, and in 1906 he entered Columbia University. After dropping out of college to pursue a chess career, he crushed U.S. champion Frank Marshall in a 1909 match by a score of eight to one, with fourteen draws. Although Capablanca was still relatively unknown, at Marshall's insistence he was invited to compete at a prestigious 1911 international tournament in San Sebastián, Spain. World-ranking competitors protested his appearance, arguing that the young Cuban lacked the experience to compete. Capablanca rebutted his doubters by winning decisively.

Negotiations soon began for a world title match with Emanuel Lasker, who had been champion since 1894, but World War I delayed the contest. The match finally occurred in 1921, and Capablanca easily defeated Lasker to win the title.

Often described in the popular press as the "Chess Machine," Capablanca did not lose a serious game between 1916 and 1924. His games were characterized by a nearly flawless positional style that gave a deceptive appearance of simplicity. He became a well-known public figure, and his popularity won for him a position in the Cuban foreign office as an ambassador-at-large promoting his homeland. Capablanca also penned a number of chess books, including *My Chess Career* (1920), *Chess Fundamentals* (1921), and *A Primer of Chess* (1935). In 1927, he lost the world title to Alexander Alekhine, who refused repeated requests for a rematch. In 1942, Capablanca died of a stroke in New York City.

Capetillo, Luisa (Oct. 28, 1879, Arecibo, Puerto Rico—Apr. 10, 1922, Río Piedras, Puerto Rico): Union leader. A prominent leader in the struggles of the working class in Puerto Rico in the early twentieth century, Capetillo was particularly interested in the plight of working-class women. She believed that their problems, including unstable families and domestic violence, could be eased if workers earned a fair wage and if women had the right to vote. Capetillo joined the Federation of Free Workers and wrote for its newspaper. In 1910, she founded her own newspaper, *La mujer* (the woman). For the next decade she traveled, stopping in New York, where she wrote for *Cultura obrera* (work culture), and in Florida and Cuba, where she worked with established unions. When she returned home, she began organizing strikes by field workers. In addition to her newspaper articles, she published several plays, essays, and books, in which she explored her visions of a better world.

Carbajal, Michael (b. 1968, Arizona): Boxer. The son of Manuel Carbajal, who won Arizona Gold Glove flyweight and bantamweight championships in the late 1940's, Michael Carbajal was one of nine children, all

Michael Carbajal after a 1990 victory over Tony DeLuca for the North American Boxing Federation junior-flyweight title. (AP/Wide World Photos)

Rod Carew makes a base hit to set a club record of at least one hit in each of twenty-three consecutive games. (AP/Wide World Photos)

of whom learned to box from their father. Carbajal fine-tuned his early skills with help from an older brother in a makeshift backyard ring. His unorthodox training paid off, as he was selected as the light-flyweight (106 pounds) member of the highly talented U.S. team for the 1988 Seoul Olympics. He suffered a controversial loss by decision and took home the Olympic silver medal.

The first member of the 1988 Olympic team to fight professionally, Carbajal became a powerful contender in the lower weight classes. Often compared to Roberto Duran, Carbajal received the nickname the "Little Hands of Stone." In July, 1990, he won the International Boxing Federation (IBF) light-flyweight title. In February, 1994, however, he lost a split decision to Humberto González in a fight that offered the first $1 million purse in a weight class under light-weight.

CARECEN. *See* **Central American Refugee Center**

Carew, Rod (Rodney Cline Carew y Scott; b. Oct. 1, 1945, Gatun, Panama): Baseball player. Carew became one of baseball's best hitters without ever playing high school or college ball. Signed by the Minnesota Twins after a tryout in 1964, the young second baseman learned quickly and made his major league debut in 1967. That year, he hit .292 and earned the American League Rookie of the Year Award.

Carew had two hundred or more hits in a season four times in his nineteen-year career and batted .300 or better every year from 1969 to 1983, winning seven American League batting titles. In 1976, Carew was moved to first base to protect him from injury, and the following season he won the American League Most Valuable Player Award, batting .388 (the highest major league mark in twenty years) and leading the league in hits, triples, and runs scored.

As a Minnesota Twin from 1967 to 1978, Carew set team records for career hits (2,085), triples (90), stolen bases (271), and batting average (.334). After a trade to the California Angels in 1979, he batted a team-leading .412 in the American League playoffs against Baltimore. In 1985, he became only the sixteenth player in history to record 3,000 hits, and he retired after the season with a total of 3,053 hits and a career .328 average.

Carew, who was selected to eighteen All-Star teams, was inducted into the National Baseball Hall of Fame in 1991. Both the Twins and the Angels retired his uniform number, 29.

Caribbean native communities: Christopher Columbus led the first well-known expedition to cross the Atlantic Ocean. Although he is credited with the discovery of America, he found the areas he explored already inhabited by various native people. The first ethnographer of the natives was a friar from the order of San Jerónimo named Ramón Pané. He compiled and wrote the first book about their myths and ceremonies. This work, published in 1498, was based on the inhabitants of Hispaniola, which he says they called Haiti. Other writers of the period did not provide many details about the people they encountered.

The lack of written information from that era, along with the decimation of the native population, has made it difficult to explore the history of the Caribbean region. It has been left to archaeologists to piece together the clues left by the various cultures.

Primary Communities. The West Indies, which include all the islands in the Caribbean Sea south of the United States, were populated mostly by the Taino. The word "Taino" means "good" or "noble." Perhaps these people chose the name to distinguish themselves from the Island CARIBS, who were fierce in comparison. The Taino inhabited the islands of Puerto Rico, Hispaniola (present-day Haiti and Dominican Republic), Jamaica, and Cuba (except for its western portion, which was inhabited by another group known as the Guanahatabey).

The Taino who lived in the Bahamas called themselves Lucayo Taino; they are also known as Lucayan Taino. Puerto Rico was inhabited by a group of Taino who called themselves BORINQUEN. Another local group that inhabited the northeastern portion of Hispaniola is known as the Ciguayan Taino.

The Island CARIBS inhabited a portion of the Caribbean, on the islands from Guadeloupe southward. They were described by early writers as fierce and cannibalistic. These traits perhaps combined with the lack of treasure and natural wealth convinced the Spanish not to explore and settle some of the smaller islands.

At one time, the Island Caribs were called Arawaks because of their similarities with Indians who lived in northeastern South America. Recent studies have indicated that the differences in language and culture between these two groups are too large for the groups to be considered as related, although the groups had extensive contact.

The Taino were further divided into three subgroups according to where they lived. The main group has come to be called the Classic Taino because they were the most populous and culturally advanced. The Clas-

Christopher Columbus' arrival at San Salvador in 1492 introduced the indigenous people to Europeans. (AP/Wide World Photos)

sic Taino inhabited all of Puerto Rico, all of Hispaniola except the westernmost tip, and the eastern tip of Cuba, with an outpost on St. Croix Island. At the time of first contact, early writers reported that there were between 100,000 and 600,000 Taino on Hispaniola. Puerto Rico and Jamaica were said to have had 600,000 inhabitants.

The two other Taino groups present at the time of Columbus were the Western and Eastern Taino. Western Taino lived on Jamaica, central Cuba, and the Bahama Islands. The Eastern Taino lived on all the Virgin Islands except St. Croix and on the islands to the north of Guadeloupe.

The densest population of Western Taino was located on Jamaica. Cultural attributes such as ornaments indicate the same class system as in the Classic Taino culture. It may be that Classic Taino influence had extended to Jamaica, although no concrete evidence of this has been located.

The final group present in 1492 was the Guanahatabey, who lived in westernmost Cuba. In the past, these people have been mistakenly called the Ciboney, a local group of Western Taino in central Cuba. Their language must have been different from that of the Western Taino, because Columbus' Taino interpreter could not communicate with them.

The Guanahatabey were the least culturally advanced of all the Caribbean people. These people subsisted by hunting and gathering rather than by agriculture. They lived in small bands rather than in villages, and no prehistoric pottery has been found in their territory.

Except for the Island Caribs encountered on later voyages, the natives who met Columbus in the Bahamas and Cuba were Western Taino. Their apparent peacefulness to Columbus may have resulted from their lack of contact with the Island Caribs. They had come into contact only with the equally peaceful Guanahatabey.

Taino Villages. The Classic Taino lived in large, permanent villages, each governed by a chief known as a

CACIQUE. A typical village contained one to two thousand people.

There were two types of dwellings. One had a conical roof and was called a *caney*. The other was rectangular in shape and was known as a *bohío*. These dwellings were arranged in an irregular fashion about a central courtyard or plaza where the chief's house was located.

The villages of the Western Taino, as well as those of the Eastern Taino, were not as large as those on Jamaica or those of the Classic Taino. They ranged in size from 120 to 225 individuals. As did the Classic Taino, the Eastern and Western Taino used communal housing, typically with more than ten residents per dwelling.

Everyday Life of the Taino. Although it is impossible to generalize about the everyday life of a Taino village because of regional differences, it is possible to combine documentary evidence with archaeological data to create a view into the past. The everyday life of the Classic Taino consisted primarily of agriculture. The Classic Taino used permanent settlements rather than temporary ones accompanying the slash-and-burn brush-clearing technique used by some of the other groups. Most of the Classic Taino settlements were located in fertile coastal or inland plains where an abundant water supply existed. The location of the settlements was important not only for agricultural purposes but also for defense against enemies.

Cultivation was accomplished on mounds of earth created by human effort. These allowed for drainage and irrigation control. The soft soil provided excellent drainage, allowing for underground storage of various root crops without rotting.

The main agricultural product of the Classic Taino was the manioc root, also known as yucca or cassava. This root was easily grown and could be preserved in the ground for more than two years. Women grated these starchy roots and would squeeze out their juice in a basketry sieve to obtain flour. This flour would be baked into bread on a griddle made from clay.

The cultivation of corn was also practiced, though it was not of much significance. Corn kernels usually were eaten from the cob instead of being ground into flour and baked into bread, as was done for most other roots and grains.

The sweet potato was also cultivated and was eaten as a boiled vegetable. Additional seed crops included peppers, beans, squashes, calabashes, and peanuts. These were boiled with meat or fish into a stew. Calabashes as well as ceramic pots were used as water containers. Wild crops that were collected included palms, guava berries, and guayiga roots as well as other less abundant fruits and vegetables.

The Taino knew how to use various fabrics, from which they would weave nets and bags. Cotton was an important crop from which were made hammocks and short skirts, which married women wore. Cotton was usually grown near the village houses to make it easy to gather. Men generally wore no clothing except for a loincloth. Unmarried women also went unclothed except for a headband, which perhaps signified availability for marriage. People of both sexes adorned themselves with feathers and wore necklaces and belts made from stone beads.

Fishing was accomplished using nets, lines, and hooks as well as spears. The fish were stored in weirs for later consumption. Turtles were also kept this way.

Most of the Caribbean islands have not been inhabited by large mammals except for ground sloths. These apparently became extinct soon after human occupation of the islands. The Taino mammalian diet consisted mostly of hutias (large ratlike rodents) and possibly dogs. Occasionally manatees were speared and eaten.

The Taino had skin of a copper color, most likely developed as protection from the relentless tropical sun. They were of medium stature and had black, coarse, straight hair.

Taino society was matrilineal, meaning that status and descent were traced through the mother rather than the father. Men lived in the village of the mother and upon marrying brought their wife or wives to that village.

Although most of the native population of the Caribbean was destroyed either through warfare or disease, methods of house construction, foods, and other cultural traits endure. In some cases, these have been combined with European and African characteristics.

—Peter E. Carr

SUGGESTED READINGS:

• Basso, Ellen B., ed. *Carib-Speaking Indians: Culture, Society, and Language.* Tucson: University of Arizona Press, 1977. Provides an overview of modern Carib-speaking societies.

• Cruxent, Jose M., and Irving Rouse. *An Archaeological Chronology of Venezuela.* 2 vols. Social Science Monographs 6. Washington, D.C.: Pan American Union, 1958-1959. Discusses the prehistory of Venezuela.

• Joyce, Thomas A. *Central American and West Indian Archaeology.* 1916. Reprint. New York: Hacker Art Books, 1973. Provides a good comparison of the differences in culture between the two areas.

• Pané, Ramón. *Relación acerca de las antigüedades de los indios*. Santo Domingo: Ediciones de la Fundacion Corripio, 1988. Describes many of the myths and rituals of the Taino.

• Rouse, Irving. *The Tainos: Rise and Decline of the People Who Greeted Columbus*. New Haven, Conn.: Yale University Press, 1992. One of many interesting works by an eminent archaeologist of Caribbean prehistory. Details the lives of the various groups who encountered Columbus and other early explorers.

• Wilson, Samuel M. *Hispaniola: Caribbean Chiefdoms in the Age of Columbus*. Tuscaloosa: University of Alabama Press, 1990. Provides an overview of the social structures of the Taino on Hispaniola.

Caribs: Indian tribe living in the Lesser Antilles. The Caribs, originally located in the northern part of South America, were highly mobile and expanded by conquest through the Lesser Antilles, conquering the Arawaks and absorbing Arawak culture. They had reached Puerto Rico by the time of the Spanish Conquest. The French, English, and Dutch later colonized the Lesser Antilles and came into contact with the Caribs. Carib influence upon the Spanish was limited.

Carib males were proud, fierce, and effective warriors. Their weapons included clubs studded with sharpened flint, bows with poisoned arrows, and javelins. The Caribs used canoes with high prows that could hold as many as one hundred warriors. For longer voyages, canoes were lashed together, with a platform constructed on top.

The Caribs relied on raids rather than trading with other groups. Small villages housing the extended family were the basis of society. The village leader, often the family head, possessed power within the village only, not across a region. Elected military leaders led the raids. Carib warriors kept Arawak women as slaves to bear male children who were reared as warriors.

The Caribs built small, wood-framed houses with oval or rectangular thatched roofs arranged around a central plaza containing a communal fireplace. Furnishings were simple, and food consisted of cassava, peanuts, peppers, beans, arrowroot, and potatoes. Fish and small animals including agouti, coneys, lizards, spiders, insects, and reptiles completed the diet. Caribs fished with long arrows or poison bark. Turtles and manatees were forbidden as food because the people feared that they would take on the slowness of those animals. Tobacco was used as money.

Caribs wore little if any clothing but wore chains of coral and stones on their legs and wrists. Caribs pierced their noses, lips, and ears. Crescents of gold and copper worn around the neck indicated rank.

The Caribs believed in an afterlife, and each individual had personal deities. Death meant a journey to heaven or hell. Brave warriors went to islands where Arawak slaves waited upon them. Cowards went to dreary places where they became the slaves of the Arawaks. Ancestors were worshipped, but more attention was given to warding off evil spirits through the use of amulets and shamans.

According to the Caribs, a live warrior's body could become the home of his dead enemies, so eating the flesh of dead enemies would give a warrior their strength and courage. Portions of the bodies not eaten were boiled, with the fat skimmed off and rubbed onto the bodies of children to give them strength.

Beginning in the first quarter of the seventeenth century, the Caribs faced the expansion of the French, English, and Dutch into the Lesser Antilles. Islands in the northern and southern ends were colonized, but the "neutral islands" in the center (Dominica, St. Lucia, Tobago, and St. Vincent) were left to the Caribs. Caribs are reputed to have met Christopher Columbus. The tribe died out soon after European arrival in the region.

Carnalismo/carnala: Philosophy of self-assertive Chicano brotherhood or sisterhood. *Carnalismo* and *carnala* identify a philosophy of Chicano brotherhood and sisterhood based on shared ethnic and cultural ancestry. This philosophy emerged as the social and political expression of *La Causa*, an activist Chicago student movement that gained momentum in the 1960's. Originally, *carnalismo* was the brotherhood code of *vatos locos*, Chicano youth gangs. Their culture was interpreted as a culture of resistance and self-assertion and was taken as the basis for a nationalist Chicano ideology. *Carnalismo* defines a model for a new cultural identity based on symbols derived from traditional Mexican culture.

Carnaval: Celebration corresponding to Mardi Gras. Carnaval celebrations originated in Brazil and are a unique part of the culture. They serve as a temporary distraction from economic problems and the day-to-day routines of Brazil's people.

The most popular, best-known, and largest celebration of Carnaval is in Rio de Janciro, Brazil. It is a five-day festival that begins with the mayor delivering the key to the city to Rei (King) Momo, who personifies indulgence.

Carnaval participants in San Francisco, California. (Lou DeMatteis)

During Carnaval, sexual taboos are suspended, and sexual and social roles are often reversed. Special events include balls, contests for the most elaborate costumes, and street performances with clowns and animals. The highlight of Carnaval is the Samba School parade. The SAMBA is a dance derived from both European and African influences. In the parade, performers dance routines revolving around a particular historical theme or legend.

Other Brazilian cities celebrate Carnaval. In the northeastern part of the country, in the state of Bahia, street festivals featuring music and dance are the most common forms of entertainment. Carnaval is a celebration in which all people can take part rather than merely attending as spectators. In all parts of Brazil, Carnaval celebrates both European and African influences on the country's heritage.

Celebrations of Carnaval in the United States are common in cities with large Hispanic populations, even those that are not necessarily Brazilian. (*See* CARNAVAL LATINO.) Carnaval is celebrated in several large cities in California, including Los Angeles, San Francisco, and San Diego. Some of the same traditions popular in Brazil, including brightly colored costumes and samba music, provide an atmosphere similar to that of Rio de Janeiro.

The most popular Carnaval celebration in the United States takes place on CALLE OCHO in Miami, Florida. The Cuban American community, led by the Cuban Kiwanis Club and other Hispanic organizations, hosts a nine-day Carnaval festival. Carnaval Miami is a huge tourist attraction with crowds in the hundreds of thousands. Well-known singers and other popular artists perform at Carnaval Miami at no cost as a means of getting national and international television coverage.

Ongoing Latin music and dance, including the TANGO and SAMBA, contribute to the party atmosphere that pervades the celebration. For children, the celebration features puppet shows, clowns, magicians, and storytellers. Although the Cuban American community sponsors Carnaval Miami, the festival is an opportunity for the multiethnic Latino population of Miami to come together. The majority of partygoers are Hispanic. The rich and varied Latino cultures are evident in the foods offered for sale; these items originated in various countries including Spain, Mexico, and the countries of Central and South America.

Carnaval Latino (New Orleans, La.): Organized by the New Orleans Hispanic Heritage Foundation and sponsored by various businesses, the Carnaval Latino in New Orleans was inaugurated in 1989. In 1994, the event moved from the famous French Quarter to City Park at Marconi Meadows, providing a less congested setting. Events include the election of the Queen of Carnaval Latino and a major parade, in addition to performances by musicians and other entertainers from several Latin American countries. Also featured is food served from booths set up by many of New Orleans' well-known restaurants. The festival has been held in June.

Carne asada: Northern Mexican-style broiled beef dish. Befitting the northern Mexican ranching tradition from which it arose, *carne asada* is beef broiled over wood or charcoal, preferably mesquite. The beef is cut distinctively, in thin strips with the grain. *Carne asada* can be cooked only until rare or until well done and usually is served with rice, BEANS, or TORTILLAS. It also can be used in TACOS or other dishes.

Carne guisada: Spicy beef stew of northern Mexico. *Carne guisada* shows how Hispano-Mexican and Anglo-American cuisine can become inextricably entwined. Traditional northern Mexican *carne guisada* is made with beef and Mexican spices including cumin, oregano, garlic, and CHILES. These items are browned in lard, then braised with water until the broth is thick. In southern Texas, *carne guisada* often has potatoes, carrots, and celery added, and the sauce is thickened with a flour slurry. Both the vegetables and thickening methods are classically Anglo-American.

Carnitas: Pork dish. *Carnitas* are bits of pork, cooked in spiced water until the water is absorbed and they are crisp on the outside. *Carnitas* are found throughout Mexico and are used primarily as a filling for tacos and other *ANTOJITOS*. They consist of slow-cooked pork bits, cooked in spiced water until most of the fat is rendered, then cooked further until the water cooks down and is absorbed, leaving them browned. Good *carnitas* are crisp on the outside and moist on the inside. In Central America, the same dish usually is called *CHICHARRONES*.

Carpas: Literally meaning "tent," *carpa* refers to a Mexican tent show. During the early twentieth century, agribusiness developed in the Mexico-United States border region. The proliferation of agricultural investment led to the establishment of substantial working-class communities heavily populated by Mexican laborers. These settlements created a base for itinerant troupes of *carpas* (tent performers) and *maromas* (acrobats) who traveled from COLONIA to *colonia*, entertaining the workers living near the fields. The *carpa* tradition was rooted in the village fair and nonverbal forms of theater such as the carnival, which existed on both sides of the border. Shows could be described as a cross between vaudeville and the circus.

Carpas developed a distinctive form of entertainment that bonded the spectators and the spectacle in a social interaction. The *carpa* players—dancers, singers, actors, and acrobats—performed songs, skits, and dances relevant to the lives of their audience. Performers often sang CORRIDOS (popular songs) about popular Mexican traditional heroes and historical events. Others kept the art of *buen hablar* (proud, public speech) alive in working-class consciousness. These speeches included the reading of poetry written by Mexican poets.

Carpas incorporated a variety of styles. Although tied to the circus traditions of clowning and acrobatics, performers skilled in the art of improvisation used various theatrical devices to maintain a lively and festive spirit. Manipulation of language and linguistic resources, along with references to crude and ribald subjects such as bodily functions, drew many laughs from the audiences. Players' thinly veiled critiques of both upper-class Mexicans and the dominant white culture also appealed to the working-class audiences. The penniless urban tramp, known as the *pelado*, was a popular comical stage persona and became a staple in *carpa* productions within the United States. The *pelado* confronted the world from the position of *rescuachismo*—a perspective of the downtrodden, the rebel, or the outsider. *Pelados* appealed particularly to Chicanos in the United States, because the characters' perspectives often mirrored those of Mexican people living in a hostile and racist Anglo-dominated U.S. culture.

From the turn of the century until the late 1940's, *carpas* were a widespread and durable form of entertainment throughout the American Southwest. Troupes often consisted of small extended families, performing under tents in rural areas and on the outer boundaries of urban barrios. Many groups depended on well-worn trucks to transport their shows and hired locals to help set up and advertise the performances.

Carpas inspired the 1960's manifestation of El TEATRO CAMPESINO. Although more political and directed at Chicano field workers, this Chicano troupe drew partly on the traditions of the *carpa* to establish the *acto*, its new form of performing art.

Carr, Vikki (Florencia Biçenta de Casillas Martínez Cardona; b. July 19, 1940, El Paso, Tex.): Singer. Carr is the daughter of Carlos Cardona, a construction engineer, and Florence Cardona. She is the eldest of seven children. The Cardona family moved to Southern California when Carr was very young. Carr was reared in the community of Rosemead, east of Los Angeles.

Carr first sang publicly in a Christmas play, when she was four years old. Carr attended parochial school until she reached high school age. She then attended Rosemead High School and participated in its musical productions. After she was graduated from high school in 1958, Carr became the soloist for Pepe Callahan's

Vikki Carr receives a star on the Hollywood Walk of Fame in 1981. (AP/Wide World Photos)

Mexican-Irish Band. Eventually, she was offered solo engagements.

During the 1960's, Carr recorded a number of albums with Liberty Records. In the late 1960's, she had three Top 40 hit records, including "It Must Be Him," which reached number three on the charts. From 1970 to 1975, she recorded for Columbia Records. The *Los Angeles Times* named her Woman of the Year for 1970. During the 1970's and 1980's, Carr appeared on television on numerous occasions. She established the Vikki Carr Scholarship Foundation in 1971 to give young Mexican Americans the opportunity for higher education. Carr remained active into the 1990's with performing and charitable work. Her 1991 album *Cosas del Amor* won a Grammy Award for Best Latin Pop Album.

Carrasco, Barbara (b. 1955): Artist. Carrasco is noted for murals and drawings that focus on farmworkers, minority history, and feminist issues. After her 1978 graduation from the University of California, Los Angeles, where she served as the first female editor of the university's Hispanic newspaper, Carrasco took part in cultural exchanges and painted murals on three continents. She designed and painted numerous public murals in Los Angeles, including the *Zoot Suit* (1978) mural on the Aquarius Theatre. In 1984, she painted a mural in Armenia with a team of artists. That year, she also was named Hispanic Artist of the Year by *Caminos* magazine. As a member of a 1986 Chicano delegation, she helped paint a youth-oriented mural in Managua, Nicaragua.

Carrasco has faced censorship conflicts over her murals. In 1983, she battled the city of Los Angeles over the political content of a mural she had been commissioned to paint for the 1984 Olympics. The controversial mural, *L.A. History—A Mexican Perspective*, depicted scenes of minority triumph and oppression, including the internment of Japanese Americans during World War II.

In the 1980's, Carrasco exhibited many works, including a miniature series on sensuality and detailed drawings honoring Mexican artist Frida Kahlo. Her work has been included in more than twenty-five exhibitions.

Carrera, Barbara (b. Dec. 31, 1945, Managua, Nicaragua): Actress and model. Carrera had a thriving career as a famous fashion model before her film debut in *The Master Gunfighter* in 1975. She was a successful model largely because of her universal, exotic look.

Her appearance at a fashion show in Cannes led to her film debut.

Carrera has appeared in varied roles. One of her most memorable was as Clay Basket in *Centennial* (1978), a twenty-six-hour adaptation of James Michener's best-selling novel. Her costar was Robert Conrad, who played Pasquinel.

In addition to *Centennial*, she also appeared in the television miniseries *Masada*. She appeared on television regularly when she played the role of Angelica Nero in the television series *Dallas* (1985-1986). Her television movies include *Sins of the Past* (1984), *Emma: Queen of the South Seas*, *Murder in Paradise*, and *Lakota Moon*.

Carrera's films include *Embryo* (1976), *The Island of Dr. Moreau* (1977), *Condorman* (1981), *I the Jury* (1982), *Lone Wolf McQuade* (1983), *Never Say Never Again* (1983), *Wild Geese II* (1985), and *Loverboy* (1989). Because of Carrera's universal look, she is cast in varied roles, from Hispanic to Native American to European.

Carrera de Gallos: Mexican game. The *Carrera de Gallos* (run of the cocks) is a game played by skilled Mexican horsemen as part of a holiday celebration. One version of this game features a rider rushing off with a rooster or dove in his hand. Other riders give chase and try to retrieve the animal. A second version features a rooster or hen that has been buried in the ground up to its neck. Riders have to pick up the bird by the neck as they ride past it at a full gallop.

Carrero, Jaime (b. 1931, Mayagüez, Puerto Rico): Writer. Carrero is an award-winning writer and playwright. Reared and educated in both New York, New York, and Puerto Rico, Carrero developed a cultural and political awareness that is common to bicultural writers and is reflected in his work. In the mid-1950's, he contributed to the new Puerto Rican poetry movement that sought to challenge established poetic forms and subjects; in the following decade, he helped set the foundation for the "Nuyorican" literary movement.

Carrero is a bilingual writer who works in several different genres, including novels, poetry, and drama. His first novel, *Raquelo tiene un mensaje* (1970; Raquelo has a message) won the Primer Premio del Ateneo Puertorriqueño, as did his play *Flag Inside* (1966). Nationalism, cultural identity, and the plight of Puerto Ricans in New York are frequent subjects of his works. Carrero is known for witty and realistic depictions of Nuyorican life and language.

Barbara Carrera. (AP/Wide World Photos)

Leo Carrillo starred as the character José Santa Cruz in the 1931 film Lasca of the Rio Grande. (AP/Wide World Photos)

Although recognized primarily as a writer, Carrero is also an accomplished painter. His other works include the novels *Los nombres* (1972; the names) and *El hombre que no sudaba* (1982; the man who did not sweat), the poetry collection *Jet neorriqueño/Neo-Rican Jetliner Poems* (1964), and the plays *Noo Jork* (1972) and *La caja de caudales FM* (1978).

Carrillo, Eduardo (b. Veracruz, Mexico): Playwright and actor. Carrillo came to Los Angeles in 1922 as a member of the Gran Compañía Cómico Dramático María Teresa Montoya. His writing covered a vast array of styles, from REVISTAS to dramas examining relevant social problems. His best-known work is *El Proceso de Aurelio Pompa* (1924), a timely examination of the persecution of a Mexican laborer. At performances of the play, Pompa's supporters gathered petition signatures and raised funds for his defense. Pompa's eventual execution was incorporated into a later version of the play.

Carrillo's other plays include *revistas* and one-acts such as *Los Angeles al día* (1922, written with Gabriel Navarro), *Malditas sean los hombres* (1924), and *En las puertas del infierno* (1925); historical plays such as *El zarco* (1924) and *Patria y honor* (1924); the Mexican Robin Hood story *El rayo de Sinaloa* (1923); and the comedy *Un crimen más* (1938).

In the 1920's, Carrillo ran a vaudeville circuit in Arizona, and his plays were contracted for performances throughout the Southwest and Mexico. Carrillo is best remembered for his incisive dramatic treatments of issues concerning the expatriate community in Los Angeles.

Carrillo, Leo (Poldo Antonio Carrillo; Aug. 6, 1880, Los Angeles, Calif.—Sept. 10, 1961, Santa Monica, Calif.): Actor. Carrillo was born to a prominent family. He first became a cartoonist, then entered vaudeville, which quickly led to Broadway. He played romantic stage roles during the 1920's and later moved to films. In Hollywood, he played both romantic leads and talkative sidekicks to the hero. He appeared in more than fifty films between 1930 and 1950. At first he played leads, as in *Love Me Forever* (1935), but later his roles were primarily comic relief. Carrillo is best remembered for the television role he played as Pancho, the witty, fractured-English-speaking partner of actor Duncan Renaldo in *The Cisco Kid*, released in the late 1950's.

In 1961, his autobiography in collaboration with Ed Ainsworth, titled *The California I Love*, attracted little credibility. It struck a chord of misrepresenting and downplaying the turbulent past. Many Latinos believed his story was falsified and sugar-coated, overlooking, minimizing, or avoiding allusions to anything Mexican. When his book is combined with the character he portrayed in *The Cisco Kid*, the result is a stereotype demeaning to Mexicans.

Carrillo always had romantic ideas of a Mexican way of life. With a sense of pride in his ethnic background, Carrillo was frequently seen at California fiestas, rodeos, and parades.

Cart War (1857): The Cart War of 1857 was a racially and economically motivated outbreak of violence against Mexicans in central Texas. Although the murders of Mexican cartmen were eventually stemmed, prejudices remained. During and after the war, many Mexicans left the area, continuing the trend of whites effectively driving Mexicans from Texas through acts of hostility.

Race relations were tense in central Texas following the Mexican American War. The considerable hostility exhibited toward Mexicans, sometimes accompanied by force, drove many from their homes. Some Texas cities Austin, Seguin, and Uvalde, for example— made efforts to purge themselves of their Mexican inhabitants. In San Antonio and Goliad, racial tension came to a head in the Cart War of 1857.

By 1856, only a little more than one-third of San Antonio's inhabitants were Mexican. About half of the city's former Mexican population had left as a result of growing hostilities and diminished economic opportunities. Of those Mexicans who remained, more than half were cartmen who transported freight along the San Antonio-Goliad Highway, an important trade route connecting San Antonio with Gulf Coast ports. Another third of the city's population was made up of Germans, who formed the bulk of the city's small merchant class. Non-German whites made up the remaining third, and it was within this group that racist feelings were strongest. By 1857, there already had been a proposal to form a vigilante committee to drive the Mexicans from San Antonio; this plan failed largely because it did not have the support of the German population.

In the summer of 1857, general antipathy toward Mexicans had become focused on a specific labor conflict. Mexican cartmen had lowered their prices. White Texan teamsters already resented competition from the Mexicans and viewed this act as a bid to monopolize the freight business. There had been occasional incidents during the two previous years of white Texans destroying the carts and merchandise of their Mexican rivals, but the situation exploded in San Antonio and Goliad in the late summer of 1857. Masked bands began attacking Mexican cartmen hauling goods to the coast; approximately seventy-five were murdered, carts were burned, and merchandise was stolen. By the fall, many feared the situation would escalate into an all-out race war.

As the assassinations continued, public outrage mounted against these blatantly race-induced acts, but civil authorities balked at taking a firm stand to stop the incidents. Many Mexican cartmen fled the area, and freight prices escalated sharply. The outcry for an end to the conflict increased—partly from humanitarian impulses, partly, no doubt, from economic motives. Outraged local citizens, joined by officials such as Mexican Minister to the United States Manuel Robles y Pezuela and Secretary of State Lewis Cass, finally were able to exert enough pressure to bring the situation under control. Although some new legislation was passed, perhaps the most effective deterrent came in November, when the TEXAS RANGERS began patrolling the highways and escorting cartmen and their goods. This marked the first time the Rangers were deployed in a civilian matter.

The assassinations ended, but no arrests were ever made. As a result of the Cart War, many Mexicans left the area, and many of those remaining quit the freight business. Racial tensions were unresolved, and Mexicans continued to be victims of extreme, and at times violent, prejudice in central Texas.

Carty, Rico (Ricardo Adolfo Jacobo y Carty; b. Sept. 1, 1939, San Pedro de Macoris, Dominican Republic): Baseball player. In a signing frenzy, Rico "Big Boy" Carty signed ten professional contracts in 1960. Once the dust settled, Carty ended up with the Milwaukee Braves. Although Carty believed himself to be a catcher, the Braves moved him to the outfield.

As a rookie in 1964, he hit for an impressive .330 average with twenty-two home runs, and for the next several years he was one of the most feared hitters in the National League. In 1968, however, he suffered from a serious case of tuberculosis and spent five months in a sanitarium, missing the entire 1968 season. Returning in 1969, Carty hit .342 despite seven shoulder dislocations. A year later, he led the league in batting with a .366 mark and was a write-in All-Star selection.

A broken knee forced Carty to miss the 1971 season. Two years later he played with the Texas Rangers,

Chicago Cubs, and Oakland A's in one season. In 1974, he was traded to the Cleveland Indians, and he began to play primarily as a designated hitter. In 1978, he was traded three times in less than eight months. Nevertheless, that season he hit a career-high thirty-one home runs before finishing his career with the Toronto Blue Jays in 1979.

Casals, Rosemary (b. Sept. 6, 1948, San Francisco, Calif.): Tennis player. Casals won a record 685 singles and doubles tournaments in a career that spanned more than twenty years. One of the first players to use a steel racket, Casals was known for her acrobatic volleys, quick hands, and nimble footwork.

In her first appearance at Wimbledon in 1966, Casals made it to the fourth round. She went on to win eleven professional singles titles and twice reached the U.S. Open finals; however, her career highlights came in doubles competition.

Coupled with her friend Billie Jean King, Casals was part of a virtually unstoppable doubles team. Together they won fifty-six professional titles, including seven Wimbledon doubles titles (including a record five open-era titles) and the first seven Virginia Slims tournaments.

Casals won twelve major doubles titles in fifteen years. Her last professional title came in 1988 with Martina Navratilova.

Casas, Melesio, II (b. Nov. 24, 1929, El Paso, Tex.): Painter. A socially conscious painter in his own right, Casas is also a founder of CON SAFOS, one of the first Chicano visual arts organizations dedicated to the cultural, political, and aesthetic development of Mexican American artists. He is considered to be a pioneer of the Chicano art movement.

Casas attended El Paso public schools and was graduated from Texas Western College in 1956. After earning his master of arts degree in 1958 from the University of the Americas in Mexico City, Mexico, he began teaching. Eventually, he became an art instructor at San Antonio College in San Antonio, Texas.

Casas' best-known paintings are part of a series he began in the 1960's and called "humanscapes." In the early humanscapes, Casas explores the effects of the media on lives and relationships by dividing the painting into two distinct halves. One half includes images—often mouths, tubes of toothpaste, or embracing couples—projected onto a movie or television screen, and the other half depicts an audience watching the image. Casas' later paintings address the social, politi-

Rosemary Casals in a 1978 match. (AP/Wide World Photos)

cal, and economic problems of Chicanos, particularly migrant workers and youths. For example, in *New Horizons Humanscape No. 15* (1970), he shows the eagle of the United Farm Workers union flag flying prominently above a field where farmworkers toil.

Castañeda, Antonia I. (b. 1942, Texas): Educator Castañeda was born into a family of migrant laborers. Her family later moved to Washington State. She earned a bachelor's degree in Spanish and education in 1966 from Western Washington State University. After receiving her master's degree in Latin American studies from the University of Washington in 1970, she served as coeditor of the anthology *Chicano Literature: Text and Context* (1972).

Castañeda began teaching in 1971. She has taught courses in Chicano history, Latin American history, and women's history at the University of Washington; Stanford University; the University of California, Davis; Pomona College; and other schools. She has written numerous research articles and won fellowships from the Ford Foundation, the American Association of University Women, and the University of California, San Diego. In 1990, she received a Ph.D. in American history from Stanford University.

Castaneda, Carlos (Carlos César Aranha Castaneda; b. Dec. 25, 1931, São Paulo, Brazil): Writer. According to immigration records, Castaneda was born in Cajamarca, Peru, six years earlier than he later claimed. He is as mysterious a figure as Don Juan, the subject of the majority of his writing. *Teachings of Don Juan: A Yaqui Way of Knowledge* (1968) became a cult hit for the late 1960's counterculture.

The author claims that Castaneda is an adopted surname and gives conflicting biographical information about himself. The questions about Castaneda's past, however, are superseded by doubts of Don Juan's existence.

Castaneda's body of work focuses on recording his experiences as an apprentice to Don Juan, a Yaqui Indian sorcerer. Describing his conflicting relationship with this Yaqui guide and his struggle to become a Yaqui "man of knowledge," Castaneda presents his books as anthropological narratives. The first book talked explicitly about using hallucinogenic drugs including PEYOTE to reach different levels of consciousness. Although that book gained notoriety for discussing drug-induced states, critics praised Castaneda's writing for its vivid depictions of witchcraft, detailed renderings of mystic experiences, and strong narrative.

Castaneda's best-known works include *A Separate Reality: Further Conversations with Don Juan* (1971), *Journey to Ixtlan: The Lessons of Don Juan* (1972), and *The Power of Silence: Further Lessons of Don Juan* (1987).

Castañeda, Carlos E. (Nov. 11, 1896, Ciudad Camargo, Mexico—Apr. 4, 1958): Historian and educator. Castañeda is best known for *Our Catholic Heritage in Texas*, the history of Texas from 1519 to 1836, and his history of the Catholic church in Texas after 1836. Because of political turmoil in Mexico, Castañeda and his family emigrated from the Mexican border town of Ciudad Camargo across the Rio Grande to Brownsville, Texas, in 1908. In 1916, as the only Mexican American in his class, he was graduated from Brownsville High School as valedictorian.

Castañeda enrolled at the University of Texas in 1917 on an academic scholarship. The following year, he enlisted in the U.S. Army, serving as a machine-gun instructor during World War I. In 1921, Castañeda was graduated as a member of Phi Beta Kappa with a B.A. in history. He earned his M.A. in 1923 and was appointed associate professor in the Spanish department at William and Mary College in Virginia.

Castañeda returned to the University of Texas as a

Carlos E. Castañeda. (AP/Wide World Photos)

librarian in 1927. The following year, he published *The Mexican Side of the Texas Revolution*, based on Mexican documents. He completed his Ph.D. requirements in 1932 with his critical editing of the "lost" *History of Texas* by Fray Juan Morfi. Its publication brought Castañeda renown and resulted in a commission from the Knights of Columbus to write a history of the Catholic church in Texas for the Texas centennial. Completed between 1936 and 1950, this project became his distinguished six-volume work, *Our Catholic Heritage in Texas*.

In 1939, Castañeda joined the history department at the University of Texas, becoming a full professor in 1946. He served as editor of the *Hispanic American Historical Review*, the *Americas Review*, and *The Handbook of Latin American Studies*. He wrote twelve books and more than eighty articles on Southwest and Mexican history.

Castanets: Wooden percussion instruments of indefinite pitch. Castanets consist of two pairs of shallow clappers, traditionally made of chestnut wood (*castaña*). The two parts of each castanet are held together by a string that, looped around the thumb, allows them to hang and to be tapped with the fingers, producing a sharp and penetrating sound in multiple rhythms. The left-hand pair, called *macho* (male), plays simple beats in a slightly lower pitch than the right-hand pair, called *hembra* (female), which plays more complicated rhythms. In existence in Roman times and the Middle ages, castanets traditionally have been played by dancers as a form of accompaniment.

Castellanos, Rosario (May 25, 1925, Mexico City, Mexico—Aug. 7, 1974, Tel-Aviv, Israel): Writer. A leading feminist, Castellanos was one of Mexico's most distinguished writers. Before her accidental death by electrocution, she published an impressive body of work including poems, essays, drama, and fiction. Although Castellanos was born in Mexico City, she was reared in Comitán, Chiapas, in southern Mexico near the Guatemalan border.

Despite growing up as a member of the Creole elite, Castellanos often critiqued the inferior status of women and the social and racial oppression of Chiapas' indigenous Indian population. In early 1994, the oppression that Castellanos duly recorded in her novels and strove to eliminate reached a critical point when Chiapas Indians led an armed revolt against the Mexican government. Their plight and struggle received worldwide attention.

Castellanos earned a graduate degree in philosophy from the National University of Mexico (UNAM). For ten years, she served as cultural director for the state of Chiapas. She taught at UNAM and other universities in the 1960's and was Mexico's ambassador to Israel in the 1970's. Her works include the novels *Balún-Canán* (1957; *The Nine Guardians*, 1959), *Oficio de tinieblas* (1962; service of darkness), and *Los convidados de agosto* (1964; the guests of August) in addition to the essay collection *El uso de la palabra* (1974; the right to speak).

Castillo, Ana (Ana Hernandez del Castillo; b. June 15, 1953, Chicago, Ill.): Writer. Castillo, an award-winning poet and novelist, began her writing career publishing poetry. She garnered critical acclaim for her first work of fiction, the epistolary novel *The Mixquiahuala Letters* (1986), which won the Before Columbus Foundation's 1987 American Book Award. Unique in its format, Castillo's first novel requires the reader to assume one of three different personas and read selected letters corresponding to that persona. Her third novel, *So Far from God* (1993), also received critical praise, winning the 1993 Carl Sandburg Literary Award.

Along with writing fiction and poetry, Castillo frequently contributes to Latina feminist scholarship. She translated (with Norma Alarcón) an influential collection of feminist essays titled *This Bridge Called My Back: Writings by Radical Women of Color* (1984, edited by Cherríe MORAGA and Gloria ANZALDÚA) from English into the Spanish *Esta puente, mi espalda: Voces de mujeres tercermundistas en los Estados Unidos* (1988), and she collected her own feminist essays in *Massacre of the Dreamers: Essays on Xicanisma* (1994).

Castillo's other works include the volumes of poetry *The Invitation* (1979), *Women Are Not Roses* (1984), and *My Father Was a Toltec* (1988). Her novel *Sapagonia* was published in 1990.

Castillo, Leonel Javier (b. June 9, 1939, Victoria, Tex.): Immigration official. The first Mexican American commissioner of the United States IMMIGRATION AND NATURALIZATION SERVICE (INS), Castillo served from 1977 to 1979. His background was in social work and politics. Before his appointment, he had worked in the Peace Corps in the Philippines, supervised a Neighborhood Center-Day Care Association and other community programs in Houston, and served as controller for the city of Houston and treasurer for the Texas Democratic Party. He also earned a master's

Leonel Castillo while he was head of the Immigration and Naturalization Service. (AP/Wide World Photos)

degree in social work, in the field of community organization. His years as INS commissioner were marked by controversy. Trying to put a modern and more humane face on the service, he encouraged agents to deemphasize capturing and deporting illegal immigrants. After resigning from the INS, Castillo formed his own business, Castillo Enterprises, and became president of Hispanic International University. He continued to be a strong advocate for immigrants' rights.

Castillo-Speed, Lillian (b. Feb. 15, 1949, La Puente, Calif.): Librarian. Castillo-Speed became coordinator of the Chicano Studies Library at the University of California, Berkeley (UC Berkeley) in 1984. She served as the principal editor of the *Chicano Periodicals Index* from 1984 to 1988 and began work as editor of the *Chicano Index* in 1989. Castillo-Speed also began developing the Chicano Database, a CD-ROM research tool, in 1990.

Castillo-Speed began an advanced degree in English at California State University, Long Beach, after earning her B.A. at the University of California, River-

side, in 1971. She transferred to the School of Library and Information Studies at UC Berkeley and earned her master's degree in 1983.

Soon after receiving her degree, Castillo-Speed was hired to direct the Chicano Indexing Project at the Chicano Studies Library at UC Berkeley. The project was the work of Chicano librarians who realized that Chicano writings, particularly the journals that had emerged in the 1960's, were not being indexed by mainstream libraries. That project led to development of the Chicano Database.

Along with her bibliographic work, Castillo-Speed has been active in efforts to keep ethnic studies libraries autonomous within their university settings. As president of Biblioteca para la Gente, a group of Northern California librarians who promote library services for speakers of Spanish, she lobbied to establish ethnic research centers in state libraries. Indicating her dedication to her field, she offered to teach a graduate course in ethnic bibliographies without pay when she learned that it was scheduled to be canceled. The course drew more students than anticipated and was soon offered on a regular basis.

Castizo: A predominantly Spanish Latino. This term describes Latinos of pure or nearly pure Spanish blood. It was used in the American Southwest by wealthy landowning families that asserted with pride their ancestral link to the conquistadores. In a society dominated by mestizos (people of mixed Spanish and indigenous ethnic origin), *castizo* was used to draw racial lines between white, MESTIZO, and indigenous people. Regardless of whether these people were in fact products of "pure" blood lines, it was important to them to assert a pro-white attitude in society as a way to maintain their top positions in the colonial hierarchy.

Castro, Fidel (Fidel Castro Ruz; b. Aug. 13, 1926 or 1927, Birán, Cuba): Dictator of Cuba. Castro was born into a relatively wealthy family. He was one of seven children. His father, Angel Castro y Argiz, had immigrated to Cuba from northwestern Spain and owned a small sugar plantation near the city of Mayarí on the eastern end of the island.

Castro received his early education at Catholic boarding schools. In 1950, he received a law degree from the University of Havana; he soon developed a practice in that city. He also demonstrated sufficient ability as a baseball player to catch the eyes of scouts

Fidel Castro meets in 1963 in the Kremlin with Soviet premier Nikita Khrushchev. (AP/Wide World Photos)

from the United States. In 1952, Castro campaigned for the Cuban House of Representatives. The government was overthrown by troops led by Fulgencio Batista on March 10 of that year, and the election was voided.

Even in his youth, Castro was aware of Cuba's economic disparity. Despite the relative wealth of his family, Castro developed a strong relationship with the rural population. While attending the university, Castro was exposed to a variety of socialist teachings, and he developed into a major advocate of such political beliefs. He also read extensively the writings of Karl Marx and Friedrich Engels, the influence of which later completed his conversion to Communism.

Running on a ticket that promised reform in the government, Carlos Prío Socarrás was elected president of Cuba in 1948. The Prío government proved no better at reform than those that preceded it, leading to its overthrow by Batista.

Observing that reforms promised by Batista would still leave the peasantry in poverty, Castro joined a growing movement to replace the Batista government. By 1953, he was head of the conspiracy. On July 26 of that year, he led a small attack against the Moncada military barracks in Santiago. Whether he believed such an uprising would lead to revolution is unclear. The attempt failed, and Castro was captured along with most of his men. He was sentenced to fifteen years in prison but was released in 1955.

After his release, Castro went to Mexico, where he organized the 26th of July movement, named for the date of his first revolt. On December 2, 1956, he tried again, landing in Oriente province and escaping to the mountains. For two years, Castro waged guerrilla warfare against Batista, finally overthrowing the government in December, 1958. In February, 1959, Castro became head of the Cuban government.

The government quickly took the form of a Communist dictatorship. No political opposition was permitted, and Castro's power over the country became absolute. Castro instituted popular reforms including the confiscation of property and expansion of educational opportunities and medical access. He also became an advocate of revolution abroad, particularly in Central and South America. Consequently, much of U.S. foreign policy from the 1960's through the 1980's was aimed at containment of Cuba. Castro developed a strong following among Third World revolutionaries, support that began to wane only with the collapse of Communism around the world during the late 1980's.

Castro, George (b. Feb. 23, 1939, Los Angeles, Calif.): Chemist. Castro is an expert in research management and physical chemistry. He received his B.S. at the University of California, Los Angeles, in 1960 and his Ph.D. in chemistry at the University of California, Riverside, in 1965. He did research at the University of Pennsylvania from 1965 to 1967 and at the California Institute of Technology from 1967 to 1968. He later worked in the area of organic photoconductors and the electronic properties of organic solids at the IBM Almaden Research Center in San Jose, California.

Castro, Raúl Hector (b. June 12, 1916, Cananea, Sonora, Mexico): Politician. In 1965, President Lyndon B. Johnson appointed Castro as ambassador to El Salvador. Five years later, Castro made his first bid for the governorship of Arizona. He ran unsuccessfully as a moderate Democrat.

Castro's second campaign in 1974 was successful. His election to the highest office in one of the most conservative U.S. states can be attributed to at least two factors. First, Castro built a strong coalition of Mexican Americans, Navajos, businesspeople, and farmers. In addition, the VOTING RIGHTS ACT OF 1965 and VOTING RIGHTS ACT OF 1970 resulted in increased efforts at the state and local levels to register voters and encourage participation of members of minority groups in the political process. Castro did not serve his full term as governor, leaving in 1977 to accept appointment by President Jimmy Carter as ambassador to Argentina.

Castro, Salvador B. (b. Oct. 25, 1933, Los Angeles, Calif.): Teacher and activist. Castro became prominent as a public figure in March of 1968, during the BLOWOUT, walkouts of students from schools in the Los Angeles area. Castro was the symbolic leader to about five thousand students, mostly Mexican Americans, who left their classrooms. Following two weeks of speeches, picketing, sit-ins, sympathy demonstrations, and mass arrests, Castro and twelve others were arrested on charges of felonious conspiracy for allegedly organizing the demonstrations. All thirteen were later cleared by the California appeals court, but Castro remained barred from teaching until 1973, when he was given an assignment at Belmont High School, which had a student population containing 70 percent Mexican Americans.

Castro began his education in Mexico, to which his parents had returned during the Great Depression. Later, he attended parochial schools in Los Angeles.

Raúl Castro delivers his inaugural address as governor of Arizona. (AP/Wide World Photos)

Sal Castro led the 1968 Blowout, a student protest. (AP/Wide World Photos)

After service in the Korean War, he enrolled at Los Angeles City College. Political activism disrupted his academic career, but he eventually earned his A.A. in 1957 and his B.A., from Los Angeles State College, in 1962. While attending college, he became active in the Democratic Party and the Mexican American Political Association. After graduation, he began teaching history and government in the city schools of Pasadena and Los Angeles.

Castro v. California (Mar. 24, 1970): VOTING RIGHTS case. This California Supreme Court case bears the designation L.A. 29693. It was brought by adult native-born citizens of California who sought to overturn their state's English-language literacy requirement for voting. The California Supreme Court accepted the arguments of the plaintiffs and found the state's English-language literacy requirement for voting unconstitutional under the Fourteenth Amendment.

Although the first European settlers of California were Spanish speakers, Spanish-speaking Californians did not enjoy full political and social equality with English-speaking Californians when this case was filed by two Los Angeles County residents, Genoveva Castro and James E. Parra, on September 13, 1967. Literate in Spanish but not in English, Castro and Parra were unable to register to vote.

Castro and Parra challenged their exclusion from the voting process on FOURTEENTH AMENDMENT grounds. They contended that they had access to sufficient information in Spanish-language newspapers and periodicals to enable them to vote intelligently. They requested the court to declare article II, section 1 of the California constitution unconstitutional for its imposition of an English-language literacy requirement on would-be voters as a condition for registration. They also requested that the court order the registration of the petitioners and other individuals who were similarly situated and order a reasonable percentage of the ballots at each election to be printed in Spanish or offer other methods of facilitating voting by those literate in Spanish.

At the trial court level, the petitioners had no success with their claim that California's English-language literacy requirement for voters was unconstitutional. In the Superior Court of Los Angeles County, Judge Ralph H. Nutter, Jr., ruled against them.

Nutter's opinion, however, failed to withstand the scrutiny of the California Supreme Court. That court held that California did not have a compelling state interest in restricting the right to vote to those literate in English. Applying the Fourteenth Amendment, the court concluded that article II, section 1 of the Cali-

fornia constitution was unconstitutional and that the English-language literacy requirement could not be applied to the petitioners nor to any other California citizens wherever resident. This decision applied not only to potential voters literate in Spanish but also to voters literate in other foreign languages who could demonstrate the same access to materials describing the state's political process as documented by the petitioners in this case.

This decision opened new avenues for participation in the political process to California citizens literate only in Spanish. The decision, in fact, made explicit reference to the state's Hispanic roots. It also provided potential protection to California citizens literate only in other foreign languages. In a state with increasing Hispanic and Asian populations, this case had crucial importance.

Catalá, Rafael (b. Sept. 26, 1942, Las Tunas, Cuba): Poet and scholar. Catalá immigrated to the United States in 1961. Although he earned his university degrees in the United States, Catalá managed to keep Cuban and Latin American literature and ideology at

Castro v. California clarified rights of voters not literate in English. (Odette Lupis)

the core of his educational pursuits. Initially he studied psychology, but once in graduate school he switched to literature. Psychology, however, never completely left his interest. Unlike most Latino writers, Catalá's interests go far beyond the provincial scope of literature and his own cultural heritage. He has a profound interest in the entire body of Latin American ideology, philosophy, and literature.

Comfortable in the realms of both science and literature, Catalá in 1980 organized Ometeca (taken from a Nahuatl word meaning "two in one"), a literary and cultural workshop aimed at fusing the thought processes of the humanities and science. He further expounded this fusion in his book of poems *Ciencia poesía* (1986; science poetry). He also has edited several collections of essays, and his editorship broadened the *Index of American Periodical Verse* to include Hispanic poets of the United States and Puerto Rico. His volumes of poetry include *Caminos/Roads* (1972), *Circulo cuadrado* (1974), *Ojo sencillo/Triqui-traque* (1975), *Copulantes* (1981), and *Escobas de millo* (1984).

Catholic church and Catholicism: The influence of the Catholic church is an integral part of the Latino experience, in both Latin America and the United States. Approximately 70 percent of U.S. Latinos are Catholic, and Latinos make up more than one-quarter of all American Catholics. The presence of Latino Catholics is particularly strong in the Southwest and in major cities such as New York, Miami, Chicago, and Los Angeles, where many parishes have a majority of Latino members. As immigrants continue to arrive in large numbers from Latin America, especially Mexico, they swell the ranks of Latino Catholics. The church has made efforts to accommodate these new parishioners with Spanish-language Masses, an array of social services, and sometimes the advocacy of immigrant rights, yet Latinos hold only a handful of leadership positions in the church that plays so powerful a role in their lives.

Overview of Church History. Catholic Christianity began about the middle of the first century A.D., when the disciples of Jesus of Nazareth were first addressed as Christians. In the beginning, Christianity was a sect

Latino parishioners participate in celebrations following the annual Mass in honor of Our Lady of Guadalupe at St. Patrick's Cathedral in New York City. (Odette Lupis)

DIOCESES WITH LARGE LATINO POPULATIONS, 1990

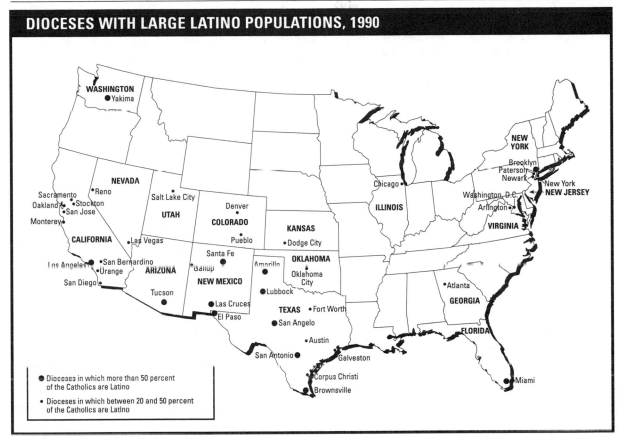

- ● Dioceses in which more than 50 percent of the Catholics are Latino
- • Dioceses in which between 20 and 50 percent of the Catholics are Latino

Source: List of dioceses provided by the National Council of Catholic Bishops, Secretariat for Hispanic Affairs.

within Judaism, but doctrinal incompatibility led to separate religions. Christianity became the official state religion of the Roman Empire, and the title of supreme priest, previously accorded to the emperor, was given to the pope, bishop of Rome. At the end of the third century, the eastern church came under imperial control while western Catholicism gained autonomy and prestige, culminating with Charlemagne's coronation in 800. Conflict between Rome and Constantinople led to the division between Roman Catholicism and Eastern Orthodox Catholics in 1054.

The relationship between church and state was strengthened during the Middle Ages with the establishment of Catholic monastic orders, universities, dioceses, canon law, and papal control over western Christian nations. Because liturgical services were in Latin, a language not understood by most people, devotion to Mary and the saints became popular. Disillusioned by excesses in the Catholic church, Martin Luther led the Protestant Reformation in rejecting papal authority, the sacramental system, the sacrificial nature of the Mass, the cult of the Virgin Mary, and the celebration of saints. New religious orders emerged with the Counter-Reformation.

At the end of the nineteenth century, Vatican I brought about the dogma of papal infallibility, asserting the correctness of the pope's authority and the church's reaction against modernism and even "Americanism." In the 1920's, concordatas or agreements with many nations and the church ensured Catholic spiritual authority, especially in heavily Catholic Latin America. In the 1960's, VATICAN II encouraged reform by extending fraternal understanding to all, including Eastern Orthodox, Protestant, and Jewish communities. Other changes included lay participation and the use of modern languages in liturgy. The pope and bishops developed guidelines on social justice, racial equality, disarmament, human rights, contraception, and abortion. Priestly celibacy, birth control, and other political issues continued to challenge the church as it pursued global expansion.

Catholicism in the New World. During the age of exploration, Portugal and Spain brought Roman Catholicism to Africa, Asia, and the New World. Explorers were followed by missionaries and colonists. Monastic orders engaged in missionary activity included Franciscans, Dominicans, and Jesuits. The first diocese in the New World was established in Puerto Rico in 1511. On the mainland of what would become the United States, Spanish Catholics established missions in Florida, New Mexico, Texas, and California. These settlements would have a significant effect on the development of those regions and the spread of Catholicism.

Although some missionary efforts were successful, there were clashes between churchmen and natives, especially when friars were perceived as supporters of the Spanish Crown in quest of material goods. Frequently, though, missionaries spoke out against the atrocities and inhumane treatment of natives by conquerors. Indians were often parceled out to the colonists for slave work. To avoid further exploitation, Catholic missionaries created self-sufficient colonies in which Indians were Christianized, trained in farming and other trades, and housed apart from the Spanish colonists. Missions, however, led to the spread of disease among Indians and to the dismantling of native cultures.

The Spanish and Portuguese consolidated their hold over Latin America between the sixteenth and the nineteenth centuries, spreading Catholicism as the dominant religion. They established governments that were and remain closely tied to Catholic church authority. Catholicism began absorbing some indigenous elements as part of the mingling of European and native Indian cultures in places such as Mexico. This process of religious syncretism continued into the late twentieth century.

Meanwhile, French explorers were opening much of what is now eastern Canada to Catholic influence. French Catholic colonists began arriving in the 1600's to convert the natives and establish schools. Roman Catholics are considered the largest single group of Christians in modern Canada.

The situation was different in the land that would become the United States. Although Spanish Catholics had established the first non-Indian communities, Catholics would never become a majority in North America. The early American colonists were Protestants who were decidedly anti-Catholic because of their own experience of religious persecution in the Old World. Of the original thirteen colonies, only Maryland had a significant number of Catholics. Catholic bishop John Carroll promoted positive Protestant-Catholic relations in the 1700's, but his was an unusual

GROWTH OF LATINO CLERGY, 1978-1993			
	1978	*1988*	*1993*
Bishops	10	20	21
Priests	1,405	1,954	2,200
Permanent deacons	400	1,284	1,800
Seminarians	804	1,211	
Sisters	1,500	2,600	
Brothers	100		

Source: Data were provided by the National Conference of Catholic Bishops, Secretariat for Hispanic Affairs.

voice. Virtually all the positions of power in colonial America were held by Protestants. This extreme imbalance held until the young nation annexed more former Spanish territory and attracted a greater diversity of immigrants.

The Growth of American Catholicism. During the nineteenth century, about five million Catholic immigrants came to the United States from Europe. In the early decades, they were mostly from Germany, Ireland, and French Canada; later, they came from southern and eastern European countries such as Italy, Poland, and the Austro-Hungarian Empire. Their arrival changed the face of American cities and the struggling American Catholic church.

The unprecedented influx of Catholics into a Protestant country was met with some hostility and suspicion. Nativist Protestant crusaders provoked a number of violent incidents and spread anti-Catholic propaganda. The response of American Catholics was generally to stick close together in their own communities, building power from within. By the turn of the twentieth century, Irish Americans had become powerful political bosses in some cities. They had also come to dominate the American Catholic church hierarchy. The election of Irish Catholic John F. Kennedy as president in 1960 symbolized a new spirit of reconciliation among the Catholic minority and Protestant majority. Many American Catholics, however, still believe they are the victims of prejudice.

Catholics began establishing their own schools during the colonial period. As their population grew and the idea of free public education gained ground in the 1800's, Catholics continued not to trust the Protestant-dominated society with the education of their children. They built an impressive system of PAROCHIAL SCHOOLS that encouraged religious loyalty to Rome and civil loyalty to the United States. These schools remain an important part of daily life for millions of American Catholics, including large numbers of Latinos.

The Latino Catholic population in the United States boomed in the mid-nineteenth century with the acquisition of lands after the Mexican American War. It was to grow steadily with migration and immigration from south of the border in the twentieth century, particularly after the immigration reforms of 1965. In states such as Texas, Latino Catholics have come to wield political power, much like the Irish a century before them, yet Latinos are still underrepresented in both political and religious arenas.

Catholicism and Latino Culture. Religion is a major factor in shaping values and cultural patterns. As a result of colonization, Spanish-speaking people in North America were primarily Catholic. Many Latinos, however, including Mexican Americans, preserved some of the rituals of their own pre-Columbian Indian cultures, as can be seen in Day of the Dead (DÍA DE LOS MUERTOS) observances. In order to make Christianity more acceptable, Spanish Catholic missionaries erected churches on the same sites where the natives used to worship. For example, Our Lady of Guadalupe shrine, founded in 1531 outside Mexico City, was the site of a former indigenous shrine. Ac-

cording to legend, the dark-skinned Virgin of GUADALUPE had appeared to a man named Juan DIEGO in Mexican garb and spoken in the Aztec language of the need for a shrine. Contemporary Mexican Americans continue their devotion to Our Lady of Guadalupe, whose image is displayed in many churches, homes, and community buildings.

Other accommodations to indigenous customs included organizing Catholic feast days in honor of the Virgin Mary or the saints to coincide with traditional religious fiestas or festivals. For some immigrants from Brazil, Cuba, and the Caribbean, such Catholic celebrations have become fused with African rituals and beliefs in an instance of *catolicismo popular* (popular or folk Catholicism). Candomblé, for example, is an Afro-Brazilian cult that involves black magic used for religious and medicinal purposes.

Latino Catholic holiday traditions have a distinctive ethnic stamp. The focus for Mexican Americans at Christmas is not the Christmas tree but *NACIMIENTOS* (nativity scenes with Mexican American themes) and *POSADAS,* processions that celebrate the birth of Jesus. Ash Wednesday, the first day of the Lenten season, is

These banners in Austin, Texas, illustrate the mixing of U.S. and Mexican Catholicism. (Bob Daemmrich)

Catholics celebrate Palm Sunday in San Antonio, Texas. (James Shaffer)

marked by somber ceremonies, and Holy Week is a high point of religious celebration in preparation for Easter Sunday. Filipinos whose roots are Asian and Latino often portray dramatic scenes of the Crucifixion on Good Friday. Portuguese Americans have elaborate Holy Ghost (Espíritu Santo) religious celebrations, including processions in which holy statues or images are paraded through the streets.

The atmosphere at Latino Catholic churches reflects their immigrant base. In areas heavily populated by Latinos, churches often bear the names of patron saints from parishioners' hometowns and villages. Services for immigrant Catholics are often conducted in Spanish. Mexican Americans play mariachi music during Mass and view the first communion for children as an occasion for religious celebration and family gatherings, which often include the parish priest. Another important church occasion for Latino families is the QUINCEAÑERA, at which fifteen-year-old girls are formally introduced to the church community.

American Catholic organizations, such as the Knights of Columbus, the Daughters of Isabella, and Our Lady of Guadalupe Society, involve the laity in church and parish activities. The Cursillo de Cristianidad, which originated in Spain in 1950, made its way to the United States a decade later via Latino Catholics in Texas (*see* CURSILLO MOVEMENT). Highly emotional weekend encounters bring together priests, nuns, and lay Catholics to experience the communitarian nature of Christianity. This charismatic approach to Roman Catholicism has been influenced by American evangelical Protestantism, a movement that continued to draw Latinos away from their traditional faith in both Latin America and the United States.

Catholic teachings about sex, sex roles, and family life have had an incalculable impact on Latino culture. The church's emphasis on procreation and a strict prohibition on contraception and abortion have made large families the norm in Latin American countries and among Latinos in the United States. This orientation, combined with church and community resistance to sex education, has made teenage pregnancy an increasing problem among Latino youth in inner cities. To ensure that Catholic values are instilled in the next generation, many families continue to enroll their children in parochial schools.

Conclusion. Although American Catholicism had European roots, it soon became a distinct culture as new immigrants acculturated to a Protestant society that valued democratic ideals, pragmatism, and representative government. Roman Catholicism in the United States was influenced by the needs of immigrant populations who, in fact, became the American Catholic church. The Latino Catholic church is founded upon identity with *el pueblo* and reflection on the lived experiences of the Christian community.

Maria A. Pacino

SUGGESTED READINGS:

• Carthy, Mary P. *Catholicism in English-Speaking Lands.* New York: Hawthorn Books, 1964. Gives information on Canada and the United States, from colonization through the 1950's.

• Considine, John J., ed. *The Religious Dimension in the New Latin America.* Notre Dame, Ind.: Fides, 1966. Presents expert views on the impact and accommodations of Roman Catholicism in Latin American countries.

• Gannon, Thomas M., ed. *World Catholicism in Transition.* New York: Macmillan, 1988. Focuses on major challenges facing Roman Catholicism in its worldwide diversity. Includes statistical data and extensive notes.

• Hennesey, James. *American Catholics.* Foreword by John Tracy Ellis. New York: Oxford University Press, 1981. Comprehensive view of Catholicism in the United States linking past with present and showing the impact of immigrants in forming church culture. Includes extensive notes.

• Maynard, Theodore. *The Story of American Catholicism.* 2 vols. Garden City, N.Y.: Image Books, 1960. Depicts distinctive Catholic characteristics of American history, outlining achievements and contributions of Catholicism in American culture. Volume II contains an extensive bibliography.

• Prest, James E. *American Catholic History.* Lanham, Md.: University Press of America, 1991. Concise perspective on American Catholicism from colonial days to the aftermath of Vatican II. The chapter on immigration and nativism is particularly enlightening.

• Rycroft, W. Stanley. *Religion and Faith in Latin America.* Philadelphia: Westminster Press, 1958. Traces the historical, social, and cultural influence of Christianity in Latin America from its beginnings until the mid-twentieth century.

• Shaughnessy, Gerald. *Has the Immigrant Kept the Faith?: A Study of Immigration and Catholic Growth in the United States, 1790-1920.* New York: Macmillan, 1925. Provides arguments and statistical tables as evidence that immigrants do not lose their "old country," Catholic roots when moving to the United States.

• Stevens Arroyo, Antonio M. *Prophets Denied Honor: An Anthology on the Hispanic Church of the United States.* Maryknoll, N.Y.: Orbis Books, 1980. Includes selections on liturgy, poetry, history, politics, and culture of Latino Catholicism. Illustrated with black-and-white photographs.

Catholic Youth Organization: Youth group. The Catholic Youth Organization is formally known as the National Federation for Catholic Youth Ministry and was founded in 1982. By the early 1990's, it had approximately 180 institutional members, a staff of eight, and fourteen regional groups. A predecessor group founded in 1951 was called the National Federation of Diocesan Catholic Youth Councils. The Catholic Youth Organization supersedes the National Catholic Youth Federation, also founded in 1951.

By the early 1990's, Catholic Youth Organization membership exceeded two million teenagers. The group sponsors locally oriented retreats, service projects, writing and oratorical contests, educational workshops, prayer groups, science fairs, play contests, photography contests, hobby shows, sports tournaments, and rallies. It bestows awards and holds regional conventions and workshops.

Católicos por la Raza: Southern California group of Chicano Catholic activists. This group was established in 1969 in Los Angeles and San Diego and consisted mostly of college students, led by law student Ricardo Cruz. Members perceived that the Catholic church was not addressing the needs of the Mexican American community, which was a large part of the church's constituency. Schools and churches in Latino neighborhoods were often in shabby condition, but parishes in wealthier non-Latino areas received more attention and resources. The aim of Católicos por la Raza was to make the church uphold its doctrine of social justice and equality.

The group's demands were met with silence from the church. On Christmas Eve of 1969, members peacefully demonstrated outside the newly built $4 million St. Basil's Cathedral. As they tried to enter for Mass, they were expelled by undercover police officers who arrested about twenty people. Católicos por la Raza ended its activity soon after the St. Basil's conflict. The organization has been credited with improving Chicano representation in Catholic clergy and influencing the church to become more active in the farmworkers' struggle.

Cavazos, Lauro F. (b. Jan. 4, 1927, the King Ranch, Tex.): Government official. After serving as the Dean of Tufts University School of Medicine, Cavazos distinguished himself as the president of Texas Tech University. President Ronald Reagan solicited his services for the post of U.S. secretary of education in 1988, making Cavazos the first Latino to hold a cabinet-level position.

President George Bush reappointed Cavazos the following year. During his tenure at the Department of Education, Cavazos played a key role in the creation of the President's Council on Educational Excellence for Hispanic Americans. He is credited with raising the awareness level in Washington regarding Latino educational concerns. Cavazos resigned in 1990.

Cedeño, César (César Cedeño y Encarnación; b. Feb. 25, 1951, Santo Domingo, Dominican Republic): Baseball player. Cedeño began his seventeen-year major league career in 1970 with the Houston Astros. A fast, line-drive-hitting outfielder, Cedeño spent twelve seasons with the team, winning Gold Glove Awards every year from 1972 to 1976 and earning four All-Star Game selections. In 1980, he helped the Astros to their first division title.

In 1982, Cedeño was traded to the Cincinnati Reds. After several disappointing seasons, he was traded to the St. Louis Cardinals late in the 1985 season. In twenty-eight games for the Cardinals, Cedeño batted .434 and hit six home runs, and his tremendous performance down the stretch helped lift the Cardinals to the National League pennant. He played briefly for the Los Angeles Dodgers before retiring following the 1986 season.

Secretary of Education Lauro Cavazos calls for a restructuring of the educational system at a 1990 press conference. (AP/Wide World Photos)

César Cedeño at bat in 1972. (AP/Wide World Photos)

Although he had a number of excellent seasons, Cedeño never lived up to the high expectations of many observers. Nevertheless, he led the National League in doubles two times, stole more than fifty bases six times, and twice batted as high as .320. He retired with a .285 career average, 199 home runs, and 550 stolen bases.

Census, treatment and counting of Latinos in the: A perennial question among Latinos, particularly prominent during the 1960's and 1970's, has been "What shall we call ourselves?" Most prefer to identify with their national origin and not with an encompassing group such as "HISPANIC" or "Latino."

It is not surprising that those in charge of collecting information had a difficult time constructing a definition for this group. Would it be persons who had ancestors from Latin America? If so, how many ancestors should those persons have, and how many generations removed? What about those whose ancestors predated the formation of these nations? Would it be persons who spoke Spanish or had a Spanish surname? Or would it be those who had parents born in these countries? Should people simply be allowed to self-identify their ethnic origin?

The Census Bureau is a U.S. federal agency with responsibility for collecting data on a wide variety of subjects. Its duties include counting the U.S. population by age, race, ethnicity, and sex. The Census Bureau has used four principal methods to identify the population living in the United States that is now referred to as persons of "Hispanic origin." The first is country of birth and country of birth of parents. The second is a Spanish surname, the third is Spanish as a mother tongue, and the fourth is Spanish origin.

The Census Bureau historically has favored questions with objective answers. For example, the Census Bureau preferred to ask a person's (and the person's parents') country of birth and language spoken at home, or to use a person's surname, rather than asking people to self-identify Hispanic origin. Thus, Census Bureau researchers preferred the first three methods to the last.

Place of Birth. Country of birth and country of birth of parents were collected in censuses from 1880 to 1970. The Census Bureau used answers to place-of-birth questions to distinguish native-born descendants of immigrants (or mixed native and foreign-born parents) from native-born individuals of native parents. Place-of-birth questions allowed the Census Bureau to identify the first and second generation of immigrants

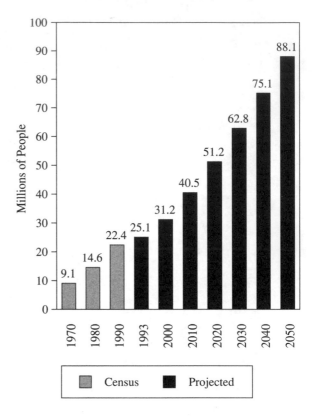

HISPANIC POPULATION 1970 TO 2050

Source: Data are from U.S. Bureau of the Census.

from Mexico, Cuba, and Central or South America (1880 to 1980), but Puerto Rico as a place of birth was collected only beginning in 1950. Place of birth of parents was last collected in 1980, but person's birthplace was collected in 1990. The main limitation of this method is that it identifies only first- and second-generation Spanish-descent persons. The loss of parental birthplace information in the 1990 census limited this method to identifying first-generation Hispanics.

Spanish Surnames. Spanish surname identification was the second way the Census Bureau identified persons of Spanish ancestry. It was used in five southwestern states from 1950 to 1970. This method involves matching a person's surname to a list of known Spanish surnames developed by the Census Bureau. The major flaw of this method of identification is that many of the "Spanish" surnames on the list are common among persons of Italian, Portuguese, and other origins. For this reason, the surname list was used only in five southwestern states (Arizona, California, Colorado, New Mexico, and Texas), where most of the

Mexican American population lived and where there were few people of non-Hispanic Latin origins. A further difficulty with Spanish surname identification was that women who married men with non-Hispanic names were lost to the Hispanic population and non-Hispanic women who married Hispanic men were incorrectly incorporated. This process was also costly, as it involved transcribing, matching, and coding.

The list of Spanish surnames used to code the 1980 census was improved based on the premise that a particular surname is Hispanic if it has a geographic distribution similar to that of the Hispanic population. This list was used to assign Hispanic origin in administrative records otherwise lacking Hispanic origin identifiers. The list was not used in the 1990 census except in a special evaluation of the 1990 census known as the post-enumeration survey.

Spanish Language. Spanish mother tongue was the third method used to identify the Hispanic population. As early as 1900, the Census Bureau solicited information about the mother tongue of respondents, which was defined as the language spoken at home when the respondent was a child. The Spanish-language popula-

tion identified in 1970 consisted of persons of Spanish mother tongue and all other persons in families in which the head or spouse reported Spanish as his or her mother tongue.

Among the problems with this method of identification is that persons may gain Spanish-language affiliation by marriage and lose it by separation or divorce. In addition, children of persons of Spanish mother tongue do not necessarily use Spanish when they become adults.

Unlike those in previous censuses, the 1980 and 1990 census language questions focused on current language usage of respondents. The questions were designed to yield information that would help to assess the need for bilingual education and other services, such as preparation of voting materials. The censuses of 1980 and 1990 had nearly identical language questions but had slightly different options in the list of possible answers. The 1990 question asked whether respondents spoke a language other than English at home and if so to identify which one, giving several examples. The question also asked how well the person spoke English, with the respondent filling in a

The census helps determine the need for bilingual voting materials. (Odette Lupis)

Members of each generation after that of immigrants become increasingly less likely to self-report themselves as being Hispanic. (James Shaffer)

circle next to "Very well," "Well," "Not well," or "Not at all."

Spanish Heritage. A method that combined three criteria was used to define persons of "Spanish heritage." The definition included persons with a Spanish surname or language use in the five states of the Southwest; persons of Puerto Rican birth or parentage in the Middle Atlantic states (New Jersey, New York, and Pennsylvania); and users of the Spanish language in the remaining forty-two states and the District of Columbia. With the exception of Puerto Ricans in the Middle Atlantic states, this measure failed to identify the various Latino subpopulations.

Spanish Origin. The previously discussed limitations led the Census Bureau to try a self-identification question on "Spanish origin or descent." Respondents were classified as "HISPANIC" if they were of Mexican, Puerto Rican, Cuban, Central or South American, or other Spanish origin or descent. The two major advan-

tages of this question were the ability to identify subpopulations and the ability to identify third-generation (or higher) persons of "Spanish descent." The primary limitation stems from the self-identification aspect of the question, because a person's conception of his or her identity might change over time.

An evaluation by the Census Bureau of the consistency of responses to the "Spanish origin" question in the 1970 census found that the likelihood of reporting a Spanish origin declined with generation. Almost everyone (99 percent) born in a "Hispanic" country (as reported in a reinterview) self-identified as being of Spanish origin in the census. About 83 percent of the second generation (at least one parent from a Hispanic country), 73 percent of the third, 44 percent of the fourth, and 6 percent of the fifth and higher generations reported being of Spanish origin in the census. Similarly, 97 percent of persons with reported Spanish origin on both sides of the family reported Spanish origin in the census, compared to only 21 percent with Spanish origin on one side of the family. Unfortunately, many non-Hispanic persons, particularly in the central or southern parts of the United States, misinterpreted the phrase "Central and South American origin" and misidentified themselves as "Hispanic" in the census. Census Bureau researchers nevertheless concluded that the self-identification item was reasonably consistent for the total population of Spanish origin and for the Mexican, Puerto Rican, and Cuban components.

The issue was settled by legislative action. On June 16, 1976, Congress passed Public Law 94-311, which required federal agencies to begin to collect and publish information relating to "Americans of Spanish origin or descent." This group was defined as "Americans who identify themselves as being of Spanish-speaking background and trace their origin or descent from Mexico, Puerto Rico, Cuba, Central and South America, and other Spanish-speaking countries." Subsequent censuses used variations of the "Spanish origin" item.

"Origin or descent" in census questions referred to the birthplace of the respondent, his or her parents, or ancestors. According to a 1976 Census Bureau report, if a respondent from the five southwestern states did not reply to this question and had a Spanish surname, he or she was assigned Mexican origin. If the question was not answered for children of persons of Spanish origin, they were assigned the origin of the parent of Hispanic origin.

All these methods were used in the 1970 census of population and housing. The methods produced estimates of the "Hispanic" population that varied widely, from a low of 5.2 million (Spanish birth or parentage) to a high of 10.1 million (Spanish language or surname).

In 1975, the Census Bureau formed its Census Advisory Committee on the Spanish Origin Population for the 1980 Census. A committee for the black population was established in 1974, and one for the Asian and Pacific Islander population in 1976. This committee, along with others, advised the director of the Census Bureau on data needs, what questions to ask in the census and how to ask them, policy issues such as whether to adjust census counts, and various statistical problems. Members of the committee were instrumental in convincing the Census Bureau to use the Spanish origin item instead of a general ethnicity question the Census Bureau tested in 1977.

Through a series of test censuses, the Spanish origin question, as it came to be known, was modified from the 1970 census design. The "Not Spanish" response was highlighted and moved to the first response category because many non-Hispanic respondents failed to answer the question. The "Central or South American" response was dropped to eliminate the misreporting of non-Hispanics in this category. Some respondents misreported in the "Mexican-American" category, thinking it referred to Mexican *or* American. "Mexican-American" was shortened to "Mexican-Amer." to reduce this type of misreporting.

The 1980 Census. The Spanish origin item was asked of all persons in the 1980 census. Instructions for the question stated that a person is of Spanish-Hispanic origin or descent if that person identifies his or her ancestry with one of the listed groups (Mexican, Puerto Rican, Cuban, and other Hispanic). Origin or descent (ancestry) could be viewed as the nationality group, the lineage, or the country in which the person or the person's parents or ancestors were born.

The 1980 census also included a general ethnicity question on the sample questionnaire. It became known as the ancestry question and asked respondents to print the ancestry group with which the person identifies. Ancestry was to be viewed in the same way as for the Spanish origin item. Persons of more than one origin who could not identify with a single group were to print their multiple ancestry (for example, German-Irish). Instructions stated that religious groups were not to be used as ancestry groups.

The answers to this question were coded into several hundred ancestry categories. The answers provided one way to identify the Hispanic population, particularly Latino groups that fall into the "Other Spanish/ Hispanic" category. The ancestry question, however, yielded a much smaller estimate of the Spanish origin population than the Spanish origin question. Some researchers recommend its use for identifying Hispanics in preference to the Spanish/Hispanic question, which encourages a Hispanic response even when respondents have only a weak ethnic identification.

The 1990 Census. The 1990 census had another, evolved, version of the 1980 Spanish/Hispanic question that was used as the principal identifier of the Hispanic population. The main difference is that persons selecting the "Other Spanish/Hispanic" category were encouraged to write in a specific group. This information was transcribed and coded only on the sample questionnaires, but it allowed the Census Bureau to publish detailed characteristics for specific groups other than Mexican, Puerto Rican, and Cuban.

Instructions for the 1990 question stated that a person is of Spanish-Hispanic origin if the person's origin

Spanish speakers are the largest U.S. language minority, prompting many schools to offer instruction in Spanish. (Impact Visuals, Mark Ludak)

(ancestry) is Mexican, Mexican American, Chicano, Puerto Rican, Cuban, Argentinean, Colombian, Costa Rican, Dominican, Ecuadoran, Guatemalan, Honduran, Nicaraguan, Peruvian, Salvadoran, from other Spanish-speaking countries of the Caribbean or Central or South America, or from Spain.

Growth Rates. It is difficult to estimate the exact growth rate between 1970 and 1980 because of changes in question format, enumeration, and processing procedures, but it is clear that the Hispanic origin population grew dramatically. Part of the growth in reported population resulted from immigration, high fertility rates, and improvements in census coverage. Census Bureau projections included continued rapid growth. Hispanic Americans may number 31 million by the year 2000, 51 million by 2020, and possibly 88 million by 2050. At projected growth rates, Hispanics will become the largest U.S. minority population between 2005 and 2010.

Spanish speakers were already the largest language minority in the United States by 1990. According to the 1990 census, more than 17 million persons over the age of five spoke Spanish at home. Nearly 55 percent of all persons in the United States who spoke a language other than English at home spoke Spanish.

Enumeration of people in the "Other Spanish/ Hispanic" category brings the discussion back to what this group should be called. Many researchers use the terms "Spanish origin" and "Hispanic" interchangeably but note that "Latino" is becoming acceptable among some groups. "Hispanic" is an official government name. "Hispanic" and "Latino" surfaced in the 1970's. In effect, they became coalition names, referring implicitly to a common culture, language, and geographic origin. Experience in designing census questions, however, showed that virtually no one of Hispanic or Spanish origin wanted a collective name, one that might indicate a collective identity. Instead, Latinos generally prefer their own national origin, although persons of Mexican origin are split among three identifiers—Mexican American, Chicano, and Mexican. Thus, there may not be any one universally accepted identifier, but collective action may someday forge a secondary collective identity.—*Jorge del Pinal*

SUGGESTED READINGS:

• Bean, Frank D., and Marta Tienda. *The Hispanic Population of the United States*. New York: Russell Sage Foundation, 1987. One of the 1980 census monographs commissioned by the Russell Sage Foundation and one of the most comprehensive analyses of the Latino population in existence.

• Choldin, Harvey M. "Statistics and Politics: The 'Hispanic Issue' in the 1980 Census." *Demography* 23 (August, 1986): 403-418. Brings together a critical discussion of how the concept of "Hispanic origin" was developed and became the way in which the Hispanic population is identified in the U.S. census of population.

• Del Pinal, Jorge, and Jesus M. Garcia. *Hispanic Americans Today*. Current Population Reports, Population Characteristics, P23-183. Washington, D.C.: Government Printing Office, 1993. This chart book presents information from the Census Bureau about the Latino population and contains a guide to census products with information about Latinos.

• Lieberson, Stanley, and Mary C. Waters. *From Many Strands: Ethnic and Racial Groups in Contemporary America*. New York: Russell Sage Foundation, 1988. A 1980 census monograph commissioned by the Russell Sage Foundation. One of the most comprehensive analyses of ethnic or ancestry populations.

• Moore, Joan. "Hispanic/Latino: Imposed Label or Real Identity." *Latino Studies Journal* 1 (May, 1990): 33 47. An important discussion of how group identities are developed and then embraced or rejected by members of the group.

• Padilla, Felix M. "Latin America: The Historical Base of Latino Unity." *Latino Studies Journal* 1 (January, 1990): 7-27. An important discussion of the emergence of a new Latino identity based on the importance of numbers for political action.

• Siegel, Jacob D., and Jeffrey S. Passel. *Coverage of the Hispanic Population of the United States in the 1980 Census: A Methodological Analysis*. Current Population Reports, Special Studies, P23-82. Washington, D.C.: Government Printing Office, 1979. The most comprehensive evaluation of the questions and methods developed at the Census Bureau to count the Hispanic population of the United States.

• U.S. Department of Commerce. Bureau of the Census. *1970 Census of Population and Housing: Procedural History*. PHC-(R)-1. Washington, D.C.: Government Printing Office, 1976. Provides a comprehensive overview of the 1970 census, questionnaires, procedures, and definitions.

• U.S. Department of Commerce. Bureau of the Census. *1980 Census of Population and Housing: History*. PHC80-R-2A and PHC80-R-2C. Washington, D.C.: Government Printing Office, 1986. This report series provides a comprehensive overview of the 1980 census, questionnaires, procedures, and definitions.

A CARECEN volunteer in Washington, D.C., completes a form for a Salvadoran client applying for legal residency. (Impact Visuals, Rick Reinhard)

- U.S. Department of Commerce. Bureau of the Census. *Persons of Hispanic Origin in the United States*. 1990 Census of Population, 1990 CP-3-3. Washington, D.C.: Government Printing Office, 1993. Presents a wealth of statistical information about Latino subgroups based on the 1990 census of population and housing.

Central American Refugee Center (CARECEN): Social service agency. The Central American Refugee Center was founded in 1981 and originally provided legal services to refugees seeking political asylum and to others needing assistance with immigration problems. CARECEN also provided English-language courses and food distribution to Central Americans in the Greater Los Angeles area. The CARECEN organization expanded its objectives by establishing a program to protect day laborers from deceptive hiring practices. In the early 1990's, CARECEN changed its name to the Central American Resource Center. The objectives of the organization changed from serving only refugees to assisting undocumented immigrants in the Greater Los Angeles area.

Centro Asturiano (Tampa, Fla.): Mutual aid society. Centro Asturiano is a mutual aid society founded in 1902 in Tampa, Florida. It is the longest-surviving and perhaps most important of the area's mutual aid societies, providing insurance and basic services for Cubans and other Latinos. Like some of Tampa's other mutual aid societies, it also sponsored a theater, which during the 1920's and 1930's hosted top names in Latino and operatic entertainment. The group was home to the Federal Theater Project, a U.S. government program funded by the Works Progress Administration that attempted to bring together Latino and Anglo theater styles and personnel for performance. The group continued to operate a theater into the 1990's.

Centro de Acción Autónoma-Hermandad General de Trabajadores (CASA-HGT): Labor organization. CASA-HGT was established by Mexican workers in

Los Angeles, California, to combat labor injustices. It is also involved in the plight of unauthorized workers.

Centro de la Raza (Seattle, Wash.): Community center. Centro de la Raza (Center of the People) was founded in 1972. At this time, the decrease in local farm labor jobs forced many workers to move to urban Seattle. A program in ENGLISH AS A SECOND LANGUAGE was developed at Seattle Central Community College in 1970 to equip these people with skills to cope in the new urban environment. The Centro de la Raza developed out of this program, expanding to provide education, training, and support services of many kinds for the Latino community. Programs include a community center that provides employment help; emergency food, shelter, and clothing; immigration and other legal referrals; a bilingual child development center; an international relations department that sponsors tours and cultural/educational presentations; and small business development. In addition, the center has public meeting facilities, a memorial park, and a network of speakers available for presentations.

Centro Español, West Tampa (Tampa, Fla.): Mutual aid society. The Centro Español was an important mutual aid society in Tampa, Florida, providing insurance and basic services for its Cuban American members. It was established in the early 1900's. As did other mutual aid societies in Tampa, it had a theatrical company and show committee that brought musical and theatrical productions to its theater. Some of these actors were Centro Español members, and some were professionals who were attracted to Tampa and the centro by the community's demand for professional theater. Many of the centro's members were cigar workers who became accustomed to quality theater through *lectores*, who read plays, fiction, and news to the workers as they prepared cigars.

Cepeda, Orlando (Orlando Manuel Cepeda y Penne; b. Sept. 17, 1937, Ponce, Puerto Rico): Baseball player. Cepeda grew up around professional baseball. His father, Perucho "The Bull" Cepeda, was among the greatest players in Puerto Rican history. Orlando, "The Baby Bull," homered for the San Francisco Giants

Orlando Cepeda was named the 1958 National League Rookie of the Year. (AP/Wide World Photos)

Mayor Alfonso Cervantes announces new appointments to the St. Louis Housing Authority in an effort to end a 1969 rent strike. (AP/Wide World Photos)

in his first major league game in 1958. The young first baseman continued to perform well that year, batting .312, leading the National League in doubles, and earning the league's Rookie of the Year Award. In 1961, he led the league with 46 home runs and 142 runs batted in, and for the next few seasons he was consistently among the league leaders in home runs and batting average.

Cepeda lost most of the 1965 season to a knee injury. Early in the 1966 season, he was traded to the St. Louis Cardinals, and he went on to win the Comeback Player of the Year Award. A year later, he was named the National League's Most Valuable Player, leading the league with 111 runs batted in as the Cardinals took the pennant and the World Series. Age and injury took their toll, however, and he was unable to sustain his brilliance. He was traded to the Atlanta Braves in 1969, and he finished his career playing briefly for the Oakland A's, Boston Red Sox, and Kansas City Royals. After the end of his major league career, he served a ten-month prison sentence for marijuana possession that may have prevented his election to the National Baseball Hall of Fame.

Ceramics. *See* **Pottery and ceramics**

Cervantes, Alfonso Juan (Aug. 27, 1920, St. Louis, Mo.—June 22, 1983, St. Louis, Mo.): Mayor of St. Louis. Cervantes, the flamboyant and controversial mayor of St. Louis for two terms running from 1965 to 1973, was a tireless promoter of his hometown. He quickly recognized the economic potential of tourism and convention business and worked incessantly to draw those benefits to St. Louis.

Cervantes may be remembered most for his struggle to gain approval of a bond issue to construct the convention center that bears his name. Two ill-fated projects—the Spanish International Pavilion and the *Santa Maria* project—detracted from his reputation as a builder of the local economy. The Spanish International Pavilion closed nine months after it opened because of financial problems. The *Santa Maria*, built for the 1965 World Fair, was moored in the Mississippi River but was destroyed by a storm within five months.

Cervantes, Lorna Dee (b. Aug. 6, 1954, San Francisco, Calif.): Poet. Cervantes is a critically acclaimed poet, a teacher, and a founder of a small press. She emerged on the literary scene in the mid-1970's. Although she is not a prolific writer, her poetry, with its feminist concerns, helped lay the foundation for the writings of other female Mexican American poets.

Women's voices and writings were often excluded in the early Chicano movement, with emphasis placed on male ideology and symbolism. In response, Cervantes founded her own press and poetry magazine, *Mango*, in San Jose, California. She started another poetry magazine, *Red Dirt*, while at the University of Colorado at Boulder, teaching in its creative writing program.

Cervantes' first book of poems, *Emplumada* (1981), was well received by Mexican American critics and scholars. Her poetry often explores female-male relationships. Cervantes is also interested in how people respond to the fleeting world around them. Like most Chicano poets who wrote between the 1960's and the 1980's, Cervantes pays particular attention to the Native American side of her Mexican American heritage and often uses symbols from nature. Her second collection of poems is titled *From the Cables of Genocide: Poems on Love and Hunger* (1991).

Cervántez, Yreina (b. 1952, Garden City, Kans.): Painter and printmaker. Cervántez is a muralist whose public art, contributions to group exhibits, and teaching have helped keep Mexican and Chicano art and art history alive after the initial surge of the Chicano movement in the 1960's and 1970's.

Cervántez grew up in San Diego, California, and earned a fine arts degree from the University of California, Santa Cruz, in 1975. Her teaching career includes an artist-in-residenceship at Self-Help Graphics in Los Angeles and a teaching assistantship at the University of California, both during the 1980's. In the early 1990's, she taught drawing, watercolor painting, and Mexican and Chicano art history for three additional California colleges, and she served as multicultural coordinator for the Los Angeles Municipal Art Gallery.

One of Cervántez's most famous works is *La Ofrenda* (1990; the offering), a Los Angeles mural that pays tribute to Latino farmworkers and spotlights the longtime leader of the United Farm Workers, Dolores HUERTA. Cervántez's other public murals include a mural project for a park in Managua, Nicaragua, and a mural for the Municipal Arts Gallery and Micheltorena Street Elementary School in Los Angeles, California.

Cha-cha: A Cuban partner dance developed from the MAMBO. The cha-cha is danced to a light bouncy rhythm, in four-four time, with the accent occurring on the first beat and the secondary accent on the third beat. The dance step, which begins on the fourth beat, is a step, followed by a glide forward or backward on the second beat, then stepping in place on the third beat. Originally called cha-cha-cha because it stressed the third and fourth beats, its stress was later changed. The cha-cha swept into ballrooms across the United States in the mid-1950's.

Chacón, Alicia Rosencrans: Government official. Chacón is a nationally recognized Hispanic leader with the distinction of being the first woman elected as a county judge in El Paso County, Texas, and being the first Hispanic judge there in more than a century. Chacón became the first woman to serve in her county's municipal government when she was elected county clerk. In 1978, President Jimmy Carter appointed Chacón as regional director of the Small Business Administration, a position in which she was the first woman to serve. She was elected to the El Paso City Council in 1983 and in 1985.

Chacón has affected the advancement of Latinos in education, employment, and public service through her participation on national boards. She was selected to serve as chairwoman of the Mexican American Legal Defense and Educational Fund. Chacón also has served as a director of the Vista Institute of Hispanic Studies, National Hispanic Leadership Agenda, and NATIONAL COUNCIL OF LA RAZA.

Chacón, Bobby (Robert Chacón; b. Nov. 28, 1951, Los Angeles, Calif.): Boxer. Chacón captured the World Boxing Council (WBC) featherweight title in 1974 with a ninth-round knockout of Alfredo Marcano. After losing the title in 1975 to Rubén Olivares, Chacón moved into the junior-lightweight class, eventually winning the WBC title in 1982 with a decision over Rafael Limon.

Bobby Chacón defeated Rafael Limon to take the WBC junior lightweight title. (AP/Wide World Photos)

Chacón, Eusebio (Dec. 16, 1869, Peñasco, N.Mex.— Apr. 3, 1948, Trinidad, Colo.): Novelist and lawyer. Chacón is one of the earliest Mexican American novelists of the American Southwest. Interest in his writings was renewed in the 1970's during the cultural reawakening brought on by the Chicano movement. An attorney by profession, Chacón received his law degree from Notre Dame in 1889, but before practicing law he taught English for two years in Mexico. Working as a Spanish translator for the United States courts, Chacón developed an acute awareness of social and legal conflicts between European Americans and Hispanics in and around Colorado.

Chacón's two novels *El hijo de la tempestad; Tras la tormenta la calma: Dos novelitas originales* (1892; the son of the storm; the calm after the storm. two original novellas) are perhaps the first two novels written in Spanish to come from the New Mexico-Colorado region. These were the only novels Chacón wrote. Adapting local contemporary issues and events to literary models originating in Spain, Chacón infused in his works a commitment to nourish Hispanic culture.

Other works by Chacón include the unpublished "La expedición de Coronado" (a lost text attributed to him) and the editorial essay "Elocuente Discurso" (1901), which defended local religion and culture.

Chacón, Felipe Maximiliano (1873, Santa Fe, N.Mex.—?): Writer. Chacón wrote only one short volume, in Spanish. The volume, titled *Obras de Felipe Maximiliano Chacón, "El Cantor Neomexicano": Poesía y Prosa* (1924; works of Felipe Maximiliano Chacón, the New Mexican bard: poetry and prose), is a three-part collection of fifty-six poems, three short stories, and seven translations of English poems into Spanish. The short story "Don Julio Berlanga" is often singled out as Chacón's best work in the collection. One of the earliest published Hispanic works of the American Southwest, Chacón's book is memorable more for its historical background than for its literary merits.

Little is known about the writer's life. Chacón was the son of a newspaper publisher. A well-educated Mexican American, Chacón made his career in journalism after attending a local college. Between 1911 and 1918, he edited Spanish-language newspapers in cities across New Mexico. He later managed the Albuquerque paper *La Bandera Americana* (the American flag). Benjamin M. Read, a renowned New Mexican historian and legislator, wrote a prologue to Chacón's book. According to Read, Chacón wrote poems and stories as a youth but did not publish any work until his adulthood.

Chacón, Peter R. (b. June 10, 1925, Phoenix, Ariz.): State legislator. Chacón was born in Arizona but received his education and shaped his career as a public servant in Southern California. Chacón earned his undergraduate degree at San Diego State University in 1953. Seven years later, he completed his master's program there.

Chacón served as a vice principal and administrator in the San Diego school system. He was first elected to represent the Seventy-ninth District in the California State Assembly in 1970, becoming the first Latino elected to the state legislature from his district. At that time, San Diego County was about 15 to 20 percent Mexican American. Chacón earned the respect of his colleagues as well as the consistent support of his constituents.

Chalupa: Mexican ANTOJITO made of fried MASA with a topping. Literally meaning "small boat," a *chalupa* resembles that vessel. The *chalupa* is made from moist *masa*, pressed into an oval with its edges pinched upward into a rim. After baking on a COMAL, it is fried in oil and the depression is filled with any filling suitable for a taco. In the state of Nuevo León in northern Mexico, the term refers to what elsewhere would be called a TOSTADA. *Gorditos* are gobs of *masa* that puff up when they are cooked like *chalupas*; they are a northern Mexican dish, usually made by street vendors.

Chamizal, Treaty of El. *See* **Treaty of El Chamizal**

Champurrado: Hot chocolate drink of Mexico. *Champurrado* is a type of ATOLE, a corn-thickened drink, and is made with fresh MASA, milk, chocolate, and *piloncillo* (raw brown sugar). Ground almonds, cinnamon, anise seeds, or other seasonings can be added. The ingredients are mixed and heated to a simmer, which is held for several minutes. The mixture is then agitated with a rotating *molinillo*, a wooden folk implement consisting of a central rod with various knobs, wheels, and disks attached. Use of the *molinillo* helps keep the *champurrado* smooth and frothy. The *molinillo* also is used in making Mexican hot chocolate. After agitation, the *champurrado* is poured, sometimes strained, and drunk.

Chang-Díaz, Franklin Ramón (b. Apr. 5, 1950, San José, Costa Rica): Astronaut. Chang-Díaz moved to

Franklin Chang-Díaz. (AP/Wide World Photos)

the United States from his native Costa Rica when he was eighteen years old and later became a naturalized U.S. citizen. He moved to the United States to study science, even though he could not speak English. He learned English quickly, then earned his B.S. in mechanical engineering from the University of Connecticut in 1973 and his Ph.D. from the Massachusetts Institute of Technology in applied physics in 1977. After his graduate studies, he worked at the Charles Stark Draper Laboratory, where he did research on fusion reactors. Chang-Díaz was selected as a mission specialist candidate in 1980 and by 1994 had participated in four space shuttle missions for the National Aeronautics and Space Administration (NASA). In addition to his work for NASA, Chang-Díaz speaks at elementary and high schools about his experiences in space and about space travel.

Charango: Musical instrument. The *charango* is indigenous to the Andean regions of South America. It is a small fretted lute, shaped like the guitar but with a smaller box and shorter strings that are either plucked or strummed. One type of *charango* is wooden, with a flat back and five double or triple courses of metal strings. This version is typical in Peru and Bolivia. The round-back *charango*, made of armadillo shell or carved wood, is found in northern Argentina and the Lake Titicaca region of Peru and Bolivia. The *charango* traditionally has been played exclusively by men, forming part of string, wind, and percussion ensembles that accompany singing and dancing.

Charreada: A colorful exhibition of horsemanship that originated in Mexico. The *charreada*, Mexico's traditional equestrian sport, began on the large cattle ranches. The horsemen, called *charros*, who worked the ranches displayed the skills they developed in herding cattle in competitions that grew into the *charreadas*. In time, these competitions began to be held in urban areas.

The Associación Nacional de Charros was begun in 1921. The *charreada* spread throughout Mexico and into the United States, and eventually there were more than seven hundred associations in Mexico, with twenty thousand members, and more than eighty associations in the United States. All aspects of being a CHARRO, such as apparel, deportment, and the rules of competition, were governed by *reglamentos*, the rules of the Federación de Charros, which was organized in 1933.

In urban areas, *charreadas* are held in structures called *charro lienzos*. The *lienzo* is an enclosed area, 65 yards long and 11 yards wide, that serves as a runway for horses and steers. Adjoining the *lienzo*, separated from it by a gate, is the *ruedo* (ring). At the opposite end of the *lienzo* from the ring are the bull pen and the *partidero*, the area from which the animals enter the *lienzo* and the *ruedo*. Running parallel to the *lienzo* is another corridor, the *devolvedero* (return route), which opens into the ring.

The *charreada* begins with the *charros* parading in to the center of the arena from the *lienzo*, their beautiful horses in perfect formation, and greeting the audience. The competition consists of events called *suertes* (feats). First, three *suertes* are executed in the *lienzo*: *cala de caballo*, in which each *charro* in turn rides his horse at a full gallop from the *partidero* to the center of the ring, then brings the horse to an abrupt full stop; the *pieales*, in which a mounted *charro* lassoes the hind legs of a running mare that is being prodded along the right side of the *lienzo*; and the *coleadero*, in which the mounted *charro* waits for a bull at the *partidero*, rides alongside it, grabs its tail and rolls it around his right leg, and then makes his horse sidestep to ground the bull.

Four *suertes* are then held in the *ruedo*. First is the *jineteo*, in which the *charro* tries to stay on the back of a bull until it stops bucking. This event is similar to steer riding in U.S. rodeos, but the ride is longer than the eight seconds required for rodeo points. Second is the *terna*, a collaboration of three *charros*: one lassoes the bull by the horns, one lassoes its hind legs, and one throws it. Next comes the *manganas*. In this event, the *charro* first rides a wild mare, then, on foot, demonstrates his skill in fancy rope work with *la reata* (the lariat) before lassoing the wild mare by its forelegs. Unlike U.S. rodeos, in which speed and strength are the primary criteria for performance, style is the main criterion in the *charreada*. The final event is the *paso de la muerte* (passage of death), in which the *charro* switches from the horse he is riding bareback, at full speed, onto the back of a wild mare. The *charreada* then ends with an *escaramuza*, a performance by a women's mounted sidesaddle drill team.

Charro: Mexican rider skilled in breaking horses. *Charro* horsemanship occupies center stage in the *charreada*, *fiesta charra*, or *jaripeo*, equestrian events inspired by work on cattle ranches. Among the events are *colear*, the felling of a steer by twisting its tail while riding on horseback; *paso de la muerte*, the passing from a tamed horse onto a bronco; and other feats based on horseback bullfighting. Typical *charro*

A charreada *in San Antonio, Texas.* (Bob Daemmrich)

Four women prepare for competition in the Tucson Charro Festival. (Ruben G. Mendoza)

dress includes the *jarano*, a wide-brimmed and high-crowned hat, short jacket, cravat, tight pants, leggings, and short boots. Some events of the CHARREADA are open to women. Female dress includes long skirts with wide hems.

Charro Days (Brownsville, Tex.): Annual festival held in late February or early March. The events begin on the Thursday before Ash Wednesday and last for four days. The term *charro*, meaning "loud" or "flashy," relates to the rancheros, Mexicans of indigenous and Spanish heritage who played a major role in Mexico's struggle for independence and were noteworthy for their extravagant clothing, such as their large sombreros, handsome jackets embroidered with silver thread, and extravagant spurs.

One of the older continuing Mexican American festivals in the United States, begun in the 1950's, Charro Days attracted more than 350,000 annual visitors by the 1990's. It originated in the tradition of the *charreada*, or Mexican rodeo, but now events include parades, concerts, fireworks, folk dances, and games.

The festival also features foodways, arts and crafts, and costume displays. More than three-fourths of the performers are Mexican or Mexican American.

Chávez, César Estrada (Mar. 31, 1927, near Yuma, Ariz.—Apr. 23, 1993, San Luis, Ariz.): Labor leader. Chávez was the grandchild of immigrants from Mexico. He spent his early childhood near Yuma, in an adobe house without running water or electricity. His family ran a small farm during the Great Depression, which was particularly hard on the Southwest. A drought in 1933, creating the "Dust Bowl," drove people from the Southwest to California.

The Chávez family moved in 1938 to Oxnard, California, where they became migrant agricultural workers. Between that time and 1952, Chávez experienced the miserable conditions under which migrant workers lived and began to form the resolve to change those conditions for the better.

In 1952, Chávez met Fred Ross, a labor organizer important in establishing the COMMUNITY SERVICE ORGANIZATION, a group intended to work with Lati-

César Chávez led strikes and boycotts primarily in California but occasionally elsewhere. (AP/Wide World Photos)

nos in the West. Chávez worked with this organization until 1962, when he decided that the most important task was to organize farm laborers.

In 1962, Chávez formed the Farm Workers Association in an attempt to organize migrant workers and improve their conditions. One of the earliest problems he encountered was the use of braceros, Mexicans who were allowed to enter the country legally as farmworkers under the BRACERO PROGRAM, instituted in 1942. Braceros were paid less than local laborers. Although growers were not supposed to hire braceros when local workers were available, this provision of the law was generally ignored.

In 1965, Filipino grape pickers began a strike against a grower in Southern California when wages were cut. Soon, the strike spread among Filipinos. Chávez persuaded his union, now called the NATIONAL FARM WORKERS ASSOCIATION, to join in the effort. The union agreed, and strikes became widespread. Inspired by the works of Martin Luther King, Jr., Chávez suggested a boycott of grapes and wine. The strike began in October, 1965, and lasted for five years, with large effects on the California grape and wine industries.

During this period, Chávez gained powerful support. When picketers arrived at California docks, longshoremen who were loading grapes refused to work. Robert F. Kennedy became a major supporter of the union and defended it in a Senate subcommittee hearing relating to violence by growers against strikers. In return, Chávez supported Kennedy in the 1968 presidential election. He served as a delegate to the Democratic National Convention.

In 1970, twenty-three California growers signed a contract with Chávez's union, now affiliated with the American Federation of Labor-Congress of Industrial Organizations and called the United Farm Workers Organizing Committee after merger with the Agricultural Workers Organizing Committee. The GRAPE BOYCOTT was lifted. Chávez's union was renamed once more in 1972, as the UNITED FARM WORKERS. Other short-lived boycotts followed in attempts to bring other growers into line with the idea of providing good wages and working conditions for migrant workers.

Although Mexican Americans and other migrant workers continued to face harsh working conditions, the status of migrant workers in the Southwest has improved over the years. The labor movement in general was influenced by the success of the nonviolent methods Chávez initiated. Largely as a result of his efforts, California's legislature in 1975 passed the AGRI-CULTURAL LABOR RELATIONS ACT, the first law in the mainland United States (Hawaii already had such a law) pertaining to collective bargaining for farmworkers.

Chávez, Denise Elia (b. Aug. 15, 1948, Las Cruces, N.Mex.): Writer. Chávez is perhaps the most prolific female Mexican American playwright in the United States. She has written more than twenty plays, about three-fourths of which had been produced by the early 1990's. *The Wait* (1970), an early work, won New Mexico University's Best Play Award that year. *Plaza* (1984) toured New Mexico and internationally, and it won places in both New York's and Edinburgh's festivals. By the 1990's, productions of Chávez's plays were common throughout the Southwest.

Even Chávez's prose has made it onto the stage. A portion of her novel *The Last of the Menu Girls* (1986) became a one-act play in 1990. The novel itself won the Puerto del Sol fiction award for 1985 and the Steele Jones Fiction Award in 1986. *The Last of the Menu Girls* is more a collection of seven narratives with the same young female Mexican American protagonist than it is a novel.

Chávez has taught theater at several universities in the Southwest and is a founding member of the National Institute of Chicana Writers. She published her first conventional novel, *Face of an Angel*, in 1990, and she selected the plays in a collection entitled *Shattering the Myth: Plays by Hispanic Women* (1993), edited by Linda Feyder.

Chávez, Dennis (Apr. 8, 1888, near Albuquerque, N.Mex.—Nov. 18, 1962, Albuquerque, N.Mex.): U.S. senator. Chávez was born into a large family. He dropped out of school in the eighth grade to help support the family but continued his studies during evenings spent at the public library.

While working for the Albuquerque city government, Chávez provided Spanish translations for Democratic Senator Andrieus Jones. Jones helped Chávez secure a clerkship in the U.S. Senate that allowed Chávez to complete law school at Georgetown University in 1920.

Chávez returned to practice law in New Mexico. Active in state Democratic Party politics, Chávez first won election to the state legislature, then defeated the Republican incumbent in his 1930 race for the U.S. House of Representatives. After being narrowly defeated by Bronson Cutting in 1934 for a U.S. Senate seat, Chávez was appointed to complete that senator's term after he died in office. Chávez was easily re-

Dennis Chávez, at left, contested his 1934 loss to Bronson Cutting; he is shown speaking with Walter George (center), chair of the Senate Elections Committee, and Houston Thompson, Cutting's attorney. (AP/Wide World Photos)

elected in 1936 and served with distinction until his death in an airplane crash. Among his many accomplishments was drafting the bill to create the FAIR EMPLOYMENT PRACTICES COMMITTEE.

Chávez, Eduardo Arcenio (b. Mar. 14, 1917, Wagon Mound, N.Mex.): Painter and sculptor. Chávez is one of a group of Hispanic artists who came of age in the 1930's and 1940's, gained valuable work experience as painters for a federal arts program, and later achieved national prominence as independent artists. He is respected for regional American murals and abstract paintings.

Chávez was introduced to art in high school, after which he studied art at the Colorado Springs Fine Arts Center. He considered himself to be primarily self-taught. In the 1930's, he painted historical murals for the WORKS PROGRESS ADMINISTRATION. In 1947, he won the Pepsi-Cola Prize for American Painting.

In the 1950's and 1960's, Chávez began to paint in more abstract forms, arranging geometric shapes on a patterned grid to suggest a beach, a mesa, a rain forest, or another particular landscape. *Xochimilcho* (1965) and *Moon Journey* (1969) are characteristic of Chávez's abstract work. His works are included in major museum collections in New York, Washington, Michigan, New Mexico, and Ohio.

In addition to his career as an artist, Chávez has taught at colleges, universities, and art schools in New York and Colorado. From 1954 to 1958, he was an instructor with the Art Students League.

Chávez, Helen (b. 1928, Brawley, Calif.): Union activist. The wife of legendary activist César CHÁVEZ, Helen Favila Chávez provided the financial and emotional support that made his work possible. The couple agreed that the needs of the people took priority and that their family would take second place. For many years, Helen Chávez worked in the fields to support the couple's eight children while her husband spent his days, without pay, organizing workers. She tutored her husband to help him make up for an inadequate education. In 1965, she was arrested for civil disobedience while participating in a labor strike after the local sheriff had forbidden demonstrators from using the word *huelga* (strike) in picketing. That year, she and César taught themselves, by reading government manuals, how to set up a credit union for the NATIONAL FARM WORKERS ASSOCIATION. For years afterward, Helen served as manager of the credit union.

Chávez, Julio César (b. July 12, 1962, Ciudád Obregón, Mexico): Boxer. Chávez was introduced to boxing by his brothers, Rodolfo and Rafael. Juan Antonio López, a former boxer who had once been ranked fifth in the world as a super-bantamweight, convinced Chávez to develop his boxing skills by training at a small gym in the suburb of Colonia Ejidal. Chávez became seriously motivated to continue boxing when he discovered that his boxing skills could be used to provide financial security for his family.

Chávez won his first championship in the super featherweight class in 1984, when he knocked out Mario Martinez for the title vacated by Hector Camacho. By 1985, when he defeated Roger Mayweather in the junior lightweight division, Chávez had a 45-0 record with 41 knockouts. Chávez then began fighting more often in the United States. Under the direction of promoter Don King, his career gained momentum.

Over the next eight years, Chávez achieved success after success in the ring. He won the World Boxing Association (WBA) lightweight title, the International Boxing Federation (IBF) lightweight title, and the World Boxing Council (WBC) super lightweight title. Chávez finally had a scare, however, in a September, 1993, welterweight match with Pernell Whitaker. After a twelve-round brawl that most observers thought Whitaker had clearly won, the judges ruled a controversial majority draw. In January, 1994, Chávez received his first loss in ninety-one fights when he was beaten by Frankie Randall. In a highly publicized rematch in May, 1994, Chávez recaptured the super lightweight title with a hotly disputed split decision.

A national hero in Mexico, Chávez has also been a popular champion among Latinos in the United States. Several songs and stories have been written about the athlete whom boxing enthusiasts have called the best pound-for-pound fighter in the world.

Chávez, Linda (b. June 17, 1947, Albuquerque, N.Mex.): Public official. Chávez has become well known for her conservative views. She completed her

Linda Chávez (right) in 1986 campaigned against Barbara Mikulski for a U.S. Senate seat. (AP/Wide World Photos)

undergraduate studies at the University of Colorado in 1970, then served on the staff for a congressional sub-committee as well as acting as a lobbyist for educational associations.

Chávez worked as an editor of various publications for the American Federation of Teachers from 1977 to 1983. During the Ronald Reagan Administration, Chávez served as staff director of the U.S. Commission on Civil Rights. She left the commission to join the White House staff as director of public liaison in 1985. The following year, Chávez ran an unsuccessful senatorial campaign in Maryland, losing to Democrat Barbara Mikulski. Chávez then briefly headed U.S. English, a conservative organization that has promoted monolingualism as public policy.

Chávez became a conservative political commentator featured on television and radio programs. As a senior fellow at the Manhattan Institute, Chávez has written on the social and political conditions of Latinos.

Chávez, Manuel (Fray Angélico Chávez; b. Apr. 10, 1910, Wagon Mound, N.Mex.): Writer. Chávez is perhaps New Mexico's greatest literary resource. A former Franciscan monk and Catholic priest, Chávez had a long, distinguished writing career. Memorable for their historical detail and spiritual introspection, Chávez's works have earned for him local and national recognition. He was awarded the Catholic Poetry Award in 1948 from the Catholic Poetry Society and a literary award in 1976 from the governor of New Mexico.

Chávez's work divides easily into three different genres: poetry, prose fiction, and historical nonfiction. Under his ordained name of Fray Angélico Chávez, he began writing autobiographical poetry concerned with issues of spirituality and Catholic faith. He also has written historical fiction depicting early Hispanic New Mexicans and their perspectives on religion and spirituality. Although he wrote religious poetry until the 1950's, Chávez has regularly turned away from creative writing and written nonfiction prose histories.

His poetry collections include *Clothed with the Sun* (1939), *Eleven Lady-Lyrics and Other Poems* (1945), *The Lady from Toledo* (1960), and *Selected Poems, with an Apología* (1969). His prose works include *The Short Stories of Fray Angélico Chávez* (1987), edited by Genaro M. Padilla, and his spiritual autobiography *My Penitente Land: Reflections on Spanish New Mexico* (1974).

Chávez Ravine development: Latinos residing near downtown Los Angeles, California, were forced to relocate from their homes in Chávez Ravine so that the city could construct a baseball stadium for the Los Angeles Dodgers.

The city of Los Angeles has enjoyed a rich history. Its charter was granted under the authority of Spain in 1781. Explored by Hernán Cortés and Francisco Vázquez de Coronado, the area remained under Spanish sovereignty until 1821, when Mexico won its independence from Spain. Throughout the city's history, there has been a strong element of involvement from all echelons of Latino society.

Norris Poulson became mayor of Los Angeles in 1953. He led efforts to lure the Brooklyn Dodgers to Los Angeles. At the time, Brooklyn's Ebbets Field was in need of major remodeling. It also was located in a dangerous part of New York.

During his mayoral campaign, Poulson criticized Los Angeles' holding of 183 acres of land at Chávez Ravine, which was designated to become a center for public housing for the poor. The Brooklyn Dodgers (later the Los Angeles Dodgers) wanted to construct a new stadium on this land, located a few miles from the heart of the city. Chávez Ravine was named after Julian Chávez, one of the city's first Latino council members. Chávez had moved to the pueblo from New Mexico in the 1840's.

The Housing Authority, backed by former mayor Fletcher Bowron, was created to implement federal law in support of the poor. On September 16, 1958, the *Los Angeles Times* ran a column expressing sports editor Paul Zimmerman's view that time was running out on the city's chances to acquire Chávez Ravine for the baseball stadium and that the city should act immediately. Local actors including Groucho Marx, Jack Benny, George Burns, and Ronald Reagan made statements in favor of terminating the Housing Authority property agreements in favor of the city of Los Angeles' proposal to use the land for a baseball stadium.

Eventually, the city of Los Angeles was successful in defeating the plan to turn the land into a low-income housing development. The stadium was built in Chávez Ravine after numerous court battles in which Latino families fought eviction from the land. On May 8, 1959, deputies forcibly removed Avena Arechiga and Aurora Vargas so that construction could begin. Victoria Augustain was forcibly removed as television cameras recorded her resistance.

Chayote: Squash with semi-hard fruit. Chayote is eaten throughout Mexico, Central America, and the Caribbean. It is a squash with green, pear-shaped fruit having the texture of the hard squashes and the non-sweet taste of the soft squashes. Domesticated in Mexico, where the Aztecs called it *chayotli*, the chayote spread to the Caribbean and Central America before the arrival of Christopher Columbus. It now is eaten in these areas as well as the eastern coast of South America. Chayotes usually are eaten boiled or stuffed and baked. Mexicans and Puerto Ricans sometimes prepare them with sugar as a dessert. Chayotes also are known as *huisquil, cho-cho*, and christophenes.

Chicago, Illinois: Home to the third largest U.S. Latino community. The 1990 census recorded nearly 900,000 Latino residents of Chicago, about 11 percent of the city's population. About two-thirds of the Latinos in the city were Mexican Americans.

History. Chicago is a major urban center of the United States. First explored in the seventeenth century, it was incorporated as a city in 1837 with a population of 4,200. During the nineteenth century, Chicago's population increased substantially as a result of its growing industrial base. This industrial growth created many job opportunities, which turned the city into a major center for immigration and internal migration. Among the new arrivals were many people of Hispanic descent.

The first Latinos to migrate to Chicago in large numbers were from Mexico. Some came in the nineteenth century, but the first major wave came after 1910. The Mexican Revolution pushed people out of Mexico, and by 1930 the U.S. Census showed 20,963 people of Mexican descent living in Chicago.

The years between 1910 and 1930 were years of relative prosperity for Chicago's Mexican Americans. The steel, railroad, and meatpacking industries provided many permanent and well-paying jobs, providing immigrants with a better standard of living than the one they had left behind.

Puerto Ricans were the second major group of Latino immigrants. They began arriving in significant numbers after World War II, when the island could no longer support its expanding population. Unlike Mexicans, Puerto Ricans began arriving after industry in Chicago had begun to decline. Employment opportunities were significantly reduced, so Puerto Ricans relied on low-paying service and light manufacturing jobs. Some who could not find work were supported by the welfare system.

The third major group of Latino migrants to Chicago were Cubans. Fidel Castro's revolution in 1959

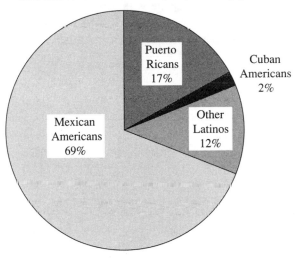

LATINO POPULATION OF CHICAGO, ILLINOIS, 1990

Total number of Latinos = 893,422; 11% of population

Puerto Ricans 17%

Cuban Americans 2%

Mexican Americans 69%

Other Latinos 12%

Source: Data are from Marlita A. Reddy, ed., *Statistical Record of Hispanic Americans* (Detroit: Gale Research, 1993), Table 110.
Note: Figures represent the population of the Chicago, Illinois-Gary, Indiana-Lake County, Wisconsin, Consolidated Metropolitan Statistical Area as delineated by the U.S. Bureau of the Census

forced thousands of Cubans to flee the island for political reasons. The majority went to Florida, particularly Miami, but many chose other major cities, including Chicago.

Most Mexican and Puerto Rican arrivals were poor, unskilled workers in search of a better life. Most Cubans, however, were middle- and upper-class people who already enjoyed a high standard of living in Cuba. They were entrepreneurs and professionals who quickly assimilated into American society. Cubans quickly established the highest standard of living of all Latino subgroups in the United States.

Although people from Mexico, Puerto Rico, and Cuba form the three major Latino groups in Chicago, people from every Latin American country have made Chicago their home. The 1990 census reported communities from Guatemala, Peru, Ecuador, Colombia, El Salvador, Honduras, and the Dominican Republic numbering more than one thousand in population.

The Late Twentieth Century. Nationality defined the residential pattern of most Latinos in Chicago by 1990. The census for that year showed that 348,040 Mexican Americans lived in Chicago, most of them in the Pilsen and Little Village neighborhoods. Mexicans began moving to the Pilsen neighborhood in the 1940's and later moved west to adjacent Little Village. On the major commercial streets of these two neighborhoods—Eighteenth Street and Twenty-sixth Street—the sidewalks were replete with stores, banks, restaurants, and other businesses with Spanish signs.

The Puerto Rican community established itself in the West Town and Humboldt Park areas, along with Logan Square. According to the 1990 census, Puerto Ricans in Chicago numbered 121,209. The Puerto Rican neighborhoods tended not to be successful commercially. Many storefronts were boarded, and residents often had to go elsewhere for employment and to fulfill their household needs.

Cubans and other Latin American populations have not had defined neighborhoods. About 66,000 Latinos, other than Mexican Americans and Puerto Ricans, lived throughout the city in 1990. Some lived in Humboldt Park, but most settled in other neighborhoods more compatible with their social status than with their cultural roots. Nevertheless, some neighborhoods had begun to take shape as Hispanic enclaves. More than 3,000 Hispanic households were located in the far north neighborhood of Rogers Park, particularly east of Clark Street.

Political Influence. The residential pattern of Latinos in Chicago has helped the community make its presence felt in the political arena. Pilsen and Little Village are roughly equivalent to the Twenty-fifth and the Twenty-second wards of the city. In the 1980's, Latino candidates were elected from these wards, Juan Solis for the Twenty-second and Jesus Garcia for the Twenty-fifth.

A third ward with strong Latino representation is the Twenty-sixth Ward, in the West Town/Humboldt Park area. Luis Gutierrez became that ward's alderman in 1987 and quickly became an outspoken and well-known politician. In 1992, he was elected to Congress from a newly created congressional district that had a high proportion of Latino residents, becoming the first Latino to represent Chicago in the U.S. Congress.

Although Latinos made progress in the political arena, the community still suffered many social ills associated with inner-city communities. About half of Latino children dropped out of high school, relegating them to a life of low-paying jobs or reliance on the welfare system.

Cultural Influences. Chicago has had a strong Latino influence in its cultural environment and has hosted many events that cater to the Latino community. One regular musical event has been the annual Viva Chicago at the Petrillo Bandshell of Grant Park in downtown Chicago. Many well-known Latino artists have performed there, including Rubén Blades and Gloria Estefan. Chicago has also hosted the annual International Latino Film Festival, screening recent films from throughout the Hispanic world. The Mexican Fine Arts Museum has been an important center for Mexican culture. It has sponsored special events that reflect Mexico's rich heritage, developed a collection of Mexican art, and encouraged local artists of Mexican descent to achieve excellence.

—Andrew Sund

SUGGESTED READINGS: • Caruso, Jorge, and Eduardo Camacho. *Hispanics in Chicago.* Chicago: The Chicago Reporter, 1985. • Fremon, David. *Chicago Politics, Ward by Ward.* Bloomington: Indiana University Press, 1988. • The Latino Institute. *Latinos in Metropolitan Chicago: A Study of Housing and Employment.* Chicago: Author, 1983. • Ropka, Gerald. *The Evolving Residential Pattern of the Mexican, Puerto Rican, and Cuban Population in the City of Chicago.* New York: Arno Press, 1980.

Chicanas: Female Mexican Americans born and/or reared in the United States. The term "Chicana" came into widespread use during the CHICANO MOVEMENT, which promoted cultural identity and pride. Women have been an integral part of Chicano organizing on every level. The struggle of Chicanas, unlike that of their male peers, is twofold. They strive to change their traditional subordinate roles within Chicano culture while at the same time defending and advancing other aspects of that culture. Chicana feminism calls for honoring the home and family structure while also recognizing that the home should not limit a Chicana's position in life. Active political and social participation is important to many Chicanas, and during the 1960's and 1970's the Chicana movement organized various groups that focused on Chicana issues.

Chicanismo: Ideology of the CHICANO MOVEMENT. Chicanismo focuses on a Chicano CULTURAL NATIONALISM. It describes the experiences of being Chicano in an Anglo environment. As a form of cultural nationalism, it assumes pride, loyalty, and self-respect within a diverse Chicano culture rather than searching for identity through assimilation into Anglo culture. The struggles and advances of the Chicano community are the most important aspects of Chicanismo, which developed in the mid-1960's in response to injustice and racism toward people of Mexican heritage.

Although the extended family and other traditional elements remain important to them, Chicanas have demanded increased participation in life outside the home. (David Bacon)

Chicano, El: Music group. El Chicano formed in 1969 in East Los Angeles. The group's first single, "Viva Tirado," was a remake of a jazz instrumental, done in El Chicano's rock/Latin/jazz style. It was the first single in history to make *Billboard* magazine's Top 40 chart in all the popular music categories. The group recorded eight albums during the 1970's, toured worldwide, shared concert bills with top rhythm-and-blues/rock performers, and was the first Chicano group to play at the Apollo Theatre. In 1978, the group went on hiatus. In the late 1980's, keyboardist Bobby Espinosa formed a new band, also called El Chicano.

Chicano dialects: Chicano dialects, varieties of Spanish and English, usually correspond to differences of other types among groups, such as geographical loca-

tion, social class, ethnicity, or age. Individuals who share important social and regional characteristics will typically speak similarly, and those who do not will often differ in certain aspects of their language usage. (*See* SPANISH LANGUAGE—VARIATIONS ACROSS LATINO GROUPS.) Furthermore, a person cannot speak a language without speaking a dialect of that language. Thus, if an individual speaks English or Spanish, he or she must speak some dialect of these languages, and one possibility is a Chicano dialect. There is no consensus as to how many Chicano dialects exist in the United States. It is difficult, if not impossible, to determine where one dialect ends and another begins.

Some researchers have categorized Chicano dialects into Chicano English and Chicano Spanish, which are mainly the English and Spanish varieties spoken in the

The dialect spoken by this United Farm Workers organizer to California farmworkers likely differs from dialects used elsewhere. (David Bacon)

southwestern United States. These dialects have their roots largely in the language varieties of Mexico. Furthermore, in the Southwest, distinctions are often made between the Chicano dialects of Texas, New Mexico, Arizona, southern Colorado, and California. These distinctions may also extend to other areas in the United States with Hispanic communities, such as Detroit and Chicago.

Chicano Spanish is a variety of Spanish that is heavily influenced by English; Chicano English is a variety of English that is influenced by Spanish. Among more narrowly defined dialects, or at least distinctive forms, are CODE SWITCHING (language alternation between Spanish and English by one speaker in a single conversation) and CALÓ (a language style used primarily by Chicano males who borrow words, "loanwords," that are common in the popular language varieties of all Southwest Spanish speakers).

Chicano dialects may differ from one another at several levels: pronunciation, vocabulary items, and the grammatical patterns of the language system (the way in which items are combined to form sentences). Whatever the level at which dialects differ, such differences are often related to social and cultural differences. In the United States, both physical and social factors are responsible for variations in both English and Spanish. The country's settlement history, its geography, and major drifts of population can explain the different characteristics of Chicano dialects. In addition, natural barriers, such as mountains and rivers, cut people off from one another, allowing for differences to emerge and be maintained. Because geographical, historical, social, and ethnic factors affect language, a Spanish-speaking farmworker in California will speak differently from a Spanish-speaking executive in Texas.

The result is that the Chicano population in the Southwest is linguistically heterogeneous. Chicano speakers vary; some are Spanish monolinguals, some are English monolinguals, and some have varying degrees of bilingualism. Some of these speakers claim Spanish as their first language, while others claim to be native speakers of English.

Chicano Film Festival (San Antonio, Tex.): The Chicano Film Festival was begun in 1976 and held annually in August. Its purpose was to promote and recognize the achievements of Chicano filmmakers. The festival showcased 16 millimeter films and videotapes entered in competition by Mexican American artists. The contest, running into June each year, was open

exclusively to U.S. citizens of Mexican descent. Sponsored by Oblate College of the Southwest, the festival featured screenings of cinematic works entered.

Chicano movement: The Chicano movement, which peaked during the late 1960's, was part of a series of social movements that were essentially struggles for self-determination and access to social, cultural, and political power.

Background. A number of events contributed to the flowering of the Chicano movement. After having participated in World War II as U.S. citizens, Mexican Americans surveyed their situation within the United States and began to resent the fact that although they had served in the military forces as full citizens, their treatment in the United States continued to reflect racism. Such treatment was evident during wartime, as seen in the zoot-suit riots, and continued afterward with countless acts of violence, including police brutality, and with ongoing de facto segregation of Mexican Americans in public institutions, including schools. A number of associations, such as the LEAGUE OF UNITED LATIN AMERICAN CITIZENS (LULAC) and the AMERICAN G.I. FORUM, had been formed to facilitate the integration of Mexican Americans, but in the 1960's, as the United States' involvement in the Vietnam War escalated, a number of participants in these groups became disillusioned with the lack of radical change. In addition, despite the War on Poverty government programs, Mexican Americans as a group continued to be poor.

Movement Figures and Issues. The Chicano movement focused on a number of issues, each of which has come to be identified with particular individuals. The farmworkers' strikes in Delano, California, which involved both Mexican and Filipino workers, was led by César CHÁVEZ, who advocated nonviolent resistance and inaugurated the GRAPE BOYCOTTS that culminated in renegotiated contracts for farmworkers. In New Mexico, Reies López TIJERINA, a descendant of early Mexican settlers, formed the Alianza Federal de los Mercedes. That organization sought to restore land grants stolen from their original owners as a result of ambiguities in the TREATY OF GUADALUPE HIDALGO that enabled U.S. citizens to appropriate the lands. In Texas, José Ángel GUTIÉRREZ formed La RAZA UNIDA PARTY and effectively pioneered the political representation of people of Mexican descent in CRYSTAL CITY. Perhaps none of the major figures of the movement was as influential for young people as Rodolfo "Corky" GONZÁLES, formerly a boxer and bailbondsman, who organized the CRUSADE FOR JUSTICE in Denver, Colorado. He is also well known for having written "I am Joaquin" (1969), a poem documenting the history of Chicanos, and for having sponsored the Denver Youth Conference (1969), at which *El PLAN ESPIRITUAL DE AZTLÁN*, a manifesto of political and cultural nationalism, was promoted.

Cultural Nationalism and Women. One of the central organizing tenets of the Chicano movement was the concept of CHICANISMO, a sentiment of nationalism that asserted the power of Chicano cultural identity and insisted on self-determination. The rhetorical force of Chicanismo and AZTLÁN mobilized thousands, including college and high school students pursuing the American dream, current and former inmates of prisons, and participants in issue-based groups.

For many women, however, the concept of Chicanismo and a family ideology that confined women to the roles of wife, mother, or sister in patriarchal terms was an oppressive force within the movement, leading to the silencing of women's opinions and denying women leadership in organizations. Women raised questions about their roles and their fundamental right to make decisions about their lives. Welfare and reproductive rights were two key areas in which CHICANAS challenged the regulation of their choices, consequently refiguring ideas about the family.

Strategies and Difficulties. The Chicano movement

César Chávez and his efforts on behalf of farmworkers formed an important part of the Chicano movement; he is shown following the defeat of Proposition 14, a California ballot initiative regarding farm labor. (AP/Wide World Photos)

José Ángel Gutiérrez organized La Raza Unida Party and led Chicano movement activists in Texas. (AP/Wide World Photos)

The spirit of the Chicano movement remained on college campuses, as shown by these UCLA students protesting cuts in the university's Chicano studies program proposed in 1993. (Impact Visuals, Ted Soqui)

encompassed many of the issues and struggles of Mexican Americans during the late 1960's and early 1970's. Sustaining coherence in the existence of so many diverse but fundamentally relevant issues proved impossible, and activists began to pursue goals separately. The movement's greatest accomplishment was facilitating the cultural, social, and political awareness of a people, who could then view themselves as a collectivity or community.

Increasingly, tensions between differing strategies of social change became unsustainable. These tensions in some cases pointed to aspects of the vision of community that needed clarification or change. What was perhaps most damaging to the Chicano movement, as to many other movements, was the infiltration of organizations by the Federal Bureau of Investigation (FBI) and persistent harassment of movement leaders and participants.

Effects. By the mid-1970's, one could say that the Chicano movement had effectively ended in its original form. Among its accomplishments, the movement can count the institutionalization of Chicano studies in colleges and universities and the enhanced conscious-

ness of the way racism operates in the United States and elsewhere, so that an ongoing battle against racism can continue to be waged. —*Dionne Espinoza*

SUGGESTED READINGS: • Acuña, Rodolfo. *Occupied America: A History of Chicanos.* 3d ed. New York: Harper & Row, 1988. • Chicano Youth Liberation Conference, Second, Denver, 1970. *Crusade for Justice: El Plan Espiritual de Aztlán.* Denver: Author, 1970. • Garcia, Alma M. "The Development of Chicana Feminist Discourse, 1970-1980." *Gender & Society* 3 (June, 1989): 217-238. • Gómez-Quiñones, Juan. *Chicano Politics: Reality and Promise, 1940-1990.* Albuquerque: University of New Mexico Press, 1990. • Gutiérrez, Ramón A. "Community, Patriarchy, and Individualism: The Politics of Chicano History and the Dream of Equality." *American Quarterly* 45, no. 1 (1993): 44-72. • Lopez, Sonia A. "The Role of the Chicana Within the Student Movement." In *Essays on la Mujer*, edited by Rosaura Sanchez and Rosa Martinez Cruz. Los Angeles: Chicano Studies Center, University of California, 1977. • Muñoz, Carlos, Jr. *Youth, Identity, Power: The Chicano Movement.* New York: Verso, 1989.